Literary Theory After Davidson

Literature & Philosophy

A. J. Cascardi, General Editor

This new series will publish books in a wide range of subjects in philosophy and literature, including studies of the social and historical issues that relate these two fields. Drawing on the resources of the Anglo-American and Continental traditions, the series will be open to philosophically informed scholarship covering the entire range of contemporary critical thought.

Already published:

J. M. Bernstein, *The Fate of Art: Aesthetic Alienation from Kant to Derrida and Adorno*
Mary Finn, *Writing the Incommensurable: Kierkegaard, Rossetti, and Hopkins*
Robert Steiner, *Toward a Grammar of Abstraction: Modernity, Wittgenstein, and the Paintings of Jackson Pollock*
Peter Bürger, *The Decline of Modernism*

Literary Theory After Davidson

Edited by

Reed Way Dasenbrock

The Pennsylvania State University Press
University Park, Pennsylvania

Library of Congress Cataloging-in-Publication Data

Literary theory after Davidson / edited by Reed Way Dasenbrock.
      p.   cm.
   Includes bibliographical references and index.
   ISBN 0-271-00895-4 (alk. paper)—ISBN 0-271-00898-9
(pbk.: alk. paper)
      1. Davidson, Donald, 1917–   —Contributions in literary
criticism.   2. Criticism—History—20th century.   3. Literature
—Philosophy.   I. Dasenbrock, Reed Way.
PN94.L4875   1993
801'.95'092—dc20   92-14885
                                                                         CIP

Published by The Pennsylvania State University Press,
Suite C, Barbara Building, University Park, PA 16802-1003

It is the policy of The Pennsylvania State University Press to use acid-free paper for
the first printing of all clothbound books. Publications on uncoated stock satisfy the
minimum requirements of American National Standard for Information Sciences—
Permanence of Paper for Printed Library Materials, ANSI Z39.48–1984.

Contents

Preface

This is a collection of essays assessing the potential significance of Donald Davidson's work in analytic philosophy for issues in literary theory. That way of defining the scope of this book obviously entails a number of presuppositions, the existence and value of something called literary theory and of something else called analytic philosophy, and finally the idea that there can be a fruitful relation between them. In what follows, neither I nor the other contributors will take the time or space to argue explicitly for these essential presuppositions, but we are all certainly aware that they have undergone some challenge. The demise of both literary theory and analytic philosophy has been both announced and predicted, and surely anyone who feels that the death of theory is near and that philosophy has entered a "postanalytic phase" will have little interest in a conversation between these two. The essential if peculiar role of presuppositions in human communication is in fact one of the things analytic philosophy has brought to light, and it would be an easy task to show in turn the philosophical and theoretical presuppositions of such critiques of literary theory and philosophy: only a literary theorist could call for or announce the death of theory; only philosophers concern themselves with the continuance or cessation of philosophy. Calling for an end to philosophy is in fact rather a stale theme in philosophy by now; as Hilary Putnam has reminded us, philosophy always buries its own undertakers.

But Northrop Frye has another wise reminder, which is that "most 'defenses of poetry' are intelligible only to those well within the defenses"; and the same is surely true of defenses of any other form of life. I therefore have eschewed the task of "explaining" or "defending" the kind of work done in the essays that follow. Readers already engaged by the kind of abstract, philosophically oriented work included here need no description of its merits; readers hostile to it for whatever reason are less likely to be swayed by anything I say here than by working through and reflecting on the essays that follow. After a generation of intense theorizing, I think that the questions of literary theory remain as open as ever, and it may in fact be possible to examine those questions more intelligently today if theory is no longer the "hotspot" of literary studies. As position replaced position, each with its fifteen minutes of fame, the glare of attention accorded theory across the 1970s and 1980s led to a marked deterioration in the quality of argumentation in theoretical discourse. Across that entire period, however, the important unremarked change in the theoretical landscape was the gradual emergence of a conversation between theorists and philosophers of a variety of persuasions. An earlier collection of essays that I edited, *Redrawing the Lines: Analytic Philosophy, Deconstruction, and Literary Theory,* is devoted to that conversation as a whole, and for a more thorough look at what developed, I would refer interested readers to the introduction and bibliography of that collection.

Literary Theory After Davidson is more prospective than retrospective, more focused around the perspective I personally hold: namely, that literary theory gains in precision, bite, and usefulness as it attends to the significant work on language and action done in the analytic tradition, in particular that done by Donald Davidson. *Literary Theory After Davidson* represents the first full-scale look at the implications of Davidson's work for literary theory. Literary theory after Davidson won't be the same as literary theory before the absorption of his work, and I hope these essays begin the process of describing what this new endeavor will look like.

Acknowledgments

It would not be inappropriate to begin these acknowledgments by re-printing those from an earlier collection I edited, *Redrawing the Lines: Analytic Philosophy, Deconstruction, and Literary Theory* (University of Minnesota Press, 1989); for in many ways this project continues from that one, and so everyone who helped with that book also helped with this. A second project that helped lead to this book was a special session on Davidson and literary theory that I organized for the 1988 annual meeting of the Modern Language Association. I'd like to thank Sam Wheeler and Shekhar Pradhan for taking part in that session with me, and I'd like to thank Charlie Altieri for inviting me to give another paper on Davidson at the MLA the next year. Michael Morton and Dave Gorman were also in that session, after which it struck me that there was a nucleus of contributors for the present book.

Many people helped between then and now. Tony Cascardi played an invaluable role as editor of the series of which this is a part, and Sandy Thatcher, Philip Winsor, and others at Penn State Press have been of great help. Charlie Altieri, Dave Gorman, and Tom Kent all had good suggestions for additional contributors, and my correspondence and conversation with Dave Gorman over the past several years on Davidson and related topics have been a constant stimulus. I also need to thank him for the most thorough and thoughtful review of anything I've ever been associated with, a review of *Redrawing the Lines* in *Poetics Today,* which helped suggest some of the lines of thought pursued in the intro-duction to this collection. I thank all the contributors for their willingness to interrupt busy schedules to contribute to this project, as well as for putting up with my persistent queries and requests as editor. My own essay in this collection benefited from comments by Stanley Fish when I delivered it at the MLA in 1988; it is the only essay in the book that has appeared elsewhere, though in quite different form, and I thank *College English* for permission to reprint. Mike Fischer, Charlie Altieri, Peter Rabinowicz, and Michael Morton all offered useful responses to that earlier version, which was also delivered as a lecture at Texas A & M University.

Closer to home, I dedicate my part of this collection, as is true of everything I write, to my wife, Feroza, and my son Hormuzdiyar. When Homi heard me refer one day to "the Davidson book," he asked me, "What is a Davidson?" I hope that he will be able to answer the question himself one day, but I'm in no hurry.

Abbreviations

The essays collected here all employ a common reference system, the parenthetical citation now recommended by the Modern Language Association and colloquially known as "new MLA." However, that system has been modified in one respect. Since Davidson's key essays and books are referred to repeatedly in the essays that follow, it seemed simpler and is surely more concise to adopt a common set of abbreviations for Davidson's published essays and books. When an abbreviation is used, it refers to one of the following works by Davidson. There are therefore no references to works by Davidson in the Works Cited for any of the essays, and the following table can also serve as a bibliography of Davidson's works—not an exhaustive one, but at least a bibliography of those of his works which the contributors found essential.

"A1987"   "Afterthoughts, 1987." In *Reading Rorty: Critical Responses to Philosophy and the Mirror of Nature (and Beyond)*. Ed. Alan Malachowski. Oxford: Basil Blackwell, 1990. 134–38.
"CTT"   "A Coherence Theory of Truth and Knowledge." In *Truth and Interpretation: Perspectives on the Philosophy of Donald Davidson*. Ed. Ernest LePore. Oxford: Basil Blackwell, 1986. 309–16.
"DD"   "Deception and Division." In *The Multiple Self*. Ed. Jon Elster. Cambridge: Cambridge UP, 1986. 79–92.
EAE   *Essays on Actions and Events*. Oxford: Clarendon, 1980.

"EE"   "Expressing Evaluations." The Lindley Lecture. University of Kansas, 1982.

"EpE"   "Epistemology Externalized." *Dialectica* 45 (1991): 191–202.

"FPA"   "First Person Authority." *Dialectica* 38 (1984): 101–12.

"II"   "Incoherence and Irrationality." *Dialectica* 39 (1985): 345–54.

ITI   *Inquiries into Truth and Interpretation.* Oxford: Clarendon, 1984.

"JII"   "Judging Interpersonal Interests." In *Foundations of Social Choice Theory.* Ed. Jon Elster and Aanund Hylland. Cambridge: Cambridge UP, 1986. 195–211.

"JJHD"   "James Joyce and Humpty Dumpty." *Midwest Studies in Philosophy* 16 (1991): 1–12.

"KOOM"   "Knowing One's Own Mind." *Proceedings and Addresses of the American Philosophical Association* 60 (1987): 441–58.

"MM"   "The Measure of the Mental." Unpublished paper.

"MS"   "The Myth of the Subjective." In *Relativism: Interpretation and Confrontation.* Ed. Michael Krausz. Notre Dame: U of Notre Dame P, 1989. 159–72.

"MTE"   "Meaning, Truth, and Evidence." In *Perspectives on Quine.* Ed. Robert B. Barrett and Roger F. Gibson. Oxford: Basil Blackwell, 1990. 68–79.

"NDE"   "A Nice Derangement of Epitaphs." In *Truth and Interpretation: Perspectives on the Philosophy of Donald Davidson.* Ed. Ernest LePore. Oxford: Basil Blackwell, 1986. 433–46.

"PEA"   "Problems in the Explanation of Action." In *Metaphysics and Morality: Essays in Honour of J.J.C. Smart.* Ed. Philip Pettit, Richard Sylvan, and Jean Norman. Oxford: Basil Blackwell, 1987. 35–49.

"PI"   "Paradoxes of Irrationality." In *Philosophical Essays on Freud.* Ed. Richard Wollheim and J. Hopkins. Cambridge: Cambridge UP, 1982. 289–305.

"PR"   "Postscript to Replies." In *Essays on Davidson: Actions and Events.* Ed. Bruce Vermazen and Merrill B. Hintikka. Oxford: Clarendon, 1985. 253–54.

"RA"   "Rational Animals." *Dialectica* 36 (1982): 317–27.

"RE"   "Replies to Essays I–IX." In *Essays on Davidson: Actions*

and Events. Ed. Bruce Vermazen and Merrill B. Hintikka.
Oxford: Clarendon, 1985. 195–229.

"RE2"   "Replies to Essays X–XII." In *Essays on Davidson: Actions and Events.* Ed. Bruce Vermazen and Merrill B. Hintikka. Oxford: Clarendon, 1985. 242–52.

"SCT"   "The Structure and Content of Truth." *The Journal of Philosophy* 87, no. 6 (1990): 279–328.

"SP"   "The Second Person." Unpublished paper.

"TUTMA"   "Toward a Unified Theory of Meaning and Action." *Grazer Philosophische Studien* 2 (1980): 1–12.

"TVK"   "Three Varieties of Knowledge." In *A. J. Ayer: Memorial Essays.* Royal Institute of Philosophy Supplement no. 30. Ed. A. Phillips Griffiths. Cambridge: Cambridge UP, 1991.

Introduction:
Davidson and Literary Theory

Donald Davidson is surely one of
the most eminent analytic philosophers alive, arguably the most eminent. His papers have been collected in two volumes by Oxford University's Clarendon Press, *Essays on Actions and Events* (1980) and *Inquiries into Truth and Interpretation* (1984). An enormous conference was held at Rutgers in 1985 on his work, and the proceedings of that conference have been collected in two equally enormous volumes published by Basil Blackwell, *Actions and Events: Perspectives on the Philosophy of Donald Davidson* (1985), edited by Ernest LePore and Brian P. McLaughlin, and *Truth and Interpretation: Perspectives on the Philosophy of Donald Davidson* (1986), edited by LePore. Yet another collection, *Essays on Davidson: Actions and Events,* edited by Bruce Vermazen and Merrill B. Hintikka, was published in 1985 by Oxford. The contributors to these three collections include virtually every other eminent analytic philosopher working today, and the way the work of Michael Dummett, Hilary Putnam, Richard Rorty, and of course many others refers to and builds on Davidson's work serves to establish the central place he occupies in contemporary analytic philosophy.

As the title of the present collection, *Literary Theory After Davidson,* should indicate, its project is really very different from these earlier collections of essays on Davidson's work. Of the twelve chapters that follow, only three are written by philosophers, the rest by literary critics

and theorists. And the question the contributors have focused on here—
no matter what their training or disciplinary identity—is what contribution Davidson's work can make to some of the ongoing debates in literary theory. The reason why this is a question worth asking is that there is
a remarkable divergence between Davidson's place in contemporary
analytic philosophy and his place in contemporary literary theory. In
philosophy, he is the central figure after W. V. Quine; but in the world of
literary theory, his work remains comparatively unknown. This is not the
result, as it once might have been, of the failure of literary theorists to
pay any attention to analytic philosophy. For a long time, there did seem
to be a wall between literary theory and analytic philosophy; this was
odd enough, given the great influence of Continental philosophy on
literary theory. But now, contemporary literary theory is liberally bor-
rowing from philosophy, not just from deconstruction and its Continental predecessors, but also from the Anglo-American analytic tradition.
J. L. Austin, Ludwig Wittgenstein, their expositors Richard Rorty and
Stanley Cavell, and, to a lesser extent, John Searle and Paul Grice have all
been influential in literary theory, widely cited if in a number of different
ways. In contrast, Davidson's work has not been extensively or systemati-
cally drawn on. One aim of the essays that follow is to redress that
imbalance, and in my judgment they do succeed in showing the great
relevance of Davidson's work to a variety of issues under discussion in
literary theory today. But I think it worth considering for a moment why
there would be this imbalance, why those on the literary side of the
fence would be so slow to take up a philosopher such as Davidson as
well as others working in the same philosophical tradition.

Although this imbalance is regrettable, I do not find it utterly inexpli-
cable. Clearly, and probably inevitably, literary theorists approach philosophy with the preconceptions of their own field, and this means that
we tend to be attracted by philosophers with a literary sense of style. So
we read Plato rather than Aristotle, Hume rather than Kant, Nietzsche
rather than Hegel. This bias has been part of what attracted theorists to
Derrida. Derrida not only writes in a unique manner (or range of manners) that has aroused admiration and imitation (if also perplexity and
annoyance); he also justifies our ingrained attitude by presenting philosophers who aim at linguistic unobtrusiveness as witting or unwitting
participants in "logocentrism." Our apprehension of the analytic tradition has been shaped by this attitude as well; the philosophers who have
had a strong influence on literary theory up to this point have been those
who have written in a style attractive to nonphilosophers. Wittgenstein,
at least the later Wittgenstein, is a more interesting and more striking

writer than Quine, Austin is livelier in his use of language than Putnam, and Rorty and Cavell comparably appeal to a literary sensibility. Like Derrida, Rorty provides theoretical support for such a preference, arguing, most pointedly in "Philosophy as a Kind of Writing," that the value of philosophy is less in representing the truth than as a kind of writing designed to shape and change our intellectual practices. Later, in *Contingency, Irony, and Solidarity*, he goes so far as to call the philosophers of which he approves "strong poets." This assumption that philosophy should aspire to the condition of poetry is perhaps even more flattering to those on the literary side of the fence than Derrida's argument that philosophy is unavoidably enmeshed in the condition of poetry.[1] Whatever the cogency of these views, their currency has been an important factor in why and—more important—how literary theorists have started to attend to analytic philosophy.

This historical fact has some ironic consequences. The first is that most literary theorists have therefore been introduced to analytic philosophy by means of Austin and Wittgenstein—which is to say, precisely backward. Analytic philosophy has always meant technical philosophy, professional philosophy, the kind of philosophy least likely to attract readers of a literary bent. The variant of analytic philosophy that was first influential for literary theorists could be called antianalytic philosophy. For the widely cited work of Austin and the later Wittgenstein are reactions against analytic philosophy, and a connection can be made between the stylistic attractiveness and the substantive stance of both men's work: the aphoristic, literary brilliance of Wittgenstein's *Philosophical Investigations* is in large measure a reaction against his own earlier work, especially the *Tractatus Logico-Philosophicus*, a reaction against its concern with logic and its confidence in philosophy's ability to solve problems. Austin is equally a philosopher reacting against the harder line of analytic philosophy concerned with logic, with philosophy of science, with solving the problems of truth and reference.[2] The explicit starting point of his seminal *How to Do Things with Words* is a critique of the logical positivism of the Vienna Circle. Precisely what delights such literary readers of Austin as Stanley Fish and Shoshana Felman—the personal voice, the offhand manner, the use of colloquial examples—is part of a conscious and deliberate rejection of the more scientific tone and approach of other varieties of analytic philosophy.

So there is a sense in which literary theorists have absorbed analytic philosophy primarily through being interested in the reaction against it. The work of Richard Rorty has been an important agent in this contradictory process: *Philosophy and the Mirror of Nature* tells us that we do not need to respect philosophy's claim to be the "master discipline," and in particular that analytic philosophy has self-deconstructed, yet *Philosophy and the Mirror of Nature* was also the first detailed introduction to contemporary analytic philosophy for many literary theorists. These claims of Rorty's have encouraged solemn pronouncements such as Cornel West's that "Rorty strikes a deathblow to modern North Atlantic [analytic] philosophy" (263); this comes from a book with the Rortyan title, *Post-Analytic Philosophy*, a title that perfectly expresses Rorty's sense that analytic philosophy is somehow moribund. Obviously, such reports of the death of analytic philosophy are greatly exaggerated, as can be shown by Rorty's own continuing reliance on the analytic work of Davidson and others (see esp. *Contingency, Irony, and Solidarity*), but their very currency has accentuated the tendency among literary theorists to absorb only the self-deconstructing eddy within analytic philosophy, not the main current. We have by and large learned about analytic philosophy by hearing accounts of its demise, and it should occasion no real surprise if that should produce an odd and partial understanding.

One of the themes in the essays that follow is that this partial take will not do, that we need to move beyond Wittgenstein and Austin, Cavell and Rorty, as interesting as these figures are, if only in order to understand the context of their work, to see why and how they are interesting. Just as Derrida's work—as a number of people have already argued[3]—can be understood only against the work of Husserl, Heidegger, and others, antianalytic philosophy can really be understood only against the background of the analytic tradition. But the paradoxical reception of analytic philosophy in literary theory means that only now are theorists beginning to look seriously at the original, harder tradition of analytic philosophy descending from Frege and Russell which is more deeply concerned with logic and with philosophy of science. And it is important to recognize that this tradition did not go away after what I am calling the antianalytic work of Austin and Wittgenstein. On the contrary. Davidson, though chronologically after Wittgenstein and Austin, is in important respects continuing in precisely the tradition they are reacting against, and he is far from alone here, as the impressive work of such living philosophers as W. V. Quine, Hilary Putnam, and Michael Dummett—not to mention a host of younger figures—demonstrates. As David Gorman has put it, "a reasoned consideration of this issue will require literary theorists to learn more than they currently know about the kind of philosophy which Austin or Wittgenstein professed to reject—and which has gone on despite these rejections, after all, massively and often impressively" (657). It is at least partially for this reason that the essays which follow generally contain a fair amount of exposition of Davidson's key concepts, exposition that should serve to introduce Davidson's work for readers unfamiliar with it as well as to highlight the relevance of that work to issues in literary theory for those who are familiar with it. The essays collected here show that by now a growing number of literary theorists are beginning to (and realizing that they need to) go beyond antianalytic philosophy to consider the main current of analytic philosophy. The time has come for a more systematic and prolonged exploration of what that main current has to offer literary theory.

So Davidson, in the essays that follow, serves both as a representative figure of a current of analytic philosophy historically ignored by literary theory as well as a figure of interest in his own right within that current. To understand Davidson's work in its complexity, one needs to understand its context in recent analytic philosophy, and a number of the essays fill out that context by discussing some of the important challenges to Davidson from within the analytic tradition. It is for this reason that other "hard" analytic philosophers, particularly Quine, Putnam, and Dummett, play important roles in some of the essays. It should be understood that my referring to these philosophers as part of a "harder" current within analytic philosophy, less skeptical than Wittgenstein or Rorty about the possibilities of philosophy and about the accomplishments of analytic philosophy, should not be taken as implying that there are no substantive disagreements among these philosophers. One can consider Davidson's work of great interest and still not accept it without reservation or challenge. In just the same way, one will encounter plenty of disagreement in the essays that follow; in no way does this collection announce the emergence of a "Davidsonian school." But even if there is no particular agreement on how we are to confront Davidson's work, there is agreement that it should be confronted, that contemporary analytic philosophy in general and Davidson's work in particular have a great deal to offer literary theory.

But I do not think many would perceive this or would feel the full force and power of Davidson's work from the discussion of his work in literary theory before the present collection. This reflects a second irony concerning the reception of analytic philosophy in literary theory which we need to discuss. Paradoxically, despite the differences among Wittgenstein, Austin, and Davidson, the reception of Davidson's work in literary theory—such as there has been—has born a remarkable resemblance to the reception accorded the other two philosophers. This has meant that theorists attending to the initial discussions about Davidson might simply see no reason to explore his work, since it seemed to have essentially the same implications for literary theory as the work of Austin and Wittgenstein. This would be a serious misunderstanding, given the differences just discussed, but those differences have not been clearly or firmly articulated for literary theorists.

Analytic philosophy has influenced literary theory in a climate shaped to a large extent by Continental philosophy, especially deconstruction, and this has had a major influence on the reception of analytic philosophy. As philosophers from the analytic tradition have become current in literary theory, the question insistently brought to bear on their work—at least since about 1975—is exactly the same: Where do they stand in relation to the one application of philosophy to literary theory everyone has heard of, deconstruction? It is perhaps less remarkable that we have asked the same question about each philosopher than that the answers to this question have also been the same. What this has meant is that the successive waves of influence of analytic philosophy on literary theory have all had the same basic shape. Despite the fundamental differences between the antianalytic philosophers such as Austin and Wittgenstein and more purely analytic philosophers like Davidson, Davidson has been treated just as Austin and Wittgenstein have been by literary theorists. In each case, the analytic philosopher was initially introduced as an opposite—in some cases, as an antidote—to deconstruction, but as the discussion continued, this opposition was transformed if not obliterated entirely. We do not have the necessary space to trace the reception of Austin and Wittgenstein in literary theory in any detail here, something I have done elsewhere (*Redrawing the Lines* 5–13), but a quick review of the use of Davidson's work that has been made in literary theory over the past decade may help show just how narrowly focused that reception has been.

The first person to have mentioned Davidson's work in the context of literary theory is Charles Altieri, in *Act and Quality* (1981). Altieri is one of the theorists concerned with the relation between the analytic tradition and deconstruction, and his strategy is generally a contrastive one, concerned with using the work of Wittgenstein in particular as a contrast to Derrida. A section of *Act and Quality* summarizes Davidson's then-uncollected work on action theory. I am not quite sure why Altieri introduces this section into his discussion, for in that discussion he is dubious about the applicability of Davidson's work to questions of literary theory. The thrust of the criticism is that Davidson's work is too narrowly analytic, too concerned with realms of action where it is possible to be tidy, to be of much use for literary theory. This leads into

Altieri's argument that Wittgenstein gives us the looser terms we need for literary theory without becoming enmeshed in skepticism about the possibility of meaning and action. Wittgenstein thus is a kind of Aristotelian mean between the extremes of Davidson and Derrida:

> I seem now to be verging on the Continental tradition in hermeneutics that lead to Derrida, because I have posited the identity of some actions as dependent upon interpretations. But rejecting formal logical analysis in favor of a hermeneutic form of intensional language does not entail indeterminacy.... Indeed, it is dissatisfaction with Davidson's methods for establishing truth-functional standards of certainty that returns us to the importance of Wittgensteinian grammar as a ground for reaching agreements in probabilistic terms. [121]

Christopher Norris's subsequent discussion of Davidson continues in this vein of contrasting Davidson and Derrida, although Norris has none of Altieri's desire to build up Wittgenstein as a mediating figure. In one of the essays included in *The Contest of Faculties* (1985), "On Not Going Relativist (Where It Counts): Deconstruction and 'Convention T,' " Norris presents an entirely different aspect of Davidson's work, his work on truth-conditional semantics. Norris's essay is primarily a reasonably cogent summary of the various charges and countercharges concerning relativism and skepticism that surround deconstruction and other forms of poststructuralism. What all of these have in common is that, accepting Saussure's notion of the arbitrary nature of the sign, they assume "all truths are 'relative to language'" (217). And Norris argues that these premises are also widely held by many analytic philosophers, particularly Quine. Davidson's focus on truth as opposed to meaning and on a critique of conventionalism is for Norris the only position that is not undercut by the ground it shares with Derrida and is thus "the only alternative to the sceptical rigours of deconstruction" (216). Now it is not at all clear from this essay whether Norris would endorse this alternative to deconstruction. The phrase "sceptical rigours of deconstruction" does not make it sound likely, and it seems clear enough from Norris's other writing that he probably would not, which makes the thrust of the entire essay a little unclear. Nonetheless, some strong claims are made by Norris for Davidson as a contrast to deconstruction for those looking for one.

These claims are extended, yet also muted, in a subsequent essay by Norris on Davidson's works, "Reading Donald Davidson: Truth, Meaning,

And Right Interpretation," in *Deconstruction and the Interests of Theory* (1988). The essay employs Norris's characteristic deconstructive strategy of describing two mutually exclusive options, but here he finds them within Davidson's work (or at least within interpretations of Davidson), summarizing a "relativist" reading of Davidson advanced primarily by Richard Rorty at odds with the Davidson presented in the earlier essay. Rorty's Davidson, "Davidson II" as Norris labels him, is one of those analytic philosophers who give up so much ground to deconstruction that they are left with little to stand on, whereas "Davidson I" remains for Norris "a considerable challenge to post-structuralist theory" (64). The distinction Norris finds crucial between Davidson I and II, between his Davidson and Rorty's, is again Davidson's notion of truth. Of these two Davidsons, it is clear that Norris feels the right reading is Davidson I, the alternative to deconstruction, yet paradoxically Davidson II is much closer to Norris's own declared position. Wherever one wants to place the "real" Davidson, a concept it is a bit surprising to find Norris relying on, the Davidson II of Norris's second essay suggests the reading of Davidson that has become more prominent. Instead of Altieri's (and Norris's earlier) Davidson, who presents the sharpest possible alternative to deconstruction, it has been argued that Davidson's position on issues in philosophy of language is in fact close to Derrida's in important respects. Rorty's discussion of Davidson which Norris summarizes tends in this direction, but far more detailed expositions of this view have been presented by Samuel Wheeler, Shekhar Pradhan, and most recently by Thomas Kent.[4]

Wheeler's work on this issue begins with a paper, "Indeterminacy of French Interpretation," which was the only paper in the two LePore anthologies that at all brings in terms familiar to literary theory, although it does not specifically discuss any literary texts.[5] Wheeler's focus is not Davidson's action theory or his truth-conditional semantics, but his more recent work on interpretation and his critique in such essays as "Communication and Convention" (*ITI* 265–80) of the conventionalist theories of language advanced by speech-act theory. Wheeler's paper argues that the critique of conventionalism advanced in "Communication and Convention" bears a particularly close resemblance to Derrida's critique of speech-act theory in "Signature Event Context" and "Limited Inc," Derrida's side of the Derrida–Searle exchange. And this is also the ground explored by Shekhar Pradhan in his "Minimalist Semantics: Davidson and Derrida on Meaning, Use, and Convention." Perhaps the central theme of analytic philosophy of language has been the distinction between what a sentence can mean and what its utterance in a specific context means. This distinction has been studied by a variety of philosophers from Strawson and Wittgenstein to Austin and Grice; the two sides of the opposition have been given various terms, such as "meaning" and "use," "sense" and "force," etc. Speech-act theory, at least as formulated by Searle, argues that we can specify in a rigorous fashion the connection between the two. We can describe the structure of use and—in some versions of the theory at least—tie that use back to the sentence being used, in effect bridging the gap opened up by analytic philosophy by analyzing the conventions of communication. Davidson and Derrida, in Wheeler's and Pradhan's presentation, both argue (if from rather different angles) that this cannot be done. Davidson's presentation of his position in "Communication and Convention" focuses on Frege's assertion sign and argues that natural language can never have such an assertion sign, a convention that obviates the need for interpretation. If an actor in a theater wanted to indicate to the audience that the theater was on fire, as opposed to there being a fictional fire inside the play, such an assertion sign would be useful. But, as Davidson points out, "It should be obvious that the assertion sign would do no good, for the actor would have used it in the first place, when he was only acting" (270). We cannot work backward from use to meaning, from force to sense, because the sense or meaning of a sentence does not control the force with which it is used or uttered. For Wheeler and Pradhan, this work on interpretation brings us close to a Derridean world of signs cut loose from their originating contexts, capable of being appropriated and cited in the drift inherent in all linguistic texts. This sense of a parallelism between the two has recently been extended to the realm of rhetoric and composition in an article by Thomas Kent in *College English*, "Beyond System: The Rhetoric of Paralogy." Following Wheeler and Pradhan's exposition, Kent argues that the two philosophers' critique of conventionalism suggests that any attempt to come up with a systematic rhetoric, a system of conventions for achieving effects, is not going to work.[6] A similar insight taken from Davidson is obviously behind Steven Knapp and Walter Benn Michaels's critique of systematic and conventionalist interpretive methods, particularly in "Against Theory 2," although they do not see the similarity to Derrida argued in these other essays and classify him as one of the bad conventionalist systematizers.

Virtually everything connecting Davidson with issues in literary theory has circled around this issue of his relation to Derrida. There are only two other issues on which Davidson's work has been brought to bear. First, Peter McCormick and Gabriele Taylor have extended Altieri's pioneering investigations into whether Davidsonian action theory can

work for the analysis of literary works. McCormick focuses less on Davidson's own work than on the work of Myles Brand, while Taylor's analysis
takes aim at Davidson's own work, but both philosophers come to essentially the same negative conclusions Altieri does: that Davidson's criteria
are too tight for literary analysis. Also critical of Davidson (or of exten-
sions of Davidson to cultural realms) is Colin MacCabe, who in "Broken
English" has criticized Davidson's position in "On the Very Idea of a
Conceptual Scheme" for allowing for "no radical confrontation with
difference" (7) and thus endorsing a kind of cultural imperialism. And a
pair of articles by Ian Saunders and Andrew Benjamin, brought together
by Christopher Norris in *Textual Practice*, debate MacCabe's claim, with
Benjamin endorsing MacCabe's critique and Saunders questioning it.
Both of these mini-*topoi* are revisited in some of the essays that follow, as
Allen Dunn and Paisley Livingston in the final two essays come to different conclusions on the applicability of Davidson's action theory for literary theory, while Steven Cole and I explicitly or implicitly argue against
MacCabe.[7] But what this shows is that the only positive contribution to
questions in literary theory that has been claimed for Davidson's work
has been in relation to Derrida.

What sense can we make of this reception of Davidson's work? First,
we need to remember that it is not Davidson who is obsessed with or
who cannot make up his mind about Derrida, for he has paid no more
attention to Derrida or the philosophical tradition in which he works
than Derrida has paid him or his tradition. We are the ones trying to
synthesize two philosophical traditions and come to some sense of what
they imply for literary theory. To a certain extent, we always find what
we are looking for in such cross-disciplinary borrowings: one looking for
an opposite to deconstruction will find one; one looking for a resemblance will also find one. But this process of translating analytic arguments into the realm of literary theory has not been at all random or
haphazard, as I hope this brief narrative has shown. The narrative has had
a preexisting shape, and that shape has been determined by the dominant presence of deconstruction and the figure of Jacques Derrida in the
minds of literary theorists. It has been because of Derrida's inescapable
presence that the question brought to a consideration of Davidson's
work has been a simple one: Where does Davidson stand in relation to
Derrida? The inescapableness of this question for literary theory can be
shown in the fact that precisely the same question has been asked of
Austin, constructed by Searle but also by Barbara Johnson, Sam Weber,
and others as an opposite to Derrida (before Felman, Fish, and others
transformed him into an ally of Derrida), and of Wittgenstein, con-

structed by Altieri, Abrams, Ellis, and others as an opposite to Derrida and subsequently construed by Staten, Winspur, Wheeler, and others as an ally, a "conservative deconstructor," to use a phrase of Wheeler's.[8] That this is an inescapable question only for us is shown by the subhead of the first section of Wheeler's essay "Indeterminacy of French Interpretation," "Who and Davidson?" Derrida is not at all the inescapable presence for a mainstream analytic philosopher that he is for literary theorists, and this is one of the factors responsible for the perplexity with which most philosophers regard the theoretical scene.

The historical logic leading literary theorists to ask about the relation between analytic philosophy and deconstruction was a powerful one, and I do not wish to reject this out of hand, as it is primarily the dialogue—both hostile and cooperative—between deconstruction and analytic philosophy under way since the 1977 Derrida–Searle exchange in *Glyph* that has led literary theorists to become aware of analytic philosophy as an intellectual tradition and resource. I have, after all, edited an earlier collection of essays devoted to that dialogue. But now that analytic philosophy has been "put into play" in literary theory, and now that we have a richer sense of the whole tradition—not just the reaction against it—surely there are other, additional questions to ask about the analytic tradition. Several of the essays that follow do touch on the relation between Derrida's work and Davidson's, but it is significant that it is the philosophers who are concerned with this question, still a fresh question for them in a way that it is not for literary theorists. Moreover, the net effect on an audience of literary theorists of finding little difference between, say, Derrida and Davidson is very different from the effect on an audience of analytic philosophers. An analytic philosopher comparing Davidson to Derrida is in a sense breaking out of his or her training to discover the interestingly different world of Derrida's work. Finding that world to be perhaps not so different may encourage further exploration, whereas literary theorists, conversant with Derrida anyway, may simply decide that Davidson (or whoever) is not worth investigating if he is little more than an analytic equivalent to Derrida. I therefore take it as a positive sign that the relation between analytic philosophy and deconstruction—though once with some justice felt to be an urgent issue—is not the (or even a) central concern of the following essays as a whole. For it is time for literary theorists to move from a monistic to a pluralistic understanding about those philosophers (and methods of philosophy) of potential interest to literary theory. It seems to me that by this point in the evolution of the conversation between philosophy and literary theory that has been under way over the past generation, we can bring other questions to bear and we can conceive of fruitful conversations between theorists and philosophers that do not revolve around the fixed star of deconstruction. Such a transformation in the attitude of theorists would of course make most analytic philosophers much more interested in the conversation, much less impatient with what strikes them as the very odd understanding of contemporary philosophy held by literary theorists of various theoretical persuasions.

One aim of this collection, therefore, is to introduce literary theorists to the diversity and complexity of Davidson's work and thus move beyond a restricted understanding of Davidson's achievement. All the contributors agree that it is work which literary theorists need to work through, become familiar with, and meet the challenge of. But this way of putting it raises perhaps a final point that needs to be discussed before turning to the essays that follow. I have referred so far to connections between literary theory and various strands of philosophy (Continental, analytic, and antianalytic) as if there were no disagreement about the general compatibility of these different traditions of thought. To put it simply, I have assumed that these different traditions are translatable. Not everyone thinks so. In particular, despite two decades of influence of analytic philosophy on literary theory, it has been argued that analytic philosophy—unlike Continental philosophy—is simply too remote from the concerns of literary theory to be of any use to it. As Ralph Flores has remarked, "whereas the Continental school is strongly committed (as in Heidegger and Derrida) to reading literature, the analytic school generally is not" (197). One must grant that Davidson's work and the analytic tradition in general do seem at a greater remove from the explicit concerns of literary theory than the work of Continental philosophers such as Nietzsche, Heidegger, and Derrida. Only occasionally has Davidson discussed topics such as metaphor that have been central concerns for literary theorists; and only recently, in such essays as "A Nice Derangement of Epitaphs," "James Joyce and Humpty Dumpty," and (his contribution to the present volume) "Locating Literary Language," has he discussed literature and literary language. This means that connecting Davidson's work to issues in literary theory involves a measure of intellectual translation and often an extension of Davidson's argument into realms he may not have been thinking about at the time. This does help explain why theorists have tended to turn to Continental—rather than analytic—philosophy, but I do not take this to be a decisive argument against any use of analytic philosophy as a resource for literary theory.

I find that even when the concerns of analytic philosophy are not of immediate relevance to the concerns of literary theory, as is sometimes the case, the method of argumentation remains relevant and has a good deal to offer literary theory. In "On the Very Idea of a Conceptual Scheme," Davidson dryly comments about the claims of Kuhn and others he is discussing that "the trouble is, as so often in philosophy, it is hard to improve intelligibility while retaining the excitement" (183). It has been even harder to do so in literary theory. Literary theorists have always loved the striking phrase, the outlandish claim, the absolute statement; preferring the excitement to intelligibility, we have tended to take such claims at face value and not subject them to careful inspection. Moreover, by this point, there are now so many schools, so many established approaches, such a diversity of authorities, that we almost do not even bother to argue with each other, to try to test the theoretical claims that fill our writings. Here, I think, analytic philosophy has a great deal to offer literary theorists as a model of careful, patient, and thorough argumentation. Davidson's analysis of Kuhn, at least in my opinion, as the lead essay reveals, shows that there is not much that is intelligible in Kuhn's claims, despite the excitement. But whether or not Davidson is right does not concern me here so much as that he provides a model of the kind of lucid analysis and discussion sharply lacking in literary theory. In my view, the kind of analytic philosophy Davidson represents is exemplary here in a way that Derrida's work is not: the contrast between, say, the exchange among Davidson, Ian Hacking, and Dummett in *Truth and Interpretation* (433–76) on which David Gorman's essay focuses and Derrida's recent response in *Critical Inquiry* to critics of his piece on Paul de Man ought to make anyone interested in rational argumentation see great value in the analytic tradition. I do not present this as a knockdown argument, for I am aware that the very notion of rational argumentation has been put into question by many and is one of the things that Derrida intends to contest in the way he responds to criticism. But this way of putting it helps to define the project of the present collection. All the contributors, no matter what their theoretical position, believe that literary theory is a field where positions can be defined and argued; moreover, they take analytic philosophy to be exemplary in its mode of argumentation.

This orientation toward analytic philosophy as a model of intellectual argumentation has had some influence on the shape of the collection, the order of the essays, as well as on its content. And although I think the essays speak for themselves and need no extensive summary here, a few comments on their order may help orient the reader. Some of the essays are more purely expository than others, concerned with laying out Davidson's work and the work of other analytic philosophers, while others are more explicitly contestatory. I have placed the more contestatory essays first, but I have also tried to arrange the essays so as to create argumentative dialogue between and among essays. Juxtaposition is therefore a function of a common focus on an aspect of Davidson's work, not agreement about it. This leads to a second principle of order which has to do with the shape of Davidson's own project. His collected essays and the previous collections of essays on his work assume a distinction between his work in philosophy of language, collected in *Inquiries into Truth and Interpretation,* and his work in action theory, collected in *Essays on Actions and Events.* The work in philosophy of language has been more immediately accessible to literary theorists, as Davidson's focus on interpretation brings the concerns of that work quite close to a central and ongoing debate in literary theory over the validity of interpretation. It is for this reason that most of the work on Davidson in literary theory, summarized above in the present introduction, focuses on *Inquiries into Truth and Interpretation,* particularly Davidson's justly famous "On the Very Idea of a Conceptual Scheme." The present collection, too, begins with work focused on Davidson's philosophy of language and on interpretation theory, particularly on conceptual schemes. We begin where the discussion has focused. But in keeping with our aim to move beyond this (or any) restricted notion of Davidson's achievement, the focus shifts as the collection continues—first to work Davidson has done since collecting his papers and, finally, in essays by Allen Dunn and Paisley Livingston, to the heretofore-neglected side of his work, that on action theory. But the essays do not fit into this scheme perfectly, for the distinction between Davidson's philosophy of language and his action theory is ultimately an artificial one; indeed, one of the themes of Davidson's recent work is the interpenetration of the two sides of his work, a theme announced in "Toward a Unified Theory of Meaning and Action" and expressed in detail in "The Structure and Content of Truth." And the following essays on Davidson's work interpenetrate as well, drawing freely on Davidson's full corpus to investigate the relevance of his work to literary theory.

What I want to suggest to literary theorists—and what I think the following essays demonstrate—is that a more thorough encounter with analytic philosophy, particularly with the "harder," mainstream tradition of analytic philosophy represented by the work of Donald Davidson, is likely to prove as rewarding for literary theory as the encounter with speech-act theory or the work of Wittgenstein. Davidson has a good deal more to offer than simply serving as a contrast or parallel to Derrida, and a thorough encounter with Davidson should provoke a comprehensive rethinking of many aspects of literary studies. Some of that rethinking is contained in the essays that follow.

NOTES

1. One critique of Rorty's proposal by a literary theorist is Michael Fischer's excellent "Redefining Philosophy as Literature."
2. David Gorman distinguishes between the two traditions and notes the imbalance in their reception in literary theory before making the shrewd observation that neither Wittgenstein nor Austin can be said to have moved as far from analytic philosophy as they claim: "Has any literary theorist, for example, noticed how wide the gap is between what might be called the official ideology of 'ordinary language' philosophy and the speech-act theory which Austin ended up creating, a theory that involves as technical an apparatus as the Russellian or Tarskian logicism which he began by attacking?" (657).
3. Staten's, Gasché's, and Llewelyn's are among the studies of Derrida that stress this point.
4. Novitz's essay should also be mentioned here, as he compares Davidson's and Derrida's views on metaphor and finds them to be essentially similar. He also finds them to be essentially misguided, however, so his work is off to one side of the sympathetic expositions of this similarity that I survey here.
5. Other essays by Wheeler in which parallels are drawn between deconstruction and recent analytic philosophy are relevant here. "The Extension of Deconstruction" draws a parallel primarily between Derrida and Quine, although Davidson is mentioned, while in "Metaphor According to Davidson and de Man," Derrida is replaced by de Man.
6. Other work by Kent connecting Davidson to issues in composition and rhetoric moves in much the same direction as this collection does, away from the Derrida question and toward a broader engagement with Davidson's work; see Kent's "Externalism and the Production of Discourse" and "On the Very Idea of a Discourse Community" as well as his chapter in the present volume. I have also contributed to this extension of Davidson's ideas to rhetoric in "A Rhetoric of Bumper Stickers."
7. I go into this question in more detail in "Teaching Multicultural Literature."
8. A more detailed narrative of all this can be found in my introduction to *Redrawing the Lines.*

WORKS CITED

Altieri, Charles. *Act and Quality: A Theory of Literary Meaning and Humanistic Understanding.* Amherst: U of Massachusetts P, 1981.

Benjamin, Andrew. "Translation and the History of Philosophy." *Textual Practice* 2, no. 2 (1988): 242–60.

Dasenbrock, Reed Way. "A Rhetoric of Bumper Stickers: What Analytic Philosophy Can Contribute to a New Rhetoric." In *Defining the New Rhetorics.* Ed. Theresa Enos and Stuart Brown. Newbury Park: Sage, 1992. 191–206.

———. "Teaching Multicultural Literature." In *Understanding Others: Cultural and*

Cross-Cultural Studies and the Teaching of Literature. Ed. Joseph Trimmer and Tilly Warnock. Urbana: NCTE, 1992. 35–46.

————, ed. *Redrawing the Lines: Analytic Philosophy, Deconstruction, and Literary Theory.* Minneapolis: U of Minnesota P, 1989.

Derrida, Jacques. "Biodegradables: Seven Diary Fragments." Trans. Peggy Kamuf. *Critical Inquiry* 15, no. 4 (1989): 812–73.

Felman, Shoshana. *The Literary Speech Act: Don Juan with J. L. Austin; or, Seduction in Two Languages.* Trans. Catharine Porter. Ithaca: Cornell UP, 1983.

Fischer, Michael. "Redefining Philosophy as Literature: Richard Rorty's 'Defence' of Literary Culture." In *Reading Rorty: Critical Responses to Philosophy and the Mirror of Nature (and Beyond).* Ed. Alan Malachowski. Oxford: Basil Blackwell, 1990. 233–43.

Fish, Stanley. "With the Compliments of the Author: Reflections on Austin and Derrida." *Critical Inquiry* 8, no. 4 (1982): 693–721.

Flores, Ralph. Review of *Redrawing the Lines* by Reed Way Dasenbrock, ed. *Philosophy and Literature* 14, no. 1 (1990): 196–97.

Gasché, Rodolfe. *The Tain of the Mirror: Derrida and the Philosophy of Reflection.* Cambridge: Harvard UP, 1986.

Gorman, David. "From Small Beginnings: Literary Theorists Encounter Analytic Philosophy." *Poetics Today* 11, no. 3 (1990): 647–59.

Kent, Thomas. "Beyond System: The Rhetoric of Paralogy." *College English* 51, no. 5 (1989): 492–507.

————. "Externalism and the Production of Discourse." *Journal of Advanced Composition* 12, no. 1 (1992): 57–74.

————. "On the Very Idea of a Discourse Community." *College Composition and Communication* 42, no. 4 (1991): 10–29.

————. "Paralogic Hermeneutics and the Possibilities of Rhetoric." *Rhetoric Review* 8, no. 1 (1989): 24–42.

Knapp, Steven, and Walter Benn Michaels. "Against Theory 2: Hermeneutics and Deconstruction." *Critical Inquiry* 14, no. 1 (1987): 49–68.

LePore, Ernest, ed. *Truth and Interpretation: Perspectives on the Philosophy of Donald Davidson.* Oxford: Basil Blackwell, 1985.

LePore, Ernest, and Brian P. McLaughlin, eds. *Actions and Events: Perspectives on the Philosophy of Donald Davidson.* Oxford: Basil Blackwell, 1985.

Llewelyn, John. *Derrida on the Threshold of Sense.* New York: St. Martin's, 1986.

MacCabe, Colin. "Broken English." *Critical Quarterly* 28, nos. 1 and 2 (1986): 3–14.

McCormick, Peter J. *Fictions, Philosophies, and the Problems of Poetics.* Ithaca: Cornell UP, 1988.

Norris, Christopher. *The Contest of Faculties: Philosophy and Theory After Deconstruction.* London: Methuen, 1985.

————. *Deconstruction and the Interests of Theory.* London: Pinter, 1988.

————. "Introduction." *Textual Practice* 2, no. 2 (1988): 219–29.

Novitz, David. "Metaphor, Derrida, and Davidson." *Journal of Aesthetics and Art Criticism* 44, no. 2 (1985): 101–14.

Pradhan, Shekhar. "Minimalist Semantics: Davidson and Derrida on Meaning, Use, and Convention." *Diacritics* 16, no. 1 (1986): 66–77.

Rorty, Richard. *Contingency, Irony, and Solidarity.* Cambridge: Cambridge UP, 1989.

———. *Philosophy and the Mirror of Nature.* Princeton: Princeton UP, 1979.

———. "Philosophy as a Kind of Writing." In *Consequences of Pragmatism: Essays, 1972–1980.* Minneapolis: U of Minnesota P, 1982. 90–109.

Saunders, Ian. "The Concept Discourse." *Textual Practice* 2, no. 2 (1988): 230–41. ✓

Staten, Henry. *Wittgenstein and Derrida.* Lincoln: U of Nebraska P, 1984.

Taylor, Gabriele. *Pride, Shame, and Guilt: Emotions of Self-Assessment.* Oxford: Clarendon, 1985.

Vermazen, Bruce, and Merrill B. Hintikka, eds. *Essays on Davidson: Actions and Events.* Oxford: Oxford UP, 1985.

West, Cornel. "Afterword: The Politics of American Neo-Pragmatism." In *Post-Analytic Philosophy.* Ed. John Rajchman and Cornel West. New York: Columbia UP, 1985. 259–75.

Wheeler, Samuel C. III. "The Extension of Deconstruction." *The Monist* 69, no. 1 (1986): 3–21.

———. "Indeterminacy of French Interpretation: Derrida and Davidson." In LePore. 477–94.

———. "Metaphor According to Davidson and de Man." In Dasenbrock, ed., *Redrawing the Lines.* 116–39.

Do We Write the Text We Read?

REED WAY DASENBROCK

Ne of the relatively unexamined
and uncontested notions in recent literary theory is the notion advanced
by Barbara Herrnstein Smith, Stanley Fish, and others that as each reader
reads a text differently, somehow the text itself is different for each
reader. Barbara Herrnstein Smith has argued this position in terms of the
actual history of the criticism of literary texts:

> presumably Hallam did read [Shakespeare's *Sonnets*], as did Dr.
> Johnson, Coleridge, Wordsworth, Hazlitt and Byron (from each of
> whom I have been quoting here): but whether any of them read
> the same poems we are reading is another question. Value alters
> when it alteration finds. The texts were the same, but it seems
> clear that, in some sense, the *poems* weren't. [5]

Or again,

> when David Hume, in "Of the Standard of Taste," observed with
> complacency that "the same Homer who pleased at Athens and
> Rome two thousand years ago is still admired at Paris and Lon-
> don," we have reason to wonder if it is indeed quite "the same"
> Homer. [15]

Given the focus of her work on evaluation, Herrnstein Smith never
explains why this might be so, but Stanley Fish gives us an explanation

that is compatible with her perception. He simply argues that "the notions of the 'same' or 'different' texts are fictions" (*Is There a Text* 169). Hume is not reading the same poem read at Athens and Rome because each of us creates the poem we read:

> Interpretation is not the art of construing but the art of constructing. Interpreters do not decode poems; they make them. [*Is There a Text* 327]

And we do so by relying upon a set of interpretive assumptions:

> either decision would give rise to a set of interpretive strategies, which, when put into action, would *write* the text I write when reading *Lycidas.* [169][1]

Although this more radical conclusion of Fish's is not one that Herrnstein Smith has explicitly drawn, it is entirely congruent with her notion that the modern Homer is not the same as the classical Homer. If our Homer and theirs are different, what causes that difference? Clearly, the interpreter, not the poet.

I hope to show four things about the notion that readers read different texts and create the text they read: 1) that this position in literary theory is a form of what Donald Davidson has called "conceptual relativism"; 2) that the arguments he has made against conceptual relativism, above all in "On the Very Idea of a Conceptual Scheme," show this position to be incoherent; 3) that Davidson's own work on radical interpretation offers a much more satisfactory account of why our interpretations of texts differ so radically; and 4) that a Davidsonian account of interpretation makes much better sense than conceptual relativist theory can of why we study literature and of what value that study can have.

Readers produce different texts as they read, according to Fish, above all because they have different beliefs: "The shape of belief . . . is responsible for the shape of interpretation" (*Doing What Comes Naturally* 43). We see different things in the world because we hold different interpretive assumptions about the world: where one person sees a sun or moon "in trouble," another sees an eclipse; where one person sees bread and wine, another sees the blood and flesh of Christ. As Imre Lakatos has put it, "there are and can be no sensations unimpregnated by expectations" (99); and it is equally true that no interpretation can be "unimpregnated by expectations." Just as what we see depends upon what we bring to the seeing, what we read depends upon what we bring to the reading. Further, we do not hold these different interpretive expectations and assumptions in isolation, but as members of a larger community:

> Thus while it is true to say that we create poetry (and assignments and lists), we create it through interpretive strategies that are finally not our own but have their source in a publicly available system of intelligibility. Insofar as the system (in this case a literary system) constrains us, it also fashions us, furnishing us with categories of understanding, with which we in turn fashion the entities to which we can point. [Fish, *Is There a Text* 332]

This interpretive system, however, is dynamic, not static. The interpretive system of one moment in time is not that of another, and this is why the texts we read/write change across time. Samuel Johnson's Milton is not Stanley Fish's Milton, and the reason for this is as much the different cultures or intellectual frames of reference in which they operate as it is any personal difference between the two interpreters.

One fact that might be said to support Fish's case is that Fish's way of thinking about these questions comes in large measure from his own contemporary "frame of reference," as his model of interpretation resembles the work of a number of contemporary thinkers, most notably Thomas Kuhn's work in *The Structure of Scientific Revolutions.* According to Kuhn, even when scientists use the same terms, they can mean utterly different things by them:

> In the transition from one theory to the next words change their meanings or conditions of applicabilities in subtle ways. Though most of the same signs are used before and after a revolution— e.g. force, mass, element, compound, cell—the ways in which some of them attach to nature has somehow changed. Successive theories are thus, we say, incommensurable. ["Reflections" 266– 67; see also *Structure* 4, 148–50]

And this notion that meaning changes even when the words are the same is identical to Fish's and Herrnstein Smith's notion that poems are somehow different for successive readers even if the words are the same. The reason for this is also the same as that advanced by Fish, theory dependence, and theory dependence leads to a situation in which different scientists cannot even communicate clearly with each other:

communication between proponents of different theories is inevitably partial, [as] what each takes to be facts depends in part on
the theory he espouses. . . . Without pursuing the matter further, I
simply assert the existence of significant limits to what the proponents of different theories can communicate to each other. [*The
Essential Tension* 338]

This emphasis on "proponents of different theories" is part of Kuhn's
insistence that the construction and maintenance of theories is inevitably
social.[2] Scientists working as members of different social groups work
within different "paradigms," and scientists with different paradigms
"work in a different world" (*Structure* 135) and "are responding to a
different world" (111). In contrast, those who hold a theory or paradigm
in common work within the same world and can communicate successfully with each other; they are, in short, an interpretive community.

Kuhn's work is certainly not the only contemporary work tending in
this direction. Although Kuhn comes closer to Fish's language than anyone else, W. V. Quine's notions of referential opacity and radical translation, the work of Edward Sapir and Benjamin Whorf on the metaphysics
of non-Western languages, and Wittgenstein's work in *On Certainty* also
can be interpreted as supporting similar formulations.[3] But Kuhn is someone Fish has cited as offering support for his position,[4] and for this
reason Donald Davidson's direct attack on Kuhn's work in "On the Very
Idea of a Conceptual Scheme" is worth the attention of literary theorists.[5] Davidson's term for Kuhn's position is "conceptual relativism," and
by this he means to call attention to Kuhn's key notion that truth (or
what is recognized as truth by a scientific community) is relative to a
conceptual scheme.[6] And although Fish has strongly dissociated himself
from the interpretive relativism or pluralism of Wayne Booth and others,[7] his Kuhnian explanation of interpretive differences is clearly the
kind of thing under attack in Davidson's essay:

Conceptual schemes, we are told, are ways of organizing experience; they are systems of categories that give form to the data of
sensation; they are points of view from which individuals, cultures, or periods survey the passing scene. [*ITI* 183]

Unfortunately, it makes no sense according to Davidson to talk in this
way about conceptual schemes or interpretive frameworks:

Conceptual relativism is a heady and exotic doctrine, or would be if we could make good sense of it. The trouble is, as so often in philosophy, it is hard to improve intelligibility while retaining the excitement. [183]

Fish's ideas about interpretation have generated a good deal of excitement, but applying Davidson's critique of Kuhn's work to Fish's notions reveals them to be ultimately unintelligible.

What is wrong with the notion of a conceptual scheme? Davidson has several objections, and I hope that I can do justice to the complexity of his argument in my necessarily brief summary. Probably the most fundamental objection is that it makes sense neither of our own beliefs nor of the beliefs of others. As speakers with beliefs about the world, we utter sentences that we hold to be true about the world. We do not hold these sentences to be true relative to a larger scheme which is true about the world; we simply hold these sentences to be true. It is unlikely that they are all true, but it is even more unlikely that they are all false. So our views about the world must not form the seamless web implied by terms like "paradigm," "conceptual scheme," or "interpretive community"; they do not necessarily all hang together as part of a scheme. Moreover, unless we hold all conceptual schemes to be true, in which case we are using the word "true" in a peculiar and private sense, then as Fish insists (*Is There a Text* 361) we must hold our own conceptual scheme to be true and those different conceptual schemes held by others to be false. But if they are incommensurable, how can we assign truth-values to them? How can we understand what in fact such schemes are, if they are truly incommensurable?

Davidson's rejoinder to this denial of translatability is simply to ask how it is that we know this or can know it. To say that someone's beliefs are unknowably different from our own is to imply that we know what those beliefs are and therefore know them to be different. Therefore, any claim to have described—or even to have perceived—a different conceptual scheme implies the very translatability it explicitly denies:

Whorf, wanting to demonstrate that Hopi incorporates a metaphysics so alien to ours that Hopi and English cannot, as he puts it, 'be calibrated', uses English to convey the contents of sample Hopi sentences. Kuhn is brilliant at saying what things were like before the revolution using—what else?—our post-revolutionary idiom. . . . The dominant metaphor of conceptual relativism, that of differing points of view, seems to betray an underlying paradox. [*ITI* 184][8]

Thus, Kuhn and others who have stressed the linguisticality of scientific explanation want to have it both ways. They want to claim that the other scheme is unknowably different from our own, but also that they know what the other scheme is. The paradox may be less important for literary theory than the attitude toward other conceptual schemes—particularly those of the past—that comes in its train:

> We may now seem to have a formula for generating distinct conceptual schemes. We get a new out of an old scheme when the speakers of a language come to accept as true an important range of sentences they previously took to be false (and, of course, vice versa). We must not describe this change simply as a matter of their coming to view old falsehoods as truths, for a truth is a proposition, and what they come to accept, in accepting a sentence as true, is not the same thing that they rejected when formerly they held the sentence to be false. A change has come over the meaning of the sentence because it now belongs to a new language.
>
> This picture of how new (and perhaps better) schemes result from new and better science is very much the picture philosophers of science, like Putnam and Feyerabend, and historians of science, like Kuhn, have painted for us. [188][9]

And, I think we can add, the picture that literary critics such as Fish and Herrnstein Smith have painted for us. (One difference is that, for them, the new scheme cannot be shown to be better than the old, just radically different.) For although this notion of how words and meanings change in important ways could be used to support a historicist program of interpretation which argues that the past meanings of words differed in ways we need to recover and understand, the language of conceptual schemes suggests instead that because these conceptual schemes and worlds differ, we cannot even know what those meanings were. This calls, not for careful historicizing, but for the kind of triumphalist modernizing represented by Stanley Fish. As we can never know Milton's own sense of his own words, all we can know is our own. Because the text changes as the world changes, the text we read/write is the only one we have.

Davidson again would ask how we can know this. Once we grant that we can mean different things by the same words, the contrasting point that our different words establish that we live in different worlds breaks down. For we can also mean the same thing by different words, and apparent incommensurabilities may conceal commensurability:

> Suppose that in my office of Minister of Scientific Language I want the new man to stop using words that refer, say, to emotions, feelings, thoughts, and intentions, and to talk instead of the physiological states and happenings that are assumed to be more or less identical with the mental riff and raff. How do I tell whether my advice has been heeded if the man speaks a new language? For all I know, the shiny new phrases . . . may in his mouth play the role of the messy old mental concepts. . . . Instead of living in different worlds, Kuhn's scientists may, like those who need Webster's dictionary, be only words apart. [*ITI* 188–89]

We do not live in different conceptual worlds, "since there is at most one world" (187). And members of the one world we all live in and share do not neatly divide into those with whom we share a conceptual scheme (members of our interpretive community) and those with whom we do not (members of other interpretive communities). This does not mean, however, as Davidson concludes, that we all necessarily live in the "same world" and can take successful translation/interpretation for granted:

> It would be equally wrong to announce the glorious news that all mankind—all speakers of language, at least—share a common scheme and ontology. For if we cannot intelligibly say that schemes are different, neither can we intelligibly say that they are one. [198]

What it means is that the world contains different speakers and interpreters, who sometimes use the same words and sometimes not, who sometimes hold the same beliefs and sometimes not. Neither Kuhn's assumption of utter intelligibility within a community nor his assumption of utter unintelligibility across communities holds up to sustained examination.

By extending this Davidsonian account to the issue of interpreting texts—which is not something Davidson has done[10]—we reveal the incoherence of the notion advanced by Herrnstein Smith and Fish that different readers read different texts. No plausible case can be made by a conceptual relativist for the position that our interpretations are so far apart that they are interpretations of different objects or texts altogether. The only evidence we could marshal for such a claim is the difference in the ways we describe our interpretations, but since the sameness in words between Johnson's Milton and Fish's was said not to establish a similarity between them, no conceptual relativist can logically argue for a difference in understanding based on a difference in the words we use. The apparent difference between Johnson's account of Milton and Fish's cannot in any way establish that they are reading different Miltons or writing the Milton they are reading. They do seem to be seeing different things in the same text; but if, when we investigate this difference, we decide that they are seeing different things, the very confidence with which we make that decision implies that we can translate Johnson's perceptions into Fish's language and, therefore, that their accounts are not incommensurable. If the reverse were true, and if we could not figure out Johnson, then we could never know whether or not he was saying exactly the same thing as Fish, just in a different language. To argue that interpreters write texts is to posit that words do not point reliably to meanings in the interpretation of texts but that they do in the interpretation of different interpretations. This is simply incoherent. How can we know so confidently the meaning of what Johnson wrote about Milton and not be able to extend that knowledge to what Milton himself wrote?

What Davidson would tell us seems right: there is at most one text just as there is at most one world, and we share that text just as we share the world.[11] That does not mean that we see the text in the same way, any more than we all speak the same language, but neither does it mean that we are seeing something utterly different. For we cannot know whether we are seeing something different unless we can understand each other's perspective, translate each other's language; and if we can understand and translate another's perspective, it cannot have the radical otherness supposed by Herrnstein Smith and Fish. It is not our different interpretive communities that keep us apart; it is simply our different interpretations.

So Davidsonian arguments reveal the incoherence of the notion that the differences in our interpretations reveal us to be reading different texts or writing the text we read. But can Davidson help us put something better in its place? For the history of the interpretation of any text is one of disagreement, and Fish's stress on interpretive communities did offer an account of why such disagreement takes place that was a considerable improvement over earlier accounts.[12] I think Davidson can help here as well, as his work on what he calls "radical interpretation" offers an account of interpretive disagreement more attractive than that offered by the notion of an interpretive community writing the text it reads.[13] These accounts overlap for a certain distance, however, and we need to specify that overlap before specifying their disagreement.

Fish and Davidson are in perfect agreement that there are no uninterpreted givens; no interpretations can be said to be neutral or objective, as all are hazarded with reference to the beliefs of the interpreter. Therefore, what we do when we encounter an object of interpretation—whether a spoken utterance, a cultural event, or a written text—is to understand that object on our own terms. Davidson's term for this is "interpretive charity." Faced with something to interpret, we interpret so as to maximize agreement, so as to credit the other speaker or writer with beliefs as much like our own as possible. According to Davidson, "charity is forced upon us": "charity is not an option, but a condition of having a workable theory" (*ITI* 197).

So far, this line of argument is in perfect keeping with the notion of interpretive communities: we interpret according to our beliefs, and our interpretations, therefore, necessarily accord with our beliefs. The difference in the two accounts is that, for Fish, this is the starting and the end point of the interpretive process. This is simply what we do as we read, and as there can be no distance between us and our beliefs, we have no alternative. There is no more escaping this than there is escape from belief: "There is no end to the ways in which you can assert your beliefs—no end to styles of self-presentation—but none of them involve the loosening of the hold they have on you" (*Doing What Comes Naturally* 21). For Davidson, in contrast, interpretive charity is where you start from but not necessarily where you end up. We begin the interpretive process by positing a broad area of agreement on beliefs and meanings. But because beliefs and meanings differ (not totally, but appreciably), interpreters find that their assumption of shared agreement on belief and meaning needs modification in places. We begin, in other words, by assuming agreement precisely because that enables us to find and make sense of disagreement. When disagreement is encountered, we then adjust our theory about the speaker's beliefs and language use in order to make sense of this anomaly. To use the terms advanced in Davidson's recent essay "A Nice Derangement of Epitaphs," we begin with a "prior theory" ("NDE" 442), a set of assumptions about the dispositions, beliefs, and language use of the speaker/writer. These are the expectations that impregnate experience. But as we encounter the anomalous, we develop a "passing theory" (442), a modified version of the prior theory adjusted to fit what we have learned about the other.[14]

So our end point is not a reification of our own prior theory, as Fish assumes, the production of a reading in strict accordance with interpretive community-specific norms. Interpreters adjust their prior theories in the direction of what they take to be a provisional agreement between speaker/writer and interpreter. This agreement is not created—as Fish would insist—by the interpreter overwhelming the text by his or her beliefs and values, but by adjusting them to the demands of the interpretive occasion.[15] But this adjustment of the interpreter to the text is not a perfect match of the two, as a theory of interpretation such as E. D. Hirsch's or as Fish's early reader-response criticism must maintain. There is (I think Davidson would hold) no necessary relation between a text and the passing theory an interpreter develops in response to it, no indisputably "correct" interpretation. Prior theories and passing theories are both irreducibly plural, and this is in accord with our actual experience of interpretation. But if there is no perfect meeting of minds, the minds that have interacted do not remain unchanged in the exchange. Certain theories are *disconfirmed,* even if none is ever indisputably confirmed. And that is the point I find particularly valuable in Davidson's model of interpretation. Prior theories are never monolithic, never an exact match of each other or an exact match for the situation. Prior theories, therefore, always undergo modification in the situation for which and in which they are advanced.

Now, why is this Davidsonian account of interpretation a better account of interpretation than that provided by Stanley Fish? First, because it is a better account of what we actually do as interpreters. Fish's own anecdotes of interpretive disagreements, like the anecdote in the essay "Is There a Text in This Class?" (*Is There a Text* 305–13), are much better explained on Davidsonian lines than on his own. The professor who misread (or mis-preread) the student's question, "Is there a text in this class?" obviously did so in keeping with his prior theory about what such a sentence was likely to mean, but he was not imprisoned within his prior theory or his beliefs about the meaning of words; he quickly constituted a passing theory and adjusted his understanding of the language to interpret this anomalous utterance. Likewise, the students in Fish's class in "How to Recognize a Poem When You See One" (*Is There a Text* 322–29), faced with the task of interpreting his list of names as a typological poem, constructed a passing theory for the text examined in this strange class with the marvelous ease that good students always exhibit. We do adjust, we do change, in order to interpret anomalous utterances, in ways that the theory of the interpretive community writing the text it reads does not quite make sense of.

But there is a crucial difference between these two anecdotes told by Fish that provides the other reason for endorsing a Davidsonian account. If an interpreter adjusts a prior theory to construct a passing theory to interpret an anomalous utterance, what happens next? With what theory does one subsequently face the world? This is not a question Davidson has explicitly discussed, but it seems to me that there are two options, and these are well illustrated in Fish's two examples. First, one could turn the passing theory into a new prior theory, incorporating the adjustments into one's beliefs. The professor who came to understand "Is there a text in this class?" as a question about his theoretical beliefs presumably retained that understanding of the sentence. He learned something from his interpretation, something that he may have found of use later. But one could also write off the passing theory as appropriate only to an anomalous situation and not incorporate it into one's future prior theory. I suspect that Fish's students never again interpreted a list of names as a typological poem. They created a passing theory for an anomalous situation; that situation passed, they had no further use for it, and what they learned did not become a part of any future prior theory.

In short, Davidson's model of interpretation allows for the possibility of learning from experience, something Fish's model of interpreters always certain of their interpretations does not and cannot. A number of critics have seen this weakness in Fish's model. Gerald Graff argues that "Fish in effect posited an interpretive world in which no reader could ever explicably experience *surprise*" (111), and Jonathan Culler has made almost the same point in his discussion of Fish: "A reader who creates everything learns nothing" (72). Interpretations are not always self-confirming; interpreters do not always produce interpretations utterly consistent with their prior beliefs and theories; theories are sometimes adjusted to fit experience rather than vice versa.

This is one of the points where Fish's reliance on contemporary philosophy of science might have helped. Kuhn and others have stressed that observation is theory-laden, but no philosopher of science argues as Fish does that observation is entirely determined by the observer's theories. There may be no neutral observation-language and there certainly is no direct, unmediated access to reality, but this does not mean that we are constrained in a prison house of our own theories. The legal theorist Ronald Dworkin has made this point well:

> It is now a familiar thesis among philosophers of science and epistemology, after all, that people's beliefs even about the facts that make up the physical world are the consequence of their

more general scientific theories. . . . If we held very different beliefs about the theoretical parts of physics and the other sciences,
we would, in consequence, divide the world into very different
entities, and the facts we "encountered" about these different
entities would be very different from the facts we now take to be
unassailable.

Now suppose we accepted this general view of knowledge and
drew from it the startling conclusion that discrete scientific hypotheses cannot be tested against facts at all, because once a
theory has been adopted there are no wholly independent facts
against which to test that theory. We would have misunderstood
the philosophical thesis we meant to apply. For the point of that
thesis is not to deny that facts constrain theories but to explain
how they do. There is no paradox in the proposition that facts
both depend on and constrain the theories that explain them.
[293]

Again, this does not mean that some miraculous, interpretation-free consensus is to be had on the far side of disagreement. But even if we do not
know the world aside from our interpretation of it, this does not mean
that the world *is* our interpretation of it. If it were, our interpretations
would never change and would never undergo successful and persuasive
refutation; but change they do, as we change and refine our theories in
accord with our changing experience.

Now, why is it so important that Davidson's theory allows the interpreter
to learn from experience, to refine one's theory in accordance with
experience? Precisely because it gives us a reason to study literature, or,
to put it another way, it explains why we find that study valuable. If
interpretations are always self-confirming, we can never learn anything
from any actual act of interpretation, except to learn once more that the
shoe fits. If an interpretation cannot be disproven, if nothing unexpected
can happen, then the only question to ask about any interpretation is
whether it is well or badly done, precisely the question most often asked
about contemporary "readings." In this context, what can we learn in
literary study or about literary study? Only how to do it the way it is
done, only the technique of being a professional. This is clearly the
pedagogy implied in Fish's "interpretive community" model of interpretation. What we can learn is to become members of the community, to
learn to do it the way it is done. If there is agreement on beliefs within
the community, what distinguishes the full member from the apprentice

is only the skill with which each interprets. The fully professional interpreter knows how to produce a reading in the way sanctioned by the
community, and that is all the knowledge that any interpreter *qua* interpreter can have.

This seems to me to be a particularly arid and impoverished notion of
what constitutes literary study, the entire world of reading reduced to
interpretation as a virtuoso performance. I can remember in graduate
school some of my fellow graduate assistants complaining that the under-
graduate students they were teaching were interested only in discussing
what literary works were about ("themes for crissake," as one colleague
memorably expressed it), as opposed to the really interesting questions
of form, technique, and—best of all—theory. And this is in miniature the
situation that obtains in many literature classrooms across the country:
from one side enters the student, with an unconscious but tenacious
prior theory that works of literature can teach us about life; from the
other, enters the professor, armed with the prior theory that literary
texts are not really about anything or that we cannot know what they are
about, doomed as we are to write the text we read according to our own
beliefs and values. How can we create a passing theory capable of creating understanding in this situation?

Davidson is of help here as well. The principle of radical interpretation tells us that we assume that those we interpret share our beliefs
until we are shown otherwise, and this is a principle reconfirmed again
and again in the literature classroom. Faced with the end of Edith Wharton's *The Age of Innocence,* it seems perfectly obvious to most under-
graduates that fifty-seven-year-old Newland Archer should walk up that
flight of stairs, take Ellen Olenska in his arms after not having seen her for
twenty-six years and "make up for all that lost time." Faced with an
ending in which he does no such thing, their first interpretive gesture is
to read the ending ironically, which is a perfect example of adjustment
so as to maximize agreement.[16] They cannot adjust Newland's actions to
fit their beliefs—even though they did so when anticipating "a happy
ending"—so they adjust Wharton's beliefs to match their own, seeing
her as criticizing Newland in the way they wish to. And here, as Fish
would suggest, they are "writing the text" in accord with their beliefs.
But that is only the first step for a good class, just as it is only the first
step in Davidsonian interpretation: making the adjustment, reflective
students ask why we need to, why Wharton did not give us the ending
we want and why she might have done so. A set of related questions is
involved here: Why did Newland Archer do what he did? Why did Edith
Wharton construct the text in this way? How do we respond to the

denouement? And, in a lively class, a discussion quickly emerges over precisely the issues we have been concerned with here: do Wharton's beliefs differ from ours, and how can we know what hers were?[17]

What emerges from this reflection? What is the value of such a discussion? In the first place, reflection takes place. Faced with an anomaly in terms of their beliefs, students encounter someone who shares many of their beliefs (about, for example, the importance of love) but not this one. To make sense of the ending, one must adjust one's prior belief that imagined gratifications—especially where love is involved—pale in comparison to realized ones; one must create a passing theory that includes the notion that some people—including Newland Archer and possibly Edith Wharton—disagree. That is undoubtedly the kind of perception one would incorporate in any future prior theory. Whether or not one also changes one's own mind about such matters in the course of reading and reflecting on *The Age of Innocence,* whether or not one thinks Newland is right, is a different question, and different readers are going to answer it in different ways. It remains open, and interestingly open, how much of the passing theory is reintegrated into the prior theory, how much one's beliefs are changed by the encounter with another's belief.

In short, to interpret another's utterance we begin by assuming provisional agreement on what we believe to be true. But that provisional, heuristic step is necessary only because, as we actually interpret, we encounter anomalies, sentences that do not seem to agree with what we hold true. Our immediate reaction when we encounter difference is to refuse that difference, to preserve the maximum of agreement; and there are times when this works, when we get away with assuming that we are saying the same thing, if in different words. But the interesting moments are when this does not work so well, when we realize that what we are interpreting does indeed express beliefs different from our own. This, for me, is the most important reason to read and to study literature: to break out of our own circle of beliefs and assumptions and to encounter another point of view. The key issue on which Fish and I disagree is whether this is possible or not. Fish recognizes that we encounter other, competing interpretations advanced by other readers; but nowhere in his system does he allow us to assign any otherness to the text itself, for it is always something we possess and have written according to our own beliefs. The problem here is not just that Fish is inconsistent, that he allows us to understand the difference between us and other critics but not the difference between us and the text. The more serious problem is that this inconsistency trivializes the study of literature by denying us any productive encounter with difference.

What is wrong with Fish's "interpretive community" model of interpretation, the notion that readers write texts, is, finally, that it is a hermeneutics of identity. The model of interpretive communities assumes, because we can understand only on our own terms, that the text cannot be understood and at the same time be understood to be different from us. And this is the problem with most contemporary methods and theories of interpretation—even deconstruction, despite all its talk of difference. In each case we understand a text by making it like us. In the words of Paul de Man, "The ideologies of otherness and of hermeneutic understanding are simply not compatible, and therefore their relationship is not a dialogical but simply a contradictory one" (105).[18] It has been my argument here that this sort of thinking reduces the reading and study of literature to an empty and formalist circle, a conversation among ourselves. What we need, in contrast, is a genuine hermeneutics of difference, particularly cultural difference,[19] an interpretive method that can understand texts different from us and understand them to be different from us. This is precisely what Davidson's theory of interpretation gives us, which is why Davidson's work on interpretation should be of interest to anyone engaged in literary study.

NOTES

1. My citations here come from *Is There a Text in This Class?* but Fish's subsequent collection of essays, *Doing What Comes Naturally*, shows that his stance on this issue has not changed. One representative formulation from the new book: "One cannot then ground the difference between literary and legal interpretation in the different kinds of texts they address, because the textual differences are themselves constituted by already differing interpretive strategies, and not the other way around" (304).

Other critics have made similar claims, both independently and in support of Fish's position. Robert Crosman, for example, claims that "the statement 'authors make meaning,' though not of course untrue, is merely a special case of the more universal truth that readers make meaning" (151). Steven Mailloux comes to a virtually identical conclusion: "In fact, literary texts and their meanings are never prior to the employment of interpretive conventions; they are always its results. Texts do not cause interpretations, interpretations constitute texts" (197).

2. Kuhn's emphases in his work after *The Structure of Scientific Revolutions*, particularly "Reflections on My Critics" and the essays collected in *The Essential Tension*, are in fact closer to Fish than *The Structure of Scientific Revolutions*: in contrast to the earlier work's stress on the paradigm as a unifying force, the later work stresses how the scientific community agrees on the paradigm (see "Reflections" 237–38, 253 and *The Essential Tension* 294–301). But this was clear enough—if less prominent—in *The Structure of Scientific Revolutions* (153, 168–74).

3. Fish's work has been related to Wittgenstein's *On Certainty* in several essays: see Law and my own "Accounting for the Changing Certainties of Interpretive Communities," a critique of Fish I now regard as insufficiently critical of many of his assumptions. It has been suggested

that Fish's position is close to Quine's, but I see no evidence of any deep engagement with Quine on Fish's part.

4. Fish cites Kuhn briefly in *Is There a Text in This Class?* (362–63) but much more frequently in *Doing What Comes Naturally* (125–26, 143, 159–60, 225, 322–23, 345, 349, 486–88), suggesting that Fish arrived at his position independently but sees Kuhn as offering support for it. Robert Scholes has argued both that Kuhn was an influence on Fish's notion of interpretive communities and that this notion "is based on a mistaken interpretation of Thomas Kuhn's paradigm theory, which is often abused by humanists for their own ends" (158; see 149–65 for the whole discussion). I agree with Scholes that the concept of interpretive communities is flawed; but I think that Kuhn's notion of paradigms has precisely the same problems, and here Scholes and I probably disagree. In any case, his focus is on the notion of interpretive communities; mine on the related but separable claim that we write the text we read, a claim that Scholes does not directly treat.

Interestingly, in *Doing What Comes Naturally*, Fish also cites Davidson as supporting his position, if only in passing: "I [stand] in the practice and convention-centered tradition that includes Ludwig Wittgenstein, W. V. Quine, Hilary Putnam, Richard Rorty, and Donald Davidson, in addition to Jacques Derrida, Michel Foucault, and other continental thinkers" (577). But there is an enormous difference in contemporary philosophy of language between a practice-centered and a convention-centered approach. Davidson has, of course, repeatedly criticized the notion central to speech-act theory that language is conventional (see "NDE" 446 as well as "Communication and Convention" [in *ITI* 265–80]), and if Fish considers himself to be in a tradition with Davidson, this seems true only in the very broad sense that Fish's general approach to literary theory is indebted to the Anglo-American analytic tradition. But such a claim fits oddly with his critique (in a number of essays in *Doing What Comes Naturally*) of the attempt to ground literary theory in philosophy.

5. It should be noted that Davidson is far from the only person to criticize Kuhn: see Lakatos and Musgrave for an entire book of essays largely critical of Kuhn; and Gutting for a collection of essays—both critical and appreciative—on Kuhn's influence. Moreover, Sir Karl Popper's essay in Lakatos and Musgrave, "Normal Science and Its Dangers," criticizes Kuhn along lines close to Davidson's: "Kuhn suggests that the rationality of science presupposes the acceptance of a common framework. He suggests that rationality *depends* upon something like a common language and a common set of assumptions.... The relativistic thesis that the framework *cannot* be critically discussed is a thesis which *can* be critically discussed and which does not stand up to criticism. I have dubbed this thesis *The Myth of the Framework*, and I have discussed it on various occasions. I regard it as a logical and philosophical mistake" (56).

6. The term "conceptual scheme" is not one Davidson has coined, as Toulmin applies it to Kuhn's position in a manner close to Davidson in an earlier article fairly sympathetic to Kuhn's work (40). I have not found Kuhn using the term, although he does accept Popper's related term, "framework," as a description of his approach ("Reflections" 242). Lakatos splits the difference between the two and refers to "conceptual framework" (132), which I think is probably the best term of the three.

7. Fish's position on relativism relies on the theory of logical types to distinguish between the first-order position of the critic and the second-order, or metacritical, position of the theorist. Relativism is a second-order position, so no one can be a relativist (*Is There a Text* 319). Although on the level of critical practice his point seems well taken, the metacritical position that emerges from Fish's work seems to be clearly relativist, granting his point that it is not a position one can occupy while actually engaged in criticism (370). His recent attack on literary theory itself (see a number of essays in *Doing What Comes Naturally*, particularly "Consequences" [315–41] and "Dennis Martinez and the Uses of Theory" [372–98]) seems to be based on the notion that one cannot attain a metacritical position above critical practice, but this is itself a metacritical position: the fact that he can make such a metacritical claim denies

his position. The interpretive relativism he has attacked, therefore, is first-order or critical relativism; the relativism that Davidson attacks is second-order or metacritical, and Fish's position seems metacritically relativist in the same way that Kuhn's is.

Barbara Herrnstein Smith seems much less offended by the term "relativism," although she is careful to distinguish her characterization of relativism from the bogeyman relativism, "a phantom heresy dreamt by anxious orthodoxy under siege" (151; see 150–84 for her full discussion). But my aim here is not to contribute to the growing literature concerning relativism, objectivism, pseudorelativism, pseudoobjectivism, and so on as much as it is to focus on the narrower claim by Fish and Herrnstein Smith that the text changes for each reader. That claim, whether relativist or not, seems incorrect, and Davidson (whose work strikes some readers as relativist, others as antirelativist) offers sound arguments against such a claim.

8. Bjørn Ramberg has argued recently that the conventional interpretation of incommensurability as "intranslatability" relied on by Davidson is incorrect, and he offers a suggestive reading of Kuhn arguing that incommensurability is "a breakdown of linguistic conventions" and, therefore, that "the meaning of what is said is in principle *theoretically recoverable*" (130). This Davidsonian reading of Kuhn is attractive, although there are certainly passages in Kuhn that are difficult to reconcile with it. In any case, even if Ramberg is right and Kuhn is more Davidsonian than anyone has realized, this does not so much affect Davidson's and my critique of Kuhnianism as it serves to differentiate Kuhn's work from the use that has been made of it.

9. Davidson's grouping together of Putnam, Feyerabend, and Kuhn here seems to me to need a little qualification. Although I am not sure precisely which of Putnam's texts Davidson has in mind, Putnam—albeit subsequently to "On the Very Idea of a Conceptual Scheme"—has criticized Kuhn and Feyerabend (see esp. "Two Conceptions of Rationality" [113–19], chapter 5 of *Reason, Truth and History*) in terms similar to Davidson's: "I wish to discuss a claim Kuhn does make in both the *SSR* and subsequent papers, and that Feyerabend made both in *Against Method* and in technical papers. This is the thesis of *incommensurability*. I want to say that this thesis, like the logical positivist thesis about meaning and verification, is a self-refuting thesis.... To tell us that Galileo had 'incommensurable' notions *and then to go on to describe them at length* is totally incoherent" (114–15). But Davidson's and Putnam's identification of Kuhn and Feyerabend on this point seems correct enough: although Feyerabend criticizes Kuhn on other grounds less pertinent to our inquiry here, he has endorsed Kuhn's language of incommensurability (202, 219–29), and in fact Kuhn cites Feyerabend in support of his views ("Reflections" 266–67).

10. See Introduction above for a discussion of the various applications of Davidson's work to questions in literary theory, which have mostly been concerned with the relation that can be established between Davidson's work and Derrida.

11. Here one needs to add the warning of the textual critic: "if indeed we do share a text." I fully endorse the point made by both Parker and McGann that too often theorists of "textuality" ignore the relevance of textual criticism. Where there is interpretive disagreement, it may on occasion stem from the fact that the critics are actually reading different texts, different versions of the same work: we may not be worlds apart, only texts apart. But my argument here will assume the unproblematic text unconsciously assumed by Barbara Herrnstein Smith ("The texts were the same, but ... the poems weren't").

12. Fish's fullest account of change is to be found in the chapter with that very title, "Change," in *Doing What Comes Naturally* (141–60). See my "Accounting for the Changing Certainties of Interpretive Communities" for a fuller discussion of why change is a problem for the notion of interpretive communities.

13. My quotations from Davidson on radical interpretation all come from "On the Very Idea of a Conceptual Scheme," but other essays in *Inquiries into Truth and Interpretation* are relevant here; see the entire section "Radical Interpretation" (*ITI* 123–79).

14. Michael Dummett has criticized the imprecision of Davidson's terms "prior theory" and "passing theory" and prefers to call them "long-range" and "short-range" theories (460, 465–66). This makes good sense to me so long as one keeps in mind the malleability of the long-range as well as the short-range theory. Dummett's response to Davidson is a fine restatement of a convention-centered view of language against Davidson's critique of the conventionalism common to Kuhn and Fish (see note 4 above).

15. This is the difference between Davidson's account of interpretation and that provided by Hans-Georg Gadamer's hermeneutics. See Greene for a critique of Gadamer in terms very close to those a Davidsonian would advance.

16. Greene is particularly illuminating on the way we ironize as a way of denying the otherness of literary texts (170–71).

17. Of course, this way of putting it violates the "intentional fallacy" of the New Critics. Davidsonian theories of interpretation, though avoiding some of the naive forms of intentionalism W. K. Wimsatt and Monroe Beardsley were inveighing against, nonetheless are thoroughly intentionalist. Understanding what someone means necessarily involves interpreting what the speaker's intentions are; Davidson's recent "The Structure and Content of Truth" (esp. 309–16) is perhaps his clearest statement of this.

18. I was led to this quotation by Hilary Putnam (in *Realism with a Human Face* 128), who stresses the similarity of this stance to Kuhn's.

19. For a fuller exploration of these issues, see my "Teaching Multicultural Literature." It has been argued by Colin MacCabe, on the other hand, that Davidson's theories allow for "no radical confrontation with difference" (7). A great deal depends here upon how one understands the adjective "radical." My sense is that Kuhn's and Fish's stress on our "radical difference" from others makes that difference seem unsurmountable, a confrontation with no meaningful outcome. Davidson's model allows for genuine confrontation precisely because the confrontation is less radical.

WORKS CITED

Crosman, Robert. "Do Readers Make Meaning?" In *The Reader in the Text: Essays on Audience and Interpretation.* Ed. Susan R. Sulieman and Inge Crosman. Princeton: Princeton UP, 1980. 149–64.

Culler, Jonathan. *On Deconstruction: Theory and Criticism After Structuralism.* Ithaca: Cornell UP, 1982.

Dasenbrock, Reed Way. "Accounting for the Changing Certainties of Interpretive Communities." *MLN* 101, no. 5 (1986): 1022–41.

———. "Teaching Multicultural Literature." In *Understanding Others: Cultural and Cross-Cultural Studies and the Teaching of Literature.* Ed. Joseph Trimmer and Tilly Warnock. Urbana: NCTE, 1992. 35–46.

De Man, Paul. "Dialogue and Dialogism." *Poetics Today* 4 (1983): 99–107.

Dummett, Michael. " 'A Nice Derangement of Epitaphs': Some Comments on Davidson and Hacking." In LePore. 459–76.

Dworkin, Ronald. "My Reply to Stanley Fish (and Walter Benn Michaels): Please Don't Talk About Objectivity Any More." In *The Politics of Interpretation.* Ed. W.J.T. Mitchell. Chicago: U of Chicago P, 1983. 287–313.

Fish, Stanley. *Doing What Comes Naturally: Change, Rhetoric, and the Practice of Theory in Literary and Legal Studies.* Durham: Duke UP, 1989.

———. *Is There a Text in This Class? The Authority of Interpretive Communities.* Cambridge: Harvard UP, 1980.

Graff, Gerald. "Interpretation on Tlon: A Response to Stanley Fish." *New Literary History* 17, no. 1 (1985): 109–17.

Greene, Thomas. "Anti-Hermeneutics: The Case of Shakespeare's Sonnet 129" (1982). In *The Vulnerable Text: Essays on Renaissance Literature.* New York: Columbia UP, 1986. 159–74.

Gutting, Gary, ed. *Paradigms and Revolutions: Appraisals and Applications of Thomas Kuhn's Philosophy of Science.* Notre Dame: U of Notre Dame P, 1980.

Kuhn, Thomas S. *The Essential Tension: Selected Studies in Scientific Tradition and Change.* Chicago: U of Chicago P, 1977.

———. "Reflections on My Critics." In Lakatos and Musgrave. 231–78.

———. *The Structure of Scientific Revolutions.* 2d ed. Chicago: U of Chicago P, 1970.

Lakatos, Imre. "Methodology of Scientific Research Programmes." In Lakatos and Musgrave. 91–195.

Lakatos, Imre, and Alan Musgrave, eds. *Criticism and the Growth of Scientific Knowledge.* Cambridge: Cambridge UP, 1970.

Law, Jules David. "Uncertain Grounds: Wittgenstein's *On Certainty* and the New Literary Pragmatism." *New Literary History* 19 (1988): 319–36.

LePore, Ernest, ed. *Truth and Interpretation: Perspectives on the Philosophy of Donald Davidson.* Oxford: Basil Blackwell, 1986.

MacCabe, Colin. "Broken English." *Critical Quarterly* 28, nos. 1 and 2 (1986): 3–14.

McGann, Jerome J. "The Monks and the Giants: Textual and Bibliographical Studies and the Interpretation of Literary Works." In *Textual Criticism and Literary Interpretation.* Ed. Jerome J. McGann. Chicago: U of Chicago P, 1985. 180–99.

Mailloux, Steven. *Interpretive Conventions: The Reader in the Study of American Fiction.* Ithaca: Cornell UP, 1982.

Parker, Hershel. "Lost Authority: Non-Sense, Skewed Meanings, and Intentionless Meanings." In *Against Theory: Literary Studies and the New Pragmatism.* Ed. W.J.T. Mitchell. Chicago: U of Chicago P, 1985. 72–79.

Popper, K. R. "Normal Science and Its Dangers." In Lakatos and Musgrave. 51–58.

Putnam, Hilary. *Realism with a Human Face.* Ed. James Conant. Cambridge: Harvard UP, 1990.

———. *Reason, Truth and History.* Cambridge: Cambridge UP, 1981.

Ramberg, Bjørn T. *Donald Davidson's Philosophy of Language: An Introduction.* Oxford: Basil Blackwell, 1989.

Scholes, Robert. *Textual Power: Literary Theory and the Teaching of English.* New Haven: Yale UP, 1985.

Smith, Barbara Herrnstein. *Contingencies of Value: Alternative Perspectives for Critical Theory.* Cambridge: Harvard UP, 1988.

Toulmin, S. E. "Does the Distinction Between Normal and Revolutionary Science Hold Water?" In Lakatos and Musgrave. 39–47.

Interpretation and Triangulation: A Davidsonian Critique of Reader-Oriented Literary Theory

THOMAS KENT

Like his fellow analytic philosophers, Donald Davidson privileges spoken discourse over written discourse, and in his now-substantial array of essays concerning the philosophy of language, he has addressed directly neither the problematics of writing nor the character of literary hermeneutics. Although Davidson clearly cannot be construed as a literary theorist, I believe that his notion of communicative interaction nonetheless sheds considerable light on the nature of literary interpretation and, in addition, provides a powerful critique of the reader-oriented hermeneutic theory held by communitarians who claim that knowledge comes into being only within the incommensurate interpretive communities in which we live.[1] With his well-known critique of conceptual schemes along with his less prominent—but, I believe, more important—conception of triangulation, Davidson's formulation of communicative interaction represents a frontal assault on the foundational assumptions about interpretation and language held by communitarians. By concentrating on the hermeneutic theory of Stanley Fish, whose work represents the example *par excellence* of communitarian theory, I would like to trace out what I believe to be this Davidsonian challenge to reader-oriented literary hermeneutics. In order to explain how Davidson's conception of communicative interaction helps us avoid some of the difficulties and philosophical contradictions intrinsic to reader-oriented theories of interpretation, I would like to consider first the presuppositions held by communitarian theorists by examining an exemplary instance of reader-oriented literary interpretation taken from Fish's *Is There a Text in This Class?*

In "What Makes an Interpretation Acceptable?" Fish attacks pluralist critics like E. D. Hirsch and Wayne Booth for their insistence that interpretive authority derives from the literary text. According to Fish, "A pluralist is committed to saying that there is something in the text which rules out some readings and allows others (even though no one reading can ever capture the text's 'inexhaustible richness and complexity')" (342). Fish argues, correctly I believe, that "the text is always a function of interpretation, [so] the text cannot be the location of the core of agreement by means of which we reject interpretations" (342). As Fish sees clearly, this position invites charges of relativism. For example, if the text is only a function of interpretation, then what makes one interpretation better than another, and if one interpretation seems more efficacious than other possibilities—always the case in literary hermeneutics—who or what decides which interpretations should be rejected? Fish responds to these questions by grounding interpretive authority in institutions or specific interpretive communities.

In an attempt to demonstrate the authority of interpretive communities, Fish cites the example of "psychoanalytic pluralism" employed by Norman Holland:

> Norman Holland's analysis of Faulkner's "A Rose for Emily" is a case in point. Holland is arguing for a kind of psychoanalytic pluralism. The text, he declares, is "at most a matrix of psychological possibilities for its readers," but, he insists, "only some possibilities . . . truly fit the matrix": "One would not say, for example, that a reader of . . . 'A Rose for Emily' who thought the 'tableau' [of Emily and her father in the doorway] described an Eskimo was really responding to the story at all—only pursuing some mysterious inner exploration." [345–46]

Although both Fish and Holland accept the motto Readers Make Meaning, Fish parts company with Holland when Holland claims that "the unacceptability of the Eskimo reading is a function of the text, of what [Holland] calls its 'sharable promptuary' . . . that public 'store of structured language' . . . that sets limits to the interpretations the words can accommodate" (346). For Fish, the Eskimo reading is unacceptable because there exists "no interpretive strategy for producing it" (346) or, stated a bit differently, there exists no interpretive community where such an interpretation might find a home. Although no interpretive strategy exists at present to authorize the Eskimo reading, Fish reminds us that such a strategy could exist:

> it is not difficult to imagine the circumstances under which [such a strategy] would establish itself. One such circumstance would be the discovery of a letter in which Faulkner confides that he has always believed himself to be an Eskimo changeling. . . . Immediately the workers in the Faulkner industry would begin to reinterpret the canon in the light of this newly revealed "belief" and the work of reinterpretation would involve the elaboration of a symbolic or allusive system . . . whose application would immediately transform the text into one informed everywhere by Eskimo meanings. [346]

In Fish's conception of literary hermeneutics, the Eskimo reading fails because it breaks too radically with the "canons of acceptability" (349) that the literary establishment holds. Because interpretive authority develops from the consensus inherent in like-minded communities, Fish emphasizes that our knowledge of the world can develop only from the institutional or conventional structures that constitute those communities. Fish emphasizes this point: "whatever seems to you to be obvious and inescapable is only so within some institutional or conventional structure, and that means that you can never operate outside some such structure" (370). According to Fish, we are prisoners of intertextuality where, "strictly speaking, getting 'back-to-the-text' is not a move one can perform, because the text one gets back to will be the text demanded by some other interpretation and that interpretation will be presiding over its production" (354). Therefore, propositional attitudes—in Fish's terms, "whatever seems to you to be obvious and inescapable" (379)—emanate from intertextuality, consensus, continuity, and the status quo.

Because interpretation always takes place within a community that shares a singular conceptual framework of beliefs and assumptions about the world, each community also possesses its own unique language in the sense that a newcomer to a community will not understand the language users in that community until the newcomer learns the conventional sign systems employed in the community. In other words, outsiders—before they can communicate at all—need to acquire a conceptual framework that supplies the necessary competence to communicate within a specific

interpretive community. Consequently, inhabitants of a particular interpretive community cannot escape the conceptual frameworks in which
they find themselves enclosed, for these conceptual frameworks actually
allow them to speak in the first place. In Fish's world, human consciousness is produced by interpretive communities, and we become the products of the interpretive communities in which we live. As Fish points out,
"One can respond with a cheerful yes to the question 'Do readers make
meanings?' and commit oneself to very little because it would be equally
true to say that meanings, in the form of culturally derived interpretive
categories, make readers" (336). When we say that readers make meaning, according to Fish, we are committed to "very little" because a reader
can say only what her "culturally derived interpretive categories"—what
I have been calling conceptual frameworks—allow her to say. A reader
cannot say whatever she pleases, for within these "culturally derived
interpretive categories" some statements will always be regarded as false.
For our purposes, the important point here is the idea that interpretation
is always relative to—we might even say controlled by—conceptual
frameworks that differ from place to place and from time to time.

A major and, I believe, insurmountable difficulty exists with this
communitarian formulation of interpretation, a difficulty that arises directly from Fish's implicit Cartesianism. When Fish accepts a Cartesian
epistemology and imagines a subjective conceptual framework which
constitutes all that we can know about the world, he obviously may
never be sure that his claims about the world—the propositional attitudes he holds—refer to anything outside his own subjective conceptual
framework. Because Fish insists that interpretation is a product of the
interpretive communities in which we always already find ourselves—
his claim, for example, that our readings of "A Rose for Emily" are
determined by the authority of different interpretive communities—he
cannot account for objects in the world or the minds of others. As Reed
Way Dasenbrock puts it, "The model of interpretive communities assumes, because we can understand only on our own terms, that the text
cannot be understood and at the same time understood to be different
from us" (17). By endorsing the idea that different conceptual frameworks supply us with unique and incommensurate ways of looking at the
world, Fish clearly advocates a brand of radical subjectivism that denies
our ability to know anything outside the interpretive community in
which we find ourselves. All we can ever know is the conceptual framework that holds together the community in which we happen to exist, a
conceptual framework that separates us from others and from the world.

To hold such a Cartesian position means that Fish possesses no convincing response to the skeptic or to those who charge him with relativism. Within this Cartesian system, the other—the "out there"—becomes unavoidably alien and lost to us, and we have no non-question-begging response to the skeptic who asks us how we know that our propositional attitudes hook onto the world or how we know that we know the mind of another. If we accept the Cartesian position, all we can do in response to the skeptic is to endorse a version of relativism: although we can never be certain that our propositional attitudes are true in the sense that they get us in touch with the thing itself or the mind of another, we can be sure that some propositional attitudes are relatively better than others because, for example, we can measure our beliefs, intentions, and so forth against other propositional attitudes by employing some sort of empirical methodology.[2] For the skeptic, however, this defense is no defense at all. For the skeptic, relativism amounts to an admission that our subjective propositional attitudes cannot be trusted to give us the knowledge necessary to make assertions about the world. Consequently, we are cast into a world where truth is unknowable and rhetoric is king.

However, I believe that Donald Davidson's conception of interpretation enables us to avoid the implicit problems found in Fish's Cartesian version of literary hermeneutics. In two seminal essays, "On the Very Idea of a Conceptual Scheme" and "A Nice Derangement of Epitaphs," Davidson lays out his views concerning the relation between interpretation and *a priori* conceptual frameworks. In "On the Very Idea of a Conceptual Scheme," Davidson argues that no conceptual framework can be discovered that organizes the way we experience the world; in "A Nice Derangement of Epitaphs," he expands this argument and takes the even more radical position that interpretation possesses no center, no generalizable metatheory, or totalizing framework that enables us to make sense of sentences. In fact, he argues that "there is no such thing as a language, not if a language is anything like what many philosophers and linguists have supposed" ("NDE" 446). Davidson's conception of language and interpretation stands in direct opposition to literary theorists like Fish, historians of science like Thomas Kuhn, and rhetoricians like Kenneth Bruffee, who share the belief that knowledge is relative to some sort of conceptual framework. Because these two essays refute the assumptions concerning the nature of interpretation held by communitarian literary theorists, they provide, I believe, a way of thinking about literary hermeneutics that is not steeped in consensus and the exclusionary power of interpretive communities.

BEYOND RADICAL SUBJECTIVISM

As I have noted, communitarians like Fish take the position that knowledge is relative to conceptual frameworks or what Davidson calls "conceptual schemes." A shared conceptual scheme is the glue that holds together an interpretive community, for members of an interpretive community will always share a conceptual scheme or, to employ Kuhn's term, a "paradigm" that allows them to experience the world in a similar fashion. According to communitarians who follow Kuhn's lead, these communal paradigms are incommensurable; that is, every paradigm possesses its own unique scheme—what Davidson describes as a "not intertranslatable" scheme (*ITI* 190)—for organizing experience so that members of one particular interpretive community see the world quite differently than members of another community. This "conceptual relativism"—Davidson's term for the idea that knowledge is relative to a conceptual scheme—allows communitarians to claim that members of different interpretive communities speak different languages. For example, Kenneth Bruffee relates plainly the conceptual-relativist position when he writes, "to teach *King Lear* seems to involve creating contexts where students undergo a sort of cultural change. This change would be one in which they loosen ties to the knowledge communities they currently belong to and join another. These two communities would be seen as having quite different sets of values, mores, and goals, and above all quite different languages" (651). Because different interpretive communities with different conceptual schemes speak "quite different languages," communitarians suggest that interpretive communities shape language and, in a sense, enable different languages to come into being. In his attack on the very idea of a conceptual scheme, Davidson makes precisely the inverse argument: an interpretive community does not create its own language; instead, language creates our sense of an interpretive community.

In his refutation of the idea that meaning is relative to incommensurate conceptual schemes, Davidson accepts the conceptual relativist position that "there is no chance that someone can take up a vantage point for comparing conceptual schemes by temporarily shedding his own" (*ITI* 185). Although having a language means having a conceptual scheme, is it possible to extend this claim and say with the communitarian that two people must possess different conceptual schemes when they speak totally different languages—languages that are, in Kuhn's terminology, incommensurate or, in Davidson's terms, not intertranslatable? Stated another way, can we agree with Edward Sapir and

Benjamin Whorf that people who speak differently see the world differently? Or, stated still another way, can we say that Milton and Eliot lived in different worlds because they employed the same words in different ways? Davidson responds to these questions by arguing 1) that the claim of incommensurate languages and, therefore, incommensurate conceptual schemes is incoherent and 2) that partial failure to understand another's language does not constitute evidence that different conceptual schemes exist. To develop this argument, Davidson examines two instances where meaning could be said to be relative to a conceptual scheme: when translatability is impossible and when there is partial failure of translatability. Because communitarians insist that literary critics—as well as scientists, historians, philosophers, artists, and so forth—who work in different interpretive communities also work, as Kuhn says, "in different worlds" (134), they must presuppose that the language of one world cannot be translated into the language of another. If the experiences and beliefs of one community were translatable into the language of another community, the claim that autonomous or even relatively autonomous interpretive communities exist would make no sense. Translatability, then, becomes the key issue.

For Davidson, what does it mean to say that different conceptual schemes are not intertranslatable? First, such a claim must mean that no neutral ground exists on which we can stand to make true statements about the world. According to communitarians, we always speak from within some interpretive community, so we cannot step outside our own community to interpret what members of other communities experience or believe. Yet, communitarians regularly translate the languages of other interpretive communities. Of course, reception-oriented literary critics like Fish do precisely the same thing, for how could they know that their interpretations of *Paradise Lost*, for example, are different than other, earlier interpretations—interpretations produced in different interpretive communities—if they did not understand the meaning of those earlier interpretations? Obviously, we cannot have a new point of view unless we have a contrasting old point of view that we understand. As Davidson points out, "The dominant metaphor of conceptual relativism, that of differing points of view, seems to betray an underlying paradox. Different points of view make sense, but only if there is a common coordinate system on which to plot them; yet the existence of a common system belies the claim of dramatic incomparability" (*ITI* 184).

Trying to defend conceptual relativism on the basis of partial failure of translatability fares no better than a defense based on incommensurability. Davidson points out the commonsense notion that to recognize a partial failure of translatability requires that we must also recognize a partial success of translatability. That is, we cannot live in different worlds and speak incommensurate languages if we recognize that someone is failing to communicate. All this problem means is that we have not employed a hermeneutic strategy that functions well enough to help us interpret what someone else desires us to understand. The upshot of Davidson's critique is clear: the claim that incommensurate interpretive communities exist is incoherent.

Because the incommensurability claim is self-contradictory and because the corollary claim that the world is separated into discrete interpretive communities is incoherent, it would be nice to suppose that we share a common scheme; it would be nice to think that all we need in order to share knowledge is a good, objective lexicon that will enable us to translate the languages of others. Unfortunately, as Davidson points out, such a desire cannot be realized either. If we cannot make intelligible the claim that conceptual schemes are different and if we also cannot make intelligible the claim that we share a common scheme, then how do we make sense of Davidson's claim that having a language means having a conceptual scheme?

I want to suggest that Davidson holds the view that a conceptual scheme is roughly equivalent to a hermeneutic strategy, where by "hermeneutic strategy" I mean a theory, loosely speaking, that helps us make sense of what others are saying. Such a strategy cannot be learned in any objective way—it does not occupy a neutral ground outside of language itself—nor does it unify language by supplying a framework that all language users share. Because we always speak from within a communicative situation, a conceptual scheme or hermeneutic strategy does not embody the world in the sense that it organizes or fits reality. Since we are thrown into an already-made world of signs—a world that is constituted by signs—we employ a conceptual scheme or hermeneutic strategy to help us make use of the languages we are thrown into. Therefore, a conceptual scheme works as a kind of guessing game—or storytelling—where each of us possesses a hermeneutic strategy that we employ in order to communicate with an other, a strategy that the other may or may not share.[3] A conceptual scheme, therefore, does not give order or structure to a reality outside of language—as the conceptual relativist would have it. Rather, language makes the conceptual scheme possible, since we construct our conceptual schemes in order to communicate within our already-made world of language. From a Davidsonian perspective, translatability—how we employ a conceptual scheme to interpret the languages of others— becomes the problematic issue; we do not need to worry about such formulations as interpretive communities or other epistemological frameworks—constructs grounded in the authority of consensus—that supposedly make interpretation possible, for as Davidson points out, these formulations can tell us little or nothing about how we actually employ language.

In "A Nice Derangement of Epitaphs," Davidson explains in more detail his view about the task of interpretation. Davidson employs the example of the malaprop to illustrate the importance of interpretation within the process of communicative interaction, and this account of interpretation unfolds from his analysis of how people who employ malaprops "get away with it":

> Here is what I mean by "getting away with it": the interpreter comes to the occasion of utterance armed with a theory that tells him (or so he believes) what an arbitrary utterance of the speaker means. The speaker then says something with the intention that it will be so interpreted. In fact this way is not provided for in the interpreter's theory. But the speaker is nevertheless understood; the interpreter adjusts his theory so that it yields the speaker's intended interpretation. The speaker has "gotten away with it". The speaker may or may not... know that he has got away with anything; the interpreter may or may not know that the speaker intended to get away with anything. What is common to the cases is that the speaker expects to be, and is, interpreted as the speaker intended although the interpreter did not have a correct theory in advance. ["NDE" 440]

Through his analysis of the malaprop, Davidson emphasizes that no transcendental or objective theory exists that will help us interpret in advance what a speaker means by her words, and Davidson extends the example of the malaprop to cover all communicative situations. He tells us, "We do not need bizarre anecdotes or wonderlands to make the point. We all get away with it all the time; understanding the speech of others depends on it" ("NDE" 440).

In order to explain how we interpret the discourses of others—what he calls "getting away with it"—Davidson argues that speakers and listeners adjust their hermeneutic strategies on the spot; they make what I have called elsewhere "hermeneutic guesses":

> Here is a highly simplified and idealized proposal about what goes on. An interpreter has, at any moment of a speech transaction,

what I persist in calling a theory. (I call it a theory, as remarked
before, only because a description of the interpreter's competence requires a recursive account.) I assume that the interpreter's theory has been adjusted to the evidence so far available
to him: knowledge of the character, dress, role, sex, of the
speaker, and whatever else has been gained by observing the
speaker's behavior, linguistic or otherwise. As the speaker speaks
his piece the interpreter alters his theory, entering hypotheses
about new names, altering the interpretation of familiar predicates, and revising past interpretations of particular utterances in
the light of new evidence. ["NDE" 441]

Davidson employs the terms "prior theory" and "passing theory" to describe this complicated communicative interaction: "For the hearer, the
prior theory expresses how he is prepared in advance to interpret an
utterance of the speaker, while the passing theory is how he *does* interpret the utterance. For the speaker, the prior theory is what he *believes*
the interpreter's prior theory to be, while his passing theory is the
theory he *intends* the interpreter to use" ("NDE" 442). In this account
of communicative interaction, both speaker and listener engage in interpretive activity; both make guesses—albeit highly accurate guesses—
about what the other knows and does not know.

     Prior theories—the guess a speaker makes about how her utterance
may be interpreted and the guess a listener makes about how to interpret an utterance—never match precisely, for speaker and listener can
never know with certainty the hermeneutic strategy the other intends to
employ in a particular communicative situation. We can never know
precisely how someone will interpret what we say, nor can we be certain
in advance about the accuracy of our interpretation of another's words.
Because the prior theory constitutes only a starting place for interpretation, it is necessary but not sufficient for effective communicative interaction. More important than the prior theory, the passing theory constitutes the hermeneutic strategy that we actually employ when we communicate. As Davidson explains: "What must be shared for communication to succeed is the passing theory. For the passing theory is the one
the interpreter actually uses to interpret an utterance, and it is the
theory the speaker intends the interpreter to use" ("NDE" 442). As a
speaker speaks and a listener listens, they both possess prior theories
that undergo modification as they speak and listen. As they guess about
the meaning of one another's sentences, they together arrive at a passing
theory, a unique hermeneutic strategy, that will enable them to under-

stand one another in their own, singular situation. Once communication takes place—once a speaker becomes satisfied that the listener has interpreted her discourse so that further discourse is unnecessary and once a listener becomes satisfied that her interpretation is close enough to the message the speaker intends—the passing theory, in a sense, disappears to become part of a prior theory that may or may not be used in future communicative situations.

This Davidsonian account of hermeneutic interaction departs significantly from the framework theory of interpretation held by communitarians like Kuhn and Fish. Because communitarians hold the view that, in Fish's words, "communication occurs within situations and that to be in a situation is already to be in possession of (or to be possessed by) a structure of assumptions, of practices understood to be relevant in relation to purposes and goals that are already in place" (318), they must also hold the view that interpretation can take place only from within an already-received socially constructed situation where there exists something usually called "linguistic competence." In fact, for the communitarian, a member of a particular interpretive community may be recognized as a member of that community only through her linguistic competence. So, as Davidson phrases the problem, "The systematic knowledge or competence of the speaker or interpreter is learned in advance of occasions of interpretation and is conventional in character" ("NDE" 436). As we have noted, however, Davidson argues that in actual linguistic communication, nothing corresponds to linguistic competence; linguistic competence, as the conception is formulated by communitarians, does not exist.

In the place of linguistic competence, Davidson posits the notion of prior and passing theories—what I have been calling "hermeneutic guessing"—because, as Davidson tells us, "In linguistic communication nothing corresponds to a linguistic competence as often described" ("NDE" 446). When we communicate, we make informed guesses about meaning; we engage in a kind of impromptu hermeneutic dance choreographed by our prior and passing theories. This dance is impromptu because it cannot be codified, systematized, or taught. Davidson is very clear on this point: neither the prior nor the passing theory can be predicted in advance of communicative interaction. Consequently, neither corresponds to the usual description of language as a shared system of conventions relative to a conceptual scheme. Davidson is so adamant about this matter that I would like to quote his remarks at some length:

> This characterization of linguistic ability [Davidson's account of prior and passing theories] is so nearly circular that it cannot be

wrong: it comes to saying that the ability to communicate by speech consists in the ability to make oneself understood, and to understand. It is only when we look at the structure of this ability that we realize how far we have drifted from standard ideas of language mastery. For we have discovered no learnable common core of consistent behavior, no shared grammar or rules, no portable interpreting machine set to grind out the meaning of an arbitrary utterance. We may say that linguistic ability is the ability to converge on a passing theory from time to time—this is what I have suggested, and I have no better proposal. But if we do say this, then we should realize that we have abandoned not only the ordinary notion of a language, but we have erased the boundary between knowing a language and knowing our way around in the world. For there are no rules for arriving at passing theories, no rules in any strict sense, as opposed to rough maxims and method- ological generalities. A passing theory really is like a theory at least in this, that it is derived by wit, luck, and wisdom from a private vocabulary and grammar, knowledge of the ways people get their point across, and rules of thumb for figuring out what deviations from the dictionary are most likely. There is no more chance of regularizing, or teaching, this process than there is of regularizing or teaching the process of creating new theories to cope with new data in any field—for that is what this process involves. ["NDE" 445–46]

For Davidson, satisfactory communication depends on our ability to interpret the beliefs and intentions of others, and interpretation depends on the efficacy and felicity of our hermeneutic guesses. Because these guesses never correspond to a linguistic code or framework that we know before we begin the process of communication, we are never prepared in advance to make sense of the world. No framework supplies for us a ready-made theory to guide or direct our interpretations; in consequence, as Davidson points out, "We must give up the idea of a clearly defined shared structure which language-users acquire and then apply to cases" ("NDE" 444). Although we certainly bring to any commu- nicative situation a lifetime of linguistic preparation, that preparation does not correspond to "linguistic competence" in the usual sense of the term.[4]

If the passing theory refutes codification and if it does not constitute "a clearly defined shared structure which language-users acquire and then apply to cases," then how does the passing theory enable us to interpret utterances and allow us to understand the propositional attitudes—beliefs, intentions, desires, and so forth—held by others? For Davidson, the passing theory, in the ontological sense, does not carry meaning; it is not a semiotic construct like a book or a string of phonemes. Instead, the passing theory—as a hermeneutic strategy—enables us to engage in a process that Davidson calls "triangulation."[5]

TRIANGULATION AND INTERPRETATION

In order to understand the utterances and propositional attitudes held by others, we must possess, according to Davidson, "three sorts of knowledge corresponding to the three apices of [a] triangle: knowledge of our own minds, knowledge of other minds, and knowledge of the shared world" ("MM" 7). The interaction among these three apices works in the following way:

> Each of two people finds certain behavior of the other salient, and each finds the observed behavior of the other to be correlated with events and objects he finds salient in the world. This much can take place without developed thought, but it is the necessary basis for thought and for language learning. For until the triangle is completed connecting two creatures and each creature with common objects in the world there can be no answer to the question whether a creature, in discriminating between stimuli, is discriminating between stimuli at the sensory surfaces or somewhere further out, or further in. It takes two to triangulate. ["MM" 7]

At least two important consequences for a theory of literary hermeneutics follow from Davidson's description of triangulation. The first concerns the nature of human subjectivity, and the second concerns the undoing of Cartesian skepticism and relativism.

For Davidson, the intimate and seemingly subjective knowledge that each of us possesses about our own mind arises only through triangulation with the other, other language users and other objects that constitute our shared world. Therefore, human subjectivity alone—in the sense of our subjective knowledge concerning our internal and nonpublic mental states—cannot account for the propositional attitudes we hold about the world. In order to hold propositional attitudes, we must communicate; for without other language users and without a shared world, no propositional attitudes could occur at all.[6] Davidson explains that "the central argument against private languages is that unless a language is shared there would be no way to distinguish between thinking one was using the language correctly and using it correctly.... If only communication can provide a check on the correct use of words, only communication can supply a standard of objectivity in other domains" ("MM" 7). For Davidson, our sense of a private language—our sense that we possess subjective propositional states that we alone can know—issues from the shared language we employ in order to communicate with one another, and not the other way around; the shared language we employ in order to communicate does not issue from a private language or nonpublic mental state.

The upshot of this argument is significant. Reduced to its bare bones, Davidson's argument takes the radically anti-Cartesian position that no subject/object split exists. According to Davidson, Cartesian subjectivity—and the problem of conceptual schemes that it engenders— emerges only when we imagine that language can be used for something other than for communication. When we understand that language's *raison d'être* is communicative interaction, then radical subjectivity—in the form of a private language or a conceptual scheme—makes no sense. In order to surmise whether our marks and noises create any effect in the world, we require at least one other language user and objects in the world that we know we share. In order to communicate, we need to triangulate.[7]

To summarize, then, Davidson argues that we cannot form concepts without communication, and communication requires triangulation. When we triangulate, we require another language user and a shared world. In order to know either the mind of another language user or objects in the world, we must match our utterances at least partially with the utterances of another. If we cannot successfully match our language with the language of another, we can never be sure what our concepts are concepts of and, therefore, we can never be sure that our concepts are concepts. Davidson explains that

> the kind of triangulation I have described, while not sufficient to establish that a creature has a concept of a particular object or kind of object, is necessary if there is to be any answer at all to the question what its concepts are concepts of. . . .
>
> The problem is not, I should stress, one of verifying what objects or events a creature is responding to; the problem is that

without a second creature responding to the first, there can be no answer to the question. And of course if there is no answer to this question, there is no answer to the question what language a creature speaks, since to designate a language as one being spoken requires that utterances be matched up with objects in the world (and not, in general, events on the surface of the skin). So we can say . . . that before anyone can speak a language, there must be another creature interacting with the speaker. But of course this cannot be enough, since mere interaction does not show how the interaction matters to the creatures involved. Unless the creatures concerned can be said to react to the interaction there is no way *they* can take cognitive advantage of the three-way relation which gives content to *our* idea that they are reacting to one thing rather than another. ["SP" 7]

In order to form the concepts that constitute our thought, we must communicate or "react to the interaction" in which we find ourselves socially situated. Of course, we do not need to employ the same language as others in order to triangulate with them; we need only arrive at a passing theory that will allow others to make good enough guesses about the sounds and marks we make.

In the process of triangulation, we cannot know our own minds—the concepts that form our thoughts—without knowing the minds of other language users; consequently, no split exists between our minds and the minds of others or between our minds and objects in a shared world. Thus, for example, my concept of a table must align—or must be able to align—with another language user's concept of a table and with an object in the world, or my concept of table cannot be said to be a concept. Davidson explains the process this way:

The only way of knowing that the second apex of the triangle— the second creature or person—is reacting to the same object as oneself is to know that the other person has the same object in mind. But then the second person must also know that the first person constitutes an apex of the same triangle another apex of which the second person occupies. For two people to know of each other that they are so related, that their thoughts are so related, requires that they be in communication. Each of them must speak to the other and be understood by the other. They don't . . . have to mean the same thing by the same words, but they must each be an interpreter of the other. ["SP" 8]

When we know our own minds, we invariably know the minds of others, for we could not know our own minds if we could not get in touch with concepts and objects outside ourselves. When we accept this Davidsonian point of view, the skeptic's question "How do you know that you are getting in touch with something beyond your own mind?" no longer makes sense, because no split exists between our minds and the minds of others. So, a Davidsonian would respond to the skeptic in this way: skepticism about the possibility of knowing an objective world occurs only when you imagine that a split exists between an "in here" and an "out there"; by understanding the nature of communicative interaction in terms of triangulation, you can stop worrying about this split, for you no longer need to fret about getting in touch with something beyond yourself; by knowing your own mind, you always already know the minds of others.

In similar fashion, a theory of communicative interaction derived from Davidson's conception of triangulation also avoids the problem of relativism. Because no split exists between an "in here" and an "out there," truth cannot correspond to something transcendental that lies outside history and social life, for no "out there" exists. Davidson points out that "communication, and the knowledge of other minds it presupposes, is the basis of our concept of objectivity, our recognition of a distinction between false and true belief. But there is no going outside this standard to check whether we have things right, any more than we can check whether the platinum-iridium standard kept at the International Bureau of Weights and Standards in Sèvres, France, weighs a kilogram" ("MM" 8). For Davidson, truth is intersubjective. However, to say that truth is intersubjective is not to say that it is relativistic. When we assert something about the world, our assertions must be in touch with reality— other language users and objects in the world—because if they were not in touch with reality, they could not be interpreted to be meaningful assertions.[8] Since our assertions connect us directly to other speakers and to objects in the world, nothing exists for our assertions to be relative to. Of course, our assertions about the world certainly may be wrong; we may discover that we have miscalculated or made an incorrect inference. But, to admit that we may be wrong about one of our assertions—that another way of understanding things is better than our current way—does not mean that we could possibly be wrong about all of our assertions. We must be right about most of our assertions or we could not get anything done in the world.[9] Consequently, one assertion cannot be as good as any other simply because at any given moment in time one assertion will always be better than another. Relativism—in the sense that no standard exists to help authorize our assertions—does not apply when we deny the Cartesian presupposition that a split exists between the mind and a world "out there."

TOWARD A DAVIDSONIAN LITERARY HERMENEUTICS

With his conceptions of the passing theory and triangulation, Davidson moves beyond reception theorists like Fish who assume a classical Cartesian stance and claim that interpretation is relative to and, consequently, determined by a conceptual scheme. Because Davidson has not elaborated a clear position regarding literary hermeneutics, however, I confess from the outset that what follows represents my view concerning the nature of such a Davidsonian position. In my appropriation of Davidson's notion of communicative interaction, then, I want to suggest that literary interpretation unfolds from two related activities: hermeneutic guessing and triangulation.

In order to interpret a text, we require a reader, other readers, and a text. These three elements obviously correspond to the three apices of Davidson's communication model where the text assumes the place of an object in the world, a reader assumes the place of a language user, and other readers assume the place of other language users. As we read, we formulate passing theories in order to align our sense of what we are reading both with interpretations held by others and with the language in the text itself. Although these passing theories never match precisely, they nonetheless allow us to interpret well enough the meaning in a text by triangulating among what we know, what the text says, and what others say about it. We should remember that this kind of triangulation is thoroughly diachronic in the sense that what we know cannot be separated from what others know and from what the text means both to us and to others. Consider, for example, the Eskimo reading cited by Fish. When we read "A Rose for Emily," we triangulate. We attempt to interpret the text in terms of a passing theory we construct from our knowledge about ourselves and the world—knowledge we derive from previous triangulation. As a passing theory, the Eskimo reading fails not because we belong to a specific interpretive community that disallows such a reading; rather, it fails because no evidence supports it. In other words, this particular passing theory cannot be made to align with the passing theories held by others or by the language in the text itself. Of course, if someone should find a letter indicating Faulkner's belief that he was an Eskimo changeling, such evidence would be enough to change our passing theories and the passing theories of others. As a result of such a find, our interpretations of the meaning of "A Rose for Emily" obviously would be modified.

This Davidsonian conception of literary hermeneutics overcomes the contradictions inherent in the radical subjectivism endorsed by Fish, for it rejects both the idea of incommensurate conceptual schemes—and therefore the idea of interpretive communities—as well as the idea of communal consensus that leads directly to relativism and skepticism. Within a Davidsonian horizon, an acceptable interpretation of "A Rose for Emily" does not depend on the consensually determined conceptual scheme held by a discrete interpretive community. Our interpretation depends instead on our ability to triangulate. In place of the consensual and authoritative interpretation allowed by the interpretive community, we have a range of possible interpretations that are more or less acceptable depending on the other readers with whom we are triangulating. If we are triangulating with freshman students, our passing theory certainly would be less complex than the passing theory we would employ when communicating with a Faulkner specialist. Both passing theories would be acceptable, however, although one would be clearly less complex than the other. By appealing to the formulation of a passing theory, we do not need to invoke something like an interpretive community in order to explain how interpretations may differ; interpretations differ because we triangulate differently in different situations. Of course, to say that a range of interpretations for "A Rose for Emily" is acceptable does not mean that all are. The Eskimo reading, for instance, is not acceptable, for that particular passing theory can be triangulated with no other existing passing theory, even the passing theory held by a first reader of Faulkner.

In addition to helping us rid ourselves of the difficulties associated with interpretive communities, a Davidsonian literary hermeneutics also allows us to explain how it is that we can understand interpretations different from our own or, stated differently, how it is that we can understand the minds of others. For Fish, the mind of the other is a cipher, for the other always resides outside the consensual interpretive community in which we reside and from which our knowledge of the world derives. The other must always be a stranger unless this outsider becomes part of our own interpretive community. For a Davidsonian, however, no outsiders exist, for, in a sense, we are all outsiders. Unlike Fish's understanding of knowledge as consensus, triangulation does not require uniform agreement among language users. On the other hand, triangulation does require that language users continually generate tenuous passing theories in order to communicate with one another, because knowledge of another's mind and the world requires communicative interaction and because communicative interaction, in turn, requires triangulation. Since we need to triangulate in order to understand others and the world, the other becomes part and parcel of the process of communicative interaction, for it is only by knowing the mind of the other that we can formulate effective passing theories. When we communicate with others by effectively but only temporarily matching our passing theories with theirs, we know their minds at that particular moment. For example, when freshman students read "A Rose for Emily" and interpret it naively, we know their minds because we are able to make sense of their passing theories, and we know the minds of Faulkner scholars for precisely the same reason. We should remember, too, that such knowledge of another's mind is not relativistic knowledge, for nothing exists for such knowledge to be relative to.

Although a literary hermeneutics derived from Davidson's work may not take the shape I have outlined here, I nonetheless believe that Davidson's conception of communicative interaction provides us with a way to talk about the interpretation of texts without getting ourselves caught up in the old problems of skepticism and relativism. Because his conceptions of triangulation and the passing theory allow us to account for the other— e.g., such objects in the world as literary texts—and because those conceptions remove the difficulties and contradictions associated with the idea of interpretive communities, Davidson's account of communicative interaction forgoes the radical subjectivism found in reception-oriented approaches to literary hermeneutics. By continuing to investigate more carefully how Davidson's philosophy of language applies to the study of those texts we consider literary, we finally might move beyond narrow dualisms such as subject/object and mind/world that continue to define the nature of contemporary literary hermeneutics.

NOTES

1. By concentrating exclusively on a communitarian theorist like Stanley Fish, I do not mean to suggest that all reader-response critics share a similar view about literary hermeneutics. At least two branches of reader-response theory exist; the psychological/phenomenological branch traces its origin to the Geneva school while the communitarian branch finds its roots in Anglo-American analytic philosophy, especially the speech-act philosophy of John Austin and John Searle. Although important methodological differences exist between these

two branches—especially between communitarians like Stanley Fish and Jonathan Culler and Freudians like Norman Holland and David Bleich—they all nonetheless share two related presuppositions about the nature of interpretation. Both branches understand meaning to be a function of the reader's subjectivity, and both endorse a version of Culler's idea of reading competence.

For the phenomenologically oriented critic, the claim that meaning is a function of the reader's subjectivity may be uncovered in Georges Poulet's reading of Edmund Husserl. Building on Husserl's phenomenological reduction of consciousness, Poulet asserts that during the reading act the individual consciousness of the reader disappears to such an extent that the reader actually begins to think the thoughts of the author. For Poulet, this kind of radical subjectivity recaptures the world of the author, and because of its transcendental nature, this recaptured world resides outside history in a timeless field of experience where it may be continually reconstituted within the reading act. Poulet's Husserlian conception of the reading experience has been modified by subsequent reception theorists, but phenomenologically oriented theorists, for the most part, retain Poulet's foundational assertion that meaning occurs primarily within the consciousness of the reader. For example, the two reception theorists who endorse most directly the radical subjectivity associated with Husserl and Poulet are Norman Holland and David Bleich. Both see interpretation as originating within the creative consciousness of the reader, and both understand the literary text to be a kind of mirror in which the reader discovers the reflected self.

On the other hand, communitarians like Stanley Fish and Jonathan Culler posit a Kantian formulation of consciousness but desire to purge from it all traces of transcendentalism and psychologism. Unlike phenomenologists such as Poulet and psychoanalytic theorists such as Holland and Bleich, communitarians displace the seat of subjectivity from the human psyche to historically and institutionally determined interpretive communities. Instead of emphasizing the individual psyche, communitarians emphasize the performative nature of language and claim that knowledge is relative to the socially constructed conventions that constitute the interpretive communities in which we live. Although communitarian critics and psychoanalytic critics disagree about the seat of subjectivity, they nonetheless agree that readers and not texts represent the origin of meaning.

Another important but less discussed presupposition held both by phenomenologists and by communitarians assumes that readers possess something Culler calls "literary competence." Literary competence corresponds closely to the idea of "linguistic competence." In general, linguistic competence describes the epistemological framework, usually conventional in nature, that a speaker possesses in advance of any specific communicative situation. Similar to linguistic competence, literary competence describes the system of conventional elements that a reader employs in order to interpret or to produce a text; again like linguistic competence, this system exists anterior to the interpretive act. One of the earliest and most influential statements describing literary competence occurs in Culler's *Structuralist Poetics*. According to Culler, what he calls a "system of conventions" constitutes a framework that enables interpretation to take place. He tells us that we should think of a poem "as an utterance that has meaning only with respect to a system of conventions which the reader has assimilated" (116). In *The Pursuit of Signs,* Culler reiterates this idea when he asserts that "the same sentence can have different meanings in poetry and prose because there are conventions that lead one to respond to it differently" (123). In Culler's view, a system of conventions allows meaning to come into being, and the competent reader will be someone who has assimilated a large number of conventions which, in turn, will enable the competent reader to, in Culler's words, "interpret works in ways which we consider acceptable, in accordance with the institution of literature" (*Structuralist Poetics* 124). Although I have been concentrating here specifically on Culler's conception of literary competence, other reception theorists share Culler's view that something exists—something roughly analogous to linguistic competence—that enables interpretation to take place. To cite only a few of the better-known examples, Hans Robert Jauss's idea of a "horizon of expectations," Wolfgang Iser's formulation of "repertoire," Steven Mailloux's designation of "interpretive conventions," and Fish's notion of "culturally derived interpretive categories" all correspond closely to Culler's conception of literary competence.

These two related presuppositions—the claim that interpretation is a subjective activity and the claim that interpretation is relative to some sort of epistemological framework—provide only a cursory description of some of the similarities and the differences among reader-response theorists. For a more detailed discussion concerning the different schools of reception theory, see Mailloux's *Interpretive Conventions*. There, he identifies three groups of theorists: phenomenologists, subjectivists, and structuralists.

2. In "Science as Solidarity," Richard Rorty discusses some of the problems connected with this idea of empirical objectivity.

3. What I have in mind here is similar to what Jean-François Lyotard means by a *petit recit,* a little story that undermines the authority of master narratives (see *The Postmodern Condition*).

4. In his book *Deconstruction and the Interests of Theory,* Christopher Norris interprets Davidson's position on this issue quite differently than I do. However, I do not think that Norris takes into account Davidson's latest work on triangulation, which I believe supports my reading here.

5. Davidson's conception of triangulation should not be confused with the conception of triangulation that ethnographers employ. These quite different formulations are similar in name only. See Doheny-Farina and Odell for a discussion of triangulation as the concept is employed in ethnographic research.

6. Davidson's argument here ensues in large part from Wittgenstein's contention that no private language and, consequently, no radical subjectivity of the Kantian sort can survive.

7. It is important to note that triangulation represents much more than simply another communication model in the tradition of structuralists like Roman Jakobson or intentionalists like John Searle. Davidson's conception of triangulation provides a means to think about communicative interaction while avoiding the old Cartesian dualisms that lead inexorably to skepticism and relativism.

8. In "Pragmatism, Davidson, and Truth," Rorty discusses Davidson's account of the relation between assertions—a subcategory of what Rorty calls "vocables"—and truth (351).

9. This claim derives from Davidson's principle of "charity" which, in turn, derives from the idea of holism. See "On the Very Idea of a Conceptual Scheme" (in *ITI*) for a discussion of the principle of charity and holism.

WORKS CITED

Austin, J. L. *How to Do Things with Words.* Cambridge: Harvard UP, 1967.

Bleich, David. *Subjective Criticism.* Baltimore: Johns Hopkins UP, 1978.

Booth, Wayne. "Preserving the Exemplar." *Critical Inquiry* 3, no. 3 (1977): 413–27.

Bruffee, Kenneth. "Collaborative Learning and the 'Conversation of Mankind,'" *College English* 46, no. 7 (1984): 635–52.

Culler, Jonathan. *On Deconstruction: Theory and Criticism After Structuralism.* Ithaca: Cornell UP, 1982.

———. *The Pursuit of Signs: Semiotics, Literature, Deconstruction.* Ithaca: Cornell UP, 1983.

————. *Structuralist Poetics.* Ithaca: Cornell UP, 1975.

Dasenbrock, Reed Way. "Do We Write the Text We Read." *College English* 53 (1991): 7–18.

Doheny-Farina, Stephen, and Lee Odell. "Ethnographic Research on Writing: Assumptions and Methodology." In *Writing in Non-Academic Settings.* Ed. Lee Odell and Dixie Goswami. New York: Guilford, 1986. 503–35.

Fish, Stanley. *Is There a Text in This Class?* Cambridge: Harvard UP, 1980.

Hirsch, E. D. *The Aims of Interpretation.* Chicago: U of Chicago P, 1976.

Holland, Norman. *5 Readers Reading.* New Haven: Yale UP, 1975.

Husserl, Edmund. *Cartesian Meditations.* Trans. D. Cairns. The Hague: M. Nijhoff, 1960.

Iser, Wolfgang. *The Implied Reader: Patterns of Communication in Prose Fiction from Bunyan to Beckett.* Trans. David Henry Wilson. Baltimore: Johns Hopkins UP, 1978.

Jakobson, Roman, and Morris Halle. *Fundamentals of Language.* The Hague: Mouton, 1956.

Jauss, Hans Robert. *Toward an Aesthetic of Reception.* Trans. Timothy Bahti. Minneapolis: U of Minnesota P, 1982.

Kent, Thomas. "Paralogic Hermeneutics and the Possibilities of Rhetoric." *Rhetoric Review* 8, no. 1 (1989): 24–42.

Kuhn, Thomas. *The Structure of Scientific Revolutions.* Chicago: U of Chicago P, 1962.

Lyotard, Jean-François. *The Postmodern Condition: A Report on Knowledge.* Trans. Geoff Bennington and Brian Massumi. Minneapolis: U of Minnesota P, 1984.

Mailloux, Steven. *Interpretive Conventions: The Reader in the Study of American Fiction.* Ithaca: Cornell UP, 1982.

Norris, Christopher. *Deconstruction and the Interests of Theory.* Norman: U of Oklahoma P, 1989.

Poulet, Georges. "Phenomenology of Reading." *New Literary History* 1 (1969): 54–70.

Rorty, Richard. "Pragmatism, Davidson, and Truth." In *Truth and Interpretation: Perspectives on the Philosophy of Donald Davidson.* Ed. Ernest LePore. Oxford: Basil Blackwell, 1986. 333–55.

————. "Science as Solidarity." In *The Rhetoric of the Human Sciences: Language and Argument in Scholarship and Public Affairs.* Ed. John S. Nelson, Allan Megill, and Donald McCloskey. Madison: U of Wisconsin P, 1987. 38–52.

Searle, John. *Speech Acts: An Essay in the Philosophy of Language.* London: Cambridge UP, 1969.

The Scrutable Subject:
Davidson, Literary Theory, and the
Claims of Knowledge

STEVEN E. COLE

*We have now not merely explored the territory of pure under-
standing, and carefully surveyed every part of it, but have
also measured its extent, and assigned to everything in it its
rightful place. This domain is an island, enclosed by nature
itself within unalterable limits. It is the land of truth—
enchanting name!—surrounded by a wide and stormy
ocean, the native home of illusion, where many a fog bank
and many a swiftly melting iceberg give the deceptive appearance of farther shores, deluding the adventurous seafarer ever
anew with empty hopes, and engaging him in enterprises
which he can never abandon and yet is unable to carry to
completion.*
      [Kant, *Critique of Pure Reason*, A236–37, B294–95]

Oone of the oddities of recent liter-
ary theory is the centrality of the notion that in crucial ways, beliefs are
essentially private—that there is something in the nature of having a
belief, or having any of the family of propositional attitudes which fall
out from the concept of belief (having desire, fear, hope, and so on),
which simply precludes public assessment. The oddity here is not in the
assumption that beliefs are private, for surely such an assumption has
defined much of the history of literary theory. Rather, the oddity comes
from trying to square this assumption with the claim that literary theory,
or more generally the study of literature, can be tied both to a *critique* of

social and public experience and to a set of positive or *normative claims* about what form social and public experience should take. The oddity is thus produced by trying to understand in conjunction the following arguments: 1) the claim that the subject and its beliefs are themselves the effects of social causal mechanisms; 2) the account of the subject as ultimately inscrutable; and 3) the insistence that the determining of the subject by social causal mechanisms should be unmasked by literary theory as a violation of the subject itself. The problem here is to determine how, given the initial definition of the subject as a congeries of effects, one can ever know either those dimensions of the subject which are claimed to resist such causation or in what sense the subject has been violated by the very conditions claimed to be necessarily the source of its existence.

There are two questions which such arguments seem to raise. The first is whether normative accounts of experience can be offered which do not in some way deny what is essential about personal identity—the "subject" in current jargon. The second question is whether we have any basis for claiming that experience is in any sense common or shared. In current literary theory, these questions are answered by claiming that shared or common experience has a determining force which is largely negative—which is to be understood in terms of the effects of ideology, the interpellation of the subject, and so on. Such shared experience is "normative" in the limited sense that it imposes norms which are the determining conditions for the subject. But continually the argument is made that such norms require the resistance of that which exceeds the determinations of the norms themselves: political emancipation is accordingly the result of a kind of structural insurrection, where the chain of signifiers of which norms are composed is revealed as somehow inadequate or incomplete. Thus, normative accounts of experience are collapsed into structural causation, and what devolves to the "subject" of emancipation are those elements of its identity which somehow stand outside the nexus of causation. In this perspective, what is unmasked by theoretical critique is a kind of exclusionary power exercised by any public regime of causation, but such critique is not so much an effort to render a normative account of how such exclusion might be surmounted as it is a kind of ontological insistence that there is an excess of signification or desire which escapes even the most cunning schemes of determination.

In what follows, I want to use Donald Davidson's account of the intersubjectivity of belief and knowledge to show why it is incoherent to claim that we can have knowledge of that which stands outside our schemes of determination, our public accounts of meaning and knowledge. Further, I want to indicate how the description of belief and knowledge as intersubjective can point toward a feasible basis for normative claims about experience. The idea here is that, within current literary theory, the suspicion of normative claims about experience comes in part from the mistaken notion that experience is itself recalcitrantly resistant to any public characterization, and thus my hope is to show how normative argument might be made plausible by showing its emergence from a more basic understanding of human experience as intractably intersubjective. I begin with an analysis of Gayatri Spivak's "essays in cultural politics," and I try to show how her analysis of the *harm* of ideology is undermined by her inability to give either an account of the subjects who experience such harm or an explanation of why such harm should be a matter of public concern. I then show how Davidson's explanations of truth and belief point to precisely the required explanation of the subject as public which Spivak's arguments lack: from a Davidsonian perspective, the deleterious effects caused by such and such a social arrangement can be identified only if we have some way of describing, and understanding, the subjects who experience those effects. Davidson, I argue, provides us with such an account of the subject, and I conclude by suggesting that his essentially Kantian construal of the conditions of possibility of intersubjective experience provides a necessary frame within which particular arguments about the normative and qualitative dimensions of experience might be made.

The central theme of all Spivak's work is what she calls "ideological victimage" (134), and given the importance of the concept, it is worth considering closely what is at stake here.[1] According to Spivak, ideology functions almost invisibly as a set of unexamined norms or assumptions which are defined as "natural" and are thus removed from what she calls "historical sedimentation" (118). Ideology in this sense determines what we count as agency, but in a thoroughly illusory fashion: "It is both the condition and the effect of the constitution of the subject (of ideology) as freely willing and consciously choosing in a world that is seen as background" (118). Free will and conscious choice are thus made possible by ideology, but they are further defined as the cause of ideology itself. What we have is obviously a vicious circle, within which the subject's illusory freedom is produced by the very ideology which is proclaimed as evidence of its freedom. The subject's belief in the freedom of will and the consciousness of choice is made possible by the assumption that such qualities of experience are "natural," but this very assumption is itself the cause of the beliefs it makes possible. Thus, the viciousness of the circle can be seen in the cunning with which the "natural" functions, for the naturalness of the assumption that freedom and consciousness define the subject is maintained by the very illusoriness which it makes possible. Because ideology is "both the condition and the effect of the constitution of the subject (of ideology)" (118), it functions with an almost seamless homeostasis, producing and reproducing precisely the kinds of subjects required for its own continued stability.

Thus far, it is hard to understand how ideology can be claimed to be a victimizer, since nothing in the account allows any description of what, exactly, might be harmed if ideology functions as that which is determinant of the very subject being harmed. The problem is that the description of ideology seems not to offer any explanation of what aspects of the subject might stand outside the determinations of ideology, and thus serve as a candidate for what ideology has itself victimized. If the subject is both the cause and the effect of ideology, and if such a relation to ideology is exhaustive of the subject itself, then there is literally nothing about the subject which ideology might victimize. Another problem is that ideology is defined in such a way that any further description of a public dimension to the subject seems precluded, yet such a dimension is required if the subject's description of itself as "victimized" is to have any force. To speak of ideology as victimizing a subject is to situate the subject within a public realm where claims about victimization might be adjudicated, but if the public is itself constituted by ideology, then there is no feasible scene of adjudication which is not itself defined by the very source of the victimization. What we can see here is that the account of ideology requires, if victimization is to be addressed, both that some notion of the subject be defined which is not determined by ideology and that such a definition of the subject have a public scope. Further, our knowledge of such a public subject which somehow escapes the web of ideology cannot itself derive from the illusory forms of knowledge proffered by ideology: it cannot, that is, be known through "conscious choice" (118), through a reliance on the "possibility of explanation" (105) and its corollary, "the presupposition of an explainable (even if not fully) universe and an explaining (even if imperfectly) subject" (105). Thus, what is required is both a description of a subject which somehow stands outside the illusory totality of ideology as well as a characterization of a kind of publicly available knowledge which relies upon none of the resources of the explanatory model of the "rationalist project" (260).

We can begin by considering Spivak's effort to offer an account of what kind of knowledge is available outside the determinations of ideology. Continually, Spivak denies that such knowledge can be conceived of as in any sense autonomous; rather, what is required is a strategic conception of ideology as somehow incomplete and thus as vulnerable to a kind of productive deconstruction: "The productive undecidability of the borderlines of politics, art, law, and philosophy, as they sustain and are sustained by the identity of a composite entity such as the state, is operated by the heterogeneous and discontinuous concept of ideology. . . . One cannot of course 'choose' to step out of ideology. The most responsible 'choice' seems to be to know it as best one can, recognize it as best one can, and, through one's necessarily inadequate interpretation, to work to change it" (120). Clearly, what Spivak wants here is to claim that the workings of ideology must inevitably fail as a totalized determination of experience and, equally, to insist that our awareness of that failure offers no confidence that we can somehow step outside that which has been exposed as inadequate. Precisely because it is ideology itself which is the determinant of an illusory freedom of choice, the exposure of ideology's heterogeneity cannot serve as the basis for a reinscription of a freely choosing subject. Ideology, Spivak argues, "is both the condition and the effect of the constitution of the subject (of ideology)" (118). The "choice" to "step out of ideology" (120) would necessarily reconstitute ideology itself, since it is exactly the illusion of such choice which ideology itself determines.

Thus, the recognition of "undecidability" would appear to warrant Paul de Man's cautionary insistence that "it *would* be naive . . . to believe that this strategy, which is not *our* strategy as subjects, since we are its product rather than its agent, can be a source of value and has to be celebrated or denounced accordingly" (122).[2] But this is exactly the conclusion that Spivak refuses, for she insists upon the possibility of an awareness of ideology being tied to a decision to "work to change" (120) what ideology has itself produced. The origin of such work is to be "interpretation," but what seems completely mysterious is how interpretation is to proceed in the face of the claim that "knowledge is made possible and sustained by irreducible difference, not identity. What is known is always in excess of knowledge. Knowledge is never adequate to its object" (254). Interpretation seems confronted with an insoluble dilemma: on the one hand, it is enjoined to "change" the workings of ideology, in large part because only such change can remediate the victimage produced by ideology; on the other hand, interpretation is precluded from ever offering adequate knowledge of precisely the object it is enjoined to change. The difficulty here is that because ideology

has itself been defined as the sole conceivable determinant of intersubjective experience, the work of interpretation has no basis for its
own account of the intersubjective, yet it is exactly such an account
which is needed if the determinations of ideology are themselves to be
changed. This brings us back to the question of whether ideology can be
seen as a victimizer: in the present context, such victimization can be
established only if *interpretation* can offer an account of how human
experience is determined which can situate ideology itself as merely a
failed evasion of that which is most basic to human experience.[3] The
argument would have to be that ideology victimizes precisely because it
denies aspects of human experience which should not be denied; but
such an argument can be made only if it can be shown that we have
knowledge of human experience which is more basic than the determinations of ideology, and which can then be the basis of the claim that
ideology should itself be changed. But interpretation, as it is defined,
explicitly excludes such knowledge ("what is known is always in excess
of knowledge" [254]) and thus has no way of fulfilling the demand that it
work to "change" what ideology has done.

The same problems appear in the attempt to define the subject which
escapes ideology as that which interpretation might use as the basis of its
own claims. Continually, what appears here is a conflict between an
attempt, on the one hand, to define the subject in terms which are
consonant with the claim that knowledge is inadequate to the subject
and, on the other hand, an attempt to give sufficient content to that
subject to allow it to serve as the basis of the normative claim about
experience embedded in the description of "ideological victimage." Consider the difference between the claim that knowledge necessarily excludes the "*radically* heterogeneous" (105) with the following account
of agency as merely an effect of ideology:

> A subject-effect can be briefly plotted as follows: that which
> seems to operate as a subject may be part of an immense
> discontinuous network ("text" in the general sense) of strands
> that may be termed politics, ideology, economics, history, sexual-
> ity, language, and so on. . . . Different knottings and configurations
> of these strands, determined by heterogeneous determinations,
> produce the effect of an operating subject. [204]

What seems clear is that the description of the "subject-effect" belies the
claim that there is any sense in which the subject can be seen as "radi-

cally heterogeneous," since such heterogeneity would preclude the kind of elaborate plotting of our knowledge of the subject which is offered by the description of the "subject-effect." What underlies this plotting is the assumption that behind the discontinuous ideological appearances of the "operating subject" is some substratum of the human which can be known, for only such a substratum leaves explicable the certainty that the appearances of the subject through the frame of ideology are merely "effects" which do not touch in any fundamental way the being we see in its appearance. From this it might seem that Spivak *is* coherent in setting against this kaleidoscope of appearance an unknowable heterogeneity, but it is important to emphasize that there is no possibility that such heterogeneity can ever be known, even in the purely negative guise of that which is excluded. The reason for such literal unknowability is precisely the impossibility of giving content to the claim that we can somehow *know* that there is something which exceeds our knowledge. Yet Spivak's entire critique of ideology as a victimizer rests upon the assumption of such knowledge, and so the conundrum is that her normative insistence that we can *know* that ideology victimizes is undermined by her insistence that knowledge is itself inconceivable in relation to that which is victimized.

It is worth noting that Spivak is herself unable to remain within the frame of a heterogeneous and unknowable Other, at least insofar as she tries to give content to the normative claim that ideological victimization must be resisted. Thus, in explaining the inadequacy of ideological accounts of identity when seen from the perspective of gender, she argues both for the possibility of accurate *knowledge* of what has been excluded by such accounts and for the possibility of basing normative claims upon such knowledge:

> Male and female sexuality are asymmetrical. Male orgasmic pleasure "normally" entails the male reproductive act—semination. Female orgasmic pleasure (it is not, of course, the "same" pleasure, only called by the same name) does not entail any one component of the heterogeneous female reproductive scenario: ovulation, fertilization, conception, gestation, birthing. The clitoris escapes reproductive framing. In legally defining woman as object of exchange, passage, or possession in terms of reproduction, it is not only the womb that is literally "appropriated"; it is the clitoris as the signifier of the sexed subject that is effaced. [151]

Stripped of the scare quotes and the jargon, what this says is that a distinction can be drawn between how women have been defined by ideology and our knowledge of what is in fact true of their experience. The important point here is that it is the appeal to truth which warrants the insistence that ideology victimizes women by causing the "efface-ment of the clitoris."

Thus, while Spivak's general account of the relation of knowledge to that which is known insists that knowledge is itself rendered indetermi-nate by the ultimate inscrutability of its objects, here instead it is pre-cisely because we *know* the truth of the female body that we are able to judge the inadequacy—indeed, the wrongness—of how that body is represented in legal definitions of "woman as object of exchange." But what warrants our belief that such knowledge can serve as the basis of a critique of how legal structures have defined women? Crucially here, there are two assumptions behind such a belief, and each stands in stark contrast to the central terms of Spivak's argument. First, the knowledge that the "clitoris escapes reproductive framing" is possible only if the clitoris itself can serve as the object of such knowledge, and it can serve this function only if knowledge itself has access to that which it knows. Second, the knowledge that we have here is assumed to have in-tersubjective validity, for what is being claimed is not that a particular clitoris has been wrongly effaced, but rather that the clitoris itself, as a defining aspect of "female orgasmic pleasure," has been excluded from public definitions of women. Thus, if we gather these two assumptions together, what we find is that Spivak's argument for a change in how women are publicly defined stands completely at odds with her attack on the "presupposition of an explainable . . . subject" (105): here, it is precisely because subjects are explainable in relation to public knowl-edge about crucial components of their identity that we are justified in attacking the exclusion of such knowledge from the legal definition of woman as an "object of exchange."

If we return to the question with which we began the discussion of Spivak—Can ideology be a victimizer?—it is now clear that the answer is yes, but only because we are able to judge ideology in relation to a publicly available knowledge about the agents of such victimization. The description of woman as an "object of exchange," and the transformation of that description into apparatuses of power and control, is "ideologi-cal" (rather than, say, a neutral fact of social experience) because it violates either what we know or what we can come to know about the agency of women. The most important issue, then, is how we can justify our claim to have such knowledge. In the account of the victimization of women by legal definitions, what is presupposed is not merely a generalized account of women in relation to which particular women might be situated. If this were all that was at stake here, then Spivak's insistence on the ultimate inscrutability of the Other would in no sense be challenged, since it would be perfectly plausible to argue that our knowledge of the relation of individual women to our generalized account has nothing to do with a knowledge of those individual women themselves. But what Spivak's account of victimization adds is the requirement that we incorporate in our generalized account precisely that dimension of individual experience which warrants the claim by an agent that she is a victim; and, here, such incorporation is possible only if we have the capacity to understand the dimension of individual experience itself. In other words, if our account of the "effacement of the clitoris" is to be more than a mere subsumption of individual female identity by an empty universal, what is required is an explanation of how we can understand that individual identity itself. For if we cannot understand such identity, if we cannot make sense of what it means for an individual woman to say that her clitoris has been publicly effaced, then we have no way of justifying our claim that we have knowledge of why such effacement should be challenged. And, of course, it is exactly the possibility of such knowledge which Spivak's insistence on the inscrutability of the Other would deny.

The opposition between the public expression, representation, or determination of personal identity, of the "subject," and the ontological inscrutability of that identity seen in itself, upon which Spivak's analysis of culture relies, has been the central focus of Donald Davidson's work. Beginning with his early attack on the notion that agency stands outside of causal explanation, and continuing through his most recent essays on the social dimension of truth, Davidson has rejected the idea that there is any cogency to the relativist or skeptical claim that there is a significant fissure separating the conditions of our knowledge from what we know. Instead, the central theme of all of Davidson's work is that our very capacity to pose questions about the limitations of our knowledge—either about the world or about other subjects—is coherent only in relation to a widespread, intersubjective agreement about both the world and the relation of individual subjects to the world. But further, such "agreement" is not in any sense a merely conventional consensus which might be somehow undermined when set against the kinds of radical contingency to which current literary theory appeals. Rather, the widespread agreement to which Davidson appeals is itself a consequence of the nature of language itself:

> Why must our language—any language—incorporate or depend upon a largely correct, shared, view of how things are? First consider why those who can understand one another's speech must share a view of the world, whether or not that view is correct. The reason is that we damage the intelligibility of our readings of the utterances of others when our method of reading puts others into what we take to be broad error. We can make sense of differences all right, but only against a background of shared belief. [*ITI* 199–200]

What language and shared belief give to a subject is a conception of truth in relation to which the subject can understand both its own identity and its relation to other subjects and to the world. In the absence of such a conception of truth, the subject would be much as Spivak describes it: indeterminate in terms of our knowledge of it, but also in terms of what it itself has the capacity to know. But precisely because the very construal of the subject is made possible by the existence of language, indeterminacy of the radical sort to which Spivak appeals is impossible. To use language, Davidson argues, is to understand truth, and thus to understand the world.

Davidson's insistence on truth as the central component of interpretation, of coming to understand the Other, is the aspect of his thought which is most likely to trouble literary theorists, since a central feature of recent literary theory has been the claim that social and political critique requires that the pretensions to truth of dominant regimes (in Foucault's sense) be exposed as indeterminate. The idea here is that appeals to truth are in some sense intrinsically repressive, and the corollary notion is that we can understand the repressive dimension of truth by setting truth-claims against social and subject-centered contingencies which truth-claims would deny. The functional connection which truth has with repression is revealed by showing the contingent dimensions of experience which truth would deny. But, as the discussion of Spivak indicated, this assumption that a contingent subject can be set against the repressive regimes of truth founders on an incapacity to account for its own knowledge of that which truth would deny. In a sense, the poststructuralist critique of the subject as I am characterizing it bases its argument on a kind of category mistake wherein the conditions of truth which underlie the very possibility of knowing what a subject might be are collapsed into specific normative claims about how the subject *should* be known—the mistake coming from a failure to understand that what allows specific normative judgments to be made (and to be disputed) is precisely the distinction we can draw between such judgments and the conditions of truth which are constitutive of the possibility of judgment itself. We are able to make normative judgments about how the subject is interpellated within public structures because of our certainty that such judgments are based upon the possibility of knowledge about that which is judged. In other words, what allows us to argue that such and such features of experience should not be repressed or denied is precisely *not* that such features are contingent in relation to dominant regimes of truth or knowledge, but rather that the features in dispute can be located within publicly available characterizations of what we know about human experience. What Davidson's account of truth is thus intended to offer is an explanation of how truth can be seen to provide a basis for our knowledge of what it means to be a subject, and the assumption is that only such a basis can explain our ability to make normative judgments about the shape which experience should take.

At the heart of Davidson's conception of truth is the claim that truth must be understood both formally (in terms of truth-conditional semantics) and holistically (in terms of the relation of any particular belief to the entire corpus of beliefs of the believer and, ultimately, of the community of all believers). Davidson's argument is that only such a conception of truth can account for the existence of communication, since what is presupposed by communication is 1) the possibility of locating particular utterances in relation to semantic rules which identify how the arrangement of words that compose an utterance is to be understood as meaningful (rather than simply a random collection of sounds or scrawls) and 2) the possibility of connecting an utterance to beliefs about the world held by the speaker. (The assumption here is that communication itself can be presupposed to exist, since a denial of its existence would simply confirm what was denied.) If the arrangement of words in an utterance were merely contingent, in the sense that we could discover no public rules determining the arrangement, then we would have no capacity to make sense of the utterance, and thus communication itself could not occur. Similarly, if we were unable to connect the utterance to a nexus of beliefs about the world held by the speaker (even if such a connection is made only implicitly), then we would be unable to make sense of what it means for the *speaker* to be making this utterance, and we would thus have no capacity to interpret his utterance as *his* communication with us. Thus, in the most general sense, what the theory of truth is designed to explain is that which must be the case about both an utterance and a speaker for communication to occur.

But Davidson's concern in showing how such a theory of truth might be established is to avoid a tautological reiteration of what we know as a consequence of possessing the required theory of truth; he wants to avoid, that is, a merely descriptive account of what occurs in actual communication. Thus, while he argues that such a theory of truth underlies even the tacit forms of interpretation which we use in making sense of utterances in a language with which we are familiar, he derives his account of truth not from such localized and familiar forms of interpretation (where it is precisely our knowledge of what it means for an utterance to be true that underlies our interpretation), but rather from what he calls "radical interpretation"—a situation in which the interpreter is confronted with a completely unfamiliar language and is thus prevented from drawing upon any of the familiar stock of immanent rules and shared ontological commitments which otherwise facilitate interpretation within a familiar language. Truth hangs upon the possibility of such radical interpretation because the relativization of truth to a particular language could not then prevent a comparable relativization to some realm of private meaning. If our only secure sense of truth is the sort of unexamined agreement which typically marks communication within a particular language, then truth itself is a merely contingent feature of such agreement and is accordingly vulnerable to the withdrawal of consent on the part of individual speakers.

Ultimately, as Davidson argues in "On the Very Idea of a Conceptual Scheme" (*ITI* 183–98), relativizing truth to a particular language fails completely to account for how we could ever conceive of such relativization, since what is implied by the act of describing how differing languages presuppose competing notions of truth is a standpoint which lies outside such relativism. In a sense, what the theory of radical interpretation is designed to test is whether such a standpoint—what Davidson calls a "common co-ordinate system" (*ITI* 184)—can be found; and the assumption is that if radical interpretation can succeed in allowing translation from a completely unfamiliar language, then such translation has succeeded only because radical interpretation has itself relied upon a theory of truth which cannot be relativized to a particular language or interpretive scheme. Thus, any theory of truth which is adequate to the demands of radical interpretation can be the basis for arguing that particular utterances, particular beliefs, can be understood because of their dependence upon the "common system" which the theory of truth allows us to understand.

Radical interpretation begins, Davidson argues, when we come to understand the role which truth would play as an interpreter struggles to understand an alien speaker.[4] Crucially in such a process, the interpreter is unable to assume any direct correlation between her own language and the language which she is interpreting, yet for interpretation to succeed, the interpreter must rely upon an assumption that what she knows to be the case for her own use of language applies in fundamental ways to the language she is attempting to interpret:

> the theory-builder must not be assumed to have direct insight into likely equivalences between his own tongue and the alien. What he must do is find out, however he can, what sentences the alien holds true in his own tongue (or better, to what degree he holds them true). The linguist will then attempt to construct a characterization of truth-for-the-alien which yields, so far as possible, a mapping of sentences held true (or false) by the linguist. Supposing no perfect fit is found, the residue of sentences held true translated by sentences held false (and vice versa) is the margin for error (foreign or domestic). Charity in interpreting the words and thoughts of others is unavoidable in another direction as well: just as we must maximize agreement, or risk not making sense of what the alien is talking about, so we must maximize the self-consistence we attribute to him, on pain of not understanding *him.* [*ITI* 27]

It is important to note that while the characterization here of charity seems to presuppose an enormous amount of precharitable insight into the relation an alien speaker has to his sentences (the fact that we apply charity when we fail to discover why this relation holds would imply that we have no problem in marking the existence of the relation itself), in fact charity begins much sooner—with an initial assumption that "we suppose, as the principle of charity says we unavoidably must, that the pattern of sentences to which a speaker assents reflects the semantics of the logical constants," for on the basis of such a supposition it is then "possible to detect and interpret those constants" ("SCT" 319). Thus, in observing the alien speaker, our only precharitable assumption is that we can observe whether a speaker assents to a sentence and that we can mark whether such assent forms part of a distinct pattern. But we are warranted in this assumption precisely because assent can be *observed* without our having knowledge of why a particular sentence warrants assent. Where charity begins is in the assumption (derived from our own use of language) that such assent emerges from a pattern, and that the pattern is reflected, in the first instance, by what Davidson calls "homophonic translation" (*ITI* 101) (roughly, the idea that the iteration of a word is the iteration of its meaning) and, secondly, by the "semantics of the logical constants," which, since we have recognized their occurrence in the pattern of sentences to which assent is given, we are then in a position to interpret.

Notoriously, this process of interpretation involves discovering "the best way to fit our logic, to the extent required to get a theory satisfying Convention T" (*ITI* 136), the convention which states "that a characterization of a truth predicate 'x is true in L' is accepted only if it entails, for each sentence of the language L, a theorem of the form 'x is true in L if and only if...' with 'x' replaced by a description of the sentence and the dots replaced by a translation of the sentence into the language of the theory" (*ITI* 204).[5] This linkage of interpretation to Convention T is notorious because it seems to reduce interpretation to a mechanical tautology of the sort involved in the biconditional " 'Snow is white' if and only if snow is white." In the present context, however, what allows such disquotation is a process of discovering, initially, homophonic translation and, ultimately, a relation between the pattern of sentences held true and our determination of the semantic devices which serve as the constants allowing our perception of a pattern: "To give a recursive theory of a language is to show that the syntax of the language is formalizable in at least the sense that every true expression may be analyzed as formed from elements (the 'vocabulary'), a finite supply of which suffice for the language" (*ITI* 57). Armed, then, with our ability to note homophonic translation and our identification of the relationship between specific sentences and recursively defined (but empirically observed) semantic functions, we are in place to begin to make sense of the Other.

But while our ability to determine such constants is a necessary condition of our interpretation of an utterance, it is by no means sufficient, since an essential aspect of interpretation involves coming to understand what it means for a speaker to hold true the sentences we are trying to interpret. Repeatedly, Davidson rejects the notion that truth can be separated from belief, arguing instead that "an utterance has certain truth conditions only if the speaker intends it to be interpreted as having those truth conditions" ("SCT" 310). Davidson insists that our awareness of such conditions requires an insight not merely into the formal semantic devices which determine the truth-conditions of sentences, but also an insight into the notion of the subject which is presupposed by the very existence of language itself:

The immediate psychological environment of linguistic aptitudes and accomplishments is to be found in the attitudes, states, and events that are described in intensional idiom: intentional action, desires, beliefs, and their close relatives like hopes, fears, wishes, and attempts. Not only do the various propositional attitudes and their conceptual attendants form the setting in which speech occurs, but there is no chance of arriving at a deep understanding of linguistic facts except as that understanding is accompanied by an interlocking account of the central cognitive and conative attitudes. ["SCT" 315]

While it might seem that what Davidson describes here is precisely the sort of indeterminate intentionality upon which much of poststructuralism relies in its insistence on the ultimate inadequacy of our knowledge, in fact for Davidson the very construal of what he calls the "psychological environment of linguistic aptitudes" is possible because such an environment is tied to a public and observable world.

Thus, Davidson argues that the central task for the interpreter in struggling to make sense of the "intensional" dimension of language (the dimension of language, that is, which requires an understanding of a "psychological environment")[6] is to understand the relation between that environment and a world which is shared by both speaker and interpreter. While Davidson has offered accounts of a number of different aspects of this relation, the most important notion here is the idea of belief, which he argues is "built to take up the slack between sentences held true by individuals and sentences true (or false) by public standards" (*ITI* 153). In his most recent essays, Davidson has increasingly argued that this "slack" is virtually invisible: in a sense, precisely what it means for a sentence to be true is that it is held true by an individual according to public standards which we can discover. The reasons why belief is tied closely to a public world are complicated; but essentially the idea is that beliefs always have content, and such content is necessarily public. As Davidson puts it, "interpretation depends (in the simplest and most basic situations) on the external objects and events salient to both speaker and interpreter, the very objects and events the speaker's words are then taken by the interpreter to have as subject matter" ("SCT" 321). Thus, in making sense of the utterance of a belief, we work to interpret its truth by seeing, in the first instance, its dependence on the familiar truth-determining devices of homophonic translation and the logical constants which determine the relations of the words; but we then look beyond such formal dimensions of language to the world itself which we share with the speaker we are interpreting. We can interpret truth here precisely because the "subject matter" of the utterance of the belief is such a shared world.

It is important to note here that truth is not, in this sense, a normative set of criteria against which particular beliefs are measured. Rather, as the notion of sentences "held true" indicates, truth becomes an issue only in the process of interpretation, only as we struggle to understand what the Other is saying. Thus, Davidson argues that there is a sense in which the notion of whether a belief is believed to be true is tautological:

> It is often wrongly thought that the semantical concept of truth is redundant, that there is no difference between asserting that a sentence *s* is true, and using *s* to make an assertion. What may be right is a redundancy theory of belief, that to believe that *p* is not to be distinguished from the belief that *p* is true. This notion of truth is not the semantical notion: language is not directly in the picture; it is part of the frame. For the notion of a true belief depends on the notion of a true utterance, and this in turn there cannot be without shared language. [*ITI* 170]

The central notion here is that truth is only rarely an issue in introspection: while I may wonder whether it is true that such and such took place, I never wonder whether it is true that I believe such and such took place. Rather, my beliefs—at least the beliefs I hold true—have an authority which cannot be questioned, for I cannot even understand what it would mean to wonder about their truth. This is not to suggest that such truth is private: rather, to have a belief is necessarily to have the ability to use language, and to use language is to situate oneself in a public world. So the idea here is, first, that an intrinsic feature of my use of language to utter my beliefs is the relation of that utterance to "the public things and events that cause [the beliefs]," (*ITI* 332) and, second, that in such use I know not merely (what you can also know) that I hold true the belief which my words are expressing, but also that I know (and you may not know) *what* I believe, which is to say that I know the relation of my belief to the objects which are its cause. But while you may need to interpret the content of my belief (i.e., you may need to discover what is causing my belief), what is not in question is the truth of my belief, since such truth inheres in precisely the fact that I have the belief which you are trying to interpret. Therefore, the question of truth becomes germane not when I am trying to make myself understood, since in such an effort a speaker "cannot wonder whether he generally means what he says" ("FPA" 110). Rather, truth becomes an issue when I am trying to understand another speaker, for there what I have to interpret is precisely what I know about myself: what the speaker's meaning is in relation "to objects and situations" ("FPA" 111) which are the causes of what he is saying. In other words, I do not ponder whether the beliefs I hold true are in fact true, because I know their relation to the objects and situations which are their cause; but when interpreting the Other, it is precisely such a relation which I need to discover.

But, crucially here, it is because I know that my own beliefs are true, insofar as I can track their relation to a public world of objects and situations, that I also know what truth will be like for the Other. My interpretation of the Other originates in my desire to understand what the Other is saying, and my presumption is that the Other wants to be understood. In such a case, "the best the speaker can do is to be *interpretable*, that is, to use a finite supply of distinguishable sounds applied consistently to objects and situations he believes are apparent to his hearer" ("FPA" 111). The speaker, insofar as he wishes to be interpretable, which is to say insofar as he uses language, utters his beliefs in the confidence that those beliefs are true and that such truth is accessible (because it originates in "a finite supply of distinguishable sounds" and because those sounds have a relation to publicly scrutable "objects and situations"). The central notion here is that truth is a primitive feature of the relation of a speaker to an utterance, and that such truth is public because 1) the "distinguishable sounds" and the "objects and situations" which compose truth are public; and 2) the primitive relation of truth which a speaker has to an utterance is a universal precondition of using language and, as such, can serve as the ground of my certainty that just as the beliefs which I hold true are true because of the relation of those beliefs to the objects which are their causes, so also the speaker whose utterances I am trying to interpret holds true the beliefs those utterances express because of a causal relation between the beliefs and their objects. As Davidson puts it, "[my] main point is that our basic methodology for interpreting the words of others necessarily makes it the case that most of the time the simplest sentences which speakers hold true *are* true. It is not the *speaker* who must perform the impossible feat of comparing his belief with reality; it is the *interpreter* who must take into account the causal interaction between world and speaker in order to find out what the speaker means, and hence what he believes" (*ITI* 332).

In considering this claim that there is a causal relation between our beliefs and the objects of those beliefs (a causal relation, say, between our belief that such and such an action is worthwhile and the action itself), it is important to keep in mind the understanding of cause at work here. Repeatedly, Davidson rejects the notion that psychological phenomena can be explained as tokens of lawlike types. He rejects the idea, that is, that a psychological phenomenon (such as having a belief) can be seen as instantiating a law which describes a necessary relation between the belief as an effect and the object as a cause: "Standing ready, as we must, to adjust psychological terms to one set of standards and physical terms to another, we know that we cannot insist on a sharp and law-like connection between them. Since psychological phenomena do not constitute a closed system, this amounts to saying they are not, even in theory, amenable to precise prediction or subsumption under deterministic laws" (*EAE* 239).[7] To claim that a particular belief has been *caused* by a particular object (or event, or experience, or situation) is not, then, to say that it will necessarily be the case that the particular belief is entailed by the existence of the particular object; it is rather to say that the particular belief could not have existed without the existence of the particular object, and thus to say that we can understand the belief by seeing its relation to that object.

Two issues are significant here. First, Davidson's claim is that the *objects* of beliefs are necessarily public in the sense that beliefs are themselves dependent upon the intersubjectivity of language and thus cannot be conceived of as having for their objects anything other than the public items whose apprehension language makes possible. Because beliefs are themselves dependent upon language, and because language is itself intersubjective, beliefs are of necessity intersubjective as well. To have a belief is to have a relation to what is publicly scrutable, both because the belief itself can come into existence only through the public resources of language and because the *objects* of the belief are themselves public—to say, "I believe *x*" is in a strong sense to say that we can understand what constitutes the "I" because we can understand that the "I" is itself causally connected with "*x*," which will be some item in the public realm. As we come to see "*x*" in relation to the "I," we will also know *why* the "I" has the belief it has, for this is exactly what it means to say that the objects of a belief cause the belief. The second issue concerns the question of what sorts of objects can serve as the cause of a belief. To say that a belief is caused by its objects is to leave open the question of what counts as an object and, thus, is to be silent concerning epistemological arguments about which sorts of objects are best qualified to serve as the objects of justified beliefs. To have a belief is, in a sense, to justify it, in the sense that any and all beliefs have as their objects any of the *things* which a language allows to serve as an object.

This, of course, brings us back to the question of truth. What warrants
or justifies a belief is not that the belief has as its object a member of an
epistemologically privileged class of entities, but rather that the belief
accords with the formal and holistic requirements of truth, requirements
which are in a strong sense constitutive of the very idea of having a
belief:

> My argument has two parts. First I urge that a correct understand-
> ing of the speech, beliefs, desires, intentions and other proposi-
> tional attitudes of a person leads to the conclusion that most of a
> person's beliefs must be true, and so there is a legitimate presump-
> tion that any one of them, if it coheres with most of the rest, is true.
> Then I go on to claim that anyone with thoughts who wonders
> whether he has a reason to suppose he is generally right about the
> nature of his environment, must know what a belief is, and how in
> general beliefs are to be detected and interpreted. These being
> perfectly general facts we cannot fail to use when we communicate
> with others, there is a pretty strong sense in which we can be said
> to know that there is a presumption in favor of the overall truthful-
> ness of anyone's beliefs, including our own. ["CTT" 314]

We can see here that what truth offers us, with respect to understanding
the Other, is a basis, first of all, for making sense of what the Other says
and, second, for using what the Other says as the basis for knowledge of
what the Other believes and what the Other desires. What allows us to
achieve such knowledge is our awareness that the belief we are struggling to understand will itself be warranted or justified just insofar as its
expression follows whatever semantic truth-conditions are required by
the language being used and insofar as we are able to make sense of the
belief by seeing its relation to the entire corpus of beliefs of the speaker,
and thus necessarily to the entire corpus of beliefs of all users of language. What truth gives us, then, is an ability to make sense of other
subjects by seeing subjects themselves as the consequences of public
articulations of beliefs: what produces the subject, and what makes the
subject publicly scrutable, is the essential role which belief plays in tying
the subject to a shared world. Of course, this process of "making sense"
of the subject is endless, but it is in no sense indeterminate. Rather, what
governs our struggle to use beliefs as the basis for understanding the
subject is precisely the requirement that we understand the beliefs holistically, in relation to the entire corpus of what is believed as well as to
the shared world which beliefs have as their object.

Crucially here, the terms of the relations among the beliefs, and their relative weight, are not stipulated in advance; thus, our struggle to understand beliefs holistically opens the possibility that the relation between the corpus of beliefs and a new belief will cause both to change, ensuring that our notion of the subject is itself open to constant revision. What we believe, and thus our understanding of ourselves as subjects, changes in relation to our development of new beliefs but also as we are exposed to the beliefs of others.[8] There is, neither in theory nor in practice, no end to this production of the subject, but what makes possible such limitless productivity is precisely the constitutive limitation of truth. The paradox, then, is that while a denial of any limitation or determination to the use of language must ultimately preclude the use of language to express or describe what it means to be a subject (thereby severely limiting and determining our notion of the subject itself), the insistence that our use of language is both limited to and determined by the necessary publicity of truth allows finally an endless capacity for language to be used as the means by which the subject can itself be revealed in all its complexity.

The focus so far has been the role which Davidson's theory of truth might play in explaining our capacity to make sense of the Other, but what has been excluded is the relationship between the possibility of such an explanation and the normative claims we might want to make about the shape which the experience of the Other *should* take. It is perfectly plausible to imagine a response to Davidson which might grant the coherence of his claim that subjects can be understood in their relations to a public world, but which might still insist that such knowledge offers no shared basis for *normative* judgments, which are determinate only in relation to the interests and values of the one who is judging. If such a response is found to be cogent, then much of the poststructuralist critique of our pretensions to know the subject which we saw in Spivak remains in force, since what is at issue there is precisely a denial that even the most compelling public description of the subject can serve as the basis for a normative claim about the shape the subject's experiences *should* take. The argument would be that while the theory of truth provides *you* with a basis for understanding what my beliefs are, such an understanding has no relation to the production of *my* interests and values, which remain an indeterminate possession of my own status as a subject. The publicly available knowledge of my beliefs is, in a sense, an *a posteriori* reconstruction of an originary experience which remains intractably private. Similarly, in my judgment of *your* beliefs, while truth assures the accuracy of my knowledge of the public dimensions of what I judge, the interests and values which motivate my judgment are as indeterminate in relation to your status as a subject as my own values and interests are when they stand as the object of *your* judgment. Unless the theory of truth can explain the *public* status of a subject's relation to its interests and values, the theory has no power to explain the possibility of normative judgment.

The central question here is thus whether the knowledge of the subject which truth provides has any real connection with the interests and values of the subject. Davidson addresses this question directly in two recent essays, "The Myth of the Subjective" and "Judging Interpersonal Interests," where he argues that an obvious consequence of the public dimension of truth is to render incoherent the very assumption that subjective states such as possessing interests or values can be identified independently of the causal (and thus public) connections which exist between the mental states of a subject and a public world. Far from standing outside our public schemes of interpretation, putatively private or indeterminate aspects of the subject which we group under the rubric of the subject's interests or values are nothing more than relations which a subject has to a shared world and, as such, raise interpretive problems no more (or less) significant than any of the issues with which we grapple as we try to understand the Other. Further, just as, in interpreting the Other, we proceed on an assumption that the world inhabited by the Other is in a fundamental sense the same as our own, so in judging the Other's interests and values do we assume a shared basis according to which our judgments are inseparable from the very process which allows us to determine that the Other *has* interests and values. Particular judgments are thus less the basis of our coming to understand the Other's interests and values than they are the consequence of a world of interests and values which is in a fundamental sense shared. In each case, that which allows our understanding both of what it means for the subject to have interests and values and of what it means to judge those interests and values is precisely this: we have no access to any notion of the subject outside of the shared world which is presupposed by our very apprehension of the subject as possessed of interests and values. We have access to the interests and values of the subject (and we can judge those interests and values) because interests and values are themselves part of the shared world which makes possible our apprehension of the subject itself.

In "The Myth of the Subjective," Davidson argues that the very delineation of a putatively "subjective" dimension to experience is the outgrowth of a misapprehension of the relation the mind has to the world. There are two issues here: the first is how to identify what are called "states of mind"; the second is how to characterize the relation such states have to the world. Not surprisingly, Davidson begins his assault on the notion that there are "subjective" states of mind by questioning what the content of such a state would be. After rehearsing the familiar empiricist argument that the mind imposes a mental "scheme" upon the "content" supplied by the senses, he then points to the difficulties involved in establishing that such a scheme could account for the relationship which states of mind have to the world. The problem is that the empiricist account of the mind assumes that the mind itself imposes its schemes upon "an ultimate source of evidence [sense data] whose character can be wholly specified without reference to what it is evidence for" ("MS" 162). Sensory data are assumed to be the basis of the subject's access to the world, but because such data are characterized as independent of the schemes we impose upon the world, we have no way of ascertaining the adequacy of the schemes themselves. Thus, while empiricism wants to keep the evidence of the senses immune from the subject, the disjunction between scheme and evidence (and the location of the scheme itself within a subjective realm standing apart from all evidence) results in a detachment of the subject from the world: "Our beliefs purport to represent something objective, but the character of their subjectivity prevents us from taking the first step in determining whether they correspond to what they pretend to represent" ("MS" 163). So long as the subject is defined as standing outside the world it experiences, and as having access to that world only by virtue of an imposition of its own organizing schemes, it has no capacity to know the connection of its beliefs with the world it experiences.

But, of course, such an account of the subject simply cannot account for the *communication* of beliefs, which, as we have seen, is possible only because beliefs themselves have as their objects a world which is shared by speakers of language. Further, because the relation between beliefs and their objects is a *causal* relation, in the sense that the beliefs are caused by their objects, there is simply no place for the uninterpreted sense data upon which the subject is presumed to impose its schemes, and thus there is no coherent account of the subjective itself. Insofar as the subjective purports to describe states of mind which are somehow independent of the public objects which are their causes, it founders on the impossibility of using language to establish such a distinction between the subjective and a public world: "There are no words, or concepts tied to words, that are not to be understood and interpreted, directly or indirectly, in terms of causal relations between people and the world (and, of course, the relations among words and other words, concepts and other concepts)" ("MS" 170). Thus, the attempt to identify a realm of subjectivity which stands outside the world is literally condemned to silence, since the attempt to communicate such a realm in language is forced to evoke the very world which the subjective itself was designed to deny.

It is important to note that this insistence that states of mind possessed by a subject are known only by their causal relations to the world is in no sense limited to those states of mind which would somehow fall within an empiricist frame. Rather, a "state of mind" is itself a relationship which the mind has to the world, and from this perspective no distinction can be made between those mental states which have as their object the causal relations among the objects of the world and those mental states which instead exhibit an affective attitude toward objects in the world. Just as in the case of the mind's apprehension of the causal relations in the world, so in the mind's values or interests the state of mind is itself caused (and thus known) by the objects which the mind values or has interest in: "states of mind like doubts, wishes, beliefs, and desires are identified in part by the social and historical context in which they are acquired; in this respect they are like other states that are identified by their causes" ("MS" 170).[9] The point here is that insofar as the subject has states of mind, those states are publicly accessible because of their relation to a public world, here defined as a "social and historical context." To say, then, that states of mind have a causal relation to their objects is to be silent about the epistemological status of the objects themselves, beyond the narrow criterion that the objects are of necessity public. This is significant because it precludes the kind of demarcation between publicly available forms of knowledge and an indeterminate realm of desire, value, or interest upon which standard defenses of the inscrutability of the subject are based. Desire, value, and interest are inconceivable from a Davidsonian perspective other than as states of mind and, as such, are as accessible to public scrutiny as any of the more commonly identified forms of public knowledge.

Indeed, Davidson concludes "The Myth of the Subjective" with the much stronger claim that public accessibility is not merely a consequence of having a mental state, but is rather constitutive of the mental itself:

> Thoughts are private, in the obvious but important sense in which property can be private, that is, belong to one person. And knowledge of thoughts is asymmetrical, in that the person who has a thought generally knows he has it in a way in which others can-

not. But this is all there is to the subjective. So far from constituting a preserve so insulated that it is a problem how it can yield
knowledge of an outside world or be known to others, thought is
necessarily part of a common public world. Not only can others
learn what we think by noting the causal dependencies that give
our thoughts their content, but the very possibility of thought
demands shared standards of truth and objectivity. ["MS" 171]

Crucially here, Davidson sees "truth and objectivity" not merely as the
necessary presuppositions of our knowledge of the Other, nor even of our
access to a world which we have in common with the Other. Rather, the
realm of thought, which in the largest sense (as including desires, values,
and so on) is that which marks the poststructuralist subject's inscrutability in relation to knowledge, is here instead made possible by the "shared
standards of truth and objectivity" which are the enabling conditions of
the subject's articulation (indeed, its apprehension) of both its own identity and its relation to the world. Thus, my interests and values, far from
demarcating a mysterious and inscrutable aspect of my identity, are instead, like all my mental states, a *consequence* of my relation to a public
realm. This is not to suggest that my particular interests and values are
determined according to lawlike relations which hold between the objects I experience and my mental states; for, as we saw earlier, Davidson
rejects the notion that psychological attributes can be reduced to
nomological regularities. Rather, my possession of interests and values is
caused in a more general way by the derivation of those interests and
values from the "standards of truth and objectivity" which constitute the
very possibility of having thoughts: the role which thought plays in linking me to the world, and in defining my relation to the world, is possible
only because that activity of linkage and relating is itself dependent upon
the constitutive presuppositions of objectivity and truth.[10]

     Accordingly, for Davidson, there is no special class of mental states or
beliefs—such as having interests or values—which can be separated out
from the publicly available access to belief which objectivity and truth
offer. I am able to understand your beliefs because of their derivation
from a public world, and accordingly I am also able to understand your
identity as a subject, since there is no component of that identity which
is not itself tied to the relations which your beliefs have to a public
world. But the question remains whether, despite my ability to *understand* your values and interests, I am not retreating to some indeterminate locus when I engage in a *judgment* of those interests and values.
The denial that subjects are in any important sense indeterminate may

be coherent as a description of the subject's relations to the world, but it does not immediately establish that my judgment of the Other's interests and values has a similar derivation from a public space.

The issue, then, is how judgment might be connected with the publicly available knowledge which I have of the Other's identity as a subject; but in order to address this issue, we need to consider the prior question of the relation between my own identity as a subject and my judgment of the Other. Thus far, the characterization of how the Other's values and interests might be known has seemed to presume a kind of independence from my own status as a subject with values and interests; it is as if, in coming to understand the Other's values and interests, I had a neutral or transparent relation to the very world which I am claiming is determinant of the values and interests of the Other which I am judging. If my account of the Other's beliefs cannot explain the *intersubjectivity* of our relation to the world, if my own judgment of the Other stands outside the very conditions which enable that judgment, then my judgment is itself precisely what the Other has claimed: an arbitrary imposition of indeterminate values and interests upon a world which has no essential connection with that which is being imposed. We need, then, to explain how the judgment of the values and interests of the Other can be seen as itself the *consequence* of the conditions of truth and objectivity which, as we have seen, enable my construal of both myself and the Other as subjects inhabiting a common world.

For Davidson, such an explanation can be provided by considering more closely the relationship between 1) the interpretation which allows me to understand the Other's interests and values and 2) my judgment of those interests and values. The assumption that interpretation and judgment can be separated is responsible for the claim that judgment is itself indeterminately related to that which it judges, but the problem with such an assumption is that it ignores the role which judgment itself (as the determination of an object according to my values and interests) plays in interpretation:

> Should we say that in interpreting others we "compare" their logic and beliefs with our own? This seems to argue for two separate stages: first we learn what they believe, and then compare. This separation cannot, I have argued, be maintained until a general basis for interpretation has been laid down. Before conscious comparison is possible, our own standards of consistency and of the general character of the world have entered essentially into the process of determining what others think. ["JII" 206]

The most important point here is that it is "standards of consistency and of the general character of the world" which constitute the very possibility of my knowledge of the Other; such standards are my own not in the sense that they are somehow opposed to the standards of the Other, but rather in the sense that they are what give me both my sense of who I am and what the world is. It is precisely because I have such standards that I am able to make sense of the Other, but in no sense are the standards subjective or private. Rather, the objectivity of those standards is confirmed by their success: my very ability to compare my beliefs with those of the Other presupposes the success not merely of my own standards in establishing what it means to have a belief, but also the adequacy of those standards to the beliefs of the Other. My own beliefs are true, and rationally consistent, and by presuming similar truth and rational consistency in the beliefs of the Other, I can come to understand them: "Interpretation takes on a normative tone. In understanding others, in attributing propositional attitudes to them, I have no choice but to consider what inconsistencies do least harm to intelligibility; inconsistency here being inconsistency as I see it. My own standards of rationality necessarily enter the process of interpretation" ("JII" 206).

Significantly here, what holds for beliefs in general holds for such particular beliefs as values and interests. Davidson argues that precisely because values and interests are themselves beliefs and, as such, are known by their causal relations to a public world, there is no coherent sense in which my own values and interests can be seen as somehow different in fundamental ways from the values and interests of the Other. Accordingly, my *judgment* of the Other's values and interests is itself made possible by the derivation of each of our values and interests from a shared world constituted by truth and objectivity:

> The "basis" of interpersonal comparisons is then provided for each of us by his own central values, both his norms of consistency and of what is valuable in itself. These norms we do not choose, at least in any ordinary sense; they are what direct and explain our choices. ["JII" 209]

What allows me to understand the values and interests of the Other is not that such understanding proceeds according to an objectivity which has no essential relation to my own values and interests; rather, it is precisely because I have values and interests that I am in a position to judge the values and interests of the Other. But further, since my values and interests are themselves coherent to me (as all my beliefs are) because of their truth and objectivity in relation to the world, I judge the Other's values and interests as themselves determined by truth and objectivity and, thus, in an important sense as indistinguishable from my own. The notion of values and interests as publicly determined is crucial here: while my particular values and interests are produced in important ways by choices I make about what to value and what to be interested in, what is not a matter of choice are the "norms of consistency," the truth and objectivity, which are the constitutive bases of the particular choices I make. Were truth and objectivity not determinant or constitutive in this way, then not only would I not be in a position to judge the values and interests of the Other, I would have no basis for knowing that the Other *had* values and interests.

Clearly, nothing in Davidson's account of the basis of our judgment of the Other's interests and values entails any particular judgment, and this may perhaps be seen as a weakness in the argument. But such a criticism would miss the force of the discussion, which is aimed less at defending particular normative judgments than at clarifying the basis, the conditions of possibility, of judgment itself. Davidson's central concern in "Judging Interpersonal Interests" is to free judgment of the debilitating anxiety that no basis can be found for how one subject judges the interests and values of another. The very construal of the subject and the Other as somehow inhabiting incommensurable worlds founders on its incapacity to explain what it means to construe the Other as possessing interests and values: from the perspective of incommensurable subjects, not only is there no basis for judgment, there is no possibility of describing the interests and values which might occasion judgment. Thus, the force of Davidson's insistence on a public world as the causal basis of values and interests (and on objectivity, norms of consistency, and rationality as the conditions of possibility for our apprehension of that world) is to establish a basis from which particular judgments might be made, a basis which Davidson argues is prior to the normative concerns which underlie particular judgments:

> there is something fundamentally wrong with the idea that interpersonal comparisons can be isolated from simple attributions of desires or interests, since comparisons are implicit in such attributions. . . . There is no reason why we cannot judge the relative strengths of our own interests and those of others, or compare the interests of two others. My point has been that we do not have to establish, argue for, or opt for, a basis of such judgments. We already have it. If it is true that the basis of interpersonal compari-

son already exists when we attribute desires to others, then we can, after all, make a clear distinction between interpersonal comparisons and normative judgments based on them. For issues of fairness, justice, and social welfare play no favoured role in our attributions to others of desires and preferences. ["JII" 210]

A world within which subject and Other confront each other as inscrutably outside any available account of knowledge is a world forced to regard normative judgments as impossibly peculiar, an imposition of the beliefs of the subject who judges upon an Other whose own beliefs are intractably alien. What Davidson allows us to see is the confusion responsible for such a conception of the world. Far from beliefs marking the inscrutability of a subject in relation to judgment, the very possession of beliefs is possible because of the relation which beliefs have to a public (and thus intersubjective) world constituted by norms of objectivity and rationality. In the absence of such norms, the subject would be not merely indeterminate, but nonexistent; yet, because such norms are themselves the basis of my identification of both myself and the Other as subjects constituted by the conditions which determine the possession of beliefs, I can proceed in the certainty that however contestable my normative judgments, those judgments are themselves the outgrowth of what it means to inhabit an intersubjective world.

I have been emphasizing Davidson's conception of the subject as the consequence of publicly determinant conditions of possibility for what it means to be a subject, and I want to conclude by returning to the question of how this conception differs from the subject as it is conceived in current literary theory. In a sense, the view of the subject which we saw in Spivak, and which is now dominant in literary studies, situates the subject as a kind of ontological absolute against which all pretensions to determinant knowledge can be exposed as inadequate. Where Davidson's focus is on the conditions of possibility which underlie our very construal of the subject, the poststructuralist strategy is instead to define the subject as itself a kind of ultimate limiting condition, an infinitely dense particularity, whose inscrutability remains in place so long as our descriptions or determinations of that particularity fail in any way to account for all conceivable descriptions or determinations. A claim that the subject can be determined or described in such and such a way is forever rendered comical by the poststructuralist insistence that all determination and description are betrayed by the infinite proliferation of possibility. Here, for example, is Spivak's explanation of how *jouissance* results from thought's inevitable discovery of its inadequate relation to the subject:

> the subject (speaking being) is more like a map or graph of knowing rather than an individual self that knows [and thus] a limit to the claim to power of knowledge is inscribed.... Thought is where this knowing-program, the mapping of knowledge, exceeds itself into and thus outlines the deliberative consciousness. Since this epistemograph is also what constitutes the subject (as well as "others" it), knowing in this para-subjective sense is also being.... Thought, as *jouissance,* is not orgasmic pleasure genitally defined, but the excess of being that escapes the circle of the reproduction of the subject. It is the mark of the Other in the subject. [258–59]

This collapse of being and otherness into the subject is the consequence of the belief that knowledge itself is a kind of secondary reproduction of an originary being. While that being is itself characterized as a consequence of what Spivak calls a "mapping of knowledge," it is significant that such knowledge is itself set over and against the being with which it struggles. What is here constituted by knowledge is little more than a recognition of an absolute subject in relation to which no particular distinctions are conceivable: the subject defined in this way is inscrutable not merely in relation to knowledge, but also in terms of any more general account of the world.

Spivak aligns her description of the subject with what she calls "such experiments as those epistemographs (maps of stages of knowing rather than the story of the growth of the individual mind that knows) of Hegel" (259), and it is useful to consider Hegel's own account of the subject which results from what Spivak characterizes as an "epistemograph." Toward the end of *Science of Logic,* Hegel dismisses the Kantian idea that a subject's relation to the good might be conceived of as distinct from a subject's phenomenal experience (the subject's experience, that is, of natural necessity), arguing instead that the determination of the subject according to what Hegel calls the "Idea of the Notion" (roughly, the relation between ethical ideals and the determinations of consciousness) must account for the totality of the subject's experience:

> When external actuality is altered by the activity of the objective Notion and its determination therewith sublated, by that very fact

the merely phenomenal reality, the external determinability and worthlessness, are removed from that actuality and it is *posited* as being in and for itself. In this process the general presupposition is sublated, namely the determination of the good as a merely subjective end limited in respect of content, the necessity of realizing it by subjective activity, and this activity itself.... The individuality of the subject with which the subject was burdened by its presupposition, has vanished along with the presupposition; hence the subject now exists as *free, universal self-identity,* for which the objectivity of the Notion is a *given* objectivity *immediately to hand,* no less truly than the subject knows itself as the Notion that is determined in and for itself. [823]

The process which Hegel describes here is one in which the subject defines itself by its dissatisfaction with the incompleteness of its relations to the world.[11] Where Davidson describes a subject as *constituted* by its relations to a public world, Hegel instead sees the public world as an outgrowth of the subject itself: the *"free, universal self-identity"* which the subject achieves is purchased at the cost of any externality, any describable relation the subject has to an independent world. Thus, paradoxically, the subject's freedom is achieved by its absorption of the very world in relation to which freedom might itself be seen as meaningful.

In a sense, Hegel begins with the world as it appears to the subject and discovers that only the subject could be responsible for such an appearance of the world; that movement from world to subject is, I want to argue, responsible for the contradictions and evasions which we saw in Spivak's attempt to describe the relation a subject might have to normative claims about the world.[12] Davidson's Kantian procedure is precisely the reverse of this: like Kant, Davidson begins with the subject, but his analysis recovers the world by showing the incapacity of the subject in itself to produce what it knows. As Davidson himself admits, there are no particular normative conclusions to be drawn from his account of the role which truth and rationality play in our knowledge, but what must be emphasized is the futility of normative argument in the absence of any agreement about how the subjects of such argument are to be identified. As Davidson puts it, before any disagreement is possible, the disputants must "interpret the words and beliefs of each other. In doing this each of necessity employs his own basis. For each, this supplies a ground of agreed-on standards, values and beliefs to which appeal can be made concerning their difference. Serious relativism provides no such common ground on which further intelligible discussion can be based" ("JII"

210). Where the Hegelian or poststructuralist subject seeks freedom in its denial of the intelligibility of any but its own determinations, and finds finally only its own absolute, the Davidsonian subject is instead constituted by the limiting certainty of the truth of its own beliefs, and discovers the freedom of endless dispute.

NOTES

1. I have chosen Spivak as the focus of discussion here because her work is, in many ways, a brilliant encapsulation of central themes in recent literary theory. Further, I have tried to locate my discussion within her own terms, since that seems the most fruitful way of exploring what is at stake in her arguments. It is my sense that real debate with the issues Spivak raises can take place only by such a procedure: to question the worth of the terminology is simply to dismiss what is actually a substantive set of arguments.

2. I examine the social dimensions of de Man's arguments in "The Dead-end of Deconstruction: Paul de Man and the Fate of Poetic Language."

3. For a good discussion of the relation of theories of ideology to normative claims about experience, see Thompson 279–302.

4. The relationship of Davidson's understanding of radical interpretation to W. V. Quine's description of the indeterminacy of translation is examined in Hookway 177–82.

5. Hacking provides a succinct explantion of Davidson's derivation of Convention T from Tarski (130–34), and a useful summary of problems philosophers have found with Davidson's use of Tarski is offered in Passmore 68–75. Norris (206–18) tries to show how Davidson's defense of Convention T can be seen to challenge poststructuralist relativism, but his argument is weakened by a failure to consider how Davidson's conception of Convention T is connected with a causal theory of belief.

6. Davidson's understanding of what counts as extensionality has apparently loosened in recent years. Thus, in "Problems in the Explanation of Action," he seems to see extensionality as merely the "strong requirement that . . . belief and desire be described in terms of their semantic contents" (43), while in "The Structure and Content of Truth" he describes "a preference for the truth of one sentence over another" as "an extensional relation that relates an agent and two sentences" (323). In each case, extensionality is made so particular to the beliefs of an agent that the required distinction to intensionality seems virtually nonexistent. Hookway has a superb account of how extensionality was intended by Quine to secure the authority of scientific discourse (78–109). Davidson's movement toward a looser conception of the constraints on semantic interpretation is criticized by Apel as weakening "the notion that sharing public meanings by communication with co-subjects of cognition is a transcendental condition of the possibility of cognition in the sense of intersubjectively valid knowledge; and thus it seems to amount to restoring the methodological solipsism of a Cartesian or Lockean epistemology" (25). However, as I argue below, Davidson's recent essays "The Myth of the Subjective" and "Judging Interpersonal Interests" provide an explanation of why the relativization of semantic constraint to a particularized speaker does not risk methodological solipsism—because the particularized speaker is itself constituted by its relation to a public world, we have as firm a basis for interpreting the speaker as that offered by the "transcendental condition of the possibility of cognition" provided by a semantic theory.

7. In "Replies to Essays X–XII" Davidson develops his insistence that the mental cannot be

seen as a closed system: "There *couldn't* be a closed system of the mental, observed or unobserved, because of the endless ways in which the mental interacts with the physical" (249). Davidson's rejection of nomological accounts of the psychological is criticized by Lycan, who argues that for Davidson "psychological 'explanation' is not genuine explanation in the sense of revealing underlying realities in nature, but is, rather, a kind of interpretative—and in part evaluative—scheme that we impose on certain beings for our own purposes of dealing with those things" (27). This opposition between the real and the evaluative is precisely what Davidson's own account of the supervenience of the mental on the physical is designed to counter, since for Davidson the ubiquity of mental–physical interaction precludes the kind of dualism assumed by consigning the evaluative to an amorphous realm of schemic imposition. The difficulty of understanding precisely how Davidson understands the relation of the mental and the physical (and, in particular, the degree to which this relation is causal) is indicated by Charlton's astonishing assertion that Davidson "subscribes to a physicalism which makes all our behavior causally determined; he thinks we are never able to behave otherwise than as we do" (32). Bishop (52–73) offers a comprehensive explanation of why the causal theory of action does not preclude individual choice and, thus, individual responsibility for actions.

8. The expansion of belief in relation to the Other is argued by Root (299–304) and by Ramberg (114–41).

9. While Davidson argues that his account of how mental states can be understood as causally connected with the objects of those states can be seen as a Kantian attempt "to explain away the appearance of contradiction" (*EAE* 209) between the mental and the physical, Allison claims that the "compatibilist" argument that the mental is supervenient on the physical should be sharply distinguished from Kant's insistence that moral freedom requires complete auton- omy from natural necessity (77–81). However, as Allison grants, a distinction is needed here between Kant's description of practical freedom in the *Critique of Pure Reason*, where such freedom is characterized as the capacity to initiate a causal series within phenomenal experi- ence, and the description of *transcendental* freedom in the *Critique of Practical Reason*, which implies that a self is free only insofar as its agency is absolutely autonomous from all phenomenal causation (54–70). While Davidson's anomalous monism would allow practical freedom insofar as it can be tied to phenomenal experience (the argument of the *Critique of Pure Reason*), his conception of truth would clearly require that any notion of noumenal agency be rejected as quite literally incommunicable, and thus outside any possible knowledge.

10. Rovane argues that, for Davidson, "one can be a self-conscious believer only if one can ascribe beliefs to others too" (423).

11. The role which dissatisfaction plays in Hegel's account of the absolute subject is exam- ined by Yack (188–223).

12. Pippin's argument that, for Hegel, "the dissatisfactions responsible for historical change . . . stem from an original failure of self-consciousness" (71) indicates the degree to which Hegel's account of a mediated subject presupposes an originary self-consciousness in relation to which any independent world is mere illusion. In this context, it is useful to remember Adorno's description of Hegelian dialectics as "the unsuccessful attempt to use philosophical concepts for coping with all that is heterogeneous to those concepts" (4).

WORKS CITED

Adorno, Theodor W. *Negative Dialectics.* Trans. E. B. Ashton. New York: Continuum, 1973.

Allison, Henry E. *Kant's Theory of Freedom.* Cambridge: Cambridge UP, 1990.

Apel, Karl-Otto. "Comments on Davidson." *Synthese* 59 (1984): 19–26.

Bishop, John. *Natural Agency: An Essay on the Causal Theory of Action.* Cambridge: Cambridge UP, 1989.

Charlton, William. *Weakness of Will: A Philosophical Introduction.* Oxford: Basil Blackwell, 1988.

Cole, Steven E. "The Dead-end of Deconstruction: Paul de Man and the Fate of Poetic Language." *Criticism* 30 (1988): 91–112.

De Man, Paul. *The Rhetoric of Romanticism.* New York: Columbia UP, 1984.

Hacking, Ian. *Why Does Language Matter to Philosophy?* Cambridge: Cambridge UP, 1975.

Hegel, G.W.F. *Science of Logic.* Trans. A. V. Miller. New York: Humanities, 1969.

Hookway, Christopher. *Quine: Language, Experience, and Reality.* Stanford: Stanford UP, 1988.

Kant, Immanuel. *Critique of Pure Reason.* Trans. Norman Kemp Smith. New York: St. Martin's, 1965.

LePore, Ernest, ed. *Truth and Interpretation: Perspectives on the Philosophy of Donald Davidson.* Oxford: Basil Blackwell, 1986.

Lycan, William G. *Judgement and Justification.* Cambridge: Cambridge UP, 1988.

Norris, Christopher. *The Contest of Faculties: Philosophy and Theory After Deconstruction.* London: Methuen, 1985.

Passmore, John. *Recent Philosophers.* LaSalle, Ill.: Open Court, 1985.

Pippin, Robert B. *Modernism as a Philosophical Problem: On the Dissatisfactions of European High Culture.* Oxford: Basil Blackwell, 1991.

Ramberg, Bjørn T. *Donald Davidson's Philosophy of Language: An Introduction.* Oxford: Basil Blackwell, 1989.

Root, Michael. "Davidson and Social Science." In LePore. 272–304.

Rovane, Carol. "The Metaphysics of Interpretation." In LePore. 417–29.

Spivak, Gayatri Chakravorty. *In Other Worlds: Essays in Cultural Politics.* New York: Routledge, 1987.

Thompson, John B. *Studies in the Theory of Ideology.* Berkeley: U of California P, 1984.

Yack, Bernard. *The Longing for Total Revolution: Philosophic Sources of Social Discontent from Rousseau to Marx and Nietzsche.* Princeton: Princeton UP, 1986.

Strict Constructionism:
Davidsonian Realism and the
World of Belief

MICHAEL MORTON

I begin with a number of consider-
ations that, on the face of it, might seem too obvious to require mention.
There are things true of the world, and things not true of it. Of the things
that are true of the world—let us call them "facts"—it is possible in a
very large number of cases for us to be absolutely certain of their truth.
No one, I think, is likely to experience the slightest difficulty in compil-
ing a list of such facts, at virtually whatever length might be desired. One
might begin, for example, with one's own name, physical attributes, and
the salient events of one's personal history; one might then broaden the
purview slightly to take in, say, such features of one's immediate environment as the present time of day, date and day of the week, and one's
current location and surroundings; and in this way one might then come,
by stages of ever-increasing epistemic scope, to survey extensive bodies
of natural scientific and historical learning. Given the exercise of even a
modicum of care and common sense in the compilation of such a list,
one will be able to say with complete and unimpeachable certainty that
it is *impossible* that any of the things on it (and countless others like
them) should not be the case.

The particular descriptions under which facts happen to be given may
vary, of course, sometimes quite considerably. One especially common

way in which such variation occurs is when a change is made from one language to another. This, however, shows nothing more than that a statement of fact in any given language can in principle always be translated into, and so expressed in, the idiom of any other. The facts themselves do not undergo any change thereby (if two statements in different languages do not express the same fact but rather different ones, then plainly the one is not a translation of the other at all). This obviously does not mean, of course, that facts are *necessary* truths. In general, I think, they are not. With very few (if, indeed, any) exceptions, whatever happens to be (or to have been) the case could equally well have been otherwise, given different circumstances. On the other hand, it would clearly be a mistake to suppose that just *any* change in the web of factuality could be seriously entertained as an alternative possibility. Could we, for example, plausibly imagine the earth, instead of occupying the position in the cosmos it actually does, being located at a distance from the sun twice that of Pluto *and,* at the same time, suppose that *everything else* in the universe, including the history of our planet and its inhabitants as well as the general laws of physics, would nevertheless remain unchanged? Surely not. What it means, again, is simply that facts are *objectively*—definitively and unalterably—the case, that the enumeration of the sum total of facts (if such a thing were possible) would constitute an exhaustive description of how the world *is* (that notion understood to include, where relevant, how it was or will be), and that true statements of fact, accordingly, represent with perfect accuracy those bits of reality with which they are concerned.[1]

Nor does it mean—and this is the more important consideration for purposes of the present discussion—that facts exist, or could even be thought to exist, *apart* from *any* description of them whatsoever. Although, so far as I am aware, there is no one yet capable of giving an account of the phenomenon entirely satisfactory in all respects, there seems to me nevertheless no alternative to the view that facts are, in some sense, *constructed* rather than given—"made" rather than "found," as it is frequently (albeit, in many cases, misleadingly) put today—in that sense constituted by us rather than simply presented to us for our inspection. The construction of facts appears to be intimately related, in particular, to our use of language and, more generally, to all the manifold activities and modes of behavior, linguistic and otherwise, that together make up what we broadly term our "form of life." The phenomenon (or metaphenomenon) of linguistic-existential constitutivism does not, however, undermine either the objectivity of facts or our ability to be entirely certain of very many of them, without the slightest possibility of error. Quite the contrary. It is precisely—indeed, I believe, *only*—the reality of linguistic-existential constitutivism that is ultimately able to guarantee either of these things. In so doing, moreover, it enables us to recognize at the same time that skeptical assaults on objectivity and certainty are not even mistaken so much as they are simply incoherent.

The fact that there have ever been such things as skeptics in the first place is perhaps something that we do not always find as remarkable as we should. To this it may be responded, of course, that there is—quite literally—nothing to be remarked upon at all here. For the overwhelming weight of the relevant logical, psychological, and pragmatic considerations is surely such as to render quite incredible the supposition that there has ever actually been a true skeptic, or could ever be one. The response strikes me as perfectly apt. I think there are few claims that so deserve to be met with skepticism on our part as the one that says of anyone (e.g., the speaker himself) that that person is philosophically a thoroughgoing skeptic. (The suggestion that the person in question might have *good reasons* for adopting the standpoint of skepticism is, in its very formulation, already so self-undermining as scarcely even to leave room for a skeptical response from us. For to have a good reason for anything is either to know or, at any rate, to believe on plausible grounds that something is the case. An appeal to *what is the case,* however, is obviously no more an option for a consistent skeptic than a resort to divine intervention as an explanatory hypothesis would be available to an atheist.) Nevertheless, it is clear that in all ages there have in fact been *professed* skeptics. As Hilary Putnam has recently noted, "the fact of self-contradiction does not seem to stop or even slow down an intellectual fashion" (*Realism* 106). Nor is it necessary to look far for evidence supporting this observation. Skepticism is nothing if not in fashion today. The critical and theoretical woods are alive with those advocating one form or another of skeptical doctrine. In itself, of course, this is not exactly news—certainly not to anyone at all familiar with the development of critical theory over the past quarter century or so. But precisely the recognition of that state of affairs merely renders all the more acute the question of *why,* then, so many have apparently found themselves irresistibly drawn to a position that a moment's reflection suffices to reveal as beset with a host of insuperable difficulties.

Before pursuing this question further, a terminological clarification is in order. A quick survey of the contemporary scene might well lead one to conclude, at least at first glance, that if there are no true skeptics out there, there are not a great many professed ones either. The fortunes of the term "skepticism," like those of many hardy perennials in the philosophical lexicon, have waxed and waned again and again over the centuries. Today, as it happens, they appear to be at something of a low ebb. For whatever reason, "skepticism" itself does not currently seem to find much favor as a philosophical designation. Few if any of those active in contemporary critical debate appear at all eager, or even willing, to have their views identified specifically with skepticism. Why this should be so may well be a question of interest in its own right. In the present context, however, it is at best an ancillary consideration and, at worst, one that actually has the potential for drawing attention away from what is really at issue. Our interest is not in the labels that people happen to employ when referring to the positions they hold. It is in those positions themselves. We want to determine as best we can what claims are actually made in connection with those positions, how and to what extent such claims can be validated, and what can be shown to follow from their acceptance. In this circumstance, the mere denial that one is oneself a skeptic, or one's theory a form of skepticism, no matter how sincerely meant, can in itself carry little or no weight. One no more succeeds in dissociating one's views from skepticism by the simple act of advertising that as one's intention than one makes oneself a supporter of democracy by doing nothing more than protesting that one is opposed to all forms of tyranny and oppression. Apart from the fact that it would obviously be a dull dictator who did not think to represent himself as the true champion of the rights of the people, history (not least the history of the twentieth century) testifies all too eloquently to the possibility of people enlisting themselves in support of what are in reality the most odious forms of totalitarianism, convinced nevertheless that in so doing they are helping to bring about the ultimate realization of democratic ideals. Broadly analogous considerations apply as well in the case of philosophical skepticism.

Both history and common usage, I believe, sanction an understanding of skepticism as consisting basically in one form or another of epistemological or ontological *denial*. Either it is held that there is no such thing as objective reality at all, or it is maintained that the truth about reality can in principle never be ascertained. In either case, the position amounts to a denial of the possibility of genuine *knowledge* of what are and are not the *facts*. With the term thus understood, however, it seems scarcely possible that anyone should fail to recognize the extent to which skepticism is in fact rife in contemporary theory. The actual nomenclature varies somewhat from one context to another, of course. But whether the preferred term be, for example, poststructuralism, deconstruction, postmodernism, antifoundationalism, neopragmatism, perspectivism, relativism ("cultural" or otherwise), nominalism ("higher" or otherwise), the "strong program," or something else entirely makes little difference for purposes of the present discussion. For all these isms, differences in detail notwithstanding, are united in a common adherence to the single, basic epistemological-ontological position just described. And it is that position alone that concerns us here. Accordingly, in what follows, I shall generally refer without further qualification or specification simply to "skepticism" (or, as the case may be, "contemporary skepticism"). And I will take it as given that, even though skepticism itself is an impossible (because self-refuting) position, the phenomenon of "professed" skepticism, however tacit or even unconscious the professing may be, is nevertheless flourishing today among critics and theoreticians in a great number and variety of fields as it seldom (if ever) has before.

To return, then, to the—on its face, still decidedly puzzling—question of *why* this development should have come about, Stanley Rosen notes that, whatever the particular field, "whether in art, mathematics, or hermeneutical philosophy, decadence manifests itself as a loss of confidence in what Husserl called 'the natural attitude' " (214). This characterization goes to the heart of the phenomenon of skepticism in particular, which I believe is properly viewed as a form of intellectual decadence (and which, not coincidentally, it seems to me, has historically always enjoyed its greatest currency in times of broad social and cultural decline).[2] Certainly there are few attitudes toward knowledge that could be thought to possess a stronger intuitive claim to the designation "natural" than the standpoint of straightforward, unvarnished realism. Some years ago, Davidson began one of his most influential and frequently cited essays with what is, in effect, a concise statement of this epistemologically "natural attitude." "A true statement," he wrote, "is a statement that is true to the facts." And he went on to say:

> This remark seems to embody the same sort of obvious and essential wisdom about truth as the following about motherhood: a mother is a person who is the mother of someone. The *property* of being a mother is explained by the *relation* between a woman and her child; similarly, the suggestion runs, the property of being true is to be explained by a relation between a statement and something else. Without prejudice to the question what the something else might be, or what word or phrase best expresses the relation (of being true to, corresponding to, picturing), I shall

take the license of calling any view of this kind a *correspondence theory* of truth. ["True to the Facts," *ITI* 37]

"Correspondence theories," Davidson notes in the same essay, although they "rest on what appears to be an ineluctable if simple idea," have nevertheless "not done well under examination." That is, of course, putting it mildly. Davidson suggests that the "chief difficulty" in this regard "is in finding a notion of fact that explains anything, that does not lapse, when spelled out, into the trivial or the empty" (37). From the standpoint of twentieth-century analytic philosophy, that is doubtless true. Historically, however, I think the problem has on the whole tended to center rather more on the other of the two principal aspects of the theory to which Davidson refers. The point on which correspondence theories have repeatedly come to grief is less the difficulty of giving an adequate account of the concept of "fact" than it is the problem of how both to explain and to confirm the relationship of "correspondence" itself. What does it even mean to say of a statement or a belief that it "corresponds" to the way things truly are? And, assuming that a satisfactory answer to that question has somehow been found, what is it, then, that in any given set of circumstances entitles us to assert with confidence that such a relationship actually obtains?

It has been suggested that all philosophical inquiry ultimately comes down to one or the other of two basic questions: What do you mean? and How do you know? The specific versions of these questions that, as just seen, can readily be brought to bear against the epistemological notion of "correspondence" have traditionally provided the points of departure for those intent on making the case for skepticism. The latter question in particular has been a favorite source of ammunition, repeatedly resorted to over the years in one form or another in an effort to reveal the supposed untenability of epistemic claims. And so long as "correspondence" was construed exclusively in what I shall refer to as "precritical" terms (in a sense to be explained presently), the skeptically inclined were in fact often able to make reasonably effective use of their weapon. For if one assumes, with regard to the mind desirous of attaining knowledge on the one hand and the prospective object of knowledge on the other, that each of these exists *prior to* the establishment of any cognitive link between them in a manner that is itself wholly unaffected by the establishment of that link; and if one views the process of acquiring knowledge, accordingly, as a matter of bringing the former in some way into a relationship of "correspondence" with the latter—in essential outline, this is the structure of what I am here calling a "precritical" epistemology—then one is indeed likely to encounter difficulties in responding to the skeptic's query as to how, even in principle, it could ever be shown conclusively that such a relationship had actually been achieved. Without a satisfactory way of meeting this challenge directly, it of course remains open to one simply to assert, more or less baldly, that nevertheless the relationship just *is* achieved—perhaps in virtue of the intrinsically unimpeachable character of "clear and distinct ideas," for example, or as a result of what is disclosed to us by "the light of nature," or through the exercise of some other faculty held to be inherently capable of underwriting our conviction that, in spite of everything, we nevertheless do indeed possess genuine knowledge of what exists "out there" in the world, both apart from and wholly independently of ourselves.

Kant's term for philosophical positions seeking to ground themselves epistemologically in this manner was, of course, "dogmatic metaphysics." Putnam notes that "before Kant almost every philosopher subscribed to the view that truth is some kind of correspondence between ideas and 'what is the case.' " And, like Davidson, Putnam, too, acknowledges that "however puzzling the *nature* of the 'correspondence' may be, the naturalness of the idea is undeniable. There is a world out there; and what we say or think is 'true' when it *gets it the way it is* and 'false' when it doesn't correspond to *the way it is*" (*Meaning* 1). What changes with Kant—the decisive transformation in thought that is the principal reason for regarding the Kantian "critical" philosophy as the most significant advance in that field since classical antiquity—is not the idea itself of truth as correspondence to reality. Indeed, it is difficult to see how any philosopher who would begin by proposing a change *here* could seriously entertain much hope of receiving a hearing at all. As Davidson has repeatedly pointed out, the notion of truth (and thus also, obviously, that of falsity) is about as conceptually *primitive* as it is possible for a notion to be.[3] What Kant does instead is to *reanalyze* from the ground up the notion of what it is for something to *be* "the way it is" in the first place. He thus, in effect, follows *avant la lettre* what might be taken as Davidson's implicit counsel in "True to the Facts." By addressing himself in the first instance to the problem of giving a satisfactory account of the notion of *fact* itself, and by answering in the way that he does the question of what it *means* for something to be a fact—objectively the case—at all, he at the same time *eliminates* altogether the problem of explaining (and *a fortiori* of warranting) the relationship of "correspondence" between thought and reality in the form in which that problem had for centuries both bedeviled the dogmatist and played into the hands of the skeptic. And it is for this reason that I adopt here the basic historical division into "precritical" and "critical" modes of thought regarding fundamental questions of the nature and status of knowledge-claims.[4]

"Critical" realism, as pioneered by Kant and Herder, reflects the need to do justice simultaneously to two equally compelling, but not at first glance immediately reconcilable, claims on our philosophical attention. The first of these is our commonsense recognition that, again, some things—the facts—are indeed objectively, definitively, and unalterably the case.[5] The second is our recognition that there neither is nor could conceivably be any such thing as unmediated—in particular, linguistically unmediated—factuality. Davidson declares flatly at the outset of "The Structure and Content of Truth": "Nothing in the world, no object or event, would be true or false if there were not thinking creatures" (279). And later in the same essay he elaborates: "Nothing would count as a sentence, and the concept of truth would therefore have no application, if there were not creatures who used sentences by uttering or inscribing tokens of them. Any complete account of the concept of truth must [therefore] relate it to actual linguistic intercourse" (300). This recognition of the ineluctable linguistic relativity of truth (and so of fact) flies in the face of the metaphysical dogmatist's conception of objective reality.[6] For the dogmatist, as noted earlier, the things that we seek to know are already there, in whatever sense of "there" may be required to yield a complete notion of existence, before we as prospective knowers ever get to them. That this view then gives rise to effectively insuperable difficulties in explaining how the gap between knower and known is bridged has been mentioned. As we are now able to see perhaps more clearly, moreover, the dogmatist confronts a still more fundamental difficulty at the purely conceptual level. The problem is to show how, on the terms of his metaphysics, it is possible even to give content to the bare notion of an "object" in the first place.

The dilemma would appear to be this. Either we are in fact able to specify some such content, in which case, however, we are evidently in possession of knowledge of the object at a point logically prior to the establishment of the epistemic linkage which, by hypothesis, first results in the attainment of knowledge of objects at all; or, on the other hand, in accordance with the internal logic of our position, we are barred in principle from saying anything whatever about the "object," in which case, however, the very notion of "object" drops below the horizon of intelligible discourse altogether. Either we must already have arrived at our destination before embarking upon the journey toward it, or we have so little conception of what the destination might consist in that the very idea of a journey toward it simply evaporates. In Davidson's words,

> the disconnection [of mind and world] creates a gap no reasoning or construction can plausibly bridge. Once the Cartesian starting point has been chosen, there is no saying what the evidence is evidence for, or so it seems. Idealism, reductionist forms of empiricism, and skepticism loom.... Our beliefs purport to represent something objective, but the character of their subjectivity prevents us from taking the first step in determining whether they correspond to what they pretend to represent. ["MS" 162–63]

As Putnam pithily characterizes the situation, dogmatic metaphysics (which he variously terms "metaphysical realism" or simply "Realism," writ large) amounts in the end to "an impossible attempt" both "to *view* the world" and to do so at the same time "*from* Nowhere" (*Realism* 28; emphasis added).[7]

All this, of course, may appear to be just so much more grist for the skeptic's mill. What is crucially important to recognize, however—and this is, in a way, the nodal point of the entire exposition, the key insight that links Herder and Kant in the eighteenth century with, among others, Davidson, Putnam, and, above all, Wittgenstein in the twentieth—is that the skeptic's *denial* of the possibility of knowledge is point for point *nothing other than* a denial of precisely what the dogmatist *asserts*. The skeptic, that is, is committed in equal measure to precisely the *same precritical* model of "correspondence" that is the foundation of the dogmatist's epistemology as well. The skeptic, too—in this respect, the mirror image of his nominal adversary—can see no *other* way of conceiving objectivity than in terms of a match between something in the mind of the knower (say, representations or ideas or some other more-or-less mysterious mental "stuff") and the object "out there," already completely formed in and of itself, a model of preexistent metaphysical plenitude. On this view, the latter is, as it were, just waiting to be latched onto by our knowledge of it in an act whereby what was *already* there within it (but, so to speak, in as yet inarticulate form) is brought into the light of day and its True Name announced. Finding, however, as he does, for reasons already indicated, insuperable difficulties in showing how knowledge *thus conceived* could ever actually come about, but seeing at the same time no other direction in which to turn for an *alternative* conception of knowledge, the skeptic jettisons

the notion of knowledge altogether, and along with it those of objectivity, factuality, and, in the end, truth itself. He preserves, in other words,
the *form* of dogmatic metaphysics, while at the same time rejecting its
substance, seeing in the latter (sensibly enough as far as it goes) merely
the expression of an unrealizable—indeed, ultimately incoherent—
philosophical project, a project, however, whose *structural* terms he
nevertheless continues tacitly to accept as exhaustively determinative
of epistemological space.

What emerges from this strangely hybrid standpoint, then, is any of a
number of versions of relativism, perspectivism, conventionalism, contextualism, and the like, most or all of which can be found in abundance
dotting the contemporary critical landscape. For the skeptic, it is *either*
full-strength dogmatic metaphysics—reality existing wholly independently of us, to be observed from the vantage of an all-transcending
"Archimedean point"—*or* it is what might be called radical interpretationism—no reality at all properly so called; that is, nothing having
anything to do with objective fact, but instead merely a multitude of
different (often, indeed, "incommensurable") "vocabularies" for talking
about . . . well, whatever it is that gets talked about. But what, after all, is
this? In particular, what is the status of the (avowedly antirealist) "vocabulary" of skepticism itself? As Putnam notes, those who advocate
what he terms "Relativist" doctrine "know very well that the majority of
their cultural peers are not convinced by Relativist arguments, but they
keep on arguing because they think they are *justified* (warranted) in
doing so, and they share the picture of warrant as independent of majority opinion" (*Realism* 22). In other words, "Relativism, just as much as
Realism, assumes that one can stand within one's language and outside it
at the same time" (23). With reference specifically to the work of Richard Rorty (certainly as influential and articulate an advocate of the skeptical position as there is active anywhere today), but with more general
application as well, Putnam notes that, at bottom, "Rorty really thinks
that metaphysical realism is *wrong.*" He believes, that is, that "we will be
better off if we listen to him in the sense of having fewer false beliefs" of
our own. At the same time, however, "this . . . is something [Rorty] cannot admit he really thinks." To do so would be to make all too clear what
Putnam (in my view, rightly) maintains is true of Rorty's neopragmatism
in any case: namely, that "the attempt to say that *from a God's-Eye View
there is no God's-Eye View* is still there, under all that wrapping" (25).
Like skeptics generally, Rorty is ineluctably involved in "a self-refuting
attempt to both have and deny an 'absolute perspective' " (26). For, as
Putnam notes in "A Comparison of Something with Something Else": "the

minute a philosopher starts trying to persuade one that some views are misleading, that giving up some notions isn't as bad as one thinks, and so forth, then he admits that there really is such a thing as getting something *right*" (79).[8]

It only appears as all the more surprising, then, that Rorty in particular should so consistently fail to recognize this fundamental difficulty at the heart of his own position, when we notice how readily he is nevertheless able to detect it in the work of other contemporary skeptics, such as Derrida. In his essay "Deconstruction and Circumvention," Rorty notes that "Derrida would like to write in [a] new way [marked by self-conscious interminability, self-conscious openness, self-conscious lack of philosophical closure], but he is caught in a dilemma" (8). The dilemma is this. Either Derrida "can . . . forget about philosophy" altogether, "demonstrating his forgetfulness by his own uncaring spontaneous activity," or he can continue to direct his attention to the philosophical tradition, with the aim of exposing in one instance after another "the dialectical dependence of the text of philosophy on its margins." The problem is that "when he grasps the first horn [of the dilemma] and forgets about philosophy, his writing loses focus and point." But the "second horn" brings with it its own "disadvantage: to remember philosophy, to tell th[e] story [of its inevitable self-deconstruction] over and over again, is to verge on doing what the philosophers do—to propound some generalization of the form 'The attempt to formulate a unique, total, closed vocabulary will necessarily . . .' " (8–9)—will necessarily result (to complete the thought that Rorty leaves unfinished) in such and such an impossible situation. In Derrida's hands, of course, it is to do a good deal more than simply to "verge" on doing "what the philosophers do," as Rorty at once goes on to make explicit:

> Derrida . . . produces a new metalinguistic jargon, full of words like *trace* and *différance,* and uses it to say Heideggerian-sounding things like "it is only on the basis of *différance* and its 'history' that we can allegedly know who and where 'we' are" (*[Margins]*, p. 7). Just insofar as Derrida tries to give arguments for such theses as "Writing is prior to speech" or "Texts deconstruct themselves"— all those slogans which his followers are tempted to regard as "results of philosophical inquiry" and as providing the basis for a method of reading—he betrays his own project. The worst bits of Derrida are the ones where he begins to imitate the thing he hates and starts claiming to offer "rigorous analyses." [9]

In sum, "grasping the second horn [of the dilemma] will produce one more philosophical closure, one more metavocabulary which claims superior status, whereas grasping the former horn will give us openness, but more openness than we really want. Literature which does not connect with anything, which has no subject and no theme . . . is just babble" (9–10). Especially coming from someone who is as much an admirer of Derrida as Rorty has often represented himself as being, this last remark seems an exceptionally candid admission. But it simply underscores all the more forcefully the impossibility of Derrida ever escaping the implications of the "precritical" trap he has laid for himself. For if it is true (and in this Rorty seems to me entirely correct) that "Derrida cannot *argue* without turning himself into a metaphysician, one more claimant to the title of discoverer of the primal, deepest vocabulary" (16), and thus rendering himself on his own terms ripe for deconstruction, it is no less true that on these same terms he cannot *not* argue without thereby removing himself to a point beyond the pale of discursive intelligibility altogether.

From the point of view of the present discussion, the chief merit of Rorty's analysis in "Deconstruction and Circumvention" lies in how thoroughly it cuts the ground out from under those who are still intent on trying to save at least something of Derrida for serious philosophy. A list of those so intent would include, among others, Newton Garver, Christopher Norris, Henry Staten, Jonathan Culler, Samuel Wheeler, and Shekhar Pradhan.[9] As Rorty in effect shows, even if claims such as Garver's that "Derrida's critique of Husserl is a first-class piece of analytical work in the philosophy of language" (ix), or Norris's, that Derrida's exchange with John Searle in the two *Glyph* pieces demonstrates the former's "commitment . . . precisely to those standards of logical rigor, consistency, and truth which deconstruction is reputed to reject out of hand" (indeed, that "Derrida wins hands down" in this exchange "as by far the more rigorous thinker") ("Limited Think" 25), or Staten's, that "Derrida has worked out a critique [of] and an alternate structure" to the tradition on the basis of genuine "arguments" (albeit arguments cast in terms of an avowedly "new logic") (127)—even if these and many other similar claims could somehow, *per impossibile,* be made good, the victory would be Pyrrhic indeed. For insofar as Derrida can be shown to be *engaged* in such projects as these at all (quite apart from whether he ever comes even remotely close to succeeding in them), that very showing already implicates him in precisely what he is ostensibly most desirous of overcoming. Rorty, to be sure, distinguishes "between an earlier and a later Derrida," claiming that the later one "*stops* doing this" sort of

thing ("Two Meanings" 214) in an "attempt to avoid the sort of 'falling
back into a kind of negative theology' " (215) that characterized his
earlier days.[10] And, whatever may be the applicability of this "earlier–
later" periodization itself to Derrida's career, it is certainly true that
there are basically two types of Derridean text, represented respectively
by such things as *Speech and Phenomena* and *Of Grammatology,* on the
one hand, and *The Post Card* and *Glas,* on the other. Yet it is far from
clear that this distinction on Rorty's part does anything to improve
Derrida's overall standing. For if, in the former sort of work, Derrida
appears as the would-be serious philosopher, ostensibly devoted to "rigorous analysis," he thereby also leaves himself open to the charge of self-
referential inconsistency that, as seen, Rorty is easily able to convict him
of. And while, on the other hand, it may be true that products of the
latter sort do not afford any such opening to the critic, they are able to
avoid prosecution only at what seems the rather high price of lapsing
into what Rorty aptly terms "babble."

Unlike Derrida, Rorty himself does not babble, of course. But, as noted
a moment ago, he is nevertheless in the end no more successful than
Derrida at finding a way out of the "precritical" dilemma; for he, too, no
less than Derrida, has limited himself to operating exclusively within the
framework of "precritical" thought. The problem appears in notably
sharp outline in his essay "The Contingency of Language." "The difficulty
faced by a philosopher ... like myself," says Rorty, "one who thinks of
himself as auxiliary to the poet rather than the physicist, is to avoid
hinting that" precisely in this capacity he himself "gets something right,
that my sort of philosophy corresponds to the way things really are. For
this talk of correspondence brings back just the idea which my sort of
philosopher wants to get rid of, the idea that the world or the self has an
intrinsic nature" (3). Of course, Rorty has no prospect whatsoever of
actually avoiding this threat to his position, arising as it does from within
the position itself. The effort to do so is tantamount to striving for the
oxymoronic condition of saying *something* without thereby actually
saying anything. What remains puzzling, again, is simply Rorty's persistent failure to recognize this state of affairs. Later in the same essay he
asserts confidently, "Conforming to my own precepts, I am not going to
offer arguments against the vocabulary I want to replace. Instead, I am
going to try to make the vocabulary I favour look attractive by showing
how it may be used to describe a variety of topics" (4). By this point in
the essay, however, as those familiar with it may recall, it is, to put it
mildly, a little late in the day to be protesting that one has no intention of
"offer[ing] arguments" or maintaining that certain propositions corre-

spond "to the way things really are." The sixty-odd column inches that
have led up to this declaration have seen Rorty develop what is nothing
if not an *argument* that a great many things—things philosophical, historical, political, literary, artistic, scientific, sociological, and doubtless
others besides—*are* precisely the way he says they are and no other. But
let it go. He is not even able to make it all the way to the end of the
paragraph that he has just begun by forswearing argumentation and
assertions of fact without falling back into the same old vice. He proposes, he says, to describe the work of several thinkers (among them
Davidson) "as so many manifestations of... a *willingness to face up to*
the contingency of the language we use." He intends "to show how *a
recognition of that contingency* leads to *a recognition of* the contingency of conscience, and *how such recognition leads* to a picture of the
history of science, culture and politics *as a history of metaphor rather
than of discovery*" (4; emphasis added). The "contingency of the language we use," in other words, as well as all which that "contingency"
entails, is not itself a merely "contingent" matter. It just *is*. And in this
circumstance the only really relevant issue is whether or not one is
willing "to face up to" that state of affairs or not. With the ground thus
prepared, Rorty can then return, as he in fact does in the remainder of
the essay, to one unqualified assertion of "the way things really are" after
another, beginning already in the immediately following paragraph,
where he turns his attention to "*spell*[*ing*] *out the consequences of* [his]
claim that only sentences can be true" (4; emphasis added).[11]

   The key "critical" realist move by which we are able to break out of
this otherwise endlessly renewed cycle of ultimate unintelligibility (dogmatism) and self-referential inconsistency (skepticism) consists in distinguishing between what we can call *construct* and *interpretation*. This
distinction is tantamount to the twofold recognition that while there is
no reality save that which is linguistically-existentially brought into being by the human beings whose reality it is, that reality is not any the less
objectively real than we intuitively take it to be for having been so
constituted. Interpretation, on the other hand, is one particular type of
activity among others, all of which take place *within* the world of human
experience. It is specifically a way of *responding to* certain sorts of facts,
and as such it does not make sense to suggest that it might be the process
by which facts themselves come into being in the first place. For what,
after all, does "objectivity" mean? As it was the great merit of Kant to
have shown in explicit fashion, the distinguishing marks of objectivity
are simply universality and necessity of judgment. That is all that anyone
has ever actually meant by objectivity and, indeed, all that anyone ever

could mean by it. The skeptic's error (the one that, as seen, he holds in common with the dogmatist) is to conflate universality and necessity of judgment with the (incoherent) notion of a universe of objects existing wholly independently of us. What Kant, Herder, Wittgenstein, and a few other philosophers (including, as I read him, Davidson) do is instead to drop the latter notion altogether and then, concentrating exclusively on the phenomenon of necessity and universality of judgment, analyze *that* phenomenon—and thus, by extension, objective reality itself—as essentially *correlative* to certain basic forms of human life, in particular the distinctively human capacity for language.

The same point emerges, as it were, from the opposite direction when we consider that the only way in which it could even make sense to suppose that our world might *not* be objectively real would be on the assumption of a level of reality somehow *more* fundamental—more "real"—than that world. Otherwise, it must be (by hypothesis) quite literally as real as anything could be. But since that assumption is in turn dependent on the (non)notion of reality as independent of us, the possibility of even coherently supposing that the world *might* not be entirely real collapses before the doubt itself can so much as take on a sufficiently well formed shape to be entertained. If there is nothing outside the web of our experience with which it could be compared, then there is also no external standard (whether of "degrees of reality" or anything else) against which it could be weighed and found wanting. We are by now accustomed to seeing one statement in particular of this "nothing out-side" principle: namely, Derrida's famous "there is no outside-the-text" (*il n'y a pas de hors-texte*), invoked in support of one after another skeptical denial of objectivity, determinacy of meaning, and the like—so much so that we do not always think to ask any longer (if, indeed, we ever did) why, after all, this should be the case. And yet, on the face of it, when viewed in the perspective of "critical" realism, it is by no means clear that the Derridean thesis actually does (or, at any rate, should) provide aid and comfort to nominalists, relativists, and others of like persuasion. If anything, quite the contrary. For if we look past the per-haps slightly eccentric, but, I think, in the end probably also harmless, metaphor of the universal "text" for a moment, it is not clear that any-thing more is really being asserted here than simply the linguistic-epistemic holism that is the essence of the "critical" realist position. Thus understood (but *only* thus understood), Derrida's denial of the possibility of an extratextual reality could comfortably take its place next to Wittgenstein's caveat in the *Investigations* that "philosophy may in no way interfere with the actual use of language. . . . It leaves everything as it is" (sec. 124). Ordinary language, as Wittgenstein is constantly trying to get us to see, is all right: "every sentence in our language . . . in order as it is" (sec. 98). It is impossible—logically impossible—that language should *not* be all right just as it is. For in order that an attribution to language of some essential flaw or shortcoming or inadequacy even be *intelligible* (quite apart from whether or not it happened to be true), there would, again, have to be something apart from language in relation to which that judgment could be made. Ascriptions of inadequacy that do not specify wherein the inadequacy lies—that is to say, in relation to what standard of (greater) perfection the thing in question is held to fall short—are simply void of content. But on the holistic view envisioned here, no such extralinguistic standard is even conceivable.

Derrida himself, it is hardly necessary to say, does not take this same view of the implications of his theory, and the reason is one we have already seen. Committed as he is, like all those intent on defending some version of skepticism, to the assumptions of a "precritical" epistemology, Derrida remains at bottom an exponent of dogmatic metaphysics, albeit merely in inverted form. In a well-known review of Culler's *On Deconstruction* (one that Putnam characterizes as "notorious" ["A Comparison" 71], although I confess I am at a loss to see why), John Searle expresses the point as follows:

> The philosophical tradition that goes from Descartes to Husserl, and indeed a large part of the philosophical tradition that goes back to Plato, involves a search for foundations: metaphysically certain foundations of knowledge, foundations of language and meaning, foundations of mathematics, foundations of morality, etc.... Derrida correctly sees that there aren't any such foundations, but he then makes the mistake that marks him as a classical metaphysician. The real mistake of the classical metaphysician was not the belief that there were metaphysical foundations, but rather the belief that somehow or other such foundations were necessary, the belief that unless there are foundations something is lost or threatened or undermined or put in question. It is this belief that Derrida shares with the tradition he seeks to deconstruct. ["Word" 77–78][12]

Precisely analogous considerations apply as well, as I have suggested, to Rorty's neopragmatism. The claim, for example, that such oppositions as the one between "objectivity" and "solidarity" have today become otiose and that our best course, accordingly, would simply be to fold the former notion into the latter and be done with it—Rorty numbers himself among those who, in his words, "wish to reduce objectivity to solidarity" ("Solidarity" 5)—itself depends decisively on the *preservation* of that very opposition, at least in concept. For if we ask, "Solidarity as opposed to what?" then it seems that either Rorty must advert to his old adversary, in which case he simply reinscribes at the center of his own discourse the antinomy he purports to deconstruct, or the question "... as opposed to what?" has no answer at all and the insistence, specifically, on "solidarity" as the touchstone for our conceptions of what to think, say, or do loses its point. Rorty, like Derrida, cannot keep from continually conjuring anew the very demon he is ostensibly intent on exorcising. Such, it seems, are the persistent toils of "precritical" metaphysics.

And thus we can see that it is to get things precisely backward to say, as Rorty does in the same essay, that the "realist ... project[s] his own habits of thought upon the pragmatist when he charges him with relativism. For the realist thinks that the whole point of philosphical thought is to detach oneself from any particular community and look down at it from a more universal standpoint" (12–13). This is certainly true of realism in the sense of metaphysical dogmatism. But since that is evidently the *only* realism of which Rorty is able to conceive, when he finds it inadequate he is then simply driven to the opposite extreme *within* the overall "precritical" framework. He retains the very same "universal standpoint" that he detects underlying his opponent's view—his theory is nothing if not a global account, claiming validity always and everywhere for all human dealings with one another or with the world at large without exception[13]—but at the same time he seeks to empty that position of any substantive, apodictic content. Notwithstanding protestations to the contrary, this is simply not a live option. To contend that one is "making [a] purely *negative* point," that one's interpretation of the notion of "truth," for example, does not really amount to a specification of the "intrinsic nature" of truth, and thus that one is not oneself formulating merely "one more positive theory about the nature of truth" (much less claiming that one's "views correspond to the nature of things"), while at the same time asserting 1) that "the term 'true' ... means the same in all cultures," 2) that that "identity of meaning" is properly analyzed as a matter of "commendation" of "well-justified beliefs" (presumably, we may suppose, for their *being*—as a matter of *fact*—"well-justified" or, alternatively, "good to believe") (6), and 3) that the presence or absence of the property of being "well-justified" (or "good to believe") is determined by reference to "the consensus of a community" (17), strikes me as patently self-contradictory.

Rorty has not by any means been alone among contemporary skeptics in representing his views as more or less in basic accord with those of Davidson. Yet it seems to me that little could be more alien to either the letter or the spirit of Davidson's work than such an association. For what Davidson in fact gives us, expressed in the idiom of contemporary analytic philosophy, is perhaps as powerful a defense of "critical" realism as has been produced by anyone in the second half of the twentieth century (or, in other words, since the death of Wittgenstein). Davidson himself has been nothing if not explicit regarding the relationship of his own views to Rorty's: "Where we differ," he writes, "if we do, is on whether there remains a question how, given that we cannot 'get outside our beliefs and our language so as to find some test other than coherence', we nevertheless can have knowledge of, and talk about, an objective public world which is not of our own making. I think this question does remain, while I suspect that Rorty doesn't think so" ("CTT" 310).[14]

Davidson's suspicion is, of course, well founded. As some of the passages cited above surely illustrate in more than ample fashion, Rorty has in fact been perfectly explicit in his own right in stating that, in his view, there is indeed no longer any such question to be pursued, at least not in anything like a useful or productive manner. Most explicit of all in this regard is doubtless his admission in "Pragmatism, Davidson and Truth," referring to the passage just cited from Davidson's "A Coherence Theory of Truth and Knowledge," that "Davidson correctly says ... that I do not think this is a good question," to which he adds at once: "I am here trying to explain what is wrong with it, and why I think Davidson too should regard it as a bad question" (342 n. 23). Near the conclusion of the same essay, however, Rorty is obliged to acknowledge that "it is an embarrassment for my interpretation of Davidson as a pragmatist that he [nevertheless continues, in spite of everything, to adhere to] the idea of 'an objective public world which is not of our making.' " From Rorty's "precritical" perspective, of course, it makes sense to see in "this formula," as he does, "no[thing] more than out-dated rhetoric" (354). From the standpoint of Davidson's "critical" realism, however, as I want to indicate here at least in outline, it reflects (in addition to common sense, of course) some deep insights into the nature and provenance of a number of our most fundamental concepts. To consider Davidson's way of dealing with the question at hand, then, is to bring into particularly sharp focus the pivotal difference between Rorty's "precritical" skepticism on the one hand and the distinctive, highly original Davidsonian version of "critical" realism on the other.

Central to Davidson's formulation of this position is his demonstration of what he terms the "veridicality of belief." Like Herder, Kant, and Wittgenstein in their own ways before him, Davidson, too, develops a *transcendental* analysis of "meaning and knowledge," the upshot of which is that skepticism cannot even "get off the ground" as a coherent position. The key to the analysis consists in "bring[ing] out essential relations among the concepts of meaning, truth and belief" in such a way as to show that "each of these concepts requires the others, but [that] none is subordinate to, much less definable in terms of, the others" ("A1987" 136). Meaning, truth, and belief, in other words, are, in Davidson's view, of necessity *co-original* with one another. The basic argument for both the "veridicality of belief" and what we might call for short the "co-originality thesis" (themselves, in turn, merely different aspects of, or ways of thinking about, a single underlying reality) appears throughout Davidson's writings. One particularly clear and effective statement of it is to be found in the essay "The Method of Truth in Metaphysics," which opens with the assertion:

> In sharing a language, in whatever sense this is required for communication, we share a picture of the world that must, in its large features, be true. It follows that in making manifest the large features of our language, we make manifest the large features of reality. [*ITI* 199]

In this way, Davidson links the pursuit of "metaphysics" with the "study [of] the general structure of our language," adverting as he does so to a long tradition in Western philosophy, represented by figures as otherwise diverse as Plato, Aristotle, Hume, Kant, Russell, Frege, Wittgenstein, Carnap, Quine, and Strawson (as I have suggested, I think he might well have included Herder in this list, too), a tradition which has taken this linkage as fundamental. Davidson's own development of the argument showing the indissolubility of language, truth, and reality, like many of the corresponding arguments in the works of his predecessors, is at once powerful and yet deceptively simple. It proceeds in two principal stages.

The first stage consists in noting that "those who can understand one another's speech must share a view of the world, *whether or not that view is correct*" (199; emphasis added). For "we damage the *intelligibility* of our readings of the utterances of others when our method of reading puts others into what we take to be broad error" (200; emphasis added). That is, if we disagree (or suppose we disagree) about *everything*, or nearly so, there will not even be a common object of that "disagreement-about" to which we can advert. In that case, however, we are no longer able to give a coherent account of what the other person is saying to begin with; and that means, in turn, that we are not actually communicating at all (which, however, by hypothesis is what we in fact are doing). "Without a vast common ground," says Davidson, "there is no place for disputants to stand in their quarrel." But since *any* belief can be seen in this way to be "identified and described only within a dense pattern of beliefs," it follows that, in order even to *attribute* a belief to someone else, that belief must of necessity form part of a whole "pattern of beliefs much like" one's own. The bare possibility of recognizing another person as engaged in intelligible linguistic behavior of any sort, and *a fortiori* the possibility of then communicating with that other person, entails that there must already be a broad coincidence of beliefs on the part of both speaker and hearer: "I can interpret your words correctly only by interpreting so as to put us largely in agreement" (200).

The first stage of the argument, which, as seen, takes us merely from communication to shared worldview, may seem entirely obvious, perhaps even tautological. On the basis of it, however, we are then able to proceed to the argument's second stage, which yields a strikingly powerful conclusion indeed. For just as it can be seen without great difficulty that "much community of belief is needed to provide a basis for communication or understanding," so, for much the same reason, it turns out that we can show that "*objective error* can occur only in a setting of largely *true belief*" (emphasis added). While the mere fact of "agreement does not make for truth" all by itself, of course, nevertheless "much of what is agreed must be true if some of what is agreed is false." For "just as too much *attributed* error risks depriving the subject of his subject matter, so too much *actual* error robs a person of things to go wrong about" (200; emphasis added). Considerations directly analogous to those which reveal the inherent impossibility of massive disagreement within the context of communication (without communication, of course, there is neither agreement nor disagreement, but simply no contact, and hence no issue is joined at all) enable us to see as well that the notion of "massive *error* about the world is [itself] simply *unintelligible*" (201; emphasis added). The point bears repeating, I think. Davidson's claim is not that any imputation to anyone (anyone we can understand, at any rate) of "massive error" about how the world is will itself necessarily be in error. The conclusion is, rather, that *no coherent sense* can be made of the *notion* of "massive error" about how the world is at all.[15]

Davidson's way of driving home this conclusion comes with an intriguing bit of philosophical-historical resonance. It is well known that Descartes, in the course of his programmatic effort to entertain the most extreme doubt possible, ultimately introduced the hypothesis of the "omnipotent deceiver." The point was not that there necessarily had to be such a being. It was simply that we could not be certain that there was not, and this, Descartes felt, was enough to shake even our apparently most well-founded and unimpeachable convictions (prior to the *cogito,* at any rate, with a healthy assist from the principle that "God is no deceiver"). Davidson invokes the possibility of an almost comparably powerful being, but draws from that possibility a rather different moral:

> We do not need to be omniscient to interpret, but there is nothing absurd in the idea of an omniscient interpreter; he attributes beliefs to others, and interprets their speech on the basis of his own beliefs, just as the rest of us do. Since he does this as the rest of us do, he perforce finds as much agreement as is needed to make sense of his attributions and interpretations; and in this case, of course, what is agreed is by hypothesis true. [201]

The fact that there is not in reality any such being (at least as far as anyone appears to be in a position to determine) is beside the point. As with Descartes' "omnipotent deceiver," but with the force of the argument reversed, it is sufficient that in principle there could be.

The overall movement of Davidson's argument here is from communication to shared worldview, and then from shared worldview to objective truth. Once the first link has been established—and this, we recall, was the one that seemed wholly unproblematic—the "omniscient interpreter" hypothesis simply helps us to see somewhat more directly that there is no way in which the second link can then *fail* to be established. For if *any* two speakers could be communicating, which is to say, interpreting each other correctly on the basis of an extensive, shared body of belief (which, as we have seen, is the only way in which communication can ever occur), *and yet* be massively in error about how the world is in reality, then it would have to be possible for an "omniscient interpreter" to be in that position as well. But that combination of genuine communication, on the one hand, and imputation by the "omniscient interpreter" of massive error to his interlocutor, on the other, contains a fundamental contradiction. For the "omniscient interpreter" cannot be communicating, any more than anyone else can, without being in general, basic agreement with his interlocutor on most things. Yet the "omniscient interpreter" cannot very well be in such *agreement* and still wish to convict the interlocutor of massive *error,* for that would be tantamount to his regarding *one and the same set of beliefs* as *simultaneously true and false*—indeed, since he is by hypothesis "omniscient," it would be tantamount to these beliefs *being* simultaneously true and false. Since this is obviously absurd, it follows that the very notion of "massive error about the world is [itself] simply unintelligible." For "to suppose it intelligible is," again, "to suppose that there could be an interpreter (the omniscient one) who correctly interpreted someone else as being massively mistaken, and this we have shown to be impossible" (201).

Thus, Davidson is able to conclude that "successful communication proves the existence of a shared, and largely true, view of the world" (201). It is worth noting that Davidson's argument blocks in advance the objection that our communication might merely *appear* to be "successful" but not truly be so in reality. For if this supposition can even be formulated as a *possible* object of belief, then it is already captured by the *first* stage of the argument, and it thereby sets in motion the chain of reasoning that culminates in its being robbed of intelligibility. We cannot coherently suppose that we are not really communicating with one another but merely appear to be doing so, for that would be tantamount to imputing to ourselves truly "massive error" about what is actually the case, which, again, we have now seen to be incoherent. The linkage established by Davidson between communication, belief, meaning, intelligibility, and truth indicates "why it is plausible to hold that by studying the general aspects of language we will be studying the most general aspects of reality" (201). In a way, of course, this conclusion simply restates the starting point of the argument. For it was precisely a consideration of certain "general aspects of language"—specifically those reflected in the phenomena of belief, communication, and interpretation—that in turn led to this very conclusion regarding the relationship of such "aspects" to "the most general aspects of reality."

If there is a circle here, however, it is in any case not a logically vicious one, for at no point in the argument was the establishment of a conclusion dependent on that conclusion having itself been previously assumed. Rather, what we have is something analogous to Heidegger's use (in *Being and Time*) of the traditional notion of the "hermeneutical circle" as a pivotal element in the existential analytic of *Dasein*.[16] Or, equivalently, we have an instance of the sort of transcendental argument-from-the-inside-out developed by Wittgenstein initially in the *Tractatus* and later amplified and elaborated in his writings after 1929. If the upshot of Davidson's argument is to show that we are always "inside" language-*cum*-reality, it also follows from his way of demonstrating this conclusion that there is in the end, properly speaking, no "outside" at all.

And that in turn removes from the "inside" any possible taint of perspectivism, relativism, contextualism, and the like. In the end, unsurprisingly enough, *all* there is turns out to be just all there *is.*[17] Like Wittgenstein, Davidson, too, is, as he says, "not interested in improving on natural language, but in understanding it" (203).

Again, I think, the contrast with Rorty's position is instructive. Rorty believes that his theory preserves us from skepticism by absolving us of any "need to ask whether our beliefs represent the world accurately." In this way, he supposes, we "give up the possibility of formulating epistemological skepticism" ("Pragmatism" 345). But, as we have seen, Rorty *denies* that there is any such thing as objective factuality, which is in turn equivalent to *denying* that "our beliefs" do in fact "represent the world accurately." His way of saving us from skepticism thus amounts, in effect, to conceding to the skeptic in advance everything the latter ever wanted and then, as it were, simply declining to discuss the whole nasty business any further. It is rather as if one were to respond to being robbed of all one's money by taking a vow of poverty. What Davidson, on the other hand, demonstrates is not that there is no "need" to ask about the relationship between our beliefs and the world; rather, there is no such *possibility* of (intelligibly) doing so. For to have a large, well-connected—that is to say, coherent—body of beliefs *is,* on Davidson's showing, in virtue of the very *nature* of belief *eo ipso* to be in the main correct about how the world is (i.e., to represent it accurately). Basically the same discrepancy in views, with the same misinterpretation of Davidson's position to which it leads, shows up again in Rorty's contention that "if one follows Davidson, one will not know what to make of the issue between realist and antirealist. For one will feel in touch with reality *all the time*" (351). For Davidson, however, one does not merely "feel" this way; one actually *is* so "in touch." Rorty, on the other hand, as an antirealist, needs to preserve the element of subjectivism implicit in the notion of "feel[ing]" one way rather than another, with its unavoidable concomitant suggestion of an ultimate gap between what we (merely) take to be so and what (in principle) really is so.

On the same page of the essay in question, Rorty expressly envisages the possibility that some group of people (the "natives" of some other culture) might "fail to find the same things red . . . as we do," and he goes on to suggest how he believes a Davidsonian would account for this anomaly. That explanation, referring as it does to "various differences in our respective environments (or the environments of our respective ancestors)" (351), strikes me as itself rather more Rortyan than Davidsonian in tenor. But the more important point here is that the very

supposition that such a state of affairs could arise at all has been shown
by Davidson's argument to be based on an incoherent set of assumptions. For in order that it should arise, two things would have to obtain:
1) that we had *correctly* interpreted the "natives" as regarding those
things red which they in fact do; and 2) that as a *result* of our (by
hypothesis) correct interpretation, we were shown to be in substantial
disagreement with them as to how the world is (for, as Wittgenstein
points out, ascriptions of color are about as fundamental as our predica-
tions get). And this, as we have seen, is precisely what Davidson shows
to be impossible. For Davidson, in other words, it is not merely a "regula-
tive principle" that we must regard any speaker's rules of linguistic
behavior as basically the same as our own if we hope to be able to
understand that speaker. Rather, Davidson's point is that this semantic-
syntactic isomorphism is *logically entailed* by the very notions of belief
and interpretation themselves. Thus, we miss what is really central to
Davidson's argument if we read him as saying merely that "any translations which portrays [*sic*] the natives as denying most of the evident
facts about their environment is automatically a bad one" (340). For we
cannot understand the "natives" as saying anything whatsoever *unless*
that something broadly coincides with what we basically hold to be true.
We cannot, that is, intelligibly impute massive error to the "natives" at
all—not even if it is only to recognize at once our own error in so doing.
The *interdependence* of meaning and belief, which is for Davidson as
fundamental a fact about our experience as there is, again entails that,
precisely to the extent that we understand others as saying *anything*
intelligible, that something must *already* coincide with what we—of
necessity, by and large correctly—hold to be true.

As Davidson puts it in "A Coherence Theory of Truth and Knowledge":

> What stands in the way of global skepticism of the senses is, in my
> view, the fact that we must, in the plainest and methodologically
> most basic cases, take the objects of a belief to be the causes of
> that belief. And what we, as interpreters, *must* take them to be is
> what they in fact *are. Communication begins where causes con-
> verge:* your utterance means what mine does if belief in its truth is
> systematically caused by the same events and objects. [317–18;
> emphasis added]

Rorty reads this passage as, in part, a restatement of "the Strawsonian
claim that you figure out what somebody is talking about by figuring out
what object most of his beliefs are true of" ("Pragmatism" 340). But the

latter sort of inquiry clearly presupposes that one *understand* the "beliefs" in question themselves, in which case one already *knows* "what [he] is talking about." If anything, Davidson's point appears to be precisely the reverse: we learn what people's beliefs are "true of" by interpreting what they are saying. But this, too, seems to me ultimately misleading. The very fact that we communicate at all presupposes *both* mutual intelligibility *and* an agreed-upon set of (largely correct) determinations of objects of belief. It is somewhat nearer the mark for Rorty to say that "Davidson is suggesting that we maximize coherence and truth first, and then let reference fall out as it may" (340). What Davidson actually shows, however, as we have now seen, is that what we *mean* by "belief" and "meaning," what is contained in these very concepts themselves, *entails* maximization of coherence insofar as intelligible discourse is occurring at all. And that, in turn, entails that "truth" and "reference" are going to "fall out" in one and only one way: namely, the way the world in fact *is.* In this sense, Davidson can legitimately say (in the best "critical" realist tradition) that "coherence yields correspondence" ("CTT" 307).

Reed Way Dasenbrock notes that "periods of great vitality in literary criticism always seem to be periods in which criticism is in close working contact with philosophy" (3). That being so, clearly much depends on what happens to be the dominant tenor of the philosophizing with which criticism comes in contact at times of such disciplinary cross-fertilization. And that, in turn, depends to a large extent on which one of the phases in a more or less regularly recurring cycle of phases in the history of philosophy (Western philosophy, at any rate) happens to be occupying center stage at the time in question. Until the latter half of the eighteenth century, there were basically two such possibilities, either dogmatism or skepticism. Since that time, chiefly by virtue of the contributions of Herder and Kant in the eighteenth century and Wittgenstein in the twentieth, there has been a third one as well, the one I have been calling "critical" realism. In "The Myth of the Subjective," Davidson begins by speaking of a "sea change in contemporary philosophical thought—a change so profound that we may not recognize that it is occurring" (159). A few pages later he elaborates:

> the most promising and interesting change that is occurring in philosophy today is that these dualisms [of scheme and content, of the objective and the subjective] are being questioned in new ways or are being radically reworked. There is a good chance

they will be abandoned, at least in their present form. The change is just now becoming evident, and its consequences have barely been recognized, even by those who are bringing it about; and of course it is, and will be, strongly resisted by many. What we are about to see is the emergence of a radically revised view of the relation of mind and the world. [163]

What Davidson is, in effect, referring to here, I believe, in accordance with what we have seen to be the dominant direction of his own philosophizing on "the relation of mind and the world," is yet another attempt to bring about what I have called the "critical turn" in philosophy—and this time to carry it through to completion.

If this is indeed the development to which we may now look forward, then certainly, from the standpoint of literary criticism in particular, it cannot come any too soon. As I noted at the outset (and as is in any case obvious to almost anyone), both the theory and the practice of literary criticism, along with much else in contemporary Western culture, have been largely dominated for some time now by outlooks broadly characterizable as "skeptical." In particular, it has become routine to claim that there is no such thing as the objectively determinate or decidable meaning of a text; in more extreme versions of the position, even the objective existence of the text itself may be denied. That such views as these have succeeded in finding any acceptance at all is to an overwhelming degree the result of what many still regard as the unassailability of the broader philosophical arguments for skepticism on which they are ultimately based. To the extent, accordingly, that those arguments come to be recognized as in fact as fatally flawed as we have here seen them to be, there would appear to be at least some reason to expect that the urge to apply their conclusions when- and wherever possible to the analysis of literary texts might likewise begin to lose some of its appeal. As to the question of what the *substantive* implications of this development might be for the analysis and interpretation of texts, here, I think, it is still too early to speak with any confidence. But just as Kant, in the preface to the second edition of the *Critique of Pure Reason,* characterized the "primary use" of his work as a "*negative*" one (Bxxiv)—namely, to demonstrate to his contemporaries why they should stop talking a certain sort of nonsense—so, it seems to me, analogous results might reasonably be hoped for from an infusion of "critical" thinking into contemporary literary theory. That is, whatever may turn out to be the things that we eventually *do* want to say about texts from such a perspective, there will in any case henceforth be a great deal that we will *not* (any longer) want to say, for the reason that we now recognize it to be incoherent. And in that development alone (should we be fortunate enough to see it actually come about), I think that much will already have been won for the larger cause of basic good sense.

NOTES

1. As Wittgenstein puts it in the *Tractatus*, "The world is all that is the case" (1), and "The world is the totality of facts, not of things" (1.1).

2. It is worth noting that Nietzsche, himself the formulator of perhaps the most sweeping and powerful version of skepticism ever conceived, took a not dissimilar view of the matter. See, for example, his analysis of the phenomenon of decadence, as well as his explicit association of his own philosophizing with that same phenomenon, in *The Case of Wagner*.

3. Davidson has made this point most recently, to my knowledge, in his 1989 John Dewey Lectures, published as "The Structure and Content of Truth": "It is a mistake to look for a behavioristic definition, or indeed any other sort of explicit definition or outright reduction of the concept of truth. Truth is one of the clearest and most basic concepts we have, so it is fruitless to dream of eliminating it in favor of something simpler or more fundamental" (314). He notes in this connection that Dewey as well "saw no harm in the idea of correspondence as long as it was properly understood. 'Truth means as a matter of course, agreement, correspondence, of idea and fact,' [Dewey] said, but immediately went on, 'but what do agreement, correspondence mean?' " (280). (This quotation of Dewey and the one immediately following are from his *Essays in Experimental Logic* 304.) Dewey's answer to his own question, cited by Davidson, seems to me both a classic instance of a nonresponse to a philosophical inquiry and, precisely as such, also a tacit corroboration of Davidson's fundamental thesis regarding the notion of truth itself: "the idea is true," says Dewey, "which works in leading us to what it purports." But surely it is obvious that we have in any case no *clearer* notion of what it is for something (much less an "idea") to "work" (much less to "lead us to what it purports") than we do of what it is for something—paradigmatically a belief or a statement—simply to be true.

4. I have argued elsewhere that Kant's effort to break the grip of "precritical" metaphysics, and thereby to point the way beyond what had been (prior to the latter half of the eighteenth century) merely a perennially renewed standoff between dogmatism and skepticism, was in large measure anticipated in the work of his one-time student, Herder. Aspects of this argument are developed, and some related issues pursued further, in both *Herder and the Poetics of Thought* and "Changing the Subject."

5. I hope it is clear that my insistence on the *unalterability* of facts, if they are to *be* facts at all, properly so called, is not tantamount to a Parmenidean denial of the reality of change. An essential part of the description of any fact is the specification of its time coordinate. To speak of factual unalterability, in other words, is simply to acknowledge the reality of time—in particular, the unrevisability of the past.

6. One respect in which I think the Herderian formulation of the "critical" realist argument may even be preferable to Kant's is the central place that Herder accords to the role of *language* in the constitution of experience. I have defended this view in "*Verum est factum:* Critical Realism and the Discourse of Autonomy," which also offers a capsule overview of some of the principal stages in the dogmatism-skepticism wars, from antiquity up through the eighteenth-century "critical turn" and thereafter.

7. Cf. "Realism and Reason," in *Meaning and the Moral Sciences* 132–33. As Putnam in

effect points out here, one particularly direct way of seeing the incoherence of "metaphysical realism" (123–25) is simply to note the impossibility of escaping theory relativity in saying anything about anything: "The fact is, *so many* properties of THE WORLD—starting with *just* the *categorial* ones, such as cardinality, particulars, or universals, etc.—turn out to be 'theory-relative' that THE WORLD ends up as a Kantian 'noumenal' world, a *mere* 'thing in itself'. If one cannot say *how* THE WORLD is theory-independently, then talk of all these theories as descriptions of 'the world' is empty" (133). On the immediately preceding page, Putnam offers a nod to Nelson Goodman in this connection. It is worth noting, however, that the central argument of Goodman's highly influential *Ways of Worldmaking* appears to be open to much the same sort of objection that Putnam himself brings against Feyerabend and Kuhn in *Reason, Truth and History*, with the one difference that the perspective in the latter case is primarily diachronic and in the former primarily synchronic. That is, it is no more possible that there should actually be a plurality of "worlds" *at any given time* (in any save a harmlessly figurative sense of the term) than that two *historical* discourses should be radically "incommensurable" with one another. For, as Putnam observes, "if this [incommensurability] thesis were really true then we could not translate other languages—or even past stages of our own language—at all. And if we cannot interpret organisms' noises at all, then we have no grounds for regarding them as *thinkers, speakers,* or even *persons.* In short, if Feyerabend (and Kuhn at his most incommensurable) were right, then members of other cultures, including seventeenth-century scientists, would be conceptualizable by us only as animals producing responses to stimuli (including noises that curiously resemble English or Italian). To tell us that Galileo had 'incommensurable' notions *and then to go on to describe them at length* is totally incoherent" (*Reason* 114–15). (On "the incoherent idea of 'incommensurable' discourse," see also Putnam, *Realism* 122ff.) Similar considerations, I think, suggest that Goodman might well have done better to call his book simply *Some Different Ways That People Have of Looking at and Talking About Various Things,* or something in that vein. Such a title would certainly have given a more accurate picture of the book's actual contents. At the same time, of course, referring as it does to nothing more than a thoroughly familiar and utterly unremarkable phenomenon of everyday life, it might also have diminished somewhat the feeling evidently experienced by some of the book's readers that they were onto something *really* philosophically exciting here.

    8. In the same essay, Putnam extends this criticism to two (or three) other prominent contemporary philosophers as well: "What Rorty and Quine and a certain quasi-fictional philosopher I call 'Kripgenstein' have in common is this: all three tell a story about how all there is is speakers and speech-dispositions, and about how we don't need any 'metaphysical' notions of truth or warranted assertibility. All three soften this austere Protagorean picture by telling us that we can, in fact, recover a surrogate for truth and rationality—as much truth and rationality as we need—from 'solidarity' (Rorty), or from the practice of scientists (Quine), or from the communal practice of deciding that certain people have 'got,' and certain people have failed to 'get,' various concepts (Kripgenstein). All three insist that their stories are *self-applicable:* that talk of the dispositions of, respectively, postmodern bourgeois liberals, scientists, and speakers who share a form of life is itself not to be thought of as a description of what is 'out there,' but simply a part of our evolving doctrine. I say this sort of transcendental Skinnerianism has got to stop! If all there is is talk and objects internal to talk, then the idea that some pictures are 'metaphysical,' or 'misleading,' and others are not is itself totally empty. . . . [It is] to privilege one story within the vast array of stories that our culture has produced in just the way [that Rorty et al.] criticize other philosophers for doing" ("A Comparison" 78–79). (In "Pragmatism, Davidson and Truth" [345–46], Rorty cites Putnam's reference to "transcendental Skinnerianism." He neglects to mention, however, that he is himself one of those of whom Putnam was speaking when he coined the expression. Indeed, in the immediate context of his essay, Rorty at least comes very close to suggesting that Putnam was actually thinking of Davidson in speaking in this way. As just seen, however, that suggestion could scarcely be further from the truth.)

9. For a (by no means exhaustive) list of such efforts on the part of these critics, see Works Cited at the end of the present essay. See also the extremely useful annotated bibliography compiled by Reed Way Dasenbrock for the collection *Redrawing the Lines,* which he edited, as well as several of the essays included in that volume.

10. The passage that Rorty cites here is from Norris's "Philosophy as *Not* Just a 'Kind of Writing,'" to which his own "Two Meanings of 'Logocentrism'" is a reply. Rorty agrees that "Norris is quite right in saying that, on [Rorty's] view, early Derrida . . . 'merely replaces one set of absolutes (truth, meaning, clear and distinct ideas) with another (trace, *différance,* and other such deconstructive key terms)'" ("Two Meanings" 214; cf. Norris, "Philosophy" 192).

11. The inability of contemporary pragmatists, relativists, perspectivists, antifoundationalists, and other would-be skeptics to put as many as two or three sentences together without positing *something* as (allegedly) a straight matter of *fact*—that is, as *objectively* the case—tends, I think, to become steadily more apparent in direct proportion to the degree of overt *politicization* of the argument in question. The best recent example of this linkage of which I am aware is the collection *Critical Terms for Literary Study,* edited by Frank Lentricchia and Thomas McLaughlin, almost all the pieces in which, beginning with McLaughlin's introduction, reflect in one degree or another this intriguing combination of professed radical interpretationism and unabashed dogmatic metaphysics.

12. In the final section of his essay, Searle addresses the question of why, in spite of its "rather obvious and manifest intellectual weaknesses," deconstruction has nevertheless "proved so influential among literary theorists" (78). In effect (if not in quite so many words), he finds the answer in a rather serious lack of philosophical sophistication or experience on the part of many of those so influenced. He notes, in particular, the "pervasive" presence among literary critics of "two . . . philosophical presuppositions," both of them "derived from" a movement that among philosophers themselves has been effectively obsolete for more than a generation now: namely, "logical positivism." "First there is the assumption that unless a distinction can be made rigorous and precise it isn't really a distinction at all. . . . Second, and equally positivistic, is the insistence that concepts that apply to language and literature, if they are to be truly valid, must admit of some mechanical procedure of verification. . . . [T]he crude positivism of these assumptions . . . is of a piece with Derrida's assumption that without foundations we are left with nothing but the free play of signifiers" (78–79).

13. He is certain, for example, that "*everybody* is ethnocentric when engaged in actual debate, no matter how much realist rhetoric about objectivity he produces in his study" (13; emphasis added).

14. The passage cited by Davidson here is from Rorty's *Philosophy and the Mirror of Nature* (178).

15. A similar argument appears (again, among many other places in Davidson's work) in the essay "Thought and Talk." There he writes: "Error is what gives belief its point. We can, however, take it as given that *most* beliefs are correct. The reason for this is that a belief is identified by its location in a pattern of beliefs; it is this pattern that *determines the subject matter of the belief, what the belief is about.* Before some object in, or aspect of, the world can become part of the subject matter of a belief (true or false) there must be endless true beliefs about the subject matter. False beliefs tend to undermine the identification of the subject matter; to undermine, therefore, the validity of a description of the belief as being about that subject. And so, in turn, *false beliefs undermine the claim that a connected belief is false*" (*ITI* 168; second and third emphasis added). Davidson's point is that we cannot intelligibly predicate something of something else, if that very predication has the effect of making it impossible to speak of that something else at all. Once we are clear on what it is for something *to be a belief* in the first place, it becomes equally clear that to ascribe massive falsity, or erroneousness, to beliefs (or, rather, to attempt to do so) is to leave *nothing* of which it could be said that

it was false (or anything else) to begin with. This surely is as palpable an instance as one could wish for of radically self-undermining predication.

16. Heidegger writes: "We cannot ever 'avoid' a 'circular' proof in the existential analytic, because such an analytic does not do *any* proving *at all* by the rules of the 'logic of consistency'. What common sense wishes to eliminate in avoiding the 'circle', on the supposition that it is measuring up to the loftiest rigour of scientific investigation, is nothing less than the basic structure of care. Because it is primordially constituted by care, any Dasein is already ahead of itself. As being, it has in every case already projected itself upon definite possibilities of its existence; and in such existentiell [*sic*] projections it has, in a pre-ontological manner, also projected something like existence and Being. *Like all research,* the research which wants to develop and conceptualize that kind of Being which belongs to existence, *is itself a kind of Being which disclosive Dasein possesses.* . . . When one talks of the 'circle' in understanding, one expresses a failure to recognize two things: (1) that understanding as such makes up a basic kind of Dasein's Being, and (2) that this Being is constituted as care. To deny the circle, to make a secret of it, or even to want to overcome it, means finally to reinforce this failure. We must rather endeavour to leap into the 'circle', primordially and wholly, so that even at the start of the analysis of Dasein we make sure that we have a full view of Dasein's circular Being" (*Being and Time* 363; see also 27–28, 194–95, and esp. 362–64).

17. Herder had already reached basically the same conclusion (and by a not entirely dissimilar route) in the 1760s. In the second edition of his *Fragments on Recent German Literature,* for example, he writes: "If it is true that without thoughts we cannot think and that we learn to think through words, it follows that *language determines the entire scope and limits of human knowledge.* . . . This general way of regarding human knowledge from the standpoint of and in terms of language must yield a *negative philosophy:* how far human nature should rise in its ideas because it cannot rise higher? how far one should express and explain oneself because one cannot express and explain oneself further? How much would one be able to sweep away here of all that we say without thereby thinking anything, that we conceive incorrectly because we say it incorrectly, that we want to say without being able to think it. The man who would develop this negative philosophy would stand at the furthest extent of human knowledge, as if at the edge of the world; and though he would be unable to raise his head over these limits and look around in the open air, he would nonetheless extend his hand in that direction and proclaim: Here is emptiness, and nothingness! And he would have attained, in another sense of the term, the highest Socratic wisdom: that of knowing nothing" (*Sämtliche Werke* II:17; emphasis added).

WORKS CITED

Cascardi, Anthony J., ed. *Literature and the Question of Philosophy.* Baltimore: Johns Hopkins UP, 1987.

Culler, Jonathan. *On Deconstruction: Theory and Criticism After Structuralism.* Ithaca: Cornell UP, 1982.

Dasenbrock, Reed Way, ed. *Redrawing the Lines: Analytic Philosophy, Deconstruction, and Literary Theory.* Minneapolis: U of Minnesota P, 1989.

Derrida, Jacques. *Margins of Philosophy.* Trans. Alan Bass. Chicago: U of Chicago P, 1982.

Dewey, John. *Essays in Experimental Logic.* New York: Dover, 1953.

Garver, Newton. Preface to Derrida, *Speech and Phenomena.* Evanston: Northwestern UP, 1973.

Goodman, Nelson. *Ways of Worldmaking.* Indianapolis: Hackett, 1978.

Heidegger, Martin. *Being and Time.* Trans. John Macquarrie and Edward Robinson. New York: Harper & Row, 1962.

Herder, Johann Gottfried. *Sämtliche Werke.* Ed. Bernhard Suphan. 33 vols. Berlin: Weidmannsche Buchhandlung, 1877–1913; reprint Hildesheim: Georg Olms Verlagsbuchhandlung, 1967.

Kant, Immanuel. *Critique of Pure Reason.* Trans. Norman Kemp Smith. New York: St. Martin's; Toronto: Macmillan, 1965.

Lentricchia, Frank, and Thomas McLaughlin, eds. *Critical Terms for Literary Study.* Chicago: U of Chicago P, 1990.

LePore, Ernest, ed. *Truth and Interpretation: Perspectives on the Philosophy of Donald Davidson.* Oxford: Basil Blackwell, 1986.

Morton, Michael. "Changing the Subject: Herder and the Reorientation of Philosophy." In Mueller-Vollmer. 158–72.

———. *Herder and the Poetics of Thought: Unity and Diversity in* On Diligence in Several Learned Languages. University Park: Pennsylvania State UP, 1989.

———. "*Verum est factum:* Critical Realism and the Discourse of Autonomy." *German Quarterly* 64 (1991): 149–65.

Mueller-Vollmer, Kurt, ed. *Herder Today.* Berlin: de Gruyter, 1990.

Nietzsche, Friedrich. *The Birth of Tragedy and The Case of Wagner.* New York: Vintage, 1967.

Norris, Christopher. "Limited Think: How Not to Read Derrida." *Diacritics* 20, no. 1 (1990): 17–36.

———. "Philosophy as *Not* Just a 'Kind of Writing': Derrida and the Claim of Reason." In Dasenbrock. 189–203.

Pradhan, Shekhar. "Minimalist Semantics: Davidson and Derrida on Meaning, Use, and Convention." *Diacritics* 16, no. 1 (1986): 66–77.

Putnam, Hilary. "A Comparison of Something with Something Else." *New Literary History* 17, no. 1 (1985): 61–79.

———. *Meaning and the Moral Sciences.* London: Routledge & Kegan Paul, 1978.

———. *Realism with a Human Face.* Cambridge: Harvard UP, 1990.

———. *Reason, Truth and History.* Cambridge: Cambridge UP, 1981.

Rajchman, John, and Cornel West, eds. *Post-Analytic Philosophy.* New York: Columbia UP, 1985.

Rorty, Richard. "The Contingency of Language." *London Review of Books,* 17 April 1986: 3–6.

———. "Deconstruction and Circumvention." *Critical Inquiry* 11, no. 1 (1984): 1–23.

———. *Philosophy and the Mirror of Nature.* Princeton: Princeton UP, 1979.

———. "Pragmatism, Davidson and Truth." In LePore. 333–55.

———. "Solidarity or Objectivity?" In Rajchman and West. 3–19.

———. "Two Meanings of 'Logocentrism': A Reply to Norris." In Dasenbrock. 204–16.

Rosen, Stanley. "The Limits of Interpretation." In Cascardi. 210–41.

Searle, John R. "The Word Turned Upside Down." *The New York Review of Books,* 27 October 1983: 74–79.

Staten, Henry. *Wittgenstein and Derrida.* Lincoln: U of Nebraska P, 1984.

Wheeler, Samuel C. III. "Indeterminacy of French Interpretation: Derrida and Davidson." In LePore. 477–94.

Wittgenstein, Ludwig. *Philosophical Investigations,* 3d ed. Trans. G.E.M. Anscombe. New York: Macmillan, 1958.

――――. *Tractatus Logico-Philosophicus.* Trans. D. F. Pears and B. F. McGuinness. London: Routledge & Kegan Paul; New York: Humanities, 1972.

Analytic Philosophy's Narrative Turn: Quine, Rorty, Davidson

The positivism that has motivated much of analytic philosophy has been challenged from two directions, represented by Wittgenstein on the one hand and by Quine on the other. Although Wittgenstein's work is undoubtedly of utmost significance for the development of philosophy as a whole, it has the basic shortcoming that it is not systematic. Even though it is not hard to read Wittgenstein, in the large, as the deconstruction of analytic philosophy, it is often not clear that this deconstruction holds onto important points in the development of analytic philosophy. Whereas Quine works from the inside, Wittgenstein often simply steps aside. Quine is essential for seeing what possibilities remain to analytic philosophy as a systematic enterprise.

The aim of this essay is to draw out one strand of the move, from within analytic philosophy, beyond positivism and empiricism. I call this strand, which has its origins in Quine, the "narrative turn." The turn is thematized as such by Richard Rorty. In telling the story of this turn, I will adopt the Rortyan mode, which has the virtue but also the vice of painting with a rather broad brush. Within this main plot structure, however, it should be understood that it is the work of Donald Davidson that brings the details to life. Rorty acknowledges this. What Rorty does not quite acknowledge, though, are the elements of Davidson's philosophy that fully break with some of the aspects of positivism and empiricism that remain in the projects of both Quine and Rorty. All the same, all three major characters are needed in the story of this turn. Quine gives us the systematic deconstruction of analytic philosophy from the inside. Davidson, in working out the details and making them all work together, provides a more developed synthesis. And Rorty, even while clinging to some apsects of the analytic tradition that are (explicitly or implicitly) jettisoned in Davidson's program, especially the atomistic individualism of the English empiricist tradition (J. S. Mill, Bertrand Russell), gives us the big picture in terms of a reconceptualization of philosophy. If we keep our eyes on the narrative turn, and on its systematic articulation in terms of elements contributed by Davidson, I think we will see that its tension with empiricism can be faithfully resolved into Rorty's reconceptualization of philosophy.

Although it may seem a not very significant point at first, it seems to me that Rorty's reconceptualization is of *analytic* philosophy, and that in some important ways the reconceptualization *remains* analytic philosophy, for better and for worse. This question will resurface both when we consider Rorty's moves in making the reconceptualization and when we raise the question of literature "as such" (as opposed to questions, such as narrativity, that obviously bear on literary studies). This question will come only at the very end, in a pair of postscripts to our story, considering in turn the idea of literature as the "destination" of philosophy and the possibility of a literary theory based on analytic philosophy.

In order to isolate the individual chapters of this particular story, the narrative will be set out as a series of titled sections. Because real stories do not have footnotes, brief references appear mainly in order to point toward details that, if fully spelled out, would detract from the main plot.

QUINE LETS THE CAT OUT OF THE BAG

Even as logical positivism was still building toward some of its more important statements, W. V. Quine was preparing for its (as Dirk Koppelberg puts it) *Aufhebung*. In 1951 he publishes his seminal "Two Dogmas of Empiricism" (in *Logical* 20–46) in which a general challenge to the hallowed analytic/synthetic distinction issues in the provocative assertion that the "ontological" status of the gods of Homeric poetry and the particles (or wavicles and what have you) of contemporary physics is coequal. What accounts for this theoretical generosity? It is the fact that, once the analytic/synthetic distinction is seen not to be ironclad, it turns out that the only distinction that will hold among different beliefs is one concerning their place in the overall web of belief. There are, then, no qualitative ontological distinctions (or, at least, none where it can be claimed that "reality is cut at the joint" [some non-Quinean analytic philosopher said this; nasty and revealing metaphor!]). Beginning with "Two Dogmas," the category of ontology itself, as first philosophy, becomes suspect. Indeed, for "post-Quineans" (the group that includes Davidson, Rorty, and Putnam among its major figures), the whole idea of "first philosophy" is itself suspect. Michael Dummett would replace onto-epistemological concerns with the philosophy of language as first philosophy (see Dummett, *Truth* 437–58; Rorty, *Objectivity* 143–46). But, if the argument replacing the analytic/synthetic distinction with the web of belief is correct, then there is no "first philosophy," period. There is no "first," for neither is there a "first knower," nor is there a "first" or "originary" web. Ultimately, as Davidson makes clear, there is no "philosophy of language," either, because there is no "language," especially as conceived of by those who are attempting to find the "first philosophy" that will ground all other intellectual endeavors (see Martin, *Matrix,* chap. 3).

What there "is" is the web. What *is* the web as it develops over time, as it is continually reconfigured, becoming, as it were, different webs at different times, but with some fundamental sense of being the same web? Surely there is an explanation here in terms of a dialectic of semantic resources, of changes in the web that result in a transformation of quantity into quality. These are not terms that analytic philosophers generally would want to get mixed up with. Their resistance is important, it seems, insomuch as it is a resistance (though not thematized as such) to the very sort of metanarrative or grand dialectic that "Two Dogmas" and subsequent essays by Quine (e.g., "Ontological Relativity" and "Epistemology Naturalized," in *Ontological* 26–68, 69–90) deconstruct. Clearly, however, the web does transform itself over time. The question is whether this transformation is a lawlike unfolding of the "original" resources of the web. To put it this way is not only to raise a Hegelian question, but further, in that we are concerned with semantic or "etymological" unfolding, a Heideggerian one. But, then, if there is no original web, where will we find the origin of the law of the form which determines subsequent transformations of the web?

GETTING THE STORY

Instead of a searcher for the Law, or Great Code, we find in Quine a hypothetical anthropologist in the field (even if a hypothetical one). In

Word and Object, Quine's anthropologist sets out to get the story on the "natives," beginning not with an attempt to understand the native's *Weltanschauung,* but rather with the problem of ostensible definition. The point is to work out a translation manual. It turns out, of course, that for Quine the problem of this manual is the problem of the relation of a language community's everyday language usage to its ontology. "Ontology," in this context, means the way that any particular language intends a scheme of individuation of objects in the world. Quine argues that translation manuals, while they may be pragmatically "accurate," cannot be known to capture adequately the foreign-language community's ontology. In this respect, the translation manual, as a theory of the other's language, is always underdetermined by the evidence. One consequence of this underdetermination is what Quine calls the "inscrutability of reference" (see *Word* 125–56; for further discussion of these issues in relation to anthropology, see Feleppa).

But to say that a translation manual is "pragmatically accurate," and in that sense adequate, is to say that we can have a conversation with the native. As Davidson argues (we will turn to these arguments in due course), that fact is crucially important. It would seem that we can indeed get the native's story. Davidson reins in some of the wilder interpretations of the "inscrutability of reference" and the related (but not identical) "indeterminacy of meaning" theses by arguing that if we could not get the native's story on some level, then we would have no basis for knowing that we were conversing with a sentient being at all. (Davidson makes this argument in "On the Very Idea of a Conceptual Scheme," *ITI* 183–98). At the end of the day, however, one wonders whether the point is not that there is an aspect of the other that cannot be translated—even if, as in so many cases with Quine and other analytic philosophers, this is a side of the story which they have kept secret even to themselves.

THE PLOT THICKENS

There is a well-known tension in Quine between the idea of the web of belief, on the one hand, and his claims about physicalism, on the other. It would be one thing if all that Quine were claiming is that, because of where we are in the story ("we" being members of Western societies in the twentieth century), we must take science as our guide to all that can be called "knowledge." For if this were the totality of Quine's claim, then he would perhaps be happy with a Rortyan formulation to the effect that the scientific *vocabulary* is simply, and contingently, the lingua franca of cognitive claims in our time and place. Quine, however, wants a stronger physicalism than that: *behaviorism* closes the gap between the web of belief and physicalism. The beginning of thought and meaning for Quine is what he calls "stimulus meaning"—in other words, the sense that we make out of "nerve hits." Ironically, the very thing that gets the ball rolling for Quine—our supposedly basic (but therefore metaphysical) connection to the world—runs very much against the grain of the rest of Quine's philosophy. "Nerve hits" play much the same role in Quine's philosophy as "knowledge by acquaintance" does in Russell's. (For Quine's development of these themes, see *Word* 31–40.) It would seem that the point of such notions of unmediated contact between self and world would be as an answer to the skeptic. As Davidson points out, this Cartesian dichotomizing of self and world in the first place is itself an invitation to skepticism (e.g., see "MS").

We will return to this question. However, there is another problem with Quine's behaviorism (and Russell's knowledge by acquaintance). Namely: even if behaviorist explanations are true, they do not offer us any way into the matrix of meaning—unless, that is, there is a "language of thought" which is inherent in the brain. Quine denies this, as do Wittgenstein, Davidson, and Rorty. If, however, the matrix of meaning is generated intersubjectively, there is no need for behaviorism in the first place. Although Quine has not come around to this position, all of the major post-Quineans have, and in ways that remain faithful to Quine's basic program (see Carol Rovane, in LePore 417–29). Indeed, in working toward a clear picture of the problems of behaviorism, Davidson has given the strongest account of intersubjectivity in analytic philosophy, and one might say that he has also transformed the Quinean project. It might be useful to note that, while Quine relies on the fictional travels of a hypothetical anthropologist, Davidson was for many years an experimental psychologist. (In fairness, we should also note that few philosophers have traveled as widely or have the legendary linguistic expertise of Professor Quine.) The upshot of Davidson's experiments was that he quit being a psychologist; to be more specific, he came to realize that there is a limit beyond which psychology cannot be a "science." In essays such as "Psychology as Philosophy" and "The Material Mind" (*EAE* 229–39, 245–59), Davidson argued that we cannot track a person's beliefs or desires unless we can also track their meanings. There is a limit, however, to how accurately we can determine what another person means by what that person says, for reasons already demonstrated by Quine. (Davidson pursues other dimensions of this question in "Expressing Evaluations.")

Quine's behaviorism is a way of illicitly sneaking a little "scrutability" back into a shared world in which interpersonal communication must forever deal with the inscrutability of reference. In a certain sense, Quine is centering the narrative on the "I," for fear of there being no center. In this case, however, if the center cannot hold, then everything falls apart. And this center, this "I," cannot hold for Quine any more than it can for Descartes once the skeptic questions what they do not: namely, the capacity of the "I" to initiate a conversation with itself. At a crucial point, then, Quine arrests the narrative, clearly worried that it might get out of control. Better to stop with science and predictability. Interestingly enough, it is clear that Quine at times recognizes these as values rather than as metaphysical absolutes. Similarly, his argument for the system of rules which he generates in his work in philosophical and mathematical logic depends ultimately, in the wake of Kurt Gödel, on the value of elegance. But perhaps there is another way, and another place from which, to tell the story.

QUINE'S HOLISM

In formulating the idea of a web of belief, Quine extended Frege's argument that a word has meaning only in the context of a sentence. We might call the various formulations of this claim "the context principle" (see Dummett, *Interpretation* 360–427). Quine (and all post-Quineans) situates sentences within a language. In the Quinean context principle, unlike Frege's, meanings are not "entities"; rather, they are "locations" in the overall web of belief. (Quine discusses "meant entities" in "Two Dogmas"; "locations" must be placed in scare quotes because, as Hilary Putnam has argued, these "meanings ain't in the head"; Davidson has extended this argument to claim that it is the wrong kind of question to ask "where" meanings are; one might wonder at the fact, all the same, that the spatial metaphor is the best, and perhaps only, one that we have.) The configuration of the web at any given point determines what meanings "mean." But what is a "point" in this instance? Seemingly we would mean "a point in time," as we have recognized that the web changes over time. However, given that we are necessarily concerned with the sort of creatures for whom there can be meaning and without which there are no meanings (in other words, *persons*—and this shall be our definition of "persons," such that the category "persons" is not necessarily limited to human beings), then we must be concerned with "historical time." Yet, unless there is a universal history that can be known from a cosmopolitan point of view, a universal "coordinate system" (as Davidson puts it), then historical time is itself a context. (The question of the social construction of time is given interesting treatment in Corlett 65–118.) Quine and other post-Quineans deny that there is a universal coordinate system; indeed, Davidson, Putnam, and Rorty deny this better and more extensively than Quine does. Historical time may be tied to a particular place, but then, as Galileo said, "It moves."

ANY OLD STORY?

The web of belief, then, must be a story that hangs together in the context of a particular culture, in particular periods and places. This must be quite a story, in some respects, because every term in the definition—web of belief, story, culture, period, and place—depends on every other term for its definition. It all works so well—and not only in our Western, contemporary, "scientific" culture—as a way of keeping us in contact with the world that we are inclined, indeed compelled, to search for the Great Code after all. Indeed, all philosophy, of whatever other designation (analytic, Continental, pragmatist, feminist, Marxist, Catholic, etc.) might be divided into two general camps: one that seeks out the Great Code and one that continually attempts to resist the temptation. (This is to put the matter tendentiously, I admit.) Perhaps in order to resist we must all the same taste of the Tree of Knowledge; let us pursue this Great Code, for it seems that our story must itself be contextualized. Even if there is no code of all codes, no context of all contexts, it is clear that every narrative, as a linguistic configuration, must have a larger context: namely, the language it is assembled from. If we pursue this question in the way that Davidson does, it seems that we come awfully close to the idea of the Great Code—close, but not quite there. There is something important about the fact that this route is the one which enables us finally to show the respectability, as it were, of analytic philosophy's narrative turn. This something, however, can be demonstrated only in the telling of Davidson's story.

DAVIDSON'S HOLISM AND TARSKI'S SATISFACTION

The web of belief is a web of sentences. In Quine's version, some sentences, close to the center of the web, are all but impervious to the judgments of experience. In our day, these would be (especially) the basic claims of logic and mathematics. Even these, argues Quine, are in principle open to empirical disconfirmation, but the experience that could cause such calamity would necessarily disturb much of the web (and therefore much of life in the web). Imagine a play, a narrative, in which nothing drastically out of the ordinary has happened (e.g., gravity has not gone haywire, people are not returning from the dead, etc.) for nine-tenths of the story; then, all of a sudden, out of nowhere, God rips open the sky and says that the rules have changed. We would call this an absurdist play, and the sense of the narrative would be difficult to determine beyond the point of, shall we say, revelation. Everything would have to be reevaluated. "Real life," it seems to me, functions more or less the same way.

Fortunately, cosmic cataclysms are relatively rare. In a certain sense they are impossible, because they cannot be made sense of and, therefore, cannot enter our matrix of meaning. In other words, imagine waking up one fine morning to the news that the basic truths of logic, beginning with the principles of identity and noncontradiction, had been changed. If this were really the case, then life would not go on as before, to say the least. But it is not clear that if these "truths," in themselves, had changed, there would be any way that the change could be assimilated— or even that the change could be known to have occurred. This should make us wonder whether there are such "truths in themselves." Quine, of course, is wondering exactly that, and he has provided the beginnings of a method whereby the very idea of such truths can be set aside by serious philosophy—set aside, that is, without thereby accepting skepticism. But then we have to look also at the outer perimeter of the web as Quine conceives it. Here we find those sentences which constantly face the tribunal of experience—claims of the sort, "There is a blackbird sitting on that windowsill" (it could turn out to be a bluebird with a very dark complexion) or "It is raining" and so on. Thinking about what makes these sentences, in principle, closer to the edge of the web, brings us once again face-to-face with the tension in Quine that we already discussed. It seems that Quine is in a double bind here. On the one hand, these sentences, which traditionally would be said to express synthetic propositions, are at the edge of the web by virtue of the particular configuration of the particular web in question. On the other hand, it appears that Quine wants to say that the special characteristic of these sentences is that their confirmation or disconfirmation depends on input from our sensory surfaces. (Without really getting into the issue here, we might question Quine's view that this aspect of his theory is in the "pragmatist" tradition, especially of James; for the category of "experience" is certainly broader and, indeed, qualitatively different for James and Dewey.) Davidson has a way of avoiding this tension.

Davidson is neither an empiricist nor a behaviorist; nor is he, contrary to Rorty ("Pragmatism, Davidson, and Truth," in LePore 333–56), a pragmatist. I would say that Davidson, like Derrida, is a contextualist. I would further say that contextualism is the only way out of the quandaries of skepticism and metaphysical realism; once one realizes that the latter is simply a kind of faith in the Great Code—the touchstone of which is the Kantian *Ding an Sich*—then the door is fully open to skepticism in any case. It should be added, of course, that Davidson's contextualism is a faithful pursuit of the projects of Frege and Quine, with help from Tarski. We should set out this contextualism in two stages: the first with reference to Quine, the second with reference to Tarski.

In Davidson's view, there are no "openings" in the web of belief, if by such openings we mean particular points of contact of the sensory surfaces of individuals with elements of the "outside world." (In "On the Very Idea of a Conceptual Scheme," Davidson refers to this dichotomy of scheme and content as a "third dogma of empiricism.") For Quine, although in principle the native's language could be translated in all sorts of ways, translations do not in fact vary so much, because our hypothetical anthropologist's sensory surfaces function (for the most part) in the same way as the native's. For Davidson, translations also will not vary that greatly, but for an entirely different reason, an "in principle" reason. As with everything in Davidson's philosophy, we will have to build up to this point.

There is only an "inside" to Davidson's web, although, once we see things this way, we might just as well say that there is only an "outside," or perhaps we may drop the spatial metaphor altogether. There are three elements to Davidson's contextualism (I have distilled this version of his contextualism through thinking about what Davidson and Derrida have in common, helped by the fine article by Shekhar Pradhan, "Minimalist Semantics.") First, there is nothing essential to the sign (or so-called basic unit of meaning, what Derrida calls the "gramme") except its ability to be situated in a context. Second, the meaning of a sign is determined by its context. Third, there is no final context or "context of all contexts."

If the web of belief (or matrix of meaning) works in this way, where is there a connection to the world? This is where Tarski comes in. Davidson has proposed a "truth conditional" theory of meaning, basing himself on Tarski's semantic theory of truth (see Tarski; also Davidson, "Truth and Meaning" and "In Defense of Convention T," in *ITI* 17–36, 65–75). In brief, Davidson proposed that the meaning of a sentence is given by its truth-conditions. In other words, we know the meaning of a sentence when we know under what conditions we would assent to its truth. Such conditions, however, cannot simply be defined as empirical, for two closely related reasons. First, in order to consider the truth of a particular sentence, I must know, in some sense, the place of that sentence in the overall scheme of the language the sentence is in. In other words, I must know the language. In some sense, this knowledge is based on experience, but it seems narrow and inaccurate to call it "empirical." Second, there are many sentences I would readily assent to that are not, in any direct way, about empirical observations—for example, "Two plus two equals four." We have it from Quine that there are no "real" analytic propositions, no propositions that are, in principle, beyond disconfirmation by experience. But then we have to accept also that there are no absolutely pure synthetic propositions either: in the determination of the meaning of any given sentence in a particular language, there is a role played by experience and a role played by the configuration of the language as a whole; and the place where one role begins and the other leaves off is determined entirely by context. In other words, what counts as "experience" is itself determined by context. The determination is, in Tarski's theory, *semantic;* the relation between meaning and truth-conditions is one of *satisfaction.* (For a useful and insightful account of Davidson's theory of truth, see Ramberg 6–15.)

Where, then, is the point of confrontation? Is it between a language as a whole and the world as a whole? For Davidson, there can be no such confrontation, nor does there need to be one. (Also see Davidson's "Reality Without Reference," in *ITI* 215–25.) The reason for this is perhaps more radical than one might expect. Before we turn to that reason, however, there are two important questions in Davidson's philosophy that need to be considered.

INTERRUPTION 1: CONCEPTUAL SCHEMES

Davidson has quite famously argued that there can be no such thing as a radical incommensurability of conceptual schemes and, therefore, that it makes no sense to speak of conceptual schemes at all. Part of Davidson's argument concerns the fact that to claim there are diffferent conceptual schemes (or that, in principle, there could be such schemes) is to set up the kind of self/world (or subject/object) dichotomy which invites skepticism (also see Davidson's "Empirical Content," in LePore 320–32). This is no answer to the conceptual schemer, of course, unless one has an answer to the skeptic. Davidson does. He claims that, in principle, I must be able to translate (by and large) the language of the other into my own language, or else I would not be able to recognize the other as a language user in the first place. If I can, in principle, translate the other's language into my own, then our "conceptual schemes" must not be radically incommensurate—indeed, satisfaction must mean for the other pretty much what it means for me—and thus it makes little sense to speak of our having different conceptual schemes or any sort of conceptual schemes at all. Put another way, from the opposite direction as it were, if I am able to have a disagreement with someone, despite the fact that this disagreement may seem to be quite "radical," it must be the case that this other person and I actually agree on quite a lot, or else we would not know what it was we were disagreeing about. In fact, our area of agreement must be quite massive, and our disagreement quite small in comparison.

But, it seems, we could encounter a problem if we extrapolate from this point. If every language can in principle be translated into every other language, then are we not in the vicinity of the Great Code, "Language itself"? Of course, the temptation is once again there. Just as there is a Hegelian temptation to go from intersubjectivity to trans-subjectivity, there is a similar temptation to go from interlinguisticality to the metalanguage. In fact, these are the same temptation. If the Cartesian dichotomy of subject and object cannot be maintained, then neither can the dichotomy of the language used by the subject and the final, "background" language be maintained. Translation and intersubjectivity explain each other not against the background of the Great Code, but rather, so to speak, against the background of the *absence* of the Great Code. The "background" is the reality of there being no final context.

Therefore, even though there are no narratives that, in principle, cannot be translated, there is no final story (no Greatest Possible Story ever told). But that is to say that there is no end to the story, and thus our particular webs are quite important. The fact that story may be traded for story does not diminish the importance of narrativity.

INTERRUPTION 2: METAPHOR

Davidson ("What Metaphors Mean," in *ITI* 245–64) is well known for arguing that the important thing about metaphors is not their meaning. We can take metaphors to have their literal meaning, but then they are almost always false; nor are they, in this case, metaphors. The important thing is not what metaphors mean, but what they "do." Metaphors are like little cataclysms in language, little invasions into the overall matrix of meaning. They stir things up. At the same time, the words and expressions that we think of as metaphorical (or "figurative" in a broader sense) are not absolutely different in kind from the rest of our language—otherwise, we would not recognize a particular sound or bit of scribbling as a metaphor, for we would not recognize it as a word or group of words.

On Davidson's account, it is just as correct to say that the definition of "literal meaning" is "not metaphorical" as it is to say that metaphors are words which are not to be taken literally. There is, and can be, no special relationship between "literal meanings" and "reality" that does not apply to metaphors. Instead, the question of what sort of language is literal, and what sort is metaphorical, once again has to be a matter of context. Metaphors are the places where the "energy" of language, its ability to call us out, to make us aware of the contextuality of language, is strongest. Metaphors, while literally false, are the places where we stop and think about meaning. The point is that there is something going on in the rest of language such that we do not ordinarily stop and think, where this "thinking" is a separate activity from our general participation in the world. Such thinking, therefore, can only be conditionally "separate." (A very interesting essay that explores these questions, in the context of a discussion of Davidson and Freud, is Marcia Cavell's "Metaphor, Dreamwork, and Irrationality," in LePore 495–507.)

NICE DERANGEMENTS

Metaphor is a nice enough derangement, as is the thinking that thinks itself out of the world. In an essay that has rightfully received a good deal of attention in recent years, "A Nice Derangement of Epitaphs," Davidson makes the argument that there is "no such thing as a language," if by a language is meant a form of rule-governed behavior. There are, ultimately, no "rules" of language—just as there is no final context. Therefore, there is no language that can confront the world. But then I must wonder if there is a "world," either, if by world is meant some sort of closed system. Perhaps there is nothing to confront because there is no "there" there, in the ordinary sense.

In "Nice Derangement," Davidson argues that there are two levels of language usage, the "background theory" and the "passing theory." The background theory is the knowledge (or, one might say, the experience) of language that I bring to any particular conversation. The passing theory is the conversation itself. The conversation will quite possibly modify the background theory—Davidson uses the example of malapropism to show the continual adjustment that is required. Indeed, there is nothing especially permanent about the background theory; it changes all the time.

RORTY'S CONTINGENCIES

In *Contingency, Irony, and Solidarity,* especially its first three chapters, Rorty draws some significant conclusions from the many threads of Davidson's philosophy. Perhaps we can sum up these conclusions in the following way: for Rorty, there is no metanarrative, only narratives, and these narratives are open-ended and contingent, in the same way that Davidson's background theory is; this is not to say, however, that we are just "making it up as we go along," because, at the very least, we are also making ourselves up as we go along. I think that this characterization captures what Rorty is saying. The only problem with his argument is the part about making ourselves up, which, in its somewhat free-floating and Nietzschean form, repeats again the tension that is in Quine (and, obviously, in some readings/readers of Nietzsche). In the end, of our three principal players, only Davidson avoids this tension.

Among analytic philosophers, however, it is Richard Rorty who most faithfully reads the more profound consequences of Davidson's philosophy. In "The Contingency of Language," Rorty argues that

> Davidson's treatment of truth ties in with his treatment of language learning and of metaphor to form the first systematic treatment of language which breaks *completely* with the notion of language as something which can be adequate or inadequate to the world or to the self. For Davidson breaks with the notion that language is a *medium*—a medium either of representation or of expression. [*Contingency* 10]

One might say, therefore, that Davidson is analytic philosophy's first truly successful critic of Cartesianism; and I would argue that, in philosophy more generally, he is joined at this point only by Derrida. What Rorty and Derrida do which adds an all-important dimension to how we understand Davidson's work—and what we *do* with it—is to argue that Cartesianism is not simply a philosophy, it is a culture. (See also Bordo on this point. I should explain that, in general, I am not especially happy with the "Rorty and Derrida" coupling that one often sees in broad references to "postmodern philosophy"; on this point, the exchange between Rorty and Christopher Norris is instructive [see Norris 139–66 and Dasenbrock 189–216; also Martin, chap. 5].) This is something the Vienna positivists understood, though from the other side: they were in favor of promoting Cartesian culture as a culture of enlightened society (they hoped to help enlightened philosophy "sink in," we might say). Wittgenstein also understood this, from the perspective of a critic of Cartesianism, but it seems that he thought of philosophy itself as the problem. In this he is joined by Heidegger, who was all the same a vastly more systematic thinker, and to some extent by Derrida, also much more systematic than Wittgenstein (on these questions, see both Nieli and Edwards). As Rorty (citing Derrida) points out, though, the Heideggerian solution to the problem of taking language as a medium "deifies" language, making humans mere emanations and, what is more important, simply transposing the philosophy of consciousness which the linguistic turn was meant to get us away from onto the face of Being itself (see Rorty, *Contingency* 11).

And yet, as some recent readers of Heidegger have argued, there is a dimension of Heidegger's thought which is quite similar to Davidson's in getting us out of a problem that still troubles Rorty's project. (On Heidegger and Davidson, see Haugeland.) We will have to build up to this part of the story.

Rorty replaces the idea of an "adequate" language, with its companion ideas of a "world" as simply "out there" and the "self" as simply "in here," with the idea of a contest of vocabularies. Vocabularies are ways that we tell stories about ourselves. To tell a new story is to invent a new vocabulary. The "hooks" of such stories are metaphors; when people have accepted a new story, they have accepted a new set of metaphors and the narrative configuration surrounding these metaphors. The "configuration," or "matrix," or "narrative" (these are all metaphors, of course) is indeed what remains centrally important. But the shape of the configuration is determined in large part by the way in which it makes room for metaphors. Remember: what metaphors do is more important than what they mean. Because of this confounding of meaning, metaphors cannot just be left lying around any old place in the matrix of meaning—that would be cataclysmic (and, therefore, would not happen). (Some social theorists have recently started thinking about the idea of revolution in these terms. It is clear that Edmund Burke already saw the possibilities— and was repulsed by them—some time ago. See Blakemore, Corlett, Rorty's *Essays,* and Martin.)

The leading characters in the contest of vocabularies are those who bring about "revolutionary achievements in the arts, in the sciences, and in moral and political thought," which "typically occur when somebody realizes that two or more of our vocabularies are interfering with each other, and proceeds to invent a new vocabulary to replace both" (Rorty, *Contingency* 12). As examples Rorty gives figures as diverse as Galileo, Hegel, Yeats, Freud, and Einstein. Because the common element among these figures is that they initiated a new way of thinking by creating a new vocabulary, Rorty calls people such as these "poets" or, using Harold Bloom's terminology, "strong critics." Given this broader usage of the word "poet," Rorty agrees with Shelley's dictum that "poets are the unacknowledged legislators of humanity."

What the poet or strong critic does *not* do is discover a "reality behind the appearances, . . . an undistorted view of the whole picture with which to replace myopic views of its parts." Instead, Rorty argues, "The proper analogy is with the invention of new tools to take the place of old tools" (*Contingency* 12). Rorty takes this analogy between vocabularies and tools from Wittgenstein, and he acknowledges one obvious drawback:

> The craftsman typically knows what job he needs to do before picking or inventing tools with which to do it. By contrast, someone like Galileo, Yeats, or Hegel (a "poet" in my wide sense of the term—the sense of "one who makes things new") is typically unable to make clear exactly what it is that he wants to do before developing the language in which he succeeds in doing it. His new vocabulary makes possible, for the first time, a formulation of its own purpose. [*Contingency* 12–13]

To invent a vocabulary is to reinvent oneself and possibly the world as well—if the vocabulary catches on. Because there is no reality behind the appearances, in the sense already specified (i.e., there is no "there" there, no final picture of the world), there is no final vocabulary.

CREATING MY OWN STORY

The only problem I have with this argument is the Nietzschean direction in which Rorty takes it. In fact, Rorty takes the argument, as he acknowledges (*Contingency* 27), in the direction of Alexander Nehemas's *Nietzsche: Life as Literature.* On one level, Rorty's argument is against authoritarianism and totalitarianism: he is opposed to the creation of a supposedly "final" vocabulary that imposes itself by force. This would be the "final solution" to the problem of meaning, and we should understand that label with all its ominous overtones. (Derrida takes up the question in these same terms in "No Apocalypse, Not Now.") I think this is a very good argument—not only because of its purpose, but mainly because it is one of the few arguments against authoritarianism which does not entirely remain, in its vocabulary and its founding metaphors, within the circuit of authoritarianism itself. But there is also a side to the argument which is still too much in debt to the methodological individualism and empiricism of most analytic philosophy, and this is where Davidson and Heidegger are needed to finish our story.

To paraphrase Marx: People make narratives, but they do not make them just as they please. Rorty recognizes this, of course, in the passage I just quoted. People make narratives in a certain context—one that is largely fixed, in a pragmatic if not in a metaphysical sense. Plato already recognized the metaphor creators as "gods" of a sort, and Rorty is in this sense a Platonist. One does not, however, have to "deify" language in the reverential tones employed especially by Heidegger (in such essays as "On the Way to Language") in order to see that there is an ongoing role played by the context principle which finally undercuts the instrumentalism proposed by Rorty. One can remain, as Davidson does, a kind of "structuralist," so long as it is recognized that the "structure" is finally open-ended. In this case, one sees narratives as always already communal, intersubjective products formed against the nonbackground (or background, written in the Derridean mode of "erasure") of a context that is always receding. The matrix of meaning is like a kind of space-time continuum. It makes no sense to ask what is "beyond" the edge, but that does not keep us from pushing toward the edge, telling stories of farther horizons. While it may be true that our poets are credited with a certain inventiveness, the larger story is told in terms of *what* is invented in and through them.

POSTSCRIPT 1:
LITERATURE AS THE DESTINATION OF PHILOSOPHY

In "The Resistance to Theory," Paul de Man discusses the idea that it is literature that philosophy has always been hiding from. In doing so, de Man claims, philosophy is ultimately hiding from itself. Rorty is the first analytic philosopher to embrace fully this line of reasoning. Post-Rortyan analytic philosophy will primarily be the attempt to invent and offer useful vocabularies. One imagines, therefore, that there will not be too many post-Rortyan analytic philosophers, as it is unlikely that the bulk of analytic philosophers will turn to this task. Philosophy will tend to bifurcate, Rorty argues, into two disciplines. Those philosophers who do not make the narrative turn will all the same be working within some system of metaphors established in the texts of some poet-philosopher, whether those texts come from Quine or Davidson, Sartre or Derrida, Chomsky, or even Rorty. There will be, in other words, details to be worked out, and this may turn out to be useful work, depending on how powerful a particular system of metaphors turns out to be. To say "powerful" here is not necessarily to say "popular," in some straightforward sense. In fact, there is the question here of a kind of Nietzschean-Foucauldian analytics of the power of institutions, as with the case, for example, of the discourse of psychiatry, whose metaphors are both popular and powerful— that is to say, people had better (in some cases at least) go along with these metaphors, or else institutional power will make itself felt. The case of Jeffrey Masson and the Freud Archives is instructive here (see Masson). The useful form for thinking about this question would be Imre Lakatos's idea of an ongoing research program. On the other side of this bifurcation, however, the honorific term "philosophy" will fall away, to be replaced by the more general "writing" or "poetry." At least that is Rorty's argument, but it remains to be seen how this will play itself out in the academic institution of philosophy.

POSTSCRIPT 2:
THE POSSIBILITY OF AN "ANALYTIC" LITERARY CRITICISM

Although it is clear that the analytic philosophy discussed in the present essay has implications for literary theory, in the broad sense that a theory of language in general has implications for "literary" language in particular, it is not clear what contribution such an "analytic literary theory" could make to the reading of particular literary texts, that is, to literary criticism. I think, however, that the possibilities lie in the general direction of "deconstruction," in the sense that Derrida's work in particular is concerned with the literariness of all language. Once the boundary between "literary" language and language in general is broken down, as it is by Davidson, one may ask two questions in particular of a given text. First, what is the text's relationship to its own linguistic configuration, in particular its system of metaphors. Second, what is the text's relationship to a supposed Great Code that underwrites textuality? That is, does the text resist or embrace such a code? (Then the question becomes one of *particulars,* really the *sine qua non* of serious literary studies.) These are the sorts of questions that Derrida raises with regard to every kind of text. It seems to me that an analytic philosophy that has made the narrative turn could move in this direction as well.

However, if a particular reading of analytic philosophy gives us merely the same opening in literary theory that has already been accomplished and articulated by deconstruction, then it would seem superfluous to take analytic philosophy in the same direction. The upshot would seem to be that there is no possibility of a distinctly analytic literary criticism. Although I will not go into this task here, I think that an extended look at Rorty's analyses of Nabokov, Orwell, and Derrida's *The Post Card* would bear this out. Such analyses, however, are interesting and important as something else—as a kind of analytic philosophy. Therefore, from the claim that there is no distinctly analytic literary criticism, I do not draw the seemingly Rortyan conclusion that there is no analytic philosophy. Rorty's own work is the best argument here: even though Rorty keeps saying that analytic philosophy has come to an end, he continues to rely on analytic arguments in his work, and his basic frame of reference remains the analytic tradition. Even if the questions that Quine, Davidson, and Rorty ask resemble some of the questions raised by Heidegger and Derrida, their procedures for working through those questions are quite different. Perhaps the difference is only "stylistic." Given the difficulties of moving from one tradition to the other, though, "style" becomes a very substantive question, to say the least. Although this conclusion is clearly inconclusive, it tells us something very interesting all the same: just where the question of style is situated in philosophy, and just where philosophy is situated in relation to style. The beginnings of a literary theory of philosophy can be found at just this point.

WORKS CITED

Blakemore, Steven. *Burke and the Fall of Language: The French Revolution as Linguistic Event.* Hanover: UP of New England, 1988.

Bordo, Susan. *The Flight to Objectivity: Essays on Cartesianism and Culture.* Albany: SUNY, 1987.

Corlett, William. *Community Without Unity: A Politics of Derridian Extravagance.* Durham: Duke UP, 1989.

Dasenbrock, Reed Way, ed. *Redrawing the Lines: Analytic Philosophy, Deconstruction, and Literary Theory.* Minneapolis: U of Minnesota P, 1989.

De Man, Paul. "The Resistance to Theory." In *The Resistance to Theory.* Minneapolis: U of Minnesota P, 1986. 3–20.

Derrida, Jacques. "No Apocalypse, Not Now (Full Speed Ahead, Seven Missiles, Seven Missives)." Trans. Catherine Porter and Philip Lewis. *Diacritics* 14, no. 2 (1984): 18–31.

Dummett, Michael. *The Interpretation of Frege's Philosophy.* Cambridge: Harvard UP, 1981.

———. *Truth and Other Enigmas.* Cambridge: Harvard UP, 1978.

Edwards, James C. *The Authority of Language: Heidegger, Wittgenstein, and the Threat of Philosophical Nihilism.* Tampa: U of South Florida P, 1990.

Feleppa, Robert. *Convention, Translation, and Understanding: Philosophical Problems in the Comparative Study of Culture.* Albany: SUNY, 1988.

Frege, Gottlob. "On Sense and Meaning." In *Translations from the Philosophical Writings of Gottlob Frege.* Trans. Max Black; ed. Peter Geach and Max Black. Oxford: Basil Blackwell, 1980.

Gibson, Roger F., Jr. *The Philosophy of W.V. Quine.* Tampa: U of South Florida P, 1982.

Haugeland, John. "Dasein's Disclosedness." In *Heidegger and Praxis.* Ed. Thomas J. Nenon. *The Southern Journal of Philosophy* 28, supp. (1990): 51–73.

Koppelberg, Dirk. *Aufhebung auf analytische Philosophie: Quine als Synthese von Carnap und Neurath.* Frankfurt: Suhrkamp, 1987.

LePore, Ernest, ed. *Truth and Interpretation: Perspectives on the Philosophy of Donald Davidson.* Oxford: Basil Blackwell, 1986.

LePore, Ernest, and Brian McLaughlin, eds. *Actions and Events: Perspectives on the Philosophy of Donald Davidson.* Oxford: Basil Blackwell, 1985.

Martin, Bill. *Matrix and Line: Derrida and the Possibilities of Postmodern Social Theory.* Albany: SUNY, 1992.

Masson, Jeffrey Moussaieff. *Final Analysis: The Making and Unmaking of a Psychoanalyst.* New York: Addison-Wesley, 1990.

Nehemas, Alexander. *Nietzsche: Life as Literature.* Cambridge: Harvard UP, 1985.

Nieli, Russell. *Wittgenstein: From Mysticism to Ordinary Language.* Albany: SUNY, 1987.

Norris, Christopher. *The Contest of Faculties: Philosophy and Theory After Deconstruction.* London: Methuen, 1985.

Pradhan, S. "Minimalist Semantics: Davidson and Derrida on Meaning, Use, and Convention." *Diacritics* 16, no. 1 (1986): 65–77.

Quine, Willard Van Orman. *From a Logical Point of View.* Cambridge: Harvard UP, 1953.

———. *Ontological Relativity and Other Essays.* New York: Columbia UP, 1969.

———. *Word and Object.* Cambridge: MIT, 1960.

Ramberg, Bjørn. *Donald Davidson's Philosophy of Language.* Oxford: Basil Blackwell, 1989.

Rorty, Richard. *Contingency, Irony, and Solidarity.* Cambridge: Cambridge UP, 1989.

———. *Essays on Heidegger and Others.* Cambridge: Cambridge UP, 1991.

———. *Objectivity, Relativism, and Truth.* Cambridge: Cambridge UP, 1991.

Tarski, Alfred. "The Concept of Truth in Formalized Languages." In *Logic, Semantics, Mathematics.* Oxford: Clarendon, 1956.

Truth-Conditions, Rhetoric, and Logical Form: Davidson and Deconstruction

SAMUEL C. WHEELER III

M

any of Derrida's deconstructive arguments start from an antiessentialist rejection of a principled line between the cognitive meanings of words and other features of words.[1] Given that the fundamental distinction between rhetoric and logic rests on cognitive meanings, such a denial entails the denial of a principled line between logic and rhetoric.[2] On my reading, deconstruction takes as an early lemma the rejection of a principled line between logic and rhetoric.[3]

As I will show below, Donald Davidson is explicitly and implicitly committed to these same starting points and lemmas. Davidson's thought starts not with Husserl and Heidegger, but with the series of reflections that leads from Frege to Quine. Davidson discusses the phenomena I characterize as "rhetorical" in terms of the concept of force and in terms of the distinction between the truth-conditions of sentences and the uses to which they are put. The present essay shows how, from these commitments and their consequences, the analytic philosophy of Davidson leads to an interchangeability of logic and rhetoric which is equivalent to Derrida's dissolution of that line.[4] As a consequence, Davidson is committed to other startling theses for which deconstruction is notorious. When properly understood, these theses are not so startling and should not be notorious, but should rather be taken as the serious basis for further work.

My argument will be a straightforward one in the analytic tradition, following the spirit of Davidson's investigations into logical form,[5] and relying on his development of the distinction between what is said and the force with which it is said.[6] One virtue of analytic philosophy is its tradition of expressing points in transparently simple paradigms. The analytic philosopher will discuss "The cat is on the mat" or "Galileo believed that the Earth moves" rather than the works of Freud and Proust. By following that analytic tradition, I show in a very simple way part of what it means to claim that rhetoric and logic are continuous. I hope thereby to remove some of the opacity that has blocked analytic philosophers from seeing what Derrida might be up to.

This result shows something about philosophical problems as well as about philosophers. Davidson and Derrida emerge from traditions which have had little contact over the past century. That they reach similar positions from analogous considerations and analogous predecessors[7] indicates that there is a common problem which comes from a background which transcends the particularities of the different traditions in which it has arisen.

Most important, that these philosophers reach similar conclusions from their disparate backgrounds and from disparate banks of texts and considerations indicates that they are getting something right. The consequences they draw from their analogous denials of naturally self-interpreting terms seem to be forced by a structure that is not peculiar to either American analytic philosophy or the French tradition. My hope is that by thinking through the problems from the points of view of both Derrida and Davidson, I can see more clearly how to think my own way through or around some of the philosophical questions that have fascinated me for a long time.[8]

LOGIC AND RHETORIC

Starting with Plato's war with the Sophists, the properties of words have been divided into two categories. On the one hand, there are the logical properties, which determine the concept or thought expressed and are the real meaning or content of the term or sentence. These are the features of words which fix the reference of a term and the truth-value of a sentence. The logical properties are thus conceived of as essences or as meanings behind the words. Most important, since the meanings of

terms are fixed by logical properties, so are the truth-values of sentences. What are known as "propositions" or the "cognitive contents" of
sentences are essentially the abstracted essence of the sequence of
words as intended on an occasion of utterance. "Logical properties" are
covered under what is categorized as "semantics."

On the other hand, there are the rhetorical properties, the various
other properties of words which can affect how those words function in
discourse. Such properties and relations are assonances, pleasant associations, the properties of having been used by Shakespeare, and anything
other than the "real meaning." The rhetorical properties spring from the
many material guises (as in the phrase "the materiality of the signifier")
in which the same *logos* or meaning can show up. The rhetoric/logic
dichotomy is yet another form of the matter/form dichotomy.[9]

The distinction between rhetoric and logic, then, is that logic draws
logical connections, relations which depend on logical properties, while
rhetoric goes from premise to conclusion using rhetorical connections,
connections which exist in virtue of accidents of words. Thus, for instance, metonymic and metaphoric connections are rhetorical. When-
ever persuasion rests on an expression's effect on a person, predicted
from our knowledge of the person's beliefs and prejudices, it is rhetorical. In fact, anything other than "meaning" in some strict sense is rhetorical.[10] Note that the rhetorical is defined by being the negation of the
logical, not by any proper feature of its own; this is characteristic of a
"binary opposition."

Logical properties are really successors of *logoi*, or Forms, which lie
behind the words and which the words express. "*Logoi*" have undergone
many incarnations, among them the "senses" that Frege thought words
expressed, the meanings that the logical positivists appealed to, and the
intentional entities of Husserl. *Logoi*, in some guise or other, serve as
foundation for many familiar philosophical concepts and distinctions
concerning language, meaning, and translation. Our thoughts are supposed to be like *logoi* or to connect directly with *logoi*. When, for
instance, we say that our thoughts can be the same whether expressed in
Latin or in English or that some of what we say is true in virtue of
meaning alone, we seem to appeal to thought-words which have many of
the same properties as Platonic Forms or Aristotelian *nous*-tokens.

Logoi have had the dual role of being the real natures of things and of
being present to thought. Plato's Forms and Aristotelian *nous*-tokens
were essences of things and not just magical representations of things.
For Aristotle, then, the thought was literally the same as the object, such
that things could be literally in mind. As essential, constituting features

of objects, the Forms that make objects be, *logoi* have diminished in scope since Plato and Aristotle. Since *logoi* are supposed to be present to thought, necessarily fitting their referents, logical judgments were necessary truths, truths which revealed the essence of their subject matter. As philosophers lost confidence in intuitions of the essence of external objects, *logoi* became restricted to those entities which philosophers thought we could intuit. While they were trying to be nonessentialist, the essentialism implicit in supposing that anything's nature could be directly intuited was retained in one form or another.

So, the British Empiricists supposed that Ideas were the tokens of thought which were directly present. An Idea of Red could not be mistaken for an Idea of Yellow. Ideas wore their sense and reference on their faces. An Idea's reference was fixed by "fitting" its referent, and this notion of "fit" ran into difficulties solved variously by Berkeley and Kant. The Idea idea finally yielded to "intentional objects" (in the phenomenological tradition) and to "meanings of words" (for the logical empiricists). That is, in the logical empiricist tradition from which Davidson and Quine free themselves, self-revealing essences were restricted to meanings of words, construed as magically represented stipulations of sets of self-revealing experiences.

As meanings of words and, thus, as objects of thought, *logoi* allow a magic language, whose tokens essentially express or are *logoi.* This magic language thereby has words which cannot be misunderstood. (We "think to ourselves" in the language of *logoi,* so this perfection gives sense to the alleged tragic inadequacy of language to express our subtler thoughts. The language of thought is perfectly expressive of all properties and nuances, unlike natural language.) To think the word is to think its meaning directly, to think a term which is nothing other than its essence. While you can be mistaken about what the word *chien* means, you cannot be mistaken about what your thought of a dog is about, or that you intend to speak of a dog. The truth-conditions of your thoughts are fixed by their very nature. So, a private language is possible with the magic language.

Unlike regular language, the language of *logoi* cannot be misinterpreted, because *logoi* reveal their meaning to the inspecting "I."[11] Put another way, the *logoi* are self-interpreting because their meaning is their essence; what it is to be this *logos* is to have as extension these objects. The history of the magic language has an interesting dialectic in this regard. The only genuinely clear candidates for "meaning by their very nature" are items which are in some way *identical* to the items they mean. Thus, Aristotelian *nous*-tokens were the entities without their matter. The problem of the magic language has been to make them "mean by their very nature" in some way short of "being the very thing." As Berkeley argued, British Empiricist ideas of red could not be mistaken for ideas of yellow only because they really meant themselves.

Even though both traditions are founded on their peculiar versions of *logoi,* neither phenomenology nor Anglo-American empiricism can be naturally comfortable with meanings. These *logoi,* the "words" of the magic language of intention and thought, must be entities which reveal their essences (and, thus, reveal necessities) to bare inspection. As sketched above, both these traditions grew out of modern philosophy's attempt to eschew intuited natural necessities. So the empiricists should have been suspicious of the magic language of *logoi,* for such a language requires that necessary truths and intrinsic natures be there in experience.

Aristotle's lesson, it seems to me, had been largely forgotten by anti-essentialist empiricists who took there to be "given" objects of any kind. For any object whatsoever, Aristotle demonstrated,[12] there must be a distinction between features the object must have to continue to be itself and features the object could lose and still exist. The very idea of a "given" object, then, presupposes that necessity and possibility are given as well. So the hope of constructing a world from mere nonmodal data must fail.[13]

Likewise, the phenomenologists ought to have been suspicious of *logoi,* since these mental words are necessarily repeatables and thus have as part of their nature what "is not yet," the past and future possibilities of reoccurrence. How can such possibilities *per se* be present? Also, if these words determine an extension, then that necessary relation to another object must somehow be totally present in the way a word is. Neither of these features of noetic content seem to be the sort of thing that can be *per se* completely present to consciousness.[14]

The rejection of *logoi,* and thus the rejection of the basis for our distinction between the rhetorical and the logical, stems from this rejection of the magic language. As I have argued elsewhere ("The Extension of Deconstruction"), such a renunciation entails Derrida's denials of principled distinctions as well as Davidson's and Quine's denials of dogmas.

DAVIDSON AS DECONSTRUCTOR

On my reading, the basic thought common to Davidson, Derrida, and Quine is that any language consisting of any kind of marks, whether marks on paper or marks in the soul, is no better than words. The marks which constitute intentions, then, are also material and are thus present to us as more than just an essence. This "nonpresence" of the true meaning goes all the way down. Every mark is subject to interpretation. If we think and intend using marks which are just like words, then the material of the word cannot be distinguished in a principled way from its form. Even marks in the soul lack a separable essence, since any mark must have materiality, accidental features which guarantee the possibility of being misunderstood. So there is no separating the logical connections and features from the rhetorical connections and features. That is, you cannot get to "meanings" which have only essential connections, which are related only to the things they are supposed to be logically related to.

Thus, the rejection of the magic language also amounts implicitly to a rejection of an absolute or ontological distinction between the logical and the rhetorical. Let us see how this distinction shows up in Davidson's theory. Davidson, in company with Quine and Derrida, holds that any representation, whether in thought or words, must be languagelike in bearing only a contingent relation to any referent. That is, there are no magical words which interpret themselves, no *logoi,* no meanings in the sense of objects which represent but are not subject to misinterpretation. The meaning of a word can be given only in other words. Without intermediaries between words and the world, supplied by the magic language, the world is what the language describes, barring a "more genuine" Language which would Really Mean the world when its Words are applied to it.[15] If there are no "natural words," then there is nothing to meaning deeper than application in circumstances. But "circumstances" are, as it were, precisely fitted to words, in the sense that the circumstances in which "Fred is a frog" is true are precisely those in which Fred is a frog. As Davidson has argued, especially in "True to the Facts" (*ITI* 37–54), there are no entities making sentences true, so an appeal to "circumstances" in which "Fred is a frog" is true adds nothing to saying that "Fred is a frog" is true if and only if Fred is a frog.

I will argue that rhetorical force and logical form must be interchangeable in Davidson's accounts of meaning, truth, and interpretation. In explaining or interpreting a particular speech act, a Davidsonian interpreter makes underdetermined choices between explaining a feature as either owing to logical form or owing to rhetorical features of the speech act. Davidson's discussions of what I am calling "rhetoric" are to be found in his papers on force, mood, and convention.[16] Davidson's discussion of force (i.e., what a sentence is presented for) makes it clear that properties like sincerity, being serious, and being sarcastic cannot be governed by conventions and, thus, cannot have a "theory" in the usual sense. "Rhetorical force," though, is always part of what is ascribed to a speech act in interpretation.

In the next section, I illustrate the interchangeability of force and truth-conditions by examining the analyses a Davidsonian might give of sentences such as "Only Fred loves Susan." Intuitively, "Only Fred loves Susan" implies that Fred loves Susan. But the implication can be interpreted equally well either as rhetorical or as owing to logical form. Hence, only relative to an underdetermined interpretation does a sentence have truth-conditions. And thus, the distinction between rhetoric and logic is an artifact of theory, not there in the phenomena.

But, since the logical form determines whether the sentence is true, this means that the interpretation of the words is being apportioned between truth and rhetorical force, so that truth itself is relative to ascriptions of rhetorical intent. This is an indeterminacy of interpretation different from those noticed in the analytic tradition of writing about the philosophy of science. Such rhetorical indeterminacy is much like what de Man discusses in describing Rousseau's account of predication, where the rhetorical use of a term as a metaphor becomes a predication.[17] This "undecidability" between figural and literal amounts to an undecidability between assigning a meaning to a rhetorical connection or to a logical content.[18] None of Derrida's deconstructions has quite the form of an undecidability between explanation by rhetoric and explanation by logical form, because "logical form" is not a concept Derrida uses. But the transfer of difficulties of interpretation between difficulties of how something is meant and what it means pervades Derrida's discussions in (for instance) "Limited Inc."

Davidson is committed explicitly and implicitly to the same positions about texts and meaning as Derrida. For Davidson, truth really functions as an analytical interpretive concept rather than as a metaphysical concept. For Davidson, truth is not correspondence in any helpful sense (see "True to the Facts"). Most important, "true" applies to sentences, not to speech acts. Thus, for Davidson, a speech act is the production of a sentence with truth-conditions for a reason. (Therefore, commands and statements such as "I hereby pronounce you man and wife" have truth-values.) So an assignment of truth-conditions determines a kind of matrix on which rhetorical force can play. But the same overall result about what a person is doing in the act of speaking can be reached by alternative assignments of logical forms and rhetorical forces. Davidsonian "truth" has little to do with the Hegelian genitive "truth of" and even less to do with the positivist tradition of taking "fact stating" to be the privileged linguistic function.

CONVERSATIONAL AND OTHER IMPLICATURES

A basic device available to a Davidsonian interpreter is a version of the theory of conversational implicature.[19] Davidsonian interpretation is really just self-conscious application of the rules of thumb we all use in understanding what's up. There is no systematizable theory much more elaborate than the supposition that much of what people do is purposeful.[20] The interpretation consists of looking for reasons to explain the properties of what is said.

Such properties include the words, of course, as well as tone, stress pattern, underlining, italicizing, and so forth. Sometimes the ascription of purposes goes astray. So if your "stress pattern" is actually the result of hiccups, I can misread an accident as intended. I misread in a different way if you are using the stress pattern deceptively.

So, how does this apply in practice? Let us start with some simple examples of "informal fallacies." Suppose I say of my university's president, "He has never been caught stealing University funds," with emphasis on the "caught." This is insulting, and the insult has two kinds of explanation.

First, and formally, the claim that he has never been caught stealing University funds is weaker than the claim that he has never stolen University funds. "Weaker" here means that if he has never stolen funds, then it follows that he has never been caught, but not vice versa. Put otherwise, the class of stealers includes the class of those caught stealing as a proper part. So, given that the person said something on purpose, and given a general protocol that his purpose was to inform us, the person can be supposed to be saying the strongest relevant things he knows. So, the remark that the guy has never been caught "implies," rhetorically speaking, that he was stealing University funds.

The protocols here are reducible to our (socially learned or, in special cases, individually learned) theories of other people's theories of us and so forth. Such theories can then be used by speakers, together with what they know about their hearers, and about their hearers' knowledge of them etc., to say what they want. Thus, there are phrases which are almost always used sarcastically.

Second, less formally, much the same kind of interpretation occurs with the interpretation of the stress on "caught." Here, there is a feature of the speech act which we take to be produced on purpose. What could the purpose be? Why accent a word? Numerous explanations may suggest themselves in the indeterminate number of contexts in which stress patterns take place and require explanation. Here, the stress is interpretable as calling attention to the cautiousness (weakness) of the "caught," thus reinforcing the conversational implicature. (Note how the meaning changes with stress on "University.")

LOGICAL FORM AND FORCE

What do the above kinds of examples have to do with issues about truth and rhetorical force? The commonsense explanations of how we understand the quirks of speech and writing not only seem to leave the relations of truth and rhetoric untouched, but, most important, seem to require a rigorous line between the meanings and the maneuvers that are possible only by playing against such meanings. That is, in order even to state an account, sentences *per se* must have meanings. How, then, do we start to show interchangeability of rhetorical force and logical form?

To begin, this rhetorical use of meanings requires only that an interpretation *take* some truth-conditions to be the truth-conditions of the sentences in question. That is, an interpretation of a feature *as* rhetorical requires a decision on truth-conditions, which are then treated as presented for different reasons; but there may be several choices as to where the line is.

That there are such choices is illustrated by the following elaborated case, which shows the relevance of innuendo to the division into rhetoric and truth-conditions. Consider sentences using "only," such as "Only Fred loves Susan" and "Only the fair deserve the brave." The tempting analysis of these "only" sentences treats them as backward-quantified truth-functional conditionals. That is, "Only Fred loves Susan" is analyzed as "For all x, if x loves Susan, then x is Fred." Likewise, "Only the fair deserve the brave" becomes "For all x, if x deserves the brave, then x is fair." (Equivalently, this may be put "For all x, x deserves the brave only if x is fair." One of the pluses of this ascription of form is that the "only" in "only if" is the same as the "only" in "Only Fred.") Call this analysis "analysis A."

The difficulty with analysis A is that the nicest conditional is the truth-functional conditional,[21] according to which "Only Fred loves Susan" and "Only the fair deserve the brave" are true when Fred does not love Susan and the fair do not deserve the brave, so long as no one else does either. The conditional is true when the antecedent is false, so a universally quantified conditional is true when the antecedent is always false.[22] So, for these sentences to be true, as analyzed, it is sufficient that no one love Susan and that no one deserves the brave. Thus, the conditional analysis would require us to accept as noncontradictory the sentences "Only Fred loves Susan, and Fred doesn't love Susan" and "Only the fair deserve the brave, and the fair do not deserve the brave." Most astonishing, perhaps, is that the proposed analysis means that "Fred loves Susan" does not follow from "Only Fred loves Susan," and "The fair deserve the brave" does not follow from "Only the fair deserve the brave."

Most speakers of English find these consequences to be compelling evidence that analysis A is mistaken. The typical judgment is that "Fred loves Susan" follows from, is a logical consequence of, "Only Fred loves Susan." Now "x is a logical consequence of y" means that "if x is true, then y is true in virtue of the forms of x and y." Thus, if someone holds that "Fred loves Susan" follows from "Only Fred loves Susan," that person must hold that "Fred loves Susan" is included in the truth-conditions of "Only Fred loves Susan." The simplest way to include "Fred loves Susan" in those truth-conditions is to add that statement as a conjunct.

Thus, the alternative logical form—analysis B—for the above "only" sentences is "For all x, if x loves Susan then x is Fred, and Fred loves Susan" and "for all x, if x deserves the brave then x is fair; and, for all x, if x is fair then x deserves the brave." This analysis is sufficient to make our inferences, and it shares many of the pleasant features of the previous analysis, albeit somewhat less elegantly. The connection between "only" and "only if" is maintained, although "only" by itself requires us to import a conjunct. The "only" is a backward conditional, still, since a person who wishes to make "Fred loves Susan" follow logically from "Only Fred loves Susan" will analyze generalities as conjunctions of a quantified conditional and an existential generalization of the antecedent.

Is alternative B, then, clearly superior? Only if there is no other way to explain our intuition that if only Fred loves Susan, then Fred loves Susan. Analysis A must explain this intuition as a recognition not of logical consequence, but rather as a recognition of what any writer or speaker producing the sentences "implies" (in the rhetorical sense).

The original analysis—analysis A—would be defended along the lines of conversational implicature, as follows. "No one loves Susan" logically implies "Only Fred loves Susan," according to analysis A. Since the person is saying "Only Fred loves Susan," then either that person is misleading us or that is the strongest thing relevant to Susan and her relationships which that person knows. The person is implying that Fred loves Susan; for although "No one loves Susan" is one way in which "Only Fred loves Susan" could come out true, it is misleading to say "Only Fred loves Susan" when you believe that no one does. In the same way, it is misleading for me to say "I will be teaching either quantum mechanics or philosophy next year" when I know I will not be teaching quantum mechanics, even though what I have said is true. I am trying to impress you by implying, rhetorically, that there is some possibility of my teaching quantum mechanics next year.

That is to say, the only way that the sentence using "only" can be true and not misleading is when the stronger remark, "No one loves Susan," is false. But that means (implies) that Fred indeed loves Susan.

FORM AND FORCE:
THE INDETERMINACY OF TRUTH-CONDITIONS

There is nothing much to choose between these accounts. The one is somewhat more elegant, but the other gets the same implications more clearly. So, in the example at hand, how can we tell which of these kinds of implication, logical or conversational, is taking place? This, take notice, amounts to a question of how we can distinguish the meaning or truth-conditions of someone's sentence from the beliefs we can assign to the person by ascribing a normal rhetorical force to the utterance or writing. But in the case of the "only" sentence, the beliefs and desires can be the same: the speaker believes that only Fred loves Sue and wants us to believe it; so he is saying something which will convey his belief. That is, if there is any difference in the nature of the phenomena between rhetorical and logical connection, then something in the soul or brain or social structure must select one account over the other. Otherwise, "rhetorical" and "logical" will be characteristics of a theory presentation; they will be organizational choices, rather than reflections of real differences in kinds of connection.

Without the existence of a magic language, looking in the person's head will tell us nothing. Listening in our own heads will tell us nothing relevant. What we will see or hear in the head are sentences in sequence, perhaps. At least that is what I hear in my own head when I ask, "What do I mean by 'guinea pig'?" and get the answer "guinea pig—little eggplants with fur." How will we be able to distinguish the conjunct "and Fred loves Susan" as a logical *part* of the sentence "Only Fred loves Susan" from the same conjunct as an automatically accompanying belief?

According to Davidsonian interpretation, there can be no ontological distinction between logical and other connections, since meaning is not the translation into a magic language but, rather, truth-definition. So nothing "in the head" will fix logical form and distinguish consequences of form from rhetorical consequences. That distinction is relative to a particular interpretation and is an artifact of the interpretation. Put another way, there is just no genuine fact of the matter concerning which connections are genuinely logical and which are implications hanging on other features of words, since there is nothing helpfully deeper than words. Of course, there is more going on in language use than words, since language use occurs in an organism with perception, states, and a brain; but none of these other phenomena is magical in the way that the special magic language of the soul was supposed to be.

Davidson agrees entirely with Derrida that there is no difference in the nature of the connection in itself. There are no *logoi* behind logic. In a way, logical and rhetorical connection are both patterns in the behavior or inner causal workings of organisms in an environment. "Logic" and "rhetoric" sort those connections in an interdependent way. Once you choose a logical form, and truth-conditions, then the rest is rhetorical connection. The difference is entirely relative to the exigencies of a presentation, much like the distinction between axiom and theorem for Quine. Rhetorical force and logical form are two analytical factors between which is apportioned the task of giving a characterization of what people say in what circumstances.

Other dichotomies Derrida attacks are also implicitly attacked by Davidson. Now Davidson remains committed to the thesis that understanding a language is a matter of having a truth-definition, that logical form is an essential analytical tool. Would this be Derrida's view?

Since I have been arguing that Davidson is committed to Derridean positions, the question arises whether Derrida is committed to Davidsonian positions about truth-definition and the importance of form. The answer is a clear yes. Derrida's whole discussion in "Speech and Phenomena," for instance, is that the ascription of a form to a sign sequence is essential to taking it as a sign sequence at all. Derrida's "Signature Event Context" likewise makes the ascription of form the core of treating sentences *as* sentences. For Derrida, structure is *ascribed* rather than "there" in the phenomena intrinsically and determinately, since there are no purely present *logoi*. But this is also Davidson's view about our theories of the other, as I have shown above. While Derrida's interests do not bring him to investigate the details of structure, or to find out how particular forms operate, this cannot mean that he denies logical form. He is just a Davidsonian rather than a Tractarian Wittgensteinian on the nature of logical form.

Davidson is completely committed to undermining those firm foundations whose disappearance is lamented by all denouncers of deconstruction. Davidson recognizes explicitly the revolutionary character of his deconstructions of the various "dogmas of empiricism" and the more general dichotomies from which he has extricated himself. In "The Myth of the Subjective," for instance, Davidson says: "The fallout from these considerations for the theory of knowledge is (or ought to be) nothing less than revolutionary" ("MS" 164).

On the surface, Davidson seems to oppose much that the explicators have taken as central to Derrida. Davidson argues for a kind of "shared meanings," against the illusion that objects are "constructed,"[23] and generally speaks with the voice of sober reason. But Derrida utters similar remarks about the impossibility of making sense of "construction" as making objects out of a given manifold.[24] Furthermore, Derrida does not deny that there are "shared meanings" in any sense that Davidson would accept. What follows from his arguments is that there are no "shared meanings" in the sense of a magic language.

There are, of course, many differences between Derrida and Davidson. I am not quite sure how many of them would turn out to be unimportant, on examination. One clear difference is in their views of the extent to which philosophical notions (e.g., the dogmas of empiricism or logocentrism) infect the rest of the culture. Wittgenstein, Quine, and Davidson are on one side of this issue, roughly holding that philosophical critiques are marginal. Heidegger and Derrida are on the other, holding that philosophical deconstructions unhinge notions throughout the culture. So, for Derrida, once certain presuppositions about "sign" have been deconstructed, we cannot really talk coherently about signs; for, given that there is nothing better than words, our words carry the connections they have and cannot be simply excised from the network of connections which give them meaning. If philosophical concepts and theories are pervasive, then, the consequences of renouncing the magic language are much more widespread. In particular, the self-referential unhinging, which makes the current discussion itself part of the object of critique, follows only if the effect of philosophy is central.

While this difference is very important, accounting for a good deal of the difference in tone between Derrida and Davidson which cannot be accounted for by different background, they still share fundamental tenets. They are as close as Aristotle and Plato, let us say. Their joint study—especially when they reach astounding conclusions, such as that rhetoric and logic are interchangeable—is rewarding.

NOTES

1. The most important arguments for the premises behind this rejection are found in "Speech and Phenomena." In Derrida's terms, the cognitive meanings of terms are *logoi*, and philosophy which accepts *logoi* is "logocentric." Another very important text on these topics is *Of Grammatology*, especially part 1.

2. The explicit development of these lines of thought as about rhetoric is most clear in Paul de Man, especially in *Allegories of Reading*, notably the chapters on Rousseau.

3. I show how these arguments would be reconstructed in analytic terms in "The Extension of Deconstruction." The basic idea is that the distinction between rhetoric and logic depends on the analytic/synthetic distinction, the fact/value dichotomy, and the cognitive/emotive distinction. Without *logoi*, none of these distinctions will be principled dichotomies.

4. Some important papers on these topics are collected in Donald Davidson's *Inquiries into Truth and Interpretation*.

5. Davidson's classic papers on logical form are collected in *Inquiries into Truth and Interpretation*; see the five essays in the section "Truth and Meaning."

6. See especially "Moods and Performances" and "Communication and Convention" (*ITI* 109–21, 265–80).

7. I develop some of these analogies in "Indeterminacy of French Interpretation: Derrida and Davidson."

8. This idea that there are "philosophical problems" which cut across traditions contradicts what some have taken to be a consequence of deconstruction. That is, such philosophical problems seem to presuppose interlinguistic *logoi* in which such questions can be formulated. But just as indeterminacy of translation allows that we can still say that Joe means that snow is white, so deconstruction of the magic language still allows that people can think about the same things. "Same," though, cannot mean "same *logos*." But that means only that "same" cannot be applied if the existence of the magic language is indeed essential to the possibility of thought and speech. That is, to insist that we cannot meaningfully speak of the "same philosophical problem" without assuming a magic language is to assume the very standpoint which deconstruction and Davidson remove. The issue is whether there is something between the perfect sameness that *logoi* (the words of the magic language) permit and nothing at all. I would argue that there is every reason to think that the terms of a natural language, including "same philosophical problem," function without needing *logoi* (I have so argued in "Wittgenstein as Conservative Deconstructor"). So, while there is no "same problem" in the sense that *logoi* would permit, we can still properly say that the discourses are troubled by the same problem. How to think about philosophical problems and distinctions without supposing the foundations that *logoi* permit is in fact one of the major philosophical problems that I hope the joint study of Derrida and Davidson can illuminate. This is not to deny that there is a very tricky problem with saying how distinctions which have had their theoretical home in a logocentric discourse can be used after the suppositions of *logoi* are abandoned. The problem is very widespread: in "Limited Inc," for example, Derrida wants to claim that Searle misreads him in "Reiterating the Differences: A Reply to Derrida," even though there can be no principled line between misreading and correct reading without a *logos* to match.

9. This self-referential sentence reminds us that a denial that a distinction can be founded on the basis of pure *logoi* does not mean that the distinction cannot be used. So there is something like the same form in different matter, and there is a difference between rhetorical and logical connection. But such differences need not imply that there is such a thing as a logical connection which is in no way rhetorical, any more than there is pure form, or a word which has nothing but the meaning it shares with other words.

10. "Pragmatics," the formal study of how the truth-values of context-dependent sentences vary according to context of utterance, would seem to fall under "logical" properties, if indeed pragmatics is able to become formal. On the other hand, to the extent that the formal theory is incomplete, pragmatics would be part of rhetoric. Or what? I think the difficulty of drawing a good line is another indication that there is no distinction in kind.

11. Derrida deconstructs the self-presenting essence required for *logoi* to supply their own interpretation ("Speech and Phenomena").

12. I take this to be a main result of Aristotle's *Metaphysics*, especially book zeta.

13. This is a different but intricately related point from those marshaled by Sellars in "Empiricism and the Philosophy of Mind." There, Sellars argues that sense data cannot both be objects and representations which can function as premises of arguments. Roughly, the properties of the sign relation, and the fact that sense data must have truth-values to function as premises, combine to undo the idea of a "given" foundation to knowledge.

14. Here I have summarized and simplified some of Derrida's arguments in "Speech and Phenomena."

15. Briefly, for Davidson, the meaning of a word is determined by what people say in what circumstances. So meaning cannot deviate from the world. Interestingly, both Davidson and Derrida hold that the issue between realism and nonrealism is a nonissue because the initial divisions, for instance into world and conceptual scheme, cannot be made coherently. They are dogmas of empiricism or deconstructible binary oppositions.

16. Namely: "Moods and Performances" and "Communication and Convention." It is interesting that, in these papers, Davidson makes many of the same points that Derrida makes in "Signature Event Context." A basic idea is that there can be no convention for the way a sentence is meant, since any such convention could be used for other purposes. For Davidson as well as for Derrida, these "marginal" nonstandard cases show the impossibility of a genuine conventional account of speech acts; for Davidson as well as for Derrida, interpretation will not be reduced to an algorithm.

17. See Paul de Man, *Allegories of Reading*, especially the chapter on Rousseau. I explore in some detail the resemblances between Davidson's and de Man's treatments of metaphor in "Metaphor in Davidson and de Man." It is striking that both de Man and Davidson treat "metaphorical meaning" as a difference in force. De Man's account of "self-deconstructing texts" involves difficulties which are too complicated for a footnote.

18. Derrida does not want to use the term "indeterminate" because that term suggests to him vagueness, fuzzy boundaries, or no definition. His term "undecidable," though, would be unacceptable to Quine and Davidson because of its Gödelian overtones. In fact, the phenomena they are labeling seem to me to be much the same: there can be distinct global interpretations, each of which is quite precise; these global interpretations can be seen as centered around the interpretation of a particular term. Derrida's clearest statement of this position is in the afterword to *Limited Inc.*

19. The most thorough presentation of the classic account of conversational implicature is Paul Grice's *Studies in the Way of Words*.

20. There is no systematizable theory because the interpretation of persons is theory formation, and there is no algorithm for that. There is no telling what new terminology or practices could come up, and no "routine" can give us ways of inventing new terms.

21. One reason to choose "only" sentences for our illustration is that the "paradoxes" of the

truth-functional conditional show up even though there is nothing especially indicating a connection or "strong" conditional in "only" sentences.

22. I am ignoring accounts on which a universal claim "presupposes" that the class in question has members. Such accounts give up too much for too little. Conversational implicature can handle the points that make presupposition have a point, and the logical theory is far more elegant.

23. The primary article here is "On the Very Idea of a Conceptual Scheme" (*ITI* 183–98).

24. The discussions of "trace" and "différance" as being "before being," as "not concepts and not beings either" (see "Différance," reprinted in *Speech and Phenomena,* and the first section of *Of Grammatology*) reflect some of the same sorts of considerations that lead Davidson to regard the idea that a "conceptual scheme" categorizes reality. That is, to have a manifold able to be sorted is already to have applied concepts and, thus, to know there can be truths about how things are prior to anything which could have a truth-definition. Derrida, admittedly, insists on trying to talk about that which, by his own account, really cannot be spoken or written about. This also manifests itself in his willingness to talk about the world as a context to which there are alternatives (see the afterword in *Limited Inc.*).

WORKS CITED

De Man, Paul. *Allegories of Reading.* New Haven: Yale UP, 1979.

Derrida, Jacques. "Limited Inc a b c." Trans. Samuel Weber. *Glyph* 2 (1977): 162–254. Reprinted in *Limited Inc.* Evanston: Northwestern UP, 1988.

———. *Of Grammatology.* Trans. Gayatri Chakravorty Spivak. Baltimore: Johns Hopkins UP, 1976.

———. "Signature Event Context." Trans. Samuel Weber and Jeffrey Mehlman. *Glyph* 1 (1977): 172–97. Reprinted in *Limited Inc.* Evanston: Northwestern UP, 1988.

———. *Speech and Phenomena and Other Essays on Husserl's Phenomenology.* Trans. David B. Allison. Evanston: Northwestern UP, 1973.

Grice, Paul. *Studies in the Way of Words.* Cambridge: Harvard UP, 1989.

Searle, John R. "Reiterating the Differences: A Reply to Derrida." *Glyph* 1 (1977): 198–208.

Sellars, Wilfrid. "Empiricism and the Philosophy of Mind." In *Science, Perception, and Reality.* London: Routledge & Kegan Paul, 1963. 127–96.

Wheeler, Samuel C. III. "The Extension of Deconstruction." *The Monist* 69, no. 1 (1986): 3–21.

———. "Indeterminacy of French Interpretation: Derrida and Davidson." In *Truth and Interpretation: Perspectives on the Philosophy of Donald Davidson.* Ed. Ernest LePore. Oxford: Basil Blackwell, 1986. 477–94.

———. "Metaphor in Davidson and de Man." In *Redrawing the Lines: Analytic Philosophy, Deconstruction, and Literary Theory.* Ed. Reed Way Dasenbrock. Minneapolis: U of Minnesota P, 1989. 116–39.

———. "Wittgenstein as Conservative Deconstructor." *New Literary History* 19, no. 2 (1988): 239–58.

On the Very Idea of a
Literal Meaning

MARK GAIPA and ROBERT SCHOLES

In many of his essays in *Inquiries into Truth and Interpretation*, Donald Davidson undertakes to clean the house of philosophy by asking his fellow residents to part with some furniture. But among his readers are those who, like ourselves, have built homes around the study of literature yet have had occasion, under the promptings of critical theory, to visit our philosophical neighbors from time to time. Although the ramshackle cottage we inhabit hardly compares with that stately house on the hill, we can see that the intellectual equipment Davidson is throwing out—in particular, talk about "conceptual schemes" and the "meaning" of metaphors—resembles the furniture that we enjoy in our less elegant domain. Metaphor, of course, lies at the heart of traditional literary interpretation, and conceptual schemes, in the form of cultural codes or ideologies, have become crucial to much of recent literary criticism. If such terms are really not proper for philosophers, then students of literature may well be concerned about the utility—or at least the fashionableness—of this equipment in their own intellectual space. We must consider the possibility that, if Davidson is right, literary studies will also need to undertake a housecleaning—one that could reach such proportions as to leave few traces of the house itself.

As Reed Way Dasenbrock's recent article "Do We Write the Text We Read?" indicates, literary scholars are already attempting to use Davidson's ideas against such theorists as Stanley Fish and Barbara Herrnstein Smith. While we are not ready to leap to the defense of Smith and Fish (who can take care of themselves), we do feel that serious scrutiny of Davidson's arguments will reveal problems that should make us hesitate before using his work as a blueprint for changes in literary study. In the pages that follow, we will attempt to show how the discussions of metaphor in "What Metaphors Mean" and of conceptual schemes in "On the Very Idea of a Conceptual Scheme" should make even philosophers hesitate before accepting Davidson's views on these matters. We take the two together because it seems to us that Davidson's discussions of metaphor and schemes are so similar as to be almost versions of the same argument. And yet, as we shall see, the arguments also "jam" one another in certain respects, generating contradictions that call into question the adequacy of either view.

In "What Metaphors Mean," Davidson argues that a proper understanding of metaphors should lead us to dispense entirely with the notion of figurative meaning: "The central mistake against which I shall be inveighing is the idea that a metaphor has, in addition to its literal sense or meaning, another sense or meaning" (*ITI* 246). Although the essay mantains a focus on metaphors, it is clear that Davidson's real target is the notion of figurative meaning in whatever guise. He describes it variously as a *special* (or *second,* or *coded,* or *hidden*) meaning; as a *poetic truth locked up* or *lodging* in the ordinary words of a metaphor; as the *cognitive* meaning of a trope that can be extracted only by a special interpretive effort. He argues that such figurative meanings do not actually exist, and that we go wrong by assuming there could ever be anything worthy of the name "meaning" that could be other than literal meaning. The distinction, then, between literal and figurative meaning can be abolished as in itself meaningless. In its place he asks us to accept another distinction between what words mean and how they are used, although how words can be used for anything but meaning is far from clear. This new distinction (between meaning and use) enables Davidson to talk about something beyond literal meaning that is nevertheless too vague and slippery to be called meaningful. On this basis, metaphors can be newly explained as a certain use we have for literal meaning, akin to such other verbal activities as lying, joking, and promising.

Figurative use, however, does not imply that figurative meaning exists. Davidson believes that the notion of figurative meaning hinges on a contradiction, and that any account of metaphor based on belief in a figurative meaning will share the same confusions: "on the one hand, the usual view wants to hold that a metaphor does something no plain prose can possibly do and, on the other hand, it wants to explain what a metaphor does by appealing to a cognitive content—just the sort of thing plain prose is designed to express" (261). The notion of metaphor Davidson is critiquing here is the interaction theory, promoted vigorously by I. A. Richards and Max Black, which sees metaphor as a source of new meaning, so special and original that ordinary language, with its overused and tired terms, can hardly hope to translate it. Because literal paraphrase is inadequate to the task of expressing a metaphor's meaning, we must, according to this theory of metaphor, at some point intuit a meaning for metaphors that we cannot fully express in other language. We find ourselves sympathetic to Davidson's critique of the extreme versions of this theory. What we shall be questioning, however, is a certain extremity in his own views. Both the strengths and the weaknesses of his position emerge if we consider together his critique of metaphor and his critique of conceptual schemes.

The problem with the interaction view of metaphor, according to Davidson, is that it pulls us in two directions at once, depicting figurative meaning as both "alongside" literal meaning and yet also somehow "beyond" it: on the one hand, metaphor has cognitive content and "conveys truths or falsehoods about the world much as plainer language does"; on the other hand, our not being able to explain it in literal terms tells us that it is a completely distinct kind (or order) of meaning, in which "the message may be considered more exotic, profound, or cunningly garbed" (246). Davidson's argument against conceptual schemes is couched in similar language. In "On the Very Idea of a Conceptual Scheme," he calls conceptual relativism "a heady and exotic doctrine" (*ITI* 183) and claims that, like figurative meaning, it, too, hinges on a contradiction: "the dominant metaphor of conceptual relativism, that of differing points of view, seems to betray an underlying paradox. Different points of view make sense, but only if there is a common co-ordinate system on which to plot them; yet the existence of a common system belies the claim of dramatic incomparability" (184).

Davidson positions the view of metaphor he is critiquing so that the proponents of metaphorical meaning must deny the possibility of paraphrase, and, by a parallel move, he positions the proponents of conceptual schemes so that they must deny the possibility of translation between one scheme and another. The elegance of these moves should be appreciated. Davidson argues that the only way you could know a metaphorical meaning was actually present would be to paraphrase it, in which case, by making it literal, you will have denied its status as metaphor. Similarly, the only way you could know an alternative conceptual scheme existed would be to describe or "translate" it, in which case you will have shown that it is not really different from the one in which the description was couched. In both cases, Davidson works by reducing to zero the distance between what we can know and what we can say. "Nothing," he writes, "could count as evidence that some form of activity could not be interpreted in our language that was not at the same time evidence that that form of activity was not speech behaviour" (185). Because "translatability into a familiar tongue [is] a criterion of languagehood" (186), nothing counts as a language that cannot be translated into English. This Wittgensteinian view seeks to undermine the basis for conceptual relativism by making our ability to identify other conceptual schemes depend upon our ability to translate them. If poetry is, as Robert Frost said, what gets lost in translation, then it could not have been meaningful in the first place.

To test this view, let us turn back to the decorative metaphor that graced our opening paragraph. How does one know a metaphor is present here? Since metaphor, according to Davidson, is a special use we have for the ordinary meaning of words, any recognition of metaphor relies on our grasping what the words in the metaphor normally mean and how they are normally used. When we read the sentence "Davidson undertakes to clean the house of philosophy by asking his fellow residents to part with some furniture," we must be able to grasp the literal meaning of the words in order to notice that there is something wrong about this way of using them together. Even without reading Davidson's book, one could guess that it is not really about interior decoration, nor is the reader likely to think that actual philosophers live happily (or unhappily) together in some stately mansion. If we could not recognize the semantic impertinence or literal impropriety of this expression (whereby we know that academic disciplines are not really dwellings), we would not be able to identify it as a metaphor. But this alone is not enough, for semantic impertinence could have, besides metaphor, other uses or aims (like deception, absurdity, irony) or even nonuses (like error). Therefore, seeing such phrases as metaphorical further requires us to credit their author with some purpose. We can articulate what it is that a metaphor is doing (what the literal words which compose it are being used for) only to the extent that we can devise "paraphrases" for it. In this example, the process entails asking—and then answering—how an academic discipline, though not really a home, is nonetheless like a home. If we are unable to begin explicating with ordinary language whatever likeness this metaphor brings to mind, not only have we not grasped the metaphor, we have not even grasped that we are confronted with a metaphor.

By claiming that we can identify as metaphors only those expressions that we can "translate" or "paraphrase," Davidson has made good on his intention to dissolve the distinction between figurative and literal meaning, for now we have but a single plane of meaning at our disposal. This move, however, brings with it a new problem: too much success at paraphrasing would seem to eliminate the existence of metaphor altogether. To forestall this possibility, Davidson relies on the distinction between meaning and use to ensure that our paraphrases have something left over, some excess of metaphorical use which, though not meaningful itself, puts us on notice that more meaning is required. All told, Davidson's theory of metaphor assures us of two things. First, we will be able to formulate a paraphrase for any metaphor we can identify, and, second, we will *not* be able to arrive at a paraphrase that is wholly satisfactory or complete. The only fully paraphrasable metaphors, in his view, are dead metaphors.

Davidson believes that we can have it both ways—insisting that no literal translation of a metaphor will do, but also maintaining that literal translations are all that we have—only if we stop trying to describe the "vision" produced by the metaphor as an essence that inspirits the metaphor and directs our understanding of it. In his view, it is a mistake to think of such a likeness as something that exists prior to the metaphor itself and that, if articulated, could reveal what the metaphor means; rather, the likeness is what a metaphor calls into being and, as such, is ultimately indistinguishable from the various literal paraphrases of it that we may provide. Only by making interpretation at once necessary and unlimited is Davidson able to dislodge cognitive content from the heart of a metaphor. By doing so he forces us to reconceive of "paraphrase" (which presumably stands outside the metaphor, occurs after it, and necessarily misrepresents its meaning) as somehow original and interior to the metaphor. With so-called paraphrase as the original condition for what metaphors mean, any interpretation of a metaphor must start with competing alternative expressions, none of which points to some more determinate originary meaning that can reconcile them all.

For Davidson, as we see it, metaphors would not exist, and we could not understand them, if we could not express in unlimited and undetermined ways what it is they call to our attention. Such a view of metaphor redresses the limitations of previous accounts by, on the one hand, refusing to posit a second realm of meaning while, on the other hand, not trivializing metaphors by reducing them to a literal equivalent. By rejecting the notion of a cognitive content that antedates the metaphor in the form of an unarticulated yet knowable likeness, Davidson folds the process of interpreting a metaphor into its identity as metaphor, thereby blurring any distinction between what the metaphor means and how it is used. He thus shows that the problem lies not in our inability to paraphrase a metaphor, but in our belief that we should be able to reconcile the various paraphrases we come up with under a central cognitive content—the "figurative meaning" that inevitably eludes our grasp.

Although we have previously argued that Davidson's view of metaphor runs parallel to his view of conceptual schemes, our above discussion marks the point where these views diverge. Whereas the endlessness of metaphorical paraphrase requires that some residue be left behind by any particular attempt to explain what a metaphor means, Davidson does not allow for such a residue when we translate another conceptual scheme into our own. This seems to imply that conceptual schemes are themselves fully literal or, as Davidson argues, that only what can be put into our language can count as language. This view, if it does not simply beg the very question under discussion, strongly suggests that conceptual schemes have to do with meaning and not with use. But language, or "speech behavior," to use his term, is made up of semantics, syntactics, and pragmatics—not just meaning but usage as well. This divergence in Davidson's views of metaphor and conceptual schemes has other implications to which we shall return, but first we must consider another problem within his theory of metaphor itself.

That problem has to do with the relative quality of different paraphrases of any given metaphor. There is ample evidence that Davidson does not consider all paraphrases equal. We believe that he would agree with us that some paraphrases of a metaphor are more relevant, resonant, or pertinent than others—even if none of them can ever be perfect or complete. This part of Davidson's theory is complicated by the way the word "paraphrase" resists literal meaning in this context. If there is no cognitive content or "meaning" there to be paraphrased, then the word "paraphrase" itself must be functioning metaphorically, with some residue of meaning always remaining to disrupt its literal significance. Moreover, if some phrases are more "para" than others, this greater adequacy would then require some basis for comparison. But Davidson observes that "the endless character of what we call the paraphrase of a metaphor springs from the fact that it attempts to spell out what the metaphor makes us notice, and to this there is no clear end" (*ITI* 263).

Philosophers like clear ends. It is a pity that there are so few of them in this world and in the language we use to talk about it. It is not clear, here, for instance, whether Davidson means there is no end to what a metaphor calls to our attention or no end to our reporting on the result of this attentive act. But surely there is no clear end to the noticing of anything in this world—or to our spelling out some version of that noticing. This does not prevent us, however, from selecting what it is important to notice and then reporting, selectively, on that. Just so, a metaphor, insofar as it "makes" us notice anything, must involve such an act of selection on the part of its maker and its paraphrasers. Most metaphors actually seem to foreground certain potentials for meaning— and, often, a rather limited set of such possibilities. Even without a "clear end," then, it should not be hard to distinguish between a paraphrase that is to the point and one that is off the wall. This is implied in Davidson's suggestion that "the legitimate function of so-called paraphrase is to make the lazy or ignorant reader have a vision like that of the skilled critic" (264).

This revealing sentence will repay a little study. If a metaphor "makes" us notice something and a paraphrase "makes" us have a vision of something, what, then, is the difference between a metaphor and a paraphrase? Both, in Davidson's formulations, seem to coerce us, to force us to be aware of something visual, something that is not verbal, not literal. But the similarity of these two coercions suggests some serious problems in Davidson's notion of metaphor. One problem, of course, is that Davidson's theory requires that paraphrase be distinctly different from metaphor—to be, in fact, literal—while his language here betrays a failure to sustain this crucial difference. Another problem has to do with the visual emphasis of both formulations. An Aristotelian "eye for resemblances" seems to lurk in both of them. This assimilation of metaphor to the visual obscures the fact that many metaphors depend more upon the matching of verbal connotations than upon any specifically visual resemblances. The final problem, and the one we are concentrating on here, lies in Davidson's failure to address the criteria that might enable us to distinguish the paraphrase of a "skilled critic" from one produced by a "lazy or ignorant" reader.

If metaphors have no meaning, then all paraphrases ought to be equal— as paraphrases—or be judged without reference to the texts they paraphrase. Davidson tries to make "use" stand in for "meaning" in this case; but if use is distinguished too clearly from meaning, it will not support the evaluations Davidson finds it necessary to invoke, precisely because it risks being meaningless. And if it cannot be distinguished clearly from meaning, then the notion of "use" is useless. If we look carefully at his discussion of T. S. Eliot's poem "The Hippopotamus," we can begin to see how untenable Davidson's distinction between use and meaning actually is. For our purposes, these are the relevant stanzas:

> The broad-backed hippopotamus
> Rests on his belly in the mud;
> Although he seems so firm to us
> He is merely flesh and blood.

> Flesh and blood is weak and frail,
> Susceptible to nervous shock;
> While the True Church can never fail
> For it is based upon a rock.

> [quoted in *ITI* 256]

In his reading, Davidson notes how the poem uses words metaphorically "to direct our attention to similarities" between the True Church and the hippopotamus, but he distinguishes this implicit metaphor from what the poem literally says: "The hippopotamus really does rest on his belly in the mud; the True Church, the poem says literally, never can fail." Davidson continues: "The poem does, of course, intimate much that goes beyond the literal meaning of the words. But intimation is not meaning" (256).

What can Davidson mean when he claims that "the *poem says literally*" that "the True Church ... never can fail"? What, precisely, can he mean by the word "literally" in this context? Surely, the notion of a poem saying something is already at least one step out of the literal and into the figurative, which means that the word "literally" itself can hardly be taken literally in this context. But let us not dwell on that. What we take him to mean is that all English-speaking people who read this poem will, at some basic level, understand the line the same way: namely, as meaning "the True Church can never fail." But suppose that some people, such as ourselves, find the literal meaning here elusive. Take the word "church" for instance. This is a word that comes with more than one "literal" or customary meaning. It can refer to a physical edifice, of course, but is used just as often to refer to an institution. The Church of Rome is a church and so is St. Peter's Cathedral. Certainly the expression "True Church," with its capital letters, looks, in its written form, like a reference to an institution. But is the institutional meaning the literal one? And if so, to which institution does it refer? Davidson might wish to argue here that "True Church" has the literal meaning of "whatever Church you think is true"—but this would merely show how the literal meaning is already determined by the way we use the word. Or, he might say that we know what "true" means and what "church" means, and that the capitalization and combination of them moves them toward the figurative. But in what sense do we begin the process of reading or writing with a simple and literal meaning for such words as "true" and "church"?

The problem here is one of determining the level at which the notion of a "literal" meaning may be said to operate. Is literal meaning supposed to be present in language only, or in its use as utterance? That is, does a word have a literal meaning before it is used or after it is used? If the literal meaning of a word is supposed to be present in language before the word is used in any specific utterance, then we should not have to resort to interpretation in order to understand the literal. If, on the other hand, the literal meaning appears only after a word is used, then use is implicated in meaning from the very beginning. A glance at any dictionary will expose the problems of the first option, for most of the words listed come not with a single literal meaning but with a range of probable or potential meanings. In any given situation, a reader or listener must sift through these possibilities, using the appropriate codes and contextual information to select the "literal" meaning for that particular case. We can come closer to a literal meaning for "True Church," for instance, if we know whether the "poem" is speaking in the code of an Anglican or a Roman Catholic—or a member of some other sect. Because different codes and contexts generate different significations out of the same signifiers, understanding always depends on these factors. The very idea of a "literal" meaning obscures the process of understanding by suggesting that clarity and specificity are a property of words which precedes their use in utterance. If what Davidson calls "use" is, as we claim, already present in the determination of what he calls "literal" meaning, then we must entertain the possibility that use goes all the way down. And this means that if we are going to deny meaning to metaphors, so must we deny meaning to literal language. The meaning/use distinction will not work, because meaning is always a product of both semantics and pragmatics, of language and use.

Davidson's theory of metaphor depends not only upon a radical distinction between meaning and use but also on a similar distinction between literal language, with its singular fixed meanings, and figurative language which requires endless interpretation. We, on the other hand, are arguing that so-called literal meanings are always to some extent interpretations and, also, that most metaphorical meanings, though not fixed, are relatively limited or clustered around a few possibilities. The extreme difficulty (if not impossibility) of sorting out literal and figurative meanings can be illustrated by looking a bit further into Davidson's own reading of Eliot's "The Hippopotamus." There, if we remember, Davidson wrote that "the True Church, the poem says literally, never can fail"; but the poem actually reads: "the True Church can never fail / For it is based upon a rock." Although we do not want to indict Davidson for selective quoting, we think it is worth noting that he defends the literal meaning of the first part of Eliot's proposition only after bracketing it off from the more metaphorical conclusion. How would things be different if Davidson had written: "the True Church, the poem says literally, is based upon a rock"? If the True Church is some unspecified Christian institution, the literal meaning would seem to be that this institution rests physically upon some particular large stone. The impossibility or "untruthfulness" of this, in Davidson's account, would be an indication that we may have a metaphor here—or a lie, or a joke. What it cannot be, according to Davidson, is an attempt "to 'say something' special, no matter how indirectly" (259).

Yet saying something special is precisely the function of this phrase, for Eliot is alluding here to a metaphor made by the founder of the "True Church," when he exploited the literal word for stone (*petra*) hiding in the name of his first pope: "Thou art Peter, and upon this rock I will build my church; and the gates of hell shall not prevail against it" (Matt. 16:18). It is as if, in English, he had said, "You are Rocky and upon this rock I will build my church." This is a metaphor based on a pun, but the meaning of it is as clear as many "literal" meanings. A proper name like Peter or Rocky refers (literally? properly?) to any individual who bears it, but it also incorporates a metaphor of toughness or reliability. It was because Peter was tough, leaping to defend Jesus physically at his arrest, that Jesus thought him strong enough to be the first pope. In the case of this particular Peter, the metaphor could be read with an almost literal directness—but only by way of the context of Peter's past behavior and a common code in which rock is a metaphor for toughness. Although this thoroughly motivated pun might be missed by any "lazy or ignorant" reader, unearthing it is not a matter of endless interpretation but, rather, as Davidson well knows, one of knowledge and thought. The complex of metaphorical meaning here is precise and focused. In fact, Jesus on this occasion is speaking in a way typical of his preaching: in parable form. A parable—which is nothing more than an extended metaphor—always has a literal meaning and an intended figurative meaning that is supposed to be as plain to the initiates as the literal meaning. "He that hath ears to hear," says Jesus, "let him hear" (Mark 4:9). Literally this means that only those with physical ears should listen; surely, however, this utterance does not open out into some limitless range of possible other meanings, but focuses rather narrowly on a second meaning just as simple as the first: "he who understands my code, let him take my meaning." Even though this second signification is implied or intimated by the first, that hardly prevents us from seeing it as a specific meaning. Such relative simplicity or directness can be found in many modern uses of metaphor, both in and out of poems. In the present case, Eliot's text operates in much the same way as that of Jesus. His use of "the True Church is based upon a rock" equally implies an audience of initiates who will find his meaning because they share his code. In place of Davidson's distinction between the "skilled" interpreter and the "lazy or ignorant" reader, we would make a distinction between those who possess the relevant intepretive protocols or codes and those who do not.

We have seen how codes legitimize the notion of "metaphorical meaning" by providing an interpretive framework that can "limit" the potentially endless ways a metaphor may be paraphrased. Possessed of such a framework, a critic is in a position to measure one paraphrase against another. By rejecting the use of codes or protocols of reading, Davidson forces himself to operate without any means of accepting or rejecting "lazy or ignorant" paraphrases. Indeed, he must wait for a metaphor to die before he can assign it meaning. As a result of this, he cannot distinguish between striking or "poetic" metaphors and more ordinary uses of figurative language, since both of these are alike "meaningless," while, at the same time, he must insist on a sharp distinction between a stale metaphor—one that may be mortally ill—and one that has been pronounced dead. Because the "death" of a metaphor is itself metaphorical, Davidson's use of this trope is revealing. By making the line between metaphorical death and life so crucial, Davidson obscures all the gradations between the most original, startling, and vigorous tropes and those which function merely to enliven or adorn ordinary conversation or academic prose. Moreover, the metaphor of death itself obscures the fact that there is no metaphor so dead that it cannot be brought back to life in the proper context, including the metaphor of the death of metaphor, which we can galvanize by just taking it seriously and literally.

Let us look, for instance, at his own example of a dead metaphor—the expression "he was burned up," which he calls "the corpse of a metaphor." Davidson says that this expression "now suggests no more than that he was very angry. When the metaphor was active, we would have pictured fire in the eyes or smoke coming out of the ears" (253). Similarly, he cites "the mouth of the bottle" as a dead metaphor because "there is nothing left to notice" here, whereas when the phrase was an active metaphor it would have caused us to notice "a likeness between animal and bottle openings" (252). But if there is nothing to notice, how did he notice it? That is, how could we distinguish an instance of "literal" language from a "dead" metaphor without noticing that the metaphor is different precisely by being, to some extent, metaphorical? Because we cannot identify a dead metaphor without simultaneously reviving it, we can conclude that all the dead metaphors we know of are not really dead.

Our argument here, it should be noted, is a Davidsonian kind of argument, which leads us to wonder why he has not made it himself and dropped the metaphor of death altogether in this case. We surmise—and it is only a surmise—that too much is at stake here for him to make this logical move. One of those stakes is the sharp distinction between meaning and use upon which his view of metaphor rests. Because a "dead metaphor" has crossed over from one side of this absolute distinction to the other—from being a "use" of another literal meaning to having a single, literal meaning of its own—it marks the point in Davidson's thinking where the endlessness of metaphorical paraphrase has given way to the finiteness of literal definition. What makes Davidson's view of the matter implausible is the way this shift must be sudden, not gradual: for, if he were to acknowledge a continuum between a dead metaphor and its past metaphoricity, he would have to confront the possibility that paraphrases of a metaphor have some bearing on its current literal meaning. This would at once make literal meaning susceptible to endless paraphrase, and metaphorical intimations susceptible to finite meaning. To avoid compromising the meaning/use distinction in this way, Davidson represses the fact that "so-called" dead metaphors retain a lingering metaphorical residue. The price for maintaining these rigid distinctions between live and dead, use and meaning, however, is an inability to account for the processes of transition from one state to the other.

By digging into the problems of evaluation (of paraphrases and of metaphors themselves) we have unearthed another problem in Davidson's view of language: the problem of how to consider and discuss semantic change. How is it that—in Davidson's own words—old words take on new uses? And, in particular, what might be the status of "literal" meaning during this process of endless change? If literal meaning is always prior to metaphorical use, why should literal meaning ever change? And, if it does, are both the new and the old meanings still "literal"—or does the old meaning simply vanish into the mists of "use"? It seems to us that problems of this sort are exactly what Thomas Kuhn's theory of schemes or "paradigms" is intended to address, which makes Davidson's hostility to that theory understandable.

Kuhn is trying to make sense of shifts within language systems or of transferences between such systems. Davidson tries to reject Kuhn's theories by refuting passages such as this one, which he quotes in "On the Very Idea of a Conceptual Scheme." We include Davidson's immediate response to it, as it will later prove important to our argument:

> "In the transition from one theory to the next words change their meanings or conditions of applicability in subtle ways. Though most of the same signs are used before and after a revolution— e.g. force, mass, element, compound, cell—the way in which some of them attach to nature has somehow changed. Successive theories are thus, we say, incommensurable" (Kuhn, "Reflections on my Critics," 267).
>
> "Incommensurable" is, of course, Kuhn and Feyerabend's word for "not intertranslatable." The neutral content waiting to be organized is supplied by nature. [*ITI* 190]

Kuhn observes that the same signs carry different meanings after a paradigm shift. It is the sameness of the signifiers, combined with the difference in signifieds, that indicates the presence of two conceptual schemes, of two different codes vying for control of certain words within language. Davidson's objection here centers on the question how we might verify such a difference between two schemes (or signifieds), if both of them make use of the same signifiers. He takes up this question in the following passage, but not without a curious reformulation of the problem as Kuhn has presented it:

> Suppose that in my office of Minister of Scientific Language I want the new man to stop using words that refer, say, to emotions, feelings, thoughts, intentions, and to talk instead of the physiological states and happenings that are assumed to be more or less identical with the mental riff and raff. How do I tell whether my advice has been heeded if the new man speaks a new language? For all I know, the shiny new phrases, though stolen from the old language in which they refer to physiologi-

cal stirrings, may in his mouth play the role of the messy old mental concepts. [*ITI* 188–89]

At first, Davidson seems to have reversed the order of things here: for if Kuhn explores the possibility of an old signifier taking on a new signified, Davidson is ostensibly addressing how a new signifier may nonetheless be used (by the new man) to refer to the old signified. Yet this difference does not affect the capacity for each scenario to raise the same issue of how one can tell from the words a person uses what conceptual scheme lies behind those words. Davidson claims that in his scenario we have "no basis for judging the new scheme to be the same as, or different from, the old" (189). But what has he really proved? Not that different codes do not exist—only that we cannot determine a meaning by the mere presence of a particular word. He has demonstrated, in short, that if words do not come with single literal meanings, then we must search beyond the confines of the speaker's mouth—that is, we must refer to cultural codes and contexts—in order to appreciate what meaning is being evoked.

Let us illustrate this point with a more humble example. In a certain novel a character is said to experience "a longing to be made love to by Duke again." What are we to suppose this means? In contemporary English, the phrase would unambiguously refer to a desire for renewed sexual intercourse. In its actual context, a novel of 1927 by E. M. Delafield, *The Way Things Are* (262), it refers, just as unambiguously, to a desire to be wooed or flirted with again, in a situation where sexual intercourse has definitely not occurred. The "same words," in the "same language," nevertheless bear significantly different (indeed, in this instance, incompatible) literal meanings. What we have here is the palpable presence of two different codes (codes which are partly social and partly linguistic) that have operated at different times within (or upon) the "same" English language. The very fact that nothing in the words themselves allows us to distinguish between the two meanings—and between the two codes—hardly proves that such a distinction is unwarranted or unintelligible. To establish a literal meaning for the words "make love" we must "translate" or "paraphrase" that expression in one way or another. Literal meaning itself always depends upon our ability to paraphrase—and especially upon the probability that most people will produce equivalent paraphrases for the same expression. A literal meaning is never more than an inductive probability and, therefore, not something that can support deductive absolutes, which, of course, is just what Davidson asks it to do.

When Davidson deals with conceptual schemes, the notion of "literal meaning" is replaced by the notion of "translatability," which is literal meaning squared, since it involves the equivalence of literal meanings in two different languages. We have been arguing that the presence of two meanings for the same expression ("make love") at different moments in linguistic or cultural history demonstrates the existence of distinct codes for those two moments. Davidson would argue, we believe, that our ability to understand both meanings demonstrates that there is only one conceptual scheme operating here, which is equivalent to the English language. The issue is partly over the proper level at which to situate "the very idea of a conceptual scheme." Davidson's theoretical argument against the existence of different conceptual schemes takes a familiar Wittgensteinian form. He assumes that the only things which could "count" as conceptual schemes would be languages, and the only way languages could be really different from one another would be if they could not be translated reciprocally. He clinches this argument by saying that if we could not translate something, we would have no way of knowing that it was a language in the first place. Anything we understand must be part of our own conceptual scheme, and what we fail to understand must remain undiscussable and, for all practical purposes, nonexistent. Accordingly, in "On the Very Idea of a Conceptual Scheme," Davidson claims that Benjamin Whorf's ability to explain Hopi concepts in English demolishes Whorf's case for the Hopi having a different scheme, just as Thomas Kuhn's ability to explain prerevolutionary modes of thought in postrevolutionary discourse demolishes Kuhn's paradigm theory. One major problem with this argument is that these cases do not demonstrate "*inter*translatability" at all—they merely demonstrate translatability in one direction. For *inter*translatability to be demonstrated, the Hopi would have to explain Whorf in Hopi, and a believer in the literal existence of phlogiston would have to explain why the word "phlogiston" can be understood only in a metaphorical sense.

Kuhn's notion of "incommensurability" allowed for the possibility of a later or more comprehensive scheme incorporating an earlier one—so that a historian of science like himself might understand the concept of phlogiston without accepting it as believable, necessary, or true. But Davidson, let us remember, translates "incommensurable" into his own language: " 'Incommensurable' is, of course, Kuhn and Feyerabend's word for 'not intertranslatable.' " Of course? By substituting the problem of translation for that of different size or scope, Davidson suppresses historical change and differences in political or linguistic power; he compounds the problem by assuming that translation in one direction

ensures the possibility of translation in the other. The difference between Kuhn's term and Davidson's translation of it—the failure of translation now ironically embodied in the concept of translation itself—
argues for a serious difference between the conceptual schemes of the
two writers. If we ask why Davidson needed to translate Kuhn 's terminology into his own, we must conclude that he did so in order to get
power over it, to make it more amenable to his own beliefs. We see this,
in short, as a mistranslation that can best be explained by a difference in
conceptual schemes, which operate not in the realm of theory but in the
realm of use.

Davidson's use of the word "translation" in connection with schematic
differences allows us to see more clearly another facet of the relationship between his view of metaphor and his view of conceptual schemes.
If we recall that writers from Friedrich Schlegel to Robert Frost have
argued that poetry is what gets lost in translation, we can begin to
understand how Davidson's theories of metaphor and of schematic differences fit together. For Davidson, translation, like literal meaning, is by
definition complete. Translatable is to untranslatable as meaning is to
use, because meanings are what gets translated. This means that only the
"literal" counts as language. We argue, however, that one of the things
which often happens in translation from one conceptual scheme to another is that what was literal in one scheme becomes metaphorical in
another.
    We can see this process at work in Davidson's own discourse when he
translates, once again, the words of others into his own, thus aligning the
worlds of others with his own beliefs, his own world:

> According to Kuhn, scientists operating in different scientific tra-
> ditions (within different "paradigms") "work in different worlds"
> (Kuhn, 134). Strawson's *The Bounds of Sense* begins with the
> remark that "It is possible to imagine kinds of worlds very differ-
> ent from the world as we know it" (15). Since there is at most one
> world, these pluralities are metaphorical or merely imagined. [*ITI*
> 186–87]

Kuhn and Strawson may believe that they are speaking literally here, but
Davidson knows better, because he knows that there is "at most one
world." But what does it mean to speak of "at most" one world, and how
is it that Davidson can claim to know this? We shall address these questions below, but first we need to examine why Davidson chooses to label

Kuhn's and Strawson's uses of the word "world" as "metaphorical" uses. Other options, of course, are to regard the plurality of such worlds as a joke, a lie, or simply an error. But, if we believe that Davidson is truly desirous of making sense of Kuhn in this matter, then, by his own account, he has little choice but to be charitable toward Kuhn: "whether we like it or not, if we want to understand others, we must count them right in most matters" (197). In this case, Davidson's principle of charity requires him to assume that those who disagree with him are speaking metaphorically rather than simply getting it wrong. Even though what Kuhn says appears to Davidson to be literally erroneous, at the same time, in some other way, Davidson must hold Kuhn to be right—and the notion of "meaningless metaphor" is perfectly designed to accommodate such a detour of contradiction. Now, however, the positivist teeth in this view of metaphor are at last revealed. The word "metaphor" refers not just to something vaguely beyond meaning, but to something specifically beyond reality as well—quite out of this world.

If the principle of charity must be invoked by Davidson in the cases of Strawson and Kuhn, it is only because, from his point of view, they initially seem to be wrong. If he agreed with them that different conceptual schemes exist and function as different worlds, then he would need no charity at all, for he would perceive them as literally meaning what they say and being correct in saying it. Earlier, we read Davidson's rejection of Kuhn's term "incommensurable" as a dramatization of what incommensurability is all about. Now, we would argue that by designating "worlds" as a metaphor, Davidson actually confirms the very same view of schemes that he wishes to deny—for he demonstrates that, when one translates across incommensurable schemes, what appears literal in one scheme will, from the perspective of the other, appear to be metaphorical. The words "literal" and "metaphorical"—it should be noted—have, under the pressure of Davidson's own use of them, shifted from signifying "determinate" versus "indeterminate," or "meaning" versus "use," to something more like "true" versus "false." Perhaps all along, for Davidson, it has been the world that makes utterances literal or metaphorical rather than some mere figuration of speech—or, rather, it has been *his* world, which he presents to us in the form of a conceptual scheme different from our own.

Kuhn's and Strawson's notions of a plurality of worlds attained their metaphorical status for Davidson because of his prior knowledge that "there is, at most, one world." How should we read this statement? If charity indeed commands us to presume Davidson correct here, then it also dictates (as we struggle to make the unfamiliar intelligible to us) that we begin with the commonsensical side of the assertion (that there is no more than one world) and work around to the side that is anything but familiar (that there may be even less than one world). How, then, does he know—i.e., what leads him to believe—that there is only one world? We assume that he is not working from a cosmic intuition here, but simply from a definition of the word "world" that requires it to connote (literally?) the notion of singleness—a notion that is more explicitly attached to the related word "universe," which wears its unity on its sleeve. There can be only one world because the word "world" refers literally to the whole enchilada—everything that is. A word, however, is a slender reed upon which to rest a notion as cosmic as the unity of the world. This particular word, after all, has more than one "literal" meaning—about a dozen more, according to *Webster's*—and many of these are specifically plural. Why should we agree that there is only one world if we cannot even limit the word "world" to a single literal meaning? If Davidson will honor only one of the word's meanings, we suspect that his choice is governed not by knowledge of the true unity of the cosmos, nor yet by the simple, literal meaning of the word "world," but by his own philosophical code and the needs of his argument.

However, even if we charitably grant the word "world" the single meaning of a single "whole" or "totality," we would still face problems in taking the word literally. Should we understand, for instance, that this single world includes everything that has existed or happened as well as everything that will exist? Or does the word refer just to what is here (where?) and now (when?)? If Davidson's "world" refers to the moment—a structuralist slice of present time—we are immediately confronted with the problem of having to stipulate as many worlds as there are moments of change. Clearly, this will not do, especially since every "whole" so described would necessarily exclude the same thing, time. Perhaps, then, we can find in the alternative a more intelligible literal meaning for Davidson's "world"—for instead of excluding time, this reading would include it, all of it, by including all the different states and stages of the universe.

This reading would leave us with One Great Scheme that underwrites English and all the other languages we have or may come upon. Here the "world" would incorporate all changes in these languages as local or temporal variants of the all-inclusive whole. But, if this universal scheme saves Davidson from having to stipulate a plurality of timeless worlds, it does so only by having him claim instead that the world, as we know it, is incomplete or unfinished. Such a reading at once sheds light on the unfamiliar side to Davidson's claim that there is "at most one world": namely, that there may be less than one world. The qualification "at most" suggests not only that the one world is unfinished, but that the one scheme unified by that world is also incomplete. On the surface this may sound reasonable, but if there is even a little bit less than one world available to us, then there is also nothing that can be called "a world" in the strict terms of Davidson's reasoning. What this suggests is that the word "world" would have no literal meaning at all, but would be metaphorical, all the way down. Because the expression "at most one world" deprives the word "world" of its literal status in Davidson's own discourse, it also takes all the logical force out of the "Since" by which he turns Kuhn's and Strawson's worlds into metaphorical ones. If Davidson's single world can be no better than figurative, how can it provide a firm basis from which to judge Kuhn's and Strawson's worlds to be merely metaphorical?

The question is rhetorical, of course. Since even Davidson does not claim to know whether there is one world or less than one, the notion of a single world remains irreducibly metaphorical. So, then, the notion of literal meaning must remain open and incomplete. This does not mean we cannot use this notion, but only that we must use it with caution; for it contains, within itself, some irreducible quantum of metaphor, induced by the unfinished state of the world itself. As an absolutist whose only perspective on the world must nonetheless be from the inside out, Davidson himself can claim no more than an approximation of the world. This makes him a somewhat reluctant or diffident absolutist. But without an absolute, he cannot sustain his objection to partial views and incommensurable schemes; nor can he find any ground, even a potential ground, that would stop the slippage of literal meanings caused by the constant pressure of use upon meaning.

To put our conclusions simply and bluntly, we do not find Davidson's objections to metaphorical meaning and conceptual schemes persuasive, primarily because they are based upon a concept of the literal which proves unworkable even in Davidson's own practice. Davidson wants us to throw out metaphorical meaning, but he has not shown us why literal meaning should not follow it out the window. He would have us stop referring to codes, but he does not tell us how otherwise to account for evaluation. He would have us stop talking about incommensurable schemes and conventional metaphors, but he does not suggest any other way to account for the changes languages go through over time. And he would forbid us to talk about schemes as producing different worlds, but he has yet to show us that the notion of one world, or less than one world, is any more intelligible than that of many worlds. As we return once more to our metaphorical home, we can say that Davidson has indeed forced us to dust off our furniture—maybe even to move it around and re-cover some pieces—but until he can offer us something better to replace our old stuff, we will have to keep on using it, knowing that even in the Big House of philosophy there are many mansions, and none of them is perfectly furnished either.

WORKS CITED

Dasenbrock, Reed Way. "Do We Write the Text We Read?" *College English* 53, no. 1 (1991): 7–18.

Delafield, E. M. *The Way Things Are.* London: Virago, 1988.

The Dream of a Common Language

SHEKHAR PRADHAN

I n his essay "A Nice Derangement of Epitaphs," published in 1986, Donald Davidson concludes that "there is no such thing as a language, not if a language is anything like what many philosophers and linguists have supposed. There is therefore no such thing to be learned, mastered or born with" (446). I do not know if Davidson is the first philosopher to claim that there is no language—perhaps Heraclitus had meant to claim that. But I am certain that Davidson is the first philosopher who has denied the existence of language in order to save literal meaning. As philosophical slogans go, literal meaning without language is startling, but no language because of literal meaning is truly astounding! But, we shall see, that is exactly what Davidson claims.

PRELIMINARIES

Davidson's philosophy of language has always given a central place to the idea of the literal meaning of a sentence or, better, of an utterance of a sentence. If we had to sum up Davidson's philosophy of language in terms of a slogan, it would be: A systematic theory of literal meaning of the expressions of a language must be in terms of a theory of truth for that language. This calls, of course, for much explanation. But I shall restrict myself to a few points of clarification as a way of setting up the background for the subsequent discussion.[1] I draw primarily on Davidson's recent John Dewey Lectures, published as "The Structure and Content of Truth," which retrospectively summarize, synthesize, and advance his earlier views on the philosophy of language.

1. In this context, by "a theory of truth" Davidson does not mean a theory about the nature of truth. He means an axiomatized theory for a certain language that gives the extension of a truth predicate for that language. It will entail theorems such as

(T) "Snow is white" is true-in-English if, and only if, snow is white.

Davidson calls such theorems "T-sentences." Each such T-sentence specifies a part of the extension of the predicate "true-in-English." Davidson's view of the relation between "true-in-English" and "true" is subtle and complicated. The interested reader should look at Davidson's insightful and lucid discussion of this issue in "The Structure and Content of Truth."

2. Davidson says:

A theory of truth for a speaker is a theory of meaning in this sense, that explicit knowledge of the theory would suffice for understanding the utterances of that speaker. It accomplishes this by describing the critical core of the speaker's potential and actual linguistic behavior, in effect, how the speaker intends his utterances to be interpreted. The sort of understanding involved is restricted to what we may as well call the literal meaning of the words, by which I mean, roughly, the meaning the speaker intends the interpreter to grasp, whatever further force or significance the speaker wants the interpreter to fathom. ["SCT" 312]

3. Although in his earlier papers he writes as if the theories of truth are theories for certain *languages,* such as English or Urdu, what he really means is that they are theories of truth for the languages of "individual speakers at various periods or even moments of their lives" ("SCT" 311).

4. Such a theory of truth for the language of an individual speaker at a certain period of her life is to be conceived of as being empirically constructed on the basis of the corpus of her utterances during that period. But the theory applies not just to those utterances; "it also specifies the conditions under which the utterance of a sentence would be true if it were uttered. This applies both to sentences actually uttered, by

telling us what would have been the case if those sentences had been uttered at other times or under other circumstances, and to sentences never uttered" ("SCT" 310). Presumably, the sentences never uttered would be composed of words that have been uttered.

5. Our ordinary semantic ways of speaking, such as "an expression's having a certain meaning," "knowing a language," "understanding what is meant by some expression," and so on, to the extent that they are intelligible, have to be understood in terms of a rational reconstruction of the project of empirically constructing and testing a truth theory for a language.

6. Thus, a language (of a certain person at a certain time) is to be identified in terms of a theory of truth for it. But since it is possible that several alternative theories of truth can be constructed on the basis of the same corpus of utterances of a speaker, those utterances may be located in different languages at the same time.

7. Davidson has sometimes cast an appropriate theory of truth for a language as a theory of interpretation for that language. It is a theory, then, which has a T-sentence for each sentence of the language such that the right-hand side of the T-sentence is taken to state the interpretation of the sentence referred to in the left-hand side. We must not be misled by the word "interpretation" here. To assign an interpretation to an utterance in this sense is just to assign it literal meaning (see item 2 above).

8. To assign an interpretation to an utterance in this sense, we need an appropriate T-sentence for that utterance. But, since there cannot be an isolated T-sentence, we must locate the utterance in a truth theory for a language (of the speaker at a given time). This is not a practical requirement of interpretation, but this is what it means to assign an interpretation to an utterance.

THE DISTINCTION THREATENED BUT SAVED

With the foregoing preliminaries out of the way, let us examine why Davidson feels the need to rescue the distinction between literal meaning and speaker meaning. According to Davidson,

> nothing should be allowed to obliterate or even blur the distinction between speaker's meaning and literal meaning. In order to preserve the distinction we must, I shall argue, modify certain

commonly accepted views about what it is to "know a language", or about what a natural language is. In particular, we must pry apart what is literal in language from what is conventional or established. ["NDE" 434]

What might obliterate or blur the distinction between speaker meaning and literal meaning? Davidson says that "the widespread existence of malaprops and their kin threaten the distinction, since here the intended meaning seems to take over from the standard meaning" ("NDE" 434). The kin of malaprops are phenomena such as perceiving a well-formed sentence when the actual utterance was incomplete or grammatically garbled, interpreting words never heard before, correcting slips of the tongue, coping with new idiolects, and handling proper names. These disparate-seeming phenomena have a feature in common: they all require the interpreter to proceed in a way not provided for by the usual meaning of the words.

The previous quotations from Davidson bring into play four types of meaning: literal meaning; speaker meaning; intended meaning; and standard meaning. In Davidson's scheme, literal meaning is, I think, intended meaning. So the literal meaning of an utterance is the meaning the speaker intended it to have. How, then, is it different from speaker meaning? Speaker meaning has to do with what the speaker intends to do with the utterance, what propositional or illocutionary or rhetorical or literary effect he wants to create, whereas the intended meaning or literal meaning has to do with what the speaker intends the utterance to be—what semantic identity is conferred on the utterance. The standard meaning of a word or an utterance, Davidson suggests, can be found in a good dictionary, which reflects past usage.

What is it about malaprops and their kin that might threaten the distinction between literal meaning and speaker meaning? In the case of malaprops, interpreters interpret the utterance differently from the usual interpretation of the words. In this respect, we may say that a malaprop is like a metaphorical or ironic or otherwise novel use of words. But the crucial difference between intepreting a malaprop and interpreting, say, a metaphor (assuming here that the metaphor is not based on a malaprop) is that, in the latter case, interpretation proceeds by assigning as literal meaning the standard meaning and figuring out the metaphorical effect or novel use on the basis of the words having that literal meaning or semantic identity. One cannot do that when interpreting a malaprop. Suppose I had titled the present essay "A Nice Arrangement of Epitaphs." If you thought I had committed a malapropism, you would not start by assigning the word "epitaph" the meaning "inscription written on a tombstone" or some such. You might have thought that by "epitaph" I meant "epithet." Then you might go on to interpret my title as being self-congratulatory or ironically self-deprecating, or whatever. In that case, interpretation would not have proceeded on the basis of the words being assigned the standard meaning. Whereas if you thought by "epitaph" I meant "inscription on a tombstone" your further understanding of my title (e.g., that I was suggesting the death or lifelessness of certain ideas) would be based on assigning my words a literal meaning that coincides with the standard meaning.

So the existence of malaprops and their kin show that even the literal meaning or semantic identity of an utterance depends on the speaker's intentions (or beliefs or expectations). Most of those who subscribe to the idea of literal meaning think of literal meaning as enshrined in words, not in the particular speaker of those words. We need not suppose that such theorists credit words with some magical intrinsic properties. To credit the word itself with literal meaning, independent of any particular speaker of the word, may be a shorthand way of referring to linguistic rules, conventions, or practices which are of course embodied in a community. In the opinion of these theorists, it is not the literal meaning of words but the speaker meaning that depends on the intentions of any particular speaker.

What is the role of language-enshrined literal meanings in the case of malaprops? They seem to be rendered irrelevant if the speaker is unaware of them. So the language-enshrined literal meanings cannot constitute the semantic identity of these expressions. But Davidson thinks any utterance of any expression must have a semantic identity and that, in cases of malapropism, the semantic identity must come from the literal meaning the speaker thinks the expression has. For that is the meaning which is relevant to the description and explanation of the further things the speaker intends to effect with his utterance. The case we are considering is special in that here the speaker is operating with a false belief about the language-enshrined meaning of the expression. But this case—though special—points to a more general conclusion: namely, the language-enshrined meaning of an expression becomes the semantic identity of an utterance of the expression only insofar as the speaker intends it and only insofar as the speaker can reasonably expect his interpreters to grasp his intention.

So now we see how the existence of malaprops and their kin threatens the distinction between literal meaning and speaker meaning: both literal meaning and what is commonly called the speaker meaning depend on the intentions of the speaker. But how does Davidson propose to save the distinction? In effect, Davidson claims that the distinction cannot be drawn as a distinction between language-enshrined meaning and the meaning determined by the speaker's intentions. Rather, it must be redrawn as a distinction between the semantic identity of an utterance and the further intended effects of the utterance. Or, better, it must be redrawn as a distinction between those further effects of the utterance which the speaker intends to achieve (speaker meaning) and those semantic properties of the utterance which it also has because of the intentions of the speaker and which figure in the explanation of how the speaker intends to achieve those further effects. It remains to be seen how, as a consequence of thus drawing the distinction, there is no language.

SEMANTIC IDENTITY AND FIRST MEANING

We must now briefly consider what it means to attribute a "semantic identity" to an expression. (Davidson himself does not use the term.) By the semantic identity of an expression (as uttered by a particular speaker on a particular occasion) I mean that which semantically distinguishes that expression or its utterance from other expressions, insofar as it *is* semantically different from those other expressions. In "Minimalist Semantics: Davidson and Derrida on Meaning, Use, and Convention," I claimed that Davidson thinks of the literal meaning of an utterance as its semantic identity and that he wants to include the minimum in the semantic identity that will still preserve some sort of explanatory role for literal meaning. In that essay, I found it not entirely inappropriate to compare Davidson's minimalist idea of semantic identity with Derrida's idea of the nonpresent remainder of a sign.

In his essay on malaprops, Davidson elects to use the term "first meaning" in place of the more familiar and misleading term "literal meaning." The semantic identity of the words, as uttered on that occasion, Davidson might say, is its first meaning. "Roughly speaking," he says, "first meaning comes first in the order of interpretation" ("NDE" 435). But this is only roughly speaking. He goes on to add that "a better way to distinguish first meaning is through the intentions of the speaker. The intentions with which an act is performed are usually unambiguously ordered by the relation of means to ends" (435). Davidson says that the first meaning of an utterance is the first intention in a means-end chain of intentions which have the Gricean reflexive property. These are intentions of the speaker which are meant to be achieved by a recognition on the part of the interpreter of those intentions.

In uttering a sentence, the speaker intends to achieve certain effects, perhaps, by the recognition of his intention to achieve those effects. For example, whatever you think I would have been up to had I used "A Nice Arrangement of Epitaphs" as the title of the present essay, you would have had to decide how I was using the word "epitaph." This is unavoidable. For my part, whatever further intentions I might have expected you to recognize in my utterance of those words, I would have expected you to do so by recognizing the meaning I wanted to confer on "epitaph." This, too, is unavoidable. But you would give "epitaph" a certain meaning only if you assumed that I intended you to give it that meaning. With such a title, then, I would have *intended to suggest* the death of certain ideas *by means of* achieving my intention that you attach a certain meaning to "epitaph," and I would have intended to achieve my intention via your recognition of my intention.

GETTING AWAY WITH IT

Now we are in a better position to see the relation between first meaning and language. But the picture cannot be completed without discussing Davidson's conception of the interpretive process. Looking at the process from the interpreter's side, Davidson says:

> The speaker wants to be understood, so he utters words he believes can and will be interpreted in a certain way. In order to judge how he will be interpreted, he forms, or uses, a picture of the interpreter's readiness to interpret him along certain lines. Central to this picture is what the speaker believes is the starting theory of interpretation that the interpreter has for him. The speaker does not necessarily speak in such a way as to prompt the interpreter to apply this prior theory; he may deliberately dispose the interpreter to modify his theory. ["NDE" 442)

If the speaker does dispose the interpreter to modify his prior theory, deliberately or not, then the speaker has "gotten away with it." Davidson adds: "The speaker may or may not . . . know that he has gotten away with anything; the interpreter may or may not know that the speaker intended to get away with anything. What is common to the cases is that the speaker expects to be, and is, interpreted as the speaker intended although the interpreter did not have a correct theory in advance" (440).

The sort of theory referred to in the above quotations is, of course, a theory of interpretation in the form of a theory of truth. Typically, both speaker and hearer come to the occasion of communication with what Davidson calls "prior theories." He explains: "For the hearer, the prior theory expresses how he is prepared in advance to interpret an utterance of the speaker. . . . For the speaker the prior theory is what he *believes* the interpreter's prior theory to be" ("NDE" 442). But in the case of "getting away with it" the hearer assigns an interpretation to the utterance different from that provided by his prior theory. Since "assigning an interpretation" is to be understood in terms of a T-sentence, and since such a T-sentence must necessarily be part of an interpretive truth theory, it follows that to assign an interpretation to an utterance different from the prior theory is, in effect, to employ a different interpretive theory. This different theory, which expresses the interpretation, Davidson calls the "interpreter's passing theory." The "speaker's passing theory," on the other hand, is the theory the speaker intends the interpreter to use, rather than (but not necessarily opposed to) the theory the speaker believes to be the interpreter's prior theory.

The terminology of prior and passing theories needs some clarification. In " 'A Nice Derangement of Epitaphs': Some Comments on Davidson and Hacking," Michael Dummett identifies the speaker's prior theory with a long-range or standing theory, whose scope is not restricted to the occasion, whereas the speaker's passing theory is about the given occasion. But this, I think, is a misinterpretation of Davidson. The prior theory could also be about a given occasion of speech, but it is held prior to the occasion of speech. For example, the speaker may think that on *this* occasion (but only this one) the interpreter will understand his utterance of "grace" to mean Grace Kelly, and he may therefore speak in such a way as to modify what he believes to be the interpreter's likely interpretation of the word "grace."

Although the scope of a prior theory may be restricted to the given occasion of interpretation, the scope of a passing theory *must* be restricted to the given occasion. Davidson writes: "Every deviation from ordinary usage, as long as it is agreed on for the moment . . . is in the passing theory as a feature of what the words mean on that occasion. Such meanings, transient though they may be, are literal" ("NDE" 442–43).

Another fundamental difference between prior and passing theories is that an interpreter may utilize a prior theory to figure out the interpretation of an utterance. It can be brought to bear in the task of interpretation. But a passing theory is merely something that *expresses* an interpretation in the form of a truth theory. Thus, Davidson writes, "knowing a passing theory is only knowing how to interpret a particular utterance on a particular occasion" ("NDE" 443).

This raises the question, Why call the interpretation of a particular utterance on a particular occasion a theory?

> The answer is that when a word or phrase temporarily or locally takes over the role of some other word or phrase (as treated in a prior theory, perhaps), the entire burden of that role, with all its implications for logical relations to other words, phrases and sentences must be carried along by the passing theory. Someone who grasps the fact that Mrs. Malaprop means "epithet" when she says "epitaph" must give "epithet" all the powers "epitaph" has for many other people. Only a full recursive theory can do full justice to these powers. ["NDE" 443]

Ian Hacking has pointed out that there is another sense of "theory" in which a passing theory is a theory. Davidson writes: "A passing theory really is like a theory at least in this, that it is derived by wit, luck, and wisdom from a private vocabulary and grammar, knowledge of the ways people get their point across, and rules of thumb for figuring out what deviations from the dictionary are most likely" ("NDE" 446). Hacking thinks that we, interlocutors, do not possess such entire-language-encompassing, recursive theories of interpretation (theory in the first sense). Rather, he thinks that, to the extent Davidson's case rests on this assumption, it becomes empirically implausible. But, as we shall see, Davidson's argument really depends on passing theories being theories in the second sense.

In a case where the speaker has "gotten away with it," the first meaning or semantic identity of the utterance is given by the speaker's passing theory. In such a case, because communication is successful, the speaker and interpreter will have the same passing theory, or nearly so. But what about a case where the interpreter fails to grasp the speaker's meaning? Is the first meaning still given by the speaker's passing theory? Davidson has recently written:

> My characterization of successful communication leaves open a range of possibilities with respect to the question what a speaker means by her words on occasion. Since the speaker must intend

to be interpreted in a certain way, she must believe her audience is equipped to interpret her words in that way. But how well justified must this belief be, and how nearly correct? I do not believe our standards for what someone's words, as spoken on a given occasion, mean are firm enough to let us draw a sharp line between a failed intention that one's words have a certain meaning and a success at meaning accompanied by a failed intention to be interpreted as intended. ["SCT" 311n.]

Although Davidson does not want to force the issue, I think his characterization of first meaning in the "Derangement" essay does force the issue to some extent. First meaning is specified by specifying the first intentions which have the Gricean reflexive property in a means-end sequence of intentions. Perhaps, for one to have an intention to do something, one must reasonably believe it possible to do it; and it is an open question as to how reasonable that belief must be. But it is not an open question, at least in the "Derangement" essay, as to whether the belief should be correct. That is because one can have intentions which are not successful, and if first meaning is specified by specifying a certain intention, then a speaker can give an utterance a first meaning even if his reflexive intention is unsuccessful; that is, even if speaker and interpreter do not share passing theories.

What I want to say, then, is that the first meaning or semantic identity of an utterance is given by the speaker's passing theory when the speaker gets away with it, and sometimes when he fails to get away with it, and even in cases where there is no question of getting away with anything. In more traditional terms, the literal meaning of a sentence as uttered by a speaker on an occasion is determined in every case by the intentions of the speaker and not by the conventional or the established or the standard meaning of the sentence: "we must pry apart what is literal in language from what is conventional or established" ("NDE" 434). And it is this conception of literal meaning or semantic identity, pried apart from the conventional or established nature of communal linguistic habits, which shows that there is no language.

WHAT IS A LANGUAGE?

At the opening of this essay I quoted Davidson as saying that "there is no such thing as a language, not if a language is anything like what many

philosophers and linguists have supposed" ("NDE" 446). Many philosophers and linguists have supposed that a language consists of a system of
expressions to which is "attached" a system of literal meanings—or, in
Saussurian terms, a system of signs and signifieds. Such theorists may
disagree about what literal meaning consists in and the nature of this
"attachment," but they do assume that a language is a repository of literal
meanings. They assume, too, that this language is communally shared
and that communication is possible because both speaker and interpreter know the language; that is, they know which literal meaning is
attached to which expression, and so they know which literal meaning is
attached to the expression used. It would follow that if language is not a
repository of literal meaning, then there is no language.

Davidson sums up this conception of language in terms of three
principles:

> (1) *First meaning is systematic.* A competent speaker or inter-
> preter is able to interpret utterances, his own or those of others,
> on the basis of semantic properties of the parts, or words in the
> utterance, and the structure of the utterance. For this to be possi-
> ble there must be systematic relations between the meanings of
> utterances.
>
> (2) *First meanings are shared.* For speaker and interpreter to
> communicate successfully and regularly, they must share a method
> of interpretation of the sort described in (1).
>
> (3) *First meanings are governed by learned conventions or
> regularities.* The systematic knowledge or competence of the
> speaker or interpreter is learned in advance of the occasions of
> interpretation and is conventional in character. ["NDE" 436]

The reference to "conventions" in principle (3) above is misleading.
The idea which (3) is meant to express is that the prior theory expresses
knowledge concerning which expression has which first meaning,
knowledge which is then applied to the specific utterance of that expression. Such knowledge may or may not be conventional in nature. On
David Lewis's analysis of convention, certain ways of satisfying conditions (2) and (3) above in the characterization of language may make
the knowledge of first meanings conventional. Suppose there is a convention of the form "Utterances of *s* are meant and interpreted as *p.*" Lewis
would analyze such a convention as follows.[2] To say there is such a
convention in a certain community C is to say that there is a regularity R
in the linguistic behavior of C of the form "Utterances of *s* are meant and

interpreted as *p,*" such that this regularity satisfies the following six conditions: i) almost everyone in C conforms to R; ii) almost everyone in C believes that the others conform to R; iii) "this belief that others conform to R gives everyone a good and decisive reason to conform to R himself" ("Languages" I:165); iv) there is general preference for conformity to R; v) there are alternatives to R which meet the last two conditions; and vi) the various facts listed in conditions i–v are matters of common or mutual knowledge. But I do not think that the existence of such regularities is essential to the conception of language sketched above.

DAVIDSON'S ARGUMENT

Davidson's argument proceeds in two stages. Stage 1: First he assumes that if there is a language, then it must play some role in describing and explaining the fact of successful communication between a speaker of that language and her interpreter. The apparatus of prior and passing theories, supplemented by the notion of strategies, is enough to describe and explain the fact of successful communication. But neither prior nor passing theories are of the right form to be a language. Hence, there need not be a language unless the existence of language can be understood in terms of the apparatus of prior and passing theories. Stage 2: In the sense in which most philosophers and linguists think of language (see the previous section), the existence of language would have to be understood as the existence of a communally shared prior theory. For communication between two people to be successful, however, they need not share a prior theory which they utilize to achieve successful communication. And, Davidson claims, in general people do not share prior theories; furthermore, each of us has different prior theories for different speakers. Hence, there are no communally shared prior theories, and language in this sense does not exist.

COMMENTS ON DAVIDSON'S ARGUMENT

In this context, by successful communication Davidson means that speaker and interpreter should converge with respect to passing theories. That is to say, the interpreter assigns that first meaning to the utterance which she is intended to assign on the basis of her recognition of the speaker's intention that she assign that first meaning to that utterance. In particular, Davidson does not consider it essential to a successful episode of communication that the interpreter come up with the interpretation relatively quickly, without expending much effort, with a fair degree of confidence, and so on. Even if these factors are not essential to a successful *episode* of communication, perhaps they are essential to the existence of a *practice* of communication. Davidson seems to assume that we need to accept the existence of a language only if its existence is required for explaining the existence of successful episodes of communication. But it seems worth asking whether we should accept the existence of language if it is necessary not just for the existence of successful episodes of communication, but also for the existence of (a certain sort of) practice of communication.

In any case, given that successful communication consists in a convergence on passing theories, we can explain this success in terms of the apparatus of passing and prior theories supplemented by the notion of stategies. When communication is "routine," the speaker's prior and passing theories will be the same, and speaker and interpreter may well have the same prior theories. But they need not. That would be one sort of case of getting away with it. Still, in every sort of case of getting away with it, the interpreter arrives at the same passing theory as the speaker even though they differ on prior theories. This capacity of the interpreter to adjust her prior theory in light of the evidence at hand is just another instance of the capacity to create new theories to cope with new data in any field. Davidson says: "there are no rules for arriving at passing theories, no rules in any strict sense, as opposed to rough maxims and methodological generalities" ("NDE" 446). These rough maxims and methodological generalities Davidson calls strategies, which he points out may differ from person to person.

Neither prior nor passing theories are of the right form to be considered a language. It is obvious that a passing theory cannot be a language. But neither can a prior theory, for "the prior theory has in it all the features special to the idiolect of the speaker that the interpreter is in a position to take into account before the utterance begins" ("NDE" 443).

Thus, if there is to be a language, it must be understood in terms of the apparatus of prior and passing theories. In particular, it must be understood as a communally shared prior theory. Such a theory would have to be prior to any communicative occasion within the time frame in which the theory is supposed to hold. The limiting case of such a linguistic community is that of one speaker and one interpreter. So, for the sake of keeping things simple, Davidson initially considers that case. He first argues that for communication to succeed in the limiting case, speaker and interpreter need not share prior theories. Success in communication consists in speaker and interpreter sharing passing theories, and the cases of "getting away with it" show that speaker and interpreter need not share prior theories in order to converge on passing theories. "Most of the time," Davidson claims, "prior theories will not be shared" ("NDE" 443), but he does not really argue for this claim. From the fact that in any given case of successful communication there need not be a shared prior theory, it does not follow that in general there need not be shared prior theories for communication to succeed—much less that, in general, prior theories are not shared. What Davidson has in mind, I assume, is that since the prior theory a person has is adjusted to the evidence available to the person, and since speaker and interpreter will in general have different evidence available to them, so, in general, they will not have the same prior theory.

The claim that, in general, members of a linguistic community do not share prior theories must strike one as suspect if one looks not just at isolated episodes of successful communication, but at what I am calling the "practice of communication." As I said earlier, this includes such facts as the ubiquitousness of successful communication among members of a linguistic community, the confidence with which speakers expect to be understood and with which intepreters interpret, the speed and ease with which most successful interpretation occurs, and the fact that one can confidently communicate with a total stranger, given that one is correct in assuming she is a member of one's linguistic community. Davidson explains this last fact thus:

> The less we know about the speaker, assuming we know he belongs to our language community, the more nearly our prior theory will simply be the theory we expect someone who hears our unguarded speech to use. If we ask for a cup of coffee, direct a taxi driver, or order a crate of lemons, we may know so little of our intended interpreter that we can do no better than to assume that he will interpret our speech along what we take to be standard lines. ["NDE" 443]

Dummett has argued that Davidson is not entitled to use the notion of a linguistic community (as he does in the above quotation) in the course of an argument to show that there are no languages; for Dummett holds that lingistic communities cannot be identified without reference to a language of that community. But Dummett is careless in his reading of the above passage. Davidson does not use the notion of a linguistic community but, rather, the notion of "our [i.e., what the speaker or the interpreter takes to be *her*] language community." What Davidson seems to have in mind is that each person has a standard or a default theory of interpretation which she uses when she has no specific information about her interlocutor other than that a more accurate theory of interpretation for the interlocutor will be sufficiently close to the default one. So *one's* language community can be defined as those persons for whom an accurate theory of interpretation would be sufficiently close to one's default theory. On the other hand, *a* language community would consist of those persons who share the same default theory and, perhaps, mutually believe that they do.

This brings us to the question, Can we explain the other features, mentioned above, of the practice of communication among a group of people without assuming that they share prior theories or default prior theories? Davidson's answer, I think, would be that such features of the practice of communication are not possible unless the participants in the practice share a great deal, including much in the way of default prior theories. He would doubtless insist, though, that no fixed set of things need be shared in order for the practice of communication among a group to have the features it has.

I agree with Davidson that no fixed set of things need be shared, but I do not think that means there need be no shared default theory. That is because the concept of "sharing a theory" or "sharing a language" is a fuzzy term. And, so, even if no fixed set of things must be shared, so long as enough parts of a default prior theory are shared by a group, that group can be said to share a prior theory. Consider a linguistic community of n people, A1, A2, ... An. Suppose A1 and A2 share their default prior theory in all details except in regard to some expression E1; A2 and A3 share their default theory in all details except in regard to some expression E2 (different from E1); A3 and A4 share their default prior theory in every detail except E3; and so on. Let us suppose further that everyone except A1 is agreed on the default interpretation of E1; everyone except A2 is agreed on E2; and so on. This example can be set up more carefully, but I think the point is obvious. No two members of this hypothetical community share a theory in all details, and there is no fixed set of things they must share. But it is also clear that in a certain sense they do share the same prior theory. So the question comes to this: For the practice of communication among a group to be successful, does the group have to share (default) prior theories to such an extent that one may say they have the same (default) prior theory? I do not think Davidson has shown that we must return a no to this question.

We have been discussing the case for a shared default prior theory. We use such a theory when communicating with unfamiliar members of our linguistic community. But what if speaker and interpreter are familiar enough with one another to have evidence about one another's linguistic dispositions? Here Davidson would say that since in general they will have somewhat different evidence, their relevant prior theories, adjusted for their evidence, will be different. Once again, however, we can make the point that although, in general in such a situation, there will be some divergence between the speaker's and the interpreter's prior theories, the divergence will not be so great that one must consider their prior theories to be different prior theories. Some may wish to be strict on this point: they may hold that any difference in two prior theories makes them two different prior theories. But I doubt that Davidson would so hold. He is willing to allow that speaker and interpreter may *share* a passing theory even though their passing theories will never completely coincide. "The *asymptote* of agreement and understanding is reached when passing theories coincide" ("NDE" 442; emphasis added). Since an asymptote is never reached, the passing theories can never totally coincide. So, presumably, Davidson cannot hold that prior theories must completely coincide to be shared.

In summary, I do not think Davidson has shown that, in general, prior theories are not shared; nor has he shown that prior theories need not be shared in general. For I think a case can be made that prior theories need to be shared in order for the practice of communication to have certain features.

A DAVIDSONIAN ARGUMENT

In this section I will sketch out another argument—an argument that I think lurks in the "Derangement" essay—for the conclusion that there is no language which does not depend on whether prior theories are shared or not.

I had earlier referred to a conception of language whereby linguistic expressions have literal meanings and whereby any token of an expression on a given occasion has that literal meaning, regardless of whether or not the speaker intends it to have that literal meaning. On this conception, literal meaning is enshrined in the language, not in the intentions of any individual speaker. We had earlier referred to this as language-enshrined meaning. Now Davidson's claim that there are no languages can be understood as the claim that there are no languages in the sense that there are no such linguistic systems with enshrined semantic properties. That is to say, if literal meaning or first meaning is not enshrined in language, then language has no semantic properties of its own. So there is no language as a bearer of semantic properties. In other words, while there may be a communally shared system of syntactic units, it does not become a communally shared language unless those syntactic units have communally shared semantic identities. It is in this sense that there is no language.

It would be perfectly reasonable to ask how a speaker manages to do what he does with certain words on a certain occasion. Let us restrict this question to the thing a speaker does by intention. This will include the illocutionary, perlocutionary, rhetorical, and literary effects of the utterance. Then we can ask how these words, in this context, can be used to produce these effects. In answering this question, one will have to credit the words used with certain properties that go beyond mere syntactic properties. This much, I think, should be uncontroversial. The assumption is that in the explanation of these effects, something we may call the "semantic properties" of the expression, as uttered on that occasion, will play a role. Indeed, we can define the concept of semantic properties in terms of such an explanatory role. Nothing else deserves to be characterized as semantic properties.

One conception of such properties are the language-enshrined literal meanings, if there are such things. Those who take this view assume that the language-enshrined literal meaning of an expression somehow figures in the explanation of any (illocutionary, perlocutionary, etc.) effects of any utterance of that expression. In "Minimalist Semantics," I characterized such a view as a "theory of semantic natures," to which I opposed what I called the "minimalist semantics" of Davidson and Derrida. We can now characterize Davidson's minimalist semantics in terms of the claim that the semantic properties which are supposed to figure in the explanation of the relevant effects of an utterance are first meanings. But an expression has a first meaning only as uttered on that occasion and only if the speaker intends it to have that first meaning. We may say that first meaning is in the utterance, not in the expression.

Davidson, we have seen, thinks that in the case of malaprops and other cases of "getting away with it," language-enshrined literal meanings, if there are any, are rendered irrelevant and can have no explanatory role in such cases. Moreover, at least in such cases, the explanatory role is fulfilled by first meanings, which are determined by the intentions of the speaker. But if the first meaning of an utterance of an expression, a meaning which is determined by the intentions of the speaker, has the power to play this explanatory role in cases of getting away with it, then it can play this role in any and every utterance of that expression. Thus, we need not invent language-enshrined literal meanings to fulfill this explanatory role: it is already filled by first meanings.

Can we find some other explanatory reason to postulate language-enshrined literal meanings? The first meaning of an utterance is supposed to figure in the explanation of certain of the further effects of the utterance. But what explains the fact that the speaker can invest that utterance with that first meaning on that occasion? Perhaps language-enshrined literal meanings can play some role there. That is, perhaps the expressions themselves, independently from the intentions of any given speaker, have certain properties which can explain how, on that occasion, the speaker could give it that first meaning. Davidson holds that for a speaker to invest an utterance of an expression with a certain meaning, she must intend, and thus reasonably expect, her interpreter to recognize her as investing that utterance with that first meaning. And, perhaps, on any given occasion, the speaker can reasonably expect her interpreter to recognize her intentions on the basis of his knowledge of certain properties of the expressions used. I see no reason why this knowledge cannot be systematic, stated by a communally shared prior theory, known in advance to speaker and interpreter alike. But we must realize that on any given occasion the speaker need not rely on this knowledge. That is what malaprops show us. Indeed, speakers use all sorts of other facts, too, such as social conventions, contextual expectations, history of interaction between the speaker and the interpreter, how the speaker thinks the interpreter is likely to understand her, and so on. Thus, although there are communally shared prior theories, and although (perhaps) there need to be communally shared prior theories in order to have a certain sort of practice of communication, the shared prior theories are not essential for a speaker to give an utterance a certain first meaning. Hence, these properties of expressions which may be stated by a communally shared prior theory are not semantic properties. So, such a system of expressions has no semantic properties, and hence there are no languages in the sense of a system of expressions having semantic properties.

The difference between this argument and the previous one is that this one rests on a certain thesis about what makes a property a semantic property and on the idea that first meaning is located in the utterance and not in the expression. It also depends on what counts as the appropriate *explanandum* for a semantic explanation; but it does not in any way depend on the claim, central to the previous argument, that in general prior theories are not shared, or need not be shared, in a linguistic community.

We have said that there needs to be a communally shared prior theory to explain certain aspects of the practice of communication, but we do not need this shared prior theory to explain how utterances have the first meaning they do or to explain the relevant sorts of further effects of utterances. And because the shared prior theory is not needed for the latter role, it cannot be said to state semantic properties. Now this may seem baffling because, in many cases, the prior theory of a speaker or an interpreter—never mind whether or not that theory is shared—may have the same content as the passing theory. If in such a case the passing theory can state the semantic properties of expressions, as uttered on that occasion, why cannot the prior theory? But we must not lose sight of what these theories represent. Prior theories represent the linguistic *dispositions* of speakers and interpreters, whereas passing theories represent bestowals of first meaning or interpretation upon utterances. That is why passing theories state or, better, express semantic properties while prior theories do not, even though *as theories* they may have the same theorems.

Another aspect of this argument deserves comment. We have represented Davidson as holding that properties of utterances deserve to be called semantic only if they figure in the explanation of certain sorts of effects of an utterance, but they cannot be called semantic if they figure only in certain other aspects of an episode of communication or in the practice of communication. Thus, properties of an utterance that help explain the ease, speed, and confidence with which communication is achieved—we may call these the "processing aspects" of that episode of communication—may not be called semantic. Roughly, we may put the distinction thus. Semantic properties of an utterance are those which must figure in the explanation of the content and force of the relevant acts performed as a result of that utterance, but properties that figure in the explanation of the processing aspects only may not be considered semantic. And, I have suggested, communally shared prior theories may be required to explain certain aspects—perhaps processing aspects—of episodes of communication as well as such aspects of the practice of communication as the ubiquitousness of successful communication.

Thus it is that in order to save the distinction between literal meaning and speaker meaning, a distinction threatened by malaprops and their kin, Davidson had to redraw it in such a way that the assumption of a common language had to be abandoned. The distinction had to be redrawn so as to locate literal meaning or semantic identity in the utterance, rather than in the language, understood now as a communally shared default prior theory. It turned out that if literal meaning was not housed in language, then language had no semantic properties. This was to banish language from the realm of the semantic. The syntactic units of what we call a language, whether or not they are communally shared, lack communally shared semantic identities. That is to say, in a certain sense, language does not exist.

One response to this argument would be to say that, even though language in the sense of a communally shared system of syntactic units having semantic identities does not exist, there can still be language in a rich enough sense. Language in this sense would be a system of syntactic units for which there exists a communally shared default prior theory.[3] So, although the properties attributed by the default prior theory to the syntactic units are not semantic properties, they nevertheless do attribute a semantically related property to the syntactic units. On Davidson's conception of a prior theory, they attribute to a syntactic unit e the property that every utterance of e (by a certain speaker, during a certain time frame) will have such and such a first meaning. That is, such properties are in the form of a hypothesis about what first meaning will be bestowed upon utterances of e. Even though such properties are not themselves semantic properties, they do refer to the first meaning of utterances of e, and to that extent they may be regarded as semantically related properties. A default prior theory would say that a *typical* utterance of e (but not every utterance of e) would have such and such first meaning.[4] Such a default prior theory would apply to those for whom a more accurate prior theory (one which is attuned to more detailed evidence regarding their linguistic behavior) would be sufficiently close to the default theory. Language in this sense may not be "anything like what many philosophers and linguists have supposed" ("NDE" 446), but it is good enough for me. Its existence helps explain certain features of the practice of communication, certain processing aspects of typical episodes of communication, as well as how in a typical instance a speaker can bestow the first meaning she does upon an utterance in that language.

NOTES

1. Ramberg, in *Donald Davidson's Philosophy of Language,* provides an excellent introduction to Davidson's project in the philosophy of language.

2. I say Lewis *would* analyze such conventions this way, instead of saying he *does*, because (as far as I know) Lewis does not write directly about such linguistic conventions. The linguistic conventions he does write about directly are of the form "It is a convention in a certain community to be truthful and trusting in such and such language."

3. Without more accurate prior theories, how does one know which of them are "sufficiently close" to the default prior theory? That is, how does one know to whom the default theory applies? Here one proceeds on all sorts of cues, such as the look of the speaker, style of clothing, accent, geographic location, and so on. Of course, such cues offer a very slim basis for judgment. But to call a theory "default" is to say that one applies the theory unless one has reason to believe otherwise. So the positive evidence needed to apply the theory need not be very strong, unless one has contrary evidence.

4. It needs to be described further what makes an utterance of some expression, *e*, *typical.* But one can say at least this much: a *typical* utterance of *e* is an utterance made by someone to whom the default prior theory can be applied and who is not trying to "get away with it."

WORKS CITED

Dummett, Michael. " 'A Nice Derangement of Epitaphs': Some Comments on Davidson and Hacking." In LePore. 459–76.
Hacking, Ian. "The Parody of Conversation." In LePore. 447–58.
LePore, Ernest, ed. *Truth and Interpretation: Perspectives on the Philosophy of Donald Davidson.* Oxford: Basil Blackwell, 1986.
Lewis, David. "Languages and Language." *Philosophical Papers.* Oxford: Oxford University Press, 1983. I:163–88.
Pradhan, Shekhar. "Minimalist Semantics: Davidson and Derrida on Meaning, Use, and Convention." *Diacritics* 16, no. 1 (1986): 65–77.
Ramberg, Bjørn. *Donald Davidson's Philosophy of Language.* Oxford: Basil Blackwell, 1989.

Davidson and Dummett
on Language and Interpretation

DAVID GORMAN

The controversy between Donald Davidson and Michael Dummett over the theses advanced in Davidson's essay "A Nice Derangement of Epitaphs" represents an extremely significant moment in the trajectory of modern analytic philosophy of language as it has developed by way of the work of Gottlob Frege, Alfred Tarski, Willard Quine, and others. It is also a particularly difficult moment to evaluate, or even to summarize, because both Davidson's essay and Dummett's response of the same title (hereafter, "Comments") presuppose the arguments and conclusions of their overall programs in the philosophy of language—two extraordinarily rich and varied bodies of ideas. While Davidson's essay can be viewed as the culmination of the work gathered in his *Inquiries into Truth and Interpretation,* it also draws out some further, scarcely anticipated consequences of the program elaborated there. In what follows, I will take it for granted that the substance of *Inquiries* and "A Nice Derangement of Epitaphs" (hereafter, "Derangement") are familiar. It would be less satisfactory to do so for Dummett's philosophy of language, scattered as it is across a very large and diffuse corpus of writings.[1] Rather than try to follow the order of the criticisms Dummett offers in "Comments," I will present a reconstruction of the ways in which Dummett's approach to language conflicts with Davidson's in "Derangement." In addition to Dummett's response, I will draw on further comments he has made in "The Origins of Analytic

Philosophy" and in chapter 4 of *The Logical Basis of Metaphysics*. In addition, I will at times be offering my own criticisms of Davidson, which are put forward, however, with the intent of extending and complementing Dummett's.

One of the things that makes the Davidson/Dummett controversy so significant is that their dispute takes place, as it were, within the same paradigm. That is to say, both thinkers accept many of the same basic or framing principles concerning the philosophy of language and, within that framework, principles concerning how to construct a theory of linguistic meaning. Dummett has described this project as one of providing "a theoretical representation of a practical ability," and he adds that it was Davidson who was the first to articulate the principles involved, in a clear, programmatic way.[2] This shared conception of how to theorize about language distinguishes any differences that Davidson might have with Dummett from those he might have with many other analytic philosophers who, like the late Paul Grice, operate with a fundamentally different conception of linguistic theory.[3] And, of course, it distinguishes Davidson's conception sharply from philosophical approaches to language (phenomenological, semiotic, and so forth) developed outside the analytic tradition.

There are many reasons to regret the lack of awareness of analytic thought among theorists of literature and the humanities generally, and the growing interest there in approaches like Davidson's is to be welcomed as a counterbalancing trend.[4] Part of my present intent, in fact, is to suggest how Dummett's work could hold at least equal interest for anyone concerned with the study of language—and to say this is, evidently, to say a great deal. Certainly one could obtain quite a profound education in the problems associated with language and with such affiliated concepts as meaning, understanding, reference, translation, and so forth by making a careful study of the series of critiques which Davidson and Dummett have offered regarding one another's arguments, a series which has been under way for two decades and of which the one occasioned by "Derangement" is only the latest.

In the interest of concision, I will omit reference to the earlier debates, and for the same reason I am also forced to scant a number of potentially fascinating aspects and avenues leading off from the current debate. Another thing which gives this controversy significance is that Davidson and Dummett are by a wide margin the best thinkers now working in the philosophical tradition running from Frege through Quine, and it will be success enough merely to suggest how multifaceted are their thoughts on language.

DAVIDSON'S PROGRAM

At the end of "Derangement," Davidson states his conclusion that "there is no such thing as a language," in a passage already much-quoted and, no doubt, fated to become a *topos* in future philosophy of language—a broad, shocking dictum as convenient for critics of the Davidsonian program to attack as it is for its defenders to rally around. Symptomatically, it is this dictum, and the arguments motivating it, upon which not only Dummett focuses, but also Ian Hacking, in his conjointly published response, "A Parody of Conversation." Debate over Davidson's conclusion, however, will be of value only so long as would-be disputants are clear as to exactly what Davidson does and does not claim in advancing his thesis, a danger particularly imminent because of the deliberately provocative way in which he has chosen to overstate the case. It is all too foreseeable that literary theorists, for example, will respond to the dictum without grasping its place in "Derangement" or—worse—without grasping how the argument made in that essay emerges from the theory elaborated in *Inquiries* and recently summarized in Davidson's John Dewey Lectures.

One possible way to misunderstand Davidson would be to miss the specificity of his claim. He does not write that there is no such thing as *language*, since to do so would amount to a direct repudiation of his whole undertaking in *Inquiries*, which is to explain how human beings are able to communicate linguistically and, particularly, to explain the role of *linguistic meaning* in communication.[5] Rather, Davidson's exact words are that "there is no such thing as *a* language," and he immediately qualifies even this qualified assertion by adding, "not if a language is anything like what many philosophers and linguists have supposed" ("NDE" 446). It may be helpful here to advert to a Saussurian distinction (which will be more familiar to many in the humanities) between *le langage* as human discourse generally and *la langue* as a codified system of rules or conventions (e.g., English, Chinese, Latin). It is the notion of *langue* rather than *langage* that comes under fire in "Derangement." Moreover, Davidson's critique of the former notion is actually only *methodological,* so to speak, although it sounds *ontological* (hence its hyperbolic quality). Davidson has no stake in denying that we can or should recognize, in practice, discrete patterns of linguistic expression like the ones labeled English, Chinese, Latin, and so on (and dialects thereof); what he denies, rather, is that the concept of such patterns has been of any use in previous attempts to theorize about language, meaning, and communication. Radical as it sounds, what we may call Davidson's "antilinguistic dictum" is of a piece with a well-established plank of the platform constructed in *Inquiries:* namely, his anticonventionalism. In concluding "Derangement" as he does, Davidson brings out a radical dimension which was always implicit in his program: "what many philosophers and linguists have supposed" about languages (in the sense of *langues*) is that they are sets of conventions. But—holding to the less misleading methodological register of expression—if the concept of linguistic convention finds no useful role to play in a satisfactorily explanatory theory of linguistic meaning, then the concept of *a* language can be of no explanatory use either. Or—reverting to the provocatively ontological register—no conventions, no languages.

If the concept of a language is denied any substantive role in the philosophy of language, then *a fortiori* the concept of *knowing* a language must be dismissed as well. Davidson continues the concluding paragraph of "Derangement" thus: "There is therefore no such thing [as a language] to be learned, mastered, or born with. We must give up the idea of a clearly defined shared structure which language-users acquire and then apply to cases" (446). Clearly, the claims cited here depend in turn on other claims belonging to Davidson's philosophy of language, and this calls for at least a condensed outline of the relevant assumptions and arguments made in *Inquiries* and "Derangement." However, what follows in the rest of this section will necessarily take the shape of an *aide-mémoire,* rather than a detailed survey of the key aspects and elements of the Davidsonian program, in order to situate Davidson's essay and Dummett's response conceptually.

Any theory of language that repudiates the notion of languages (and of knowing languages) is clearly a very austere one, and conceptual parsimony is as pronounced a quality of Davidson's work as it is of the work of his teacher, Quine. The theoretical hope which motivates Davidson's program is that the main features of linguistic communication can be explained adequately by appeal to just two kinds of notion: on the one hand, that of a *truth-theory;* on the other, that of *radical interpretation.* A truth-theory is an abstract semantic structure, pairing conditions of truth and falsity with sentences; Tarski developed the prototypical version of such a theory in connection with purely formalized languages, and although Tarski denied that parallel structures can be read directly into natural languages, Davidson, in his early writings, begins with the contention that the acquisition of some such structured theory must form the core of each person's linguistic ability.[6] Crucially, however, Davidson does not see that any individual's truth-theory will necessarily be uniform with any other individual's. To communicate effectively, then, we must learn to adjust our truth-theories to each other's, so that we associate the same conditions of truth with at least some sentences.

Thus, the other basic element of human linguistic ability—radical interpretation—Davidson hypothesizes to be a propensity to formulate strategies for recognizing other people's truth-theories and for helping them recognize ours. The interpretation involved is characterized as "radical" because, as part of his theoretical program of austerity, Davidson disallows appeal to any concepts standing in the intersubjective middle ground between the truth-conditions which each speaker attaches to sentences (and which constitute the whole of meaning in Davidson's strict definition) and the manifold possible communicative activities which involve sentences (and which for him belong entirely to the field of interpretation).[7] This restriction stands sharply in contrast to many other programs in the philosophy of language (if not all, as Davidson rather exaggeratedly claims), insofar as other theories presume that linguistic communication must occur in virtue of at least some kinds or degrees of commonly shared beliefs among individuals concerning linguistic usage. Anything of this sort Davidson views as a convention, and from this definition follows his aforementioned anticonventionalism.[8]

In speaking of Davidson as disallowing and restricting various conceptual options, I mean of course that he disallows them from the theoretical apparatus of a properly explanatory account of human linguistic behavior; and this brings out another characteristic quality of his program—that is, its extremely abstract or theoretical nature. Davidson does not really deny that there are conventions of language, any more than he denies that there are languages; instead, his point is that, at best, such things are matters of practical simplification for language users and that *in principle* linguistic communication can occur in their absence. The methodological assumption deriving from this is that theorists of meaning must focus on accounting for the abstract situation. Once this has been accomplished, however, Davidson's claim is that justice has been done to whatever is openly observable in linguistic activity: conventions and the like are secondary phenomena, of little philosophical interest (it is implied) in comparison with the basic dichotomy of truth-conditions and interpretive strategies. The vision of language that emerges from this program (to crystallize in "Derangement") is one of human linguistic behavior as a highly dynamic, open-ended activity in which we constantly adjust our linguistic usage with the intent of helping our listeners adjust their truth-theories to converge sufficiently with ours to enable communication. In Davidson's summary:

the interpreter uses his theory to understand the speaker; the speaker uses the same (or an equivalent) theory to guide his speech. For the speaker, it is a theory about how the interpreter will interpret him. Obviously this principle does not demand that speaker and interpreter share the same language. It is an enormous convenience that many people speak in similar ways, and therefore can be interpreted in more or less the same way. But in principle communication does not demand that any two people share the same language. What must be shared is the interpreter's and the speaker's understanding of the speaker's words. ["NDE" 438]

In "Derangement," Davidson is mainly concerned to clarify one point in his program, which is that the strategic adjustments involved need only be *temporary* and *local.* That is to say, the convergence of speaker's and listener's beliefs as to the truth-conditions of a sentence being used in a linguistic encounter does not—in principle—have to involve any overall convergence between the truth-theories each person brings to the encounter (and may well take away from it unmodified). Davidson calls the latter their "prior" theories; Dummett suggests it would be more helpful to call them "long-range" theories ("Comments" 459–60). The crucial distinction that Davidson wants to draw in "Derangement" is between these "prior" (or "long-term") assignments of truth-conditions to sentences and the extent to which, purely within the duration of some linguistic encounter, both participants arrive at common assignments for the sentences in use at the time, which Davidson calls the participants' "passing" theories (and Dummett, perhaps more helpfully, their "short-term" theories). If this is all that needs to be shared, however, then by implication the concept of a language or of knowing a language drops out as superfluous or, rather, as far more rich and complex a notion than is necessary to explain what happens between speaker and listener. In his essay, Davidson focuses on the seemingly marginal linguistic phenomenon of malapropism precisely because it involves the violation or circumvention of linguistic convention and yet is as open to correct interpretation as those expressions which do follow the rules. Davidson sees in malapropism the prototype of linguistic creativity, and the generalized version of his argument in "Derangement" is that even though no system of linguistic conventions can anticipate such innovation, linguistic innovation nevertheless takes place all the time and presents no obstacle to understanding; thus, interpreters must really proceed on some other basis than that of applying rules or recognizing conventions. The following extract, along with the one quoted in the preceding paragraph, reveals the core of Davidson's arguments without the hyperbole of his conclusion:

> there are no rules for arriving at [convergent] passing theories, no rules in any strict sense, as opposed to rough maxims and methodological generalities. A passing theory really is like a theory at least in this, that it is derived by wit, luck, and wisdom from a private vocabulary and grammar, knowledge of the ways people get their point across, and rules of thumb for figuring out what deviations from the dictionary are most likely. There is no more chance of regularizing, or teaching, this process than there is of regularizing or teaching the process of creating new theories to cope with new data in any field—for that is what this process involves. ["NDE" 446]

Davidson's case in "Derangement" turns crucially on his distinction between prior and passing theories. The apparatus is meant to explain how we can come to understand an unfamiliar utterance. When talking with Mrs. Malaprop, for example, if we begin to notice that she regularly confuses near-homonyms, that observation will give us a clue on the basis of which, when she speaks of "a nice derangement of epitaphs," we can hypothesize that she means "a nice arrangement of epithets." This represents an adjustment to our passing theory, since we did not equate, in the present example, "epitaphs" with "epithets" prior to our linguistic encounter with her, nor are we likely to do so subsequently; our aim in adjusting our theory is to achieve a temporary match with Mrs. Malaprop's theory. The clues guiding our interpretation are given only unintentionally by Mrs. Malaprop, although speakers can also plant them deliberately in their discourse, albeit within certain limits. Davidson indicates these limits by alluding to the case, often cited but seldom understood by literary theorists, of Humpty Dumpty explaining to Alice that when he says "glory" he means "a nice, knockdown argument," and that he is free to decide what he will mean by whatever he says. This conception of meaning is wrong, argues Davidson, because "you cannot change what words mean . . . merely by intending to"; still, it is not utterly off-track either, because "you can change the meaning provided you believe (and perhaps are justified in believing) that the interpreter has adequate clues for the new interpretation" (439). Humpty fails to provide clues of the relevant sort and so is reduced to telling Alice what he intends "glory" to mean—telling her in words whose meaning he has to accept while doing so. Davidson's crucial point, then, has to do not primarily with strategic intention in linguistic activity, but with the strategic opportunities for convergent interpretation which are provided to a listener, deliberately or not, by a speaker's words.

If the distinction embodied by the prior/passing apparatus can be made to work, then Davidson can justify his antilinguistic conclusion by allowing that the speaker's and listener's prior theories may be as conventional or languagelike as one chooses, so long as it is agreed that only their passing theories matter in communication. But Dummett finds reasons to think that this distinction cannot be made out, and we will turn now to his criticisms of "Derangement." Some of the reasons that he offers against the prior/passing distinction have to do with considering it primarily as a piece of technical apparatus in the theory of meaning, and we will begin with these aspects of "Comments." Intermixed with them, however, are arguments that count, instead, against that larger image of language and interpretation which motivates Davidson's program and its conclusions, and it is with these that we will end.

DUMMETT'S CRITIQUE: THE STATUS OF THEORIES

A number of the more technical points touched upon in Dummett's "Comments" might be called minor or clarifactory ones, such as the suggestion that Davidson's terminology of "passing" and "prior" be replaced with "short-term" and "long-term." (I will continue to follow Davidson's usage here, although of course Dummett's alternatives will feature within any quotations from "Comments.") Along the same lines, perhaps, are suggestions that Davidson has not eliminated the concepts of convention or individual language from his theory of meaning, but has only redefined them in an unusually restrictive way, which however is not discontinuous with standard conceptions, despite what is claimed in "Derangement." An instance of this response would be Dummett's observation that Davidson, while he depends as much as any theorist on a distinction between language generally and individual languages, has reduced the latter concept from that of a "common language," shared by many, to something resembling an idiolect, but even narrower, a concept "not of the general speech habits of an individual at a particular time, but, rather, his habits of speech when addressing a particular hearer at that time" (469; see also "Origins" 198).[9]

One could make a similar point about conventions in Davidson's later work. If a "linguistic convention" is defined as an (intersubjectively) recognized procedure for realizing some communicative transaction, then what the argument of "Derangement" shows is not that there are no recognized procedures for communicating linguistically, but only that they properly belong to the very *short term* of linguistic activity, arising and disappearing in the course of a conversation in their *primary* instance while, if some become stabilized or entrenched in the middle or long terms of various people's linguistic dispositions, this is only a derivative, secondary occurrence, an "enormous convenience" for facilitating communication but theoretically ("in principle") unnecessary for its achievement.

Dummett also offers technical objections that cut considerably deeper, however. Davidson's resistance to making essential use of such concepts as language and convention follows, on our analysis, from his sharp dichotomization of linguistic meaning and of activities using language, and particularly from his desire to confine the scope of linguistic meaning to an austere minimum: namely, that of truth-conditions on sentences. In "Derangement" he reemphasizes the point, writing that "part of the burden of this paper is that much that [interpreters] can do ought not to count as part of their basic *linguistic* competence" (437). This puts a great explanatory burden, however, on the concepts of truth and truth-conditions, on the one hand, and interpretive "maxims" and "stratagems," on the other. What compounds the problem is that Davidson applies the term "theory" to both of these things, but in different ways, so that his use of the term is ambiguous at best and question-begging at worst. Davidson's tendency is to conflate the notion of a theory of meaning as a theory *about* a language with the notion of language as consisting in mastery *of* a theory—indeed, he is quite blunt about this assimilation early in "Derangement" when he states, "I shall henceforth assume there is no harm in calling such a method [of interpretation] a theory, as if the interpreter were using the theory we use to describe his competence" (438). It is just here, however, that Dummett begins to pick the essay apart.

What tends to get lost amid the variety of theories which Davidson recognizes (speaker's, hearer's, prior, passing, truth-, meaning-, etc.) is the basic idea of linguistic ability or competence. The familiar version of this idea is that of *knowing a language*, which is just the concept that Davidson wants to exclude from any significant explanatory role, of course. But it would be question-begging to set up a general description of linguistic activity in a way which, in effect, precludes the introduction of the concept in advance, and this is what Davidson's account does if Dummett's analysis is right:

> In this talk of theories, we need to take care what we consider each theory to be a theory of. According to Davidson, the speaker's long-range theory is a theory of what the hearer's long-range theory is; we may call any theory about what another theory is a second-order theory. . . . We must beware, however, of representing all theories as of the second order. We cannot say both that the speaker's theory is a theory about what the hearer's theory is, and that the hearer's theory is a theory about what the speaker's theory is, without falling into an infinite regress: there must be some first-order theory. A first-order theory is simply a theory of meaning. . . .
>
> We must distinguish between three things: a language; a theory of meaning for that language; and a second-order theory. A language is an existing pattern of communicative speech: it is not a theory, but a phenomenon. A theory of meaning for that language, as conceived by Davidson, is a theory of the content of expressions belonging to it—what that content is and how it is determined by the composition of the expressions. It does not itself employ the notion of meaning, but can be recognized as an adequate representation of the meanings of the words and expressions of the language. It serves to explain how the language functions, that is, to explain the phenomenon of speech in that language; but it does so only indirectly. This is so because the theory itself contains no reference to speakers or to their beliefs, intentions or behaviour, linguistic or non-linguistic. Instead it uses theoretical terms such as "true" applying to certain expressions of the language. . . .
>
> A second-order theory is of a quite different character. If it is a long-range theory, it consists of a set of beliefs about what the expressions of some language mean, or about what certain individuals intend or take them to mean; if it is a short-range theory, then about what certain specific utterances are intended or taken to mean. ["Comments" 466–67]

One might object that Dummett is here guilty of question-begging of a kind inverse to that which Davidson stands accused of: namely, presupposing that languages *do* exist and that the concept *is* central in the way that Davidson means to question. However, little hangs on where or whether a theorist uses the *term* "language," but rather on what *concept* a theorist attaches to it. Dummett's express definition of "a language" as "an existing pattern of communicative speech" applies perfectly well to the linguistic encounters upon which Davidson focuses; it does not involve any concept of a shared system of conventions, which is Davidson's description of the standard notion of a language. Moreover, Dummett's initial point stands quite independently of any dispute here: unquestionably, Davidson tends to characterize theories as being *about* other theories. It is not only that, in order to avoid confusion, a hierarchy of higher- and lower-order theories needs to be recognized: it is that, in order to avoid regress, there must also be a *base* for any such hierarchy, consisting of a place where theories of any sort encounter the phenomena for which they are supposed to account.

A natural place for this would be the listener's prior (or, in Dummett's terms, long-range) theory, described as the set of a person's general expectations as to how anyone will address him or her. But now we are approaching a fairly traditional conception of someone's "knowing a language," because there seems no other way to characterize the nature of someone's general expectations. Let us say that this set of expectations or this body of knowledge which the listener possesses about patterns of address constitutes a theory; then it must be a first-order theory. The next question, naturally, concerns the order of the speaker's prior theory. If it also belongs to the first order—consisting, presumably, of the speaker's expectations as to how he or she will be understood—then Davidson's argument seems virtually to have short-circuited, because all we are now postulating is two individuals possessed of a variety of broad assumptions about how utterances will be understood, and that is what knowing a language involves if anything is. Yet the way in which the distinctions between theories are drawn in "Derangement" seems to preclude this reading: all of Davidson's descriptions of the speaker's prior theory suggest that it belongs to the second order, because they make essential mention of the speaker's beliefs about the hearer's theory. Meanwhile, there is no question that the speaker's and the listener's passing (or short-range) theories are both of the second order, since they are theories which speaker and listener form in the context of their prior theories, and each may feel the need to modify his or her long-term assumptions about the other, if only for the short term.[10]

Here, a defender of Davidson's approach can interrupt to say that the status of the prior theories is an incidental matter. What remains crucial, the Davidsonian will remind us, is the distinction between prior and passing theories on *both* the speaker's and the listener's side. So long as the passing theories do not resemble languages, so long as an individual's formulation of such a theory does not resemble learning a language, it makes no difference whether the prior theories are languagelike, on any definition of this concept. And passing theories do not in fact resemble these things, as Davidson emphasizes:

> A passing theory is not a theory of what anyone (except perhaps a philosopher) would call an actual natural language. "Mastery" of such a language would be useless, since knowing a passing theory is only knowing how to interpret a particular utterance on a particular occasion. Nor could such a language, if we want to call it that, be said to have been learned, or to be governed by conventions. Of course things previously learned were essential to arriving at the passing theory, but what was learned could not have been the passing theory. ["NDE" 443]

This objection, though tidy, does not suffice to shake off the problems involved in Davidson's plethora of theories. For the absolute insulation that he wants to maintain between prior and passing theories will not hold. There seems to be no way to justify granting the status of "theory" *both* to the prior and the passing theories while simultaneously insisting that the content of the two sets differs. The distinction between first- and second-order theories will not suffice, especially if (as we have seen that we must conclude) the speaker's *prior* theory is of the second order. This generates a dilemma. Davidson explains that he "persists" in calling passing as well as prior theories *theory* "only because a description of the interpreter's competence requires a recursive account" (441)—in other words, because the competence involved must be structured (a requirement that Davidson extends to the speaker as well, certainly). The resulting dilemma is that while the requirement clearly seems to apply to the prior theory, it does not seem to apply to a passing theory. Dummett writes that

> Davidson appears to conceive of [the short-range] theory as massively reduplicating the long-range theory . . . but there seems no good reason for this: if we think of the two theories as used in conjunction, the short-range theory may be taken as bearing on only those utterances for which the long-range one does not yield the correct interpretation. The short-range theory, so viewed, will not be a structured theory, but only a collection of disconnected propositions. ["Comments" 466]

Davidson's basic claim, that only the passing theories of a speaker and listener need to converge in order for them to communicate, loses all plausibility if the passing theories amount to mere "disconnected propositions." His own description of what happens aims to forestall this, however:

> Why should a passing theory be called a theory at all? For the sort of theory we have in mind is, in its formal structure, suited to be the theory for an entire language, even though its expected field of application is vanishingly small. The answer is that when a word or phrase temporarily or locally takes over the role of some other word or phrase (as treated in a prior theory, perhaps), the entire burden of that role, with all its implications for logical relations to other words, phrases, and sentences, must be carried along by the passing theory. Someone who grasps the fact that Mrs. Malaprop means "epithet" when she says "epitaph" must give "epithet" all the powers "epitaph" has for many other people. Only a full recursive theory can do justice to these powers. ["NDE" 443]

But, on this account, the passing theory just *is* the prior theory (or a "massive" duplicate of it, as Dummett says), and there is no believable way to claim that a speaker or hearer could "converge" on such a complex recursive structure. Rather, most of what is in the prior theory must carry over into the passing theory (where it is modified in certain ways), breaking the insulation between the two upon which Davidson's claims depend. The dilemma, to summarize, is that either there is not enough content ascribable to a passing theory to account for successful communication, in which case we must advert to a far more languagelike conception of the prior theory to carry the explanatory burden, or else (on the only description of the content of the passing theory that Davidson gives us), the passing theory already includes or duplicates the prior theory, thus including or duplicating whatever is languagelike about it.

The problem being emphasized here was already implicit in a passage, quoted previously, in which Davidson grants that "of course things previously learned [are] essential to arriving at the passing theory," while also maintaining that "what was learned could not have been the passing theory" ("NDE" 443). Davidson's case relies on suggesting that whatever is involved in the convergence of two individuals' passing theories happens in isolation, in a crucial way, from their prior theories. But here he is allowing—as of course he must—that passing theories evolve in *some* context, and that there are factors "essential" to this context, including previously acquired information of various sorts: this can be nothing other than the information belonging to the prior theory. The lack here of a clean demarcation emerges most strongly in a case which, though obvious, Davidson seems never to consider—the situation where a speaker successfully communicates with a hearer and where no malapropisms or innovative language uses of any kind arise, only standard or familiar uses of familiar expressions. The whole need for the concept of a passing theory, in Davidson's presentation, has to do with linguistic creativity: this is what calls for adjustments, on the part of both the speaker and the listener, of linguistic dispositions; and Davidson is certainly correct to insist on how common this sort of creativity is. However, he certainly cannot deny that communication *can* take place without deviations of any sort—and what role would the concept of passing theories have to play in that sort of situation? I suppose Davidson would say that, in such cases, the passing theories involved are isomorphic to the prior ones; but this, as I said, only brings out the point that the two concepts cannot be differentiated enough to justify the conclusion that the notion of language (or of knowing a language) remains superfluous for the purposes of a theory of meaning.

DUMMETT'S CRITIQUE: PERSPECTIVES ON LANGUAGE

To all this it might be conceded that, while Davidson has failed to elaborate some of the technical elements of his theory of meaning in a satisfactory way (or at least has failed to present them satisfactorily in "Derangement"), the underlying image of language remains untouched and compelling. Each of us who has acquired linguistic ability (not *a* language, note) has done so by virtue of having internalized a truth-theory. When another person speaks, we interpret what is said by attempting to read our truth-theory into that person's utterances, adjusting the theory (temporarily and locally) as necessary to make the best overall sense of what is being said. When we have learned conventional patterns of utterance and when we share those with a speaker, or with someone listening to us speak, the need for this kind of radical interpretation is, conveniently, greatly reduced. But these shared conventions (languages as they are usually considered) are incidental to what is essentially involved in linguistic communication: namely, truth-theories and interpretive strategies. However, as

Dummett argues, this background picture is also unsatisfactory in itself. Indeed, the complicated ambiguities and confusions of the technical apparatus introduced by Davidson to provide a case for his program appear symptomatic of some dominating image of this sort, rather than constitutive of it. Therefore, it remains to give critical consideration to Davidson's theory within a wider perspective concerning questions of meaning and interpretation, because that is where theorists concerned with language stand to learn the most—positively and negatively—from his inquiries. Numerous interrelated issues and problems will arise in any broad evaluation of Davidson's program, especially in the turn that it has taken with "Derangement," as Dummett brings out especially well in his various responses.

UNDERSTANDING

One basic problem of this sort, pointed out by Hacking and underscored by Dummett, has to do with the extended or ambiguous sense in which Davidson uses the term "interpretation" in such recent essays as "Derangement." When describing the receptive participant in the linguistic encounter, Davidson alternates between calling that person the "hearer" and calling him or her the "interpreter," and the implicit equivalence thereby established between interpreting discourse and overhearing it already represents a very large expansion of the former notion's sense: surely what we ordinarily understand as interpretation is a more specific phenomenon. Davidson is virtually forced to elide any possible discriminations here by the burden which the evolution of his theory has led him to place on the concept of interpretation. Under this rubric, Davidson includes everything that relates to human communication except a bare grasp of the truth-conditions of sentences. He has extended the concept so far that it is no longer really clear what remains for a grasp of truth-conditions to *be*. As with his multiplicitous use of "theory," what Davidson avoids here is any direct characterization of what is most basic to a language user's activities with respect to language: namely, his or her *understanding* of that activity. Interpretation, in its narrower and more familiar sense, is a process that we initiate in order to achieve understanding. In the first place, it presupposes a lack of understanding, or at least a problem in understanding; but, in the second place, it also presupposes some amount of prior, achieved understanding, which provides the informational base upon which any interpretation must be built. This second presupposition is, as Dummett notes, an important theme of Wittgenstein's: interpretation must *start* somewhere (in a belief or an activity, say) which is not itself an interpretation; otherwise, we have a conceptual regress. But Davidson, by treating everything that goes on between speaker and listener (as they try to adjust their theories to converge) as interpretation, makes it impossible to see where the whole process can begin, for either party. Dummett expands upon this and links it to the first presupposition:

> interpretation, in the strict sense, is of necessity an exceptional occurrence. . . . In the normal case, the speaker simply says what he means. By this I do not mean that he first has the thought and then puts it into words, but that, knowing the language, he simply speaks. In the normal case, likewise, the hearer simply understands. That is, knowing the language, he hears and thereby understands; given that he knows the language, there is nothing that his understanding the words consists in save his hearing them. There are, of course, many exceptional cases. They occur, for the speaker, whenever he uses a word with which he suspects the hearer may be unfamiliar, whenever he very deliberately uses a subtle or humorous figure of speech, when he is conscious of knowing the language imperfectly or believes his hearer to do so. They occur, for the hearer, when the speaker misuses an expression, or uses an unfamiliar one, or employs a difficult figure of speech, or, again, when one or other is speaking in a language he is not fully at home in. These are just the cases that aroused Davidson's interest. They are, however, in the nature of things, atypical cases: if taken as prototypes for linguistic communication, they prompt the formulation of an incoherent theory. ["Comments" 471–72]

The incoherence mentioned by Dummett is not only the relatively technical kind which we have discussed in connection with Davidson's use of various concepts of "theory." Now we find this incoherence reproduced on a more intuitive level in connection with such nontechnical notions as understanding and interpretation. This aspect of the dispute between Dummett and Davidson should hold special interest, of course, for literary theorists and others concerned with interpretation. The negative side of the emphasis built into Davidson's program on the open-endedness of linguistic action emerges in such later papers as "Derangement," where he seems to treat the interpretive process as if it were open on *both* ends—as something that not only has no set conclusion, but no set beginning—and Dummett and Hacking are right to argue that this must be incorrect for a range of "normal" cases taken as basic to communication ("Comments" 463–65; "Parody" 449–51). This objection—which critical theorists would do well to reflect upon, in conjunction with Davidson's ideas about interpretation—is epitomized in Dummett's invocation of the Wittgensteinian theme: "there is a way of understanding a sentence or an utterance that does not consist in putting an interpretation on it" (464).

A Davidsonian might attempt several responses. One, used by Ramberg in his book, is dismissive: "For Dummett and Hacking, to interpret an utterance is to render it in your own idiolect; what already *is* expressed in your own idiolect is not interpreted, you somehow just get it" (108). This response will not work. Ramberg makes it sound as if Davidson's theory promises to reveal what understanding consists in (namely, the interpretive procedures which Davidson describes speakers and listeners as following), while his critics treat understanding discourse as a mysteriously given phenomenon ("you somehow just get it"). However, the fact is, for Hacking and especially for Dummett, the development of an informative characterization of understanding is a fundamental task for the philosophy of language; yet neither believes that an account of understanding can be based on the concept of interpretation.

A more sophisticated response, which Ramberg also attempts, is to advert to the emphasis on the dynamic nature of the linguistic situation that orients so much of Davidson's thought about language: "It is the fact that language is not static, that interpretation is modelled by the continuous creation of truth-theories and not by the knowledge of any one truth-theory, that allows a discrepancy between convention and truth-theory to appear" (111). Granted that the words are those of an expositor, their spirit seems convincingly Davidsonian. The suggestion is that while a listener (let us say) tries to adjust his or her truth-theory strategically to approximate the speaker's and thus to interpret what is spoken, the speaker's language—in the sense, that is, of his or her linguistic propensities—undergoes constant change, so that total convergence between listener's and speaker's truth-theories never occurs (which does not preclude, of course, that more than enough of the relevant part of the two theories will match sufficiently well for any particular thought of the speaker to be communicated successfully). What Ramberg calls "convention," by which he means patterns of understanding of the sort on which Davidson's critics insist, can on this basis be dismissed as a by-product of the underlying phenomenon, as an image of how someone speaks that is arbitrarily stabilized from the always-evolving character of a person's discursive tendencies. This "fluid" quality of meaning is something which can be grasped far better, Ramberg concludes, by a listener conceptualized as a radical interpreter than by one modeled as a conventional understander, since the latter can do only as well as the former in grasping discourse, and will often do much less well:

> In so far as we practice communication as speakers of a language, that is, by relying on conventions, and not as radical interpreters, the potential lag between the convention-bound use of language and the radical interpretation of language represents a possible diffusion of meaning, a blurring of linguistic understanding. To speak a language, in other words, is necessarily always to be in danger of misunderstanding what is said. [112]

At this point I think that we are right to feel cheated, or at least to feel that this emphasis on the dynamics of language has more to do with its convenience in deflecting criticism than with bringing out the mechanisms of meaning and understanding. The "discrepancy" or "gap" for which Ramberg argues here, far from being dramatically important, seems evanescent. He explicitly allows that someone conceived of as knowing *a* language *can* understand an utterance as well as a radical interpreter, and Ramberg is reduced to warning that a listener of the first kind faces the danger of "misinterpreting"—which is hardly a danger from which the radical interpreter is exempt! Nor does it seem more than a distraction from the issue to insist that the ways people speak undergo constant change, for acceptance of this point is in no way precluded by acceptance of the Wittgensteinian point that some understanding must not involve interpretation.

NORMATIVITY
Another possible response to Dummett's objection, consideration of which will lead us into further important topics in the philosophy of language, would be to question conceptions of the "normal" or "typical" cases of communication on which the objection rests. In "Comments," Dummett explains what he means by a normal case, and he does so in a way that brings out another basic problem in Davidson's rejection of the concept of a language. In the normal situation of communication, where by hypothesis no interpretation is involved,

> speaker and hearer treat the words [spoken] as having the meanings that they do in the language. Their so treating them does not consist in their having any beliefs about the other person, but,

rather, in their engaging in the way they do in the conversation, reacting as they do to what the other says, and, perhaps, acting accordingly after it is over. They may be compared to players of a game. A game with two or more players is a social activity; but the players' grasp of the rules does not consist in any theories they have about the knowledge of the rules on the part of the other players. It is manifested by their playing the game in accordance with the rules (or cheating by surreptitiously breaking them), that is, in their acting in a manner that makes sense only in the light of the rules. [472]

Aside from any problems of ambiguity or regression already noted in the apparatus of speaker's and hearer's theories as consisting in beliefs about *each other's beliefs,* Davidson's whole conception of the relevant patterns of competence of those involved in linguistic activity as consisting in beliefs about *each other* is misguided, Dummett claims. What "makes sense" of their behavior, from the viewpoint of the theorist of meaning, is surely instead their beliefs—or, if not explicit beliefs, then their tacit dispositions—in regard to patterns of such activity, patterns which must be understood as *normative.* That the concept of a language is a normative one, and as such indispensable to a theory of linguistic behavior, is the core of the view that Dummett advocates against Davidson's. As users of language, Dummett is fond of saying, we "hold ourselves responsible" to patterns of meaning that make up our ordinary, pretheoretical notion of what a language is.

It is important to understand what normativity does *not* entail or imply. The game example, which Dummett uses only to introduce this conception, has the potential to mislead us here. The normativity of language does not imply that speakers are bound by fixed rules. For one thing, unlike the rules of a game such as chess, the rules or patterns of the language game are subject to constant change (a quite obvious and important point which I was not intending to deny when criticizing Ramberg for making an obfuscating appeal to it). For another thing, deviations from the norms, which would amount to cheating in a genuine game, are perfectly in order and indeed quite significant activities in the use of language; and Dummett points out that this is the valuable insight from which Davidson began in "Derangement," although it has led him to false conclusions. These two qualifications are in fact related, since linguistic deviation is the basis for language change. Further, the normativity of language does not consist—cannot consist, Dummett emphasizes—in a set of *rules,* as it can and usually does in the case of a game; in the case of language, the norms involved are indeed *patterns,* patterns of what we earlier saw Dummett call "practical activity," for which the philosopher of language aims to find a "theoretical representation."[11] Finally, normativity does not mean that those involved in the linguistic encounter must fully or perfectly share any explicit beliefs or tacit commitments. Indeed, Dummett's main point is that divergences between individuals' ways of speaking, or "idiolects" as he calls them in preference to Davidson's suspect use of "theories," are explicable only as divergences from a *norm,* which is that of the sociolect or "common language."[12] We can summarize the drift of these ideas by saying that, for Dummett, the innovating uses of language upon which Davidson concentrates are possible only as taking place against a background of normative patterns, with the same holding true for the possibility of interpreting such new uses.[13]

Thus, the divergent idiolects of different speakers, it is being argued, do not result principally from the differences in their ideas about each other's patterns of language use, but from the differences in their ideas about what the sociolect is. One case that brings this out, and thus brings out the indispensability of the concept of knowing a language for a theory of meaning, is the case where we have *no idea* how to begin understanding someone else's discourse. The Davidsonian line is to say that this is precisely the situation of radical interpretation; but, without returning to the technical intricacies of the conception involved, we might simply ask what is wrong with the more intuitive way of describing the situation as one of my not knowing the language of the speaker. As Dummett writes:

> In what does the fact that I know no Yoruba consist? Not, surely, in the fact that I have no tendency to form the same short-range (passing) theory of the utterances of a Yoruba speaker on a particular occasion as he has. . . . It consists, in Davidson's terms, in my lacking any long-range theory whatever for Yoruba speakers; or, rather, since a great many Yoruba speakers also know English, in my lacking any such theory for them when they are speaking Yoruba. It thus appears that there is no way to characterize this piece of ignorance on my part without appeal to the concept of a language. ["Comments" 465]

It is useful to compare this to the case mentioned in a passage from "Comments," quoted earlier, where Dummett contrasts the normal case, a speaker and listener who know the same language, against the "exceptional" case, "when one or [the] other is speaking a language he is not fully at home in"—when one or both "is conscious of knowing the language imperfectly" (472). This kind of situation, he argues, provides an exemplary opening for the realization of Davidson's model, because strategic interpretive adjustments will certainly need to be made by the participants for communication to be achieved. Yet the strategic adjustments needed do *not* derive (notwithstanding what the analysis supporting Davidson's model implies) from attempts by either participant to start from scratch and overcome ignorance by means of radical interpretation; rather, they derive from attempts to *compensate* by means of interpretation (radical or otherwise) for any gaps that either may begin to find in their mutual linguistic understanding. To put it more concisely, the need for interpretive strategies of the Davidsonian type derives from the extent of the language users' grasp of linguistic norms; the norms are not a sort of incidental side effect of the strategies.[14]

As Davidson generalizes his "radical" model (as we may call it), Dummett generalizes his "normative" one. In fact, *all* users of natural language are to some degree in the position of "knowing the language imperfectly"—not always (for that would erase the distinction between normal and exceptional cases), but often enough to make the concept of *imperfect* knowledge of a language crucial for a theorist of meaning. For Dummett, this is a virtue rather than a shortcoming of the normative view of language. The idea that no one has perfect linguistic knowledge does not depend simply on the complexity of natural languages, which is a contingent quality. The point is, first, not just that no one can know every word of, for example, English, but that no one *needs* to know every word to be counted as a fully competent English speaker; for a word or other expression to have a meaning in English is just for *someone* to know it, and for this knowledge to be recognized in some public way. This phenomenon Dummett calls (using a phrase of Hilary Putnam's) the "social division of linguistic labour" (or of linguistic knowledge, as I would prefer). A second, deeper aspect of this phenomenon is that someone can effectively *use* words in communication without fully knowing what they mean, so long as the user is prepared to defer in appropriate ways to the usage of those who have greater knowledge, to hold him- or herself responsible (*à la* Dummett) to that usage, and to accept correction as necessary from those whose knowledge is authoritative.[15] The normative or authoritative conception of language seems to me as undeniable as the analogous conception of games, which after all are *constituted* by their rules; however, it also generates fascinating difficulties because, again in contradistinction to the case of games, neither the norms of language nor the (divided) authority of its users is given from the outside but, rather, is immanent *in* the activity of using language, in a way which is difficult to specify and which generates a striking paradox, in fact. Dummett describes that paradox in *Basis:*

> if [a] game ceases to have rules, it ceases to be a game, and, if there cease to be right and wrong uses of a word, the word loses its meaning. The paradoxical character of language lies in the fact that while its practice must be subject to standards of correctness, there is no ultimate authority to impose those standards from without. The only ultimate determinant of what the standards of correctness are is the general practice of those recognised as primary speakers of the language.... Those who inveigh against a prescriptive attitude to... language sometimes stigmatise as superstitious the idea that a word may have a meaning "in itself," as opposed to what a speaker means by it on a given occasion: but, when Alice told Humpty-Dumpty that "glory" does not mean "a nice knock-down argument," she was not being superstitious. [85]

The meaning of "glory," or of any word, is a matter of norms, and no individual, *as* an individual, is free to change that meaning; nevertheless, the norms themselves are only a matter of the linguistic practice of various individuals, and that practice can and will change collectively, taking the norms and thus the meanings along with it, so to speak. The difficulty of this conception of language and meaning lies in the difficulty of characterizing the immanent, collective constitution of linguistic norms. However, the problems of a normative conception of language are those of any *social* conception of a practice, as Dummett often reiterates, and language is above all a social practice, interwoven with other such shared activities; it is precisely a sense of this perspective which Dummett finds missing from Davidson's account of language as it has developed toward the conclusions of "Derangement." A theory of meaning that does full justice to the social character of language may be very hard to develop, as Dummett often admits; but the Davidsonian approach, as it stands, would simply render it impossible, in a way which we will now turn to consider.

PUBLICITY

What Davidson's current approach denies or at least ignores, Dummett claims, is the *publicity* of language. Of course, Dummett must allow that

Davidson's official stance goes against this claim completely. For what is the whole logic of Davidson's theory, as we have surveyed it, if not one according to which the analysis of meaning is limited to openly observable elements? Yet, in matters as abstract and complex as this, a gap may easily open between overall intent and actual result, particularly with respect to theoretical emphasis. This emphasis may not easily be captured in a grid of large, simple dichotomies like private/public or individual/social. In an attempt to articulate the points at issue, however, Dummett recruits two familiar characters in these discussions, Humpty and Alice:

> There are two natural pictures of meaning. One depicts words as carrying meanings independently of speakers. It was to this conception that Alice was appealing when she objected to Humpty Dumpty, "But 'glory' doesn't mean 'a nice knock-down argument'." According to Alice, Humpty Dumpty could not mean that by the word, because the word itself did not have it in it to bear that meaning. The opposite picture is that which Humpty Dumpty was using. On this conception, it is the speaker who attaches the meaning to the word by some inner mental operation; so anyone can mean by "glory" whatever he chooses. Each picture is crude; each is easily ridiculed by a philosopher or linguist. But each theorist of language tends to offer a more sophisticated version of one picture or the other. Davidson's is a version of the second picture. His reason for denying that, by "glory," Humpty Dumpty could, in speaking to Alice, mean "a nice knock-down argument" is quite different from Alice's: it is that Humpty Dumpty knew that Alice would not understand him as meaning that. If he had expected her so to understand him, and had intended him to do so, then his intention, or . . . expectation, would have conferred that meaning on the word as uttered by him. ["Comments" 470]
>
> . . . .
>
> The view that I am urging against Davidson is an adaptation of Alice's picture, according to which words have meanings in themselves, independently of speakers. Of course, they do not have them intrinsically, and hence independently of anything human beings do. They have them in virtue of belonging to the language, and hence in virtue of the existence of a social practice. But they have them independently of any particular speakers. No speaker needs to form any express intention, or to hold any particular theory about his audience, or, indeed, about the language, in

order to mean by a word what it means in the language: he has only to know the language and to utter the word in an appropriate context, such as that of a sentence. In particular cases, he may have some interpretation in mind; but he could not have an interpretation in mind in every case. This is to say that we cannot grasp senses without any vehicle for them, and associate those senses to the words as a semaphore associates flag positions to letters: to invest a word with sense is just to grasp the pattern of its use. [473]

As will be seen, many of the themes and ideas under consideration here are drawn together in these passages, which are fundamental to thinking about Davidson's argument in "Derangement," in my opinion, whether or not Dummett is correct.

There are a number of considerations which might count for or against the correctness of Davidson's views, and it would only overburden an already long discussion to do more than indicate them very briefly—despite their complexity—by way of conclusion. On the other hand, what all this reveals is the intellectual power of these debates over meaning and understanding, debates still far too little studied outside the close confines of analytic philosophy of language and philosophical logic.

One example which would be crucial in adjudicating the competing claims of these rival "pictures of meaning" is that of *names*. For Davidson, proper names and the way in which we learn them are a primary instance of the general phenomenon that "Derangement" is devoted to analyzing, because "adding a name to one's way of interpreting a speaker depends on no rule clearly stated in advance" but, rather, calls for an innovation in our "method of interpretation," which must coincide with the speaker's ("NDE" 440). For Dummett, by contrast, proper names such as place names are especially vivid examples of the doctrine of the division of linguistic knowledge, since it is not just that no one knows the meaning of every place name, or that everyone has at best a partial knowledge of many such names, but that there are some names of which *no one* can be said to have a full understanding. For, as Dummett puts it in "Origins," the uses of these names "exist only as interwoven with a multitude of non-linguistic practices: the existence of roads and shipping routes, and, in our time, of railways and air flights, and even of travel agencies, enters essentially into the language-game, to use Wittgenstein's phrase, that involves the use of place-names" (195); and the sum of this lies beyond the intellectual grasp of any individual.

One of the oddities of Dummett's approach to the theory of meaning becomes especially salient here, in his emphasis on the pervasiveness of partial or defective knowledge on the part of language users with respect to their own language. If Davidson's approach has the strange consequence that there is no such thing as a language, Dummett comes to a conclusion that seems equally counterintuitive: namely, that when we speak, we often do not know just what we mean, if knowledge of meaning entails a full and accurate understanding of our own words and sentences. In Davidson's only further comments thus far on the arguments in "Derangement," he defends his approach precisely in such terms:

> A malapropism or slip of the tongue, if it means anything, means what its promulgator intends it to mean. There are those who are pleased to hold that the meanings of words are magically independent of the speaker's intentions; for example that they depend on how the majority, or the best-informed, or the best-born of the community in which the speaker lives speak, or perhaps how they would speak if they took enough care. This doctrine entails that a speaker may be perfectly intelligible to his hearers, may be interpreted exactly as he intends to be interpreted, and yet may not know what he means by what he says. . . . For the purpose of the present enterprise, that of understanding truth and meaning, we should, I think, stick as closely as possible to what is made directly available to an audience by a speaker, and this is the relevant state of the speaker's mind. ["SCT" 310–11]

Although the critique of Dummett implicit here needs more development, this may be Davidson's best line of defense for his doctrines concerning language and interpretation after "Derangement."[16]

However, a strong point remains on Dummett's side which we have hardly considered. Namely: Davidson's theory, as it stands, is open to the charge of psychologism; that is, of appealing to the existence of inner mental states not open to observation. Dummett emphasizes this point in "Origins":

> We need to be told by what means I can recognise the other speaker as having the same theory of meaning as I do: that is, what use one who assigns certain truth-conditions to the sentences of a language will make of those sentences. All talk in this connection of discerning a speaker's intentions is mere gesturing in the desired

direction, until that connection between truth and meaning—and
hence between truth-conditions and linguistic practice—which
we were presumed to know has been made explicit to us. [202; see
196–203]

A first step in this direction would be to broaden the conception of the
basic linguistic situation on which Davidson focuses, that of speaker and
listener. Davidson's assumption seems to be that, since this is the minimal situation of communication, nothing is lost in focusing on it exclusively; but it is arguable that, far from revealing what is most basic to
linguistic communication, focus on this scenario excludes or blurs much
upon which communication depends—most important, perhaps, that it
requires not only a linguistic *encounter,* as I have been calling it throughout, but also a linguistic *transaction,* where both parties speak *and*
listen. Until then, Davidson's paradigm situation is indeed only a "parody
of conversation," although ironically it is Dummett rather than Hacking
who drives this point home:

> In his picture, there is no interaction, no exchange of the roles of
> speaker and hearer: the hearer remains mute throughout the con-
> versation or, rather, monologue. The hearer can therefore seek
> from the speaker no elucidation of what he has said: and it is this
> artificial restriction that deprives the notion of incorrect use of its
> interest for Davidson. Figures of speech and other deliberately
> non-standard uses apart, a speaker holds himself responsible to
> the accepted meanings of words and expressions in the language
> or dialect he purports to be speaking; his willingness to withdraw
> or correct what he has said when made aware of a mistake about
> the meaning of a word in the common language therefore distin-
> guishes erroneous uses from intentionally deviant ones. He can-
> not become aware of any mistake if the only other party to the
> dialogue is constrained to silence, and for this reason Davidson
> takes no note of this feature of his linguistic behaviour. ["Com-
> ments" 462]

A point that has echoed through much of this discussion is Davidson's
assumption that his analyses of communication in terms of truth and
radical interpretation need apply only *in principle.* That is to say, if it
can be shown that linguistic intercourse could be, so to speak, reconstructed using only such austere principles, then Davidson can claim to
have revealed the essence of the phenomenon and can happily allow

that, in actuality, linguistic activity goes on in very different ways, involving shared conventions and the like. This assumption in turn depends upon a further assumption of Davidson's that, as Dummett puts it in a passage quoted earlier, a theory of meaning "serves to explain how . . . language functions . . . but it does so only indirectly" ("Comments" 467). The theory works indirectly because Davidson does not hold that we can *impute* it to language users: it amounts only to a description of information such that, if someone *did* know it, that person could speak a given language. In other words, a Davidsonian theory of meaning is intended to describe a body of knowledge *equivalent* to whatever it is those who have language mastery know, but not *identical* with it (see "SCT" 312). However, Dummett's assumption here, which underlies a great deal of his writing on Davidson, runs nearly to the contrary. The Wittgensteinian maxim which guides him is that linguistic meaning must be "manifest," as he often puts it, in linguistic use; and so, any indirect description of linguistic activity such as Davidson's program aims to create requires that it be linked, in some way and at some point, to a *direct* description of linguistic activity. For Dummett, Davidson's whole project remains up in the air until—and unless—the resulting theory can be shown to be amenable to the addition of "linking principles" which can provide the "connection" Dummett writes of "between truth-conditions and linguistic practice" (see "Origins" 202; cf. *Basis* 103–5 and "Comments" 466–67).

One last point haunting our considerations has been Dummett's distinction between language as a phenomenon or "practical ability" and a theory of meaning as a (first-order) "theoretical representation" of it. In the course of responding to Davidson, however, Dummett has had to revise at least this part of his view. If such a neat separation of the two were possible, there would be no obvious objection to Davidson's indirect strategy for a theory of meaning, since it treats the theory as effectively equivalent to whatever is involved in the ability; but, Dummett now holds, mastery of a language is a complex capacity, involving both a certain degree of explicit theoretical knowledge and a degree of implicit practical ability, which problematizes the form that an adequate theory of meaning must take and renders any neat equivalence impossible. This comes out, as Dummett explains in "Origins," when we ask what mode of knowledge is involved when we say that someone "knows" the meaning of a word: "on the one hand, it is . . . *conscious* knowledge; but on the other, it cannot in all cases be explicit, verbalisable knowledge, if only because it would be circular to explain someone's understanding of the words of his language as consisting, in every case, in an ability to define them verbally" (205). And he regards this as an open problem in the philosophy of language (see "Origins" 203–7 and *Basis* 93–95, 105).

The underlying weakness of Davidson's theory, in the form it takes in "Derangement," comes down to the vision it presents of a world where everyone might speak entirely differently but where, however slowly and laboriously, people could nonetheless communicate with each other through language. It is entirely doubtful whether this is possible, even in principle. On the other side, the power of Davidson's recent work on language lies in how plausible an account of linguistic communication he succeeds in giving with the extraordinarily reduced stock of concepts he has allowed himself. From Hume through the Logical Empiricists to Quine, the history of modern philosophy has shown repeatedly how such reductionist programs, when handled by a thinker of genius, can prove illuminating even when unsuccessful. Davidson's work continues that tradition. More than that, it challenges us to supply what it lacks, and I have suggested that part of what is lacking is encapsulated in the general principles advocated by Dummett—that not all understanding can involve interpretation; that language must be analyzed as a norma- tive social practice; and that the mechanisms of meaning, whatever they may be, are inherently public. Although these principles enmesh anyone attempting to develop a theory of meaning in many further problems, still they point the road on which progress lies.[17]

NOTES

1. Dummett's work has primarily taken the form of an extended commentary on Frege's philosophy, particularly his philosophy of language. There is much material of fundamental importance in these writings, but the corpus now fills some six volumes, approaching two thousand pages in length, so that we are badly in need of a survey and guide to this work comparable to Ramberg's on Davidson. The most accessible summary presentation of Dum- mett's thought is his own essay "Can Analytic Philosophy Be Systematic, and Ought It to Be?"; for his philosophy of language, the opening pages of "The Philosophical Basis of Intuitionistic Logic" (215–32) are clearest. Also of importance, though quite difficult, are his two essays named "What Is a Theory of Meaning?" (which discuss Davidson's program at length). In addition to these writings and the others cited elsewhere in the present essays, two recent works of interest are Dummett's "Language and Truth" and "Language and Communication."

2. The entire passage from which this quotation is taken provides a good overview of the significance of Davidson's program in the context of analytic philosophy of language; see "What Is a Theory of Meaning? (II)" 68–70.

3. For Grice's philosophy of language, see now his collected papers on this and other topics, *Studies in the Way of Words,* and the essays by and about Grice in the festschrift for him

edited by Grandy and Warner (for which, in fact, "Derangement" was originally written). On the antithesis, characterized by Strawson as a "Homeric struggle," between Gricean and Davidsonian theories of meaning, see Strawson's (pro-Gricean) inaugural lecture along with McDowell's (Davidsonian) corrective and the further correctives to be found in Dummett's "Language and Communication."

4. Dasenbrock's anthology represents a pioneering attempt to connect and confront literary theory with analytic philosophy, as I discuss in a review essay titled "From Small Beginnings." Other efforts in this area include my earlier essay "Discovery and Recovery in the Philosophy of Language" and Avni's recent, ambitious volume.

5. As Davidson expresses it in his introduction to *Inquiries*, the guiding question there is: "What is it for words to mean what they do?" (xviii). The query is of course an ancient one; what is new is the kind of answer the Davidsonian program would provide, completing a revolution in thought about language that began with Frege a century ago. Some familiarity with Frege's celebrated semantic essays is presupposed by Davidson's program; see Frege, *Translations from the Philosophical Writings* 21–78.

6. This explains why so much of *Inquiries* takes the form of commentaries on Tarski (see essays 1–5 and the book's index). Nor has Davidson's concern with Tarski waned, and the first of the John Dewey Lectures offers further commentary ("SCT" 279–95). A good, informal presentation of Tarski's quite technical work is to be found in Chapter 9 of Blackburn, with a helpful emphasis on its role in the Davidsonian program.

7. On radical interpretation, see essays 9–12 of *Inquiries*. The concept is modeled on Quine's ideas about "radical translation," which are also vital background for understanding *Inquiries*, "Derangement," and "The Structure and Content of Truth." See chapter 2 of Quine's great treatise *Word and Object* or (less intellectually arduous) the opening two essays in his *Ontological Relativity*.

8. See especially essays 8, 17, and 18 of *Inquiries* for arguments against a variety of conventionalist lines in the philosophy of language, including Dummett's. Far from being a radical departure from Davidson's previous work, "Derangement" fits quite comfortably into this series of writings.

9. Davidson considers this kind of attitude, but moves to dismiss it: "We could hold that any theory on which a speaker and interpreter converge is a language; but then there would be a new language for every unexpected turn in the conversation, and languages could not be learned and no one would want to master most of them" ("NDE" 445). As we will see, there are several things to consider before we accept such a quick refutation.

10. Davidson summarizes his distinctions as follows: "For the hearer, the prior theory expresses how he is prepared in advance to interpret an utterance of the speaker, while the passing theory is how he *does* interpret the utterance. For the speaker, the prior theory is what he *believes* the interpreter's prior theory to be, while his passing theory is the theory he *intends* the interpreter to use" ("NDE" 442). Note that both speaker-side theories are defined in explicitly second-order terminology ("believes," "intends"), while the description of the hearer's prior theory avoids the intentional idiom ("is prepared in advance to . . .") and thus can be assigned to the first order. Finally, the hearer's passing theory is described neutrally here, although elsewhere Davidson makes it clear that beliefs are involved in how a hearer "does interpret."

11. Why Dummett holds that linguistic norms cannot amount only to explicitly known rules, in contrast to those of a game, is made clear in this passage of "Comments": "The players of the game can probably state the rules, perhaps only haltingly, if challenged to do so, even though they seldom actually advert to those rules when playing. Speakers of a language know the meanings of the words belonging to it, but are frequently unable to state them; it is in principle impossible for their knowledge of the language, if it be their mother-tongue, to consist in its entirety in knowledge that they could state" (472).

12. Dummett summarizes his case for the priority of sociolect over idiolect in *Basis:* "A language is not to be characterised as a set of overlapping idiolects. Rather, an idiolect is constituted by the partial and imperfect grasp that a speaker has of a language, which is related to the language as a player's grasp of the rules of a game is related to the game. It is largely determined by what the speaker rightly or wrongly takes the meanings of words in the language to be; the concept of such an idiolect therefore cannot be anterior to that of a common language" (87).

13. If this argument conveys a sense of *déjà vu,* that is because of the remarkable similarity it bears to the celebrated case Davidson has made ("On the Very Idea of a Conceptual Scheme" [*ITI* 183–98]) for the intelligibility of false beliefs as dependent on the existence of a broad background of true beliefs. What is more remarkable, perhaps, is that while Davidson has made so much of this line of thinking as it bears on belief—where it seems to me somewhat dubious—he has not even noted the potentially parallel application to the case of meaning, where the argument not only seems more plausible in itself, but is quite damaging to the line Davidson actually has taken, in recent writings, on meaning and interpretation.

14. In *Basis* Dummett writes: "only by assuming [someone] to understand or, occasionally, to misunderstand the words he uses can we give any substance to attributing to him one or another intention in using them: if someone has no idea what he is doing, he can have no purpose in doing it rather than something else. This becomes vivid when we try to understand the utterances of a foreigner with an imperfect grasp of the language: we assign quite different intentions to him from those we should assign to a native speaker who used the same words" (92).

15. For more on this, see "Origins" 193–96 and *Basis* 82–84, where the example used in both cases is "gasket": I can convey something fully intelligible to you by saying, "My car needed a gasket repaired," even if neither of us could say what a gasket *is;* the authoritative speaker in this case is a garage mechanic, and it is to the mechanic's use that we tacitly appeal in this transaction and to which we would defer if challenged on our usage.

16. In the passage quoted, Davidson is explicitly criticizing not Dummett, but a younger philosopher of rather similar outlook, Tyler Burge, who has developed a line on the theory of meaning which he calls an "anti-individualistic" one and by which he means (among other things) a social one. Interested readers can follow the debate in Davidson's "Knowing One's Own Mind" (448–50 and notes) and "The Structure and Content of Truth" (310–11) and in Burge's "Intellectual Norms and the Foundations of Mind" (sec. 1) and "Wherein Is Language Social?" (184–87).

17. Since the present essay was drafted, Davidson has extended some of the themes of "Derangement" in an essay entitled "James Joyce and Humpty Dumpty." Its potential interest for literary critics should be evident, although I do not see that it adds a great deal to the *philosophical* arguments analyzed here.

WORKS CITED

Avni, Ora. *The Resistance of Reference: Linguistics, Philosophy, and the Literary Text.* Baltimore: Johns Hopkins UP, 1990.

Blackburn, Simon. *Spreading the Word: Groundings in the Philosophy of Language.* New York: Oxford UP, 1984.

Burge, Tyler. "Intellectual Norms and the Foundations of Mind." *Journal of Philosophy* 83 (1986): 697–720.

———. "Wherein Is Language Social?" In George 175–91.

Dasenbrock, Reed Way, ed. *Redrawing the Lines: Analytic Philosophy, Deconstruction, and Literary Theory.* Minneapolis: U of Minnesota P, 1989.

Dummett, Michael. "Can Analytic Philosophy Be Systematic, and Ought It to Be?" In *Truth and Other Enigmas* 437–58.

———. "Language and Communication." In George 192–212.

———. "Language and Truth." In *Approaches to Language.* Ed. Roy Harris. New York: Pergamon, 1983. 95–125.

———. *The Logical Basis of Metaphysics.* Cambridge: Harvard UP, 1991.

———. " 'A Nice Derangement of Epitaphs': Some Comments on Davidson and Hacking." In LePore 459–76.

———. "The Origins of Analytic Philosophy." *Lingue e Stile* 23 (1988): 3–49, 171–210.

———. "The Philosophical Basis of Intuitionistic Logic." In *Truth and Other Enigmas* 215–47.

———. *Truth and Other Enigmas.* Cambridge: Harvard UP, 1978.

———. "What Is a Theory of Meaning?" In *Mind and Language.* Ed. Samuel Guttenplan. Oxford: Clarendon, 1975. 97–138.

———. "What Is a Theory of Meaning? (II)." In *Truth and Meaning: Essays in Semantics.* Ed. Gareth Evans and John McDowell. Oxford: Clarendon, 1976. 67–137.

Frege, Gottlob. *Translations from the Philosophical Writings of Gottlob Frege,* 3d ed. Ed. and trans. Peter Geach and Max Black. Totowa: Rowman & Littlefield, 1980.

George, Alexander, ed. *Reflections on Chomsky.* New York: Basil Blackwell, 1989.

Gorman, David. "Discovery and Recovery in the Philosophy of Language: Dummett and Frege." *Diacritics* 13 (1983): 43–62.

———. "From Small Beginnings: Literary Theorists Encounter Analytic Philosophy." *Poetics Today* 11, no. 3 (1991): 647–59.

Grandy, Richard, and Richard Warner, eds. *Philosophical Grounds of Rationality: Intentions, Categories, Ends.* Oxford: Clarendon, 1986.

Grice, Paul. *Studies in the Way of Words.* Cambridge: Harvard UP, 1989.

Hacking, Ian. "A Parody of Conversation." In LePore 447–58.

LePore, Ernest, ed. *Truth and Interpretation: Perspectives on the Philosophy of Donald Davidson.* Oxford: Basil Blackwell, 1986.

McDowell, John. "Meaning, Communication, and Knowledge." In *Philosophical Subjects: Philosophical Essays Presented to P. F. Strawson.* Ed. Zak van Straaten. New York: Oxford UP, 1980. 117–35.

Quine, W.V.O. *Ontological Relativity and Other Essays.* New York: Columbia UP, 1969.

———. *Word and Object.* Cambridge: MIT, 1960.

Ramberg, Bjørn. *Donald Davidson's Philosophy of Language.* Oxford: Basil Blackwell, 1989.

Strawson, P. F. "Meaning and Truth." In *Logico-Linguistic Papers.* London: Methuen, 1971. 170–89.

What Causal Explanation Leaves Out: Davidson's Causal-Action Theory as a Tool for Practical Judgment

ALLEN DUNN

Since the publication of Donald Davidson's "Actions, Reasons, and Causes" in 1963, there has been a growing consensus among Anglo-American philosophers that an agent's reasons for an action constitute the causes of that action. Prior to the publication of that essay, most philosophers working in the analytic tradition had accepted Wittgenstein's claim that to know an agent has acted for certain reasons is not to know cause and effect, since causal laws are essentially nomological and based upon induction, while reasons are teleological and do not yield such laws. Although Davidson claimed that the reasons which cause human actions are not governed by universal laws, the shift from Wittgenstein's teleological theory of action to Davidson's causal theory was widely supposed to have demolished some of the most important differences separating the human sciences from the positive sciences. It seems, however, that to the extent literary critics have thought about the philosophy of action at all, most have remained confirmed Wittgensteinians, committed to the assumption popularized in von Wright's *Explanation and Understanding* that a phenomenological language of human understanding is governed by notions of teleology while the explanatory languages of the sciences are governed by the laws of causality. In the present essay I will consider what implications Davidson's causal theory of action might have for literary critics. Specifically, I will consider two related questions: Does the causal theory of action provide a viable and compelling alternative to the phenomenological models of action which are most often employed by literary critics? and, if not, Will a causal theory of action help to refine or elaborate the explanatory models which literary critics characteristically employ?

My answer to both questions is no, although my response to the second is heavily qualified. I do not think that Davidson's causal theory of action, as it now stands, provides a viable alternative to the loosely phenomenological accounts of action commonly favored by literary critics; neither do I think that Davidson's causal theory of action in its present form is likely to add much to such phenomenological accounts, although such a theory may help clarify or model certain forms of rational choice. My pessimistic response to the questions posed does not reflect a blanket judgment on the viability of Davidson's causal theory of action. Such a judgment would far exceed the scope of the present essay. Davidson's theory may help explain the general conditions under which actions become intelligible, and it may play an indispensable role in his theory of truth. Anyone familiar with Davidson's work must be impressed by the breadth and coherence of his thought. There are two reasons, however, for my belief that, in its present form, Davidson's theory of action cannot replace or supplement phenomenological accounts. The first is practical or procedural: several technical problems must be overcome before a causal theory can be applied with the requisite rigor, and frequently it seems that the effort required to formalize the elements in a causal explanation is disproportionate to the results. I will mention some of these problems in passing, but they are peripheral to the main thrust of my argument. As I argue below, the second and more substantial barrier to using Davidson's theory for literary criticism is that, as Davidson himself admits, a causal theory of action does not attempt to give an introspective account of the experience of decision making and acting.[1] Such introspective accounts, I will maintain, are crucial to moral and aesthetic descriptions of action. Nothing in Davidson's causal theory argues against the usefulness or validity of such accounts, but causal explanation typically reduces our deliberations about actions (whether our own or those of others) to a pattern of deductive reasoning that sometimes seems irrelevant or extrinsic to the deliberations themselves.

I will begin by sketching some of the essential features of Davidson's causal-action theory and some of the responses to that theory by Davidson's various critics. Next, I will analyze "Hume's Cognitive Theory of Pride," in which Davidson uses his causal theory to reconstruct Hume's arguments about pride. This causal explanation of a mental disposition reveals some of the more general problems that I see in the causal theory of action. In the third and final section of the present essay, I will apply Davidson's causal theory to two literary texts in order to illustrate what I consider to be some of the shortcomings in his descriptions of actions and complex mental states. I also consider what special problems the characteristic features of *literary* representations might pose for a Davidsonian description of action.

Most theories of action begin with the assumption that an action is distinguished from an event by the fact that action involves mental events or actions. The goal of a theory of action, therefore, is to give adequate descriptions of actions, mental events, and their relationship. Davidson assumes that actions as well as events have an objectlike particularity that allows them to be incorporated as nouns or noun phrases in truth-functional sentences.[2] This gives ontological priority to the event/action, and it means that all actions can also be described as events. For instance, the intentional action of raising an arm may also be described in purely physiological terms as an event. Agency or intentionality is just one frame of reference that can be used in describing such an event. This assumption is crucial to Davidson's project because it gives actions/events an identity that is not dependent upon intention; intention is merely one possible way of describing a particular occurrence. By contrast, those who favor a teleological description of action commonly insist that the act of intending itself provides the definition of the action intended. Davidson's approach to defining and delimiting actions is characterized as austere because it sharply distinguishes an action from its consequences, intended or otherwise.

Davidson's approach to the mental events that cause action is equally parsimonious. Actions are distinguished from events, he insists, because they are rationalized by primary reasons. In "Actions, Reasons, and Causes," he defines a primary reason as a combination of a *pro* attitude and a belief:

> Whenever someone does something for a reason, therefore, he can be characterized as (*a*) having some sort of pro attitude toward actions of a certain kind, and (*b*) believing (or knowing, perceiving, noticing, remembering) that his action is of that kind. Under (*a*) are to be included desires, wantings, urges, prompt-

ings, and a great variety of moral views, aesthetic principles, economic prejudices, social conventions, and public and private
goals and values in so far as these can be interpreted as attitudes
of an agent directed toward actions of a certain kind. [*EAE* 3–4]

Davidson formulates two theses about primary reasons:

1. In order to understand how a reason of any kind rationalizes
an action it is necessary and sufficient that we see, at least in
essential outline, how to construct a primary reason.
2. The primary reason for an action is its cause. [4]

Thus, the primary reason that explains an action is, in fact, an informal or
practical syllogism, and the logical relationship between the *pro* attitude
and the belief state is the cause of the action that it rationalizes. A *pro*
attitude is a commitment to the desirability of a certain state of affairs,
and a belief state expresses the conviction that a specific action will
bring about that state of affairs. Together, they cause the action that they
explain. Davidson insists, however, that the fact that reasons are the
causes of actions does not mean that they are determined by a law or
lawlike generalization: "The practical syllogism provides a model neither
for a predictive science of action nor for a normative account of evaluative reasoning" (16).

By his own account, this much of Davidson's argument from "Actions,
Reasons, and Causes" has remained unchanged, but he has modified
certain assertions that he made there. He has, first of all, retracted the
claim that the "propositional expressions of the reasons for an action are
deductively related to the proposition that corresponds to the action as
explained by those reasons" ("Introduction," *EAE* xii). That is, the propositional content of a *pro* attitude cannot be expressed as a universalized
conditional statement. This means that a *pro* attitude cannot be incorporated in a first-order logic, but as Ernest LePore and Brian McLaughlin
point out, it does not preclude the *pro* attitude from being treated in
some other type of logical system (13). Davidson has also modified his
claim in "Actions, Reasons, and Causes" that there are no intentions. In
that essay he argued that intention adds nothing to the description of an
action—that is to say, intention is syncategorematic (*EAE* 8). He has
since come to believe that although intentions may add nothing to *pro*
attitudes, they exist as "all-out, unconditional judgement[s]" that a specific course of action is superior to alternatives ("Intending," *EAE* 99).

Davidson's evolving causal theory of action has generated an enormous body of commentary. Those who in principle accepted the theory and attempted to give it practical application have concerned themselves with refining Davidson's formulations so that true instances of rationalized action can be distinguished from anomalous events. These philosophers have, among other things, sought ways to avoid what Myles Brand calls antecedential and consequential waywardness (17ff.). Davidson's much-discussed example of antecedent waywardness, for example, involves a mountain climber who realizes that he could save himself from danger by letting go of the rope from which his partner is hanging. The thought of betraying his partner so upsets him that he accidentally releases his grip. Despite the fact that the appropriate *pro* attitude is present here, this is not a cause of rationalized action. The challenge (a challenge met in several different ways) facing the causal-action theorist is to provide a description of the connection between mental events and actions that rules out such cases.

A more serious difficulty with Davidson's theory, one acknowledged both by Davidson's supporters and by his opponents, is the notion of a *pro* attitude. I would summarize this difficulty by observing that Davidson's notion of a *pro* attitude is too general in principle but also too simply one-dimensional in the examples he gives. Wilfrid Sellars observes:

> what disturbs me about Davidson's account [of *pro* attitudes] is that in his examples he tends to stress the onslaught of factual thoughts and leaves the relevant pro-attitudes to be relatively long term dispositions which constitute the mental background of the functioning of reasons. [190]

More specifically, in his examples Davidson tends to describe mental events in terms of a fairly simple cognitive model which largely ignores the role that factors such as affect, desire, and social conditioning play in motivating action.[3] Davidson is willing to admit that these motives might be important; but, as Brand notes, he gives us no clues about how they may be distinguished and related (45).

Among Anglo-American philosophers of action, both those applying and those criticizing Davidson's causal-action theory tend to push his theory in one of two directions, directions he explicitly resists. As I mentioned above, Davidson insists that a primary cause for an action "provides a model neither for a predictive science of action nor for a normative account of evaluative reasoning" ("Actions," *EAE* 16). Yet, critics and followers alike persist in attempting to assimilate Davidson's theory either to the physicalism/naturalism of a predictive science or to the rational-decision theory that would provide a normative account of reasoning. The physicalists insist that action theory should yield a program wherein so-called mental events can be described in or translated into physical events. Davidson, who describes himself as an asymmetrical monist, agrees that all events are physical events (monism); the mental, for Davidson, is a conceptual rather than an ontological category like the physical. Nonetheless, Davidson insists that there is no way to reduce mental meanings to physical phenomena. The relationship between the two is, he claims, necessarily asymmetrical. Similarly, Davidson resists those who would treat the primary causes of actions as typically primitive forms of a logic of choice. He notes that those among his critics who, like Carl Hempel, want to use the logic of a rational-choice theory to explain human action often use logical models prescriptively to explain what should happen, rather than descriptively to show what does happen, in mental events. Davidson does seem to be receptive to the idea of using a descriptive form of logical modeling to elaborate his theory of action, but it is not clear how this might alter his account of primary reasons.[4] These competing agendas for causal-action theory raise two crucial questions. First is the question of the status such a theory will grant to the folk-psychological descriptions of action (nonsystematic intuitive accounts of mental states) that are found in everyday language. Many naturalists seem to favor abandoning such descriptions entirely. The second and closely related question is what role causal-action theory will play in other (nonphilosophical) disciplines. The answers to these questions will determine to what extent causal-action theory will become developed within existing disciplinary frameworks and to what extent it will be developed in opposition to them.

Paradoxically, it seems that Davidson's commitment to the folk-psychological descriptions of everyday language is the source both of his causal-action theory's appeal (for those who are committed to working in such a medium) as well as its limitations: it gives us no formal theory—phenomenological, cognitive, or neurophysiological—that would allow us to develop a more complex notion of a *pro* attitude. It is also ironic that those who have developed Davidson's theory using models borrowed from cognitive psychology and research in artificial intelligence might well produce more that is practically useful for phenomenological accounts of action, although this has yet to be established as the case.

Although there has been little written on the literary applications of Davidson's causal-action theory, two studies have been published that identify some of the apparent difficulties in such an application. In *Act and Quality,* Charles Altieri argues that Davidson's commitment to the description of actions/events as objectlike particulars renders him incapable of describing certain qualities of human action that can be described using expressivist theories of action; in *Fictions, Philosophies, and the Problems of Poetics,* Peter McCormick analyzes the psychological models of cognition and motivation that have been employed by causal-action theorists and finds that these models provide inadequate description of literary representations of action.

Altieri, who defends a modifed teleological view of action, claims that by giving priority to the objectlike particularity of events as well as actions, Davidson "may collapse human actions into event descriptions" (116). "The issue," according to Altieri, "boils down to whether examples can convince us that even if no explanation is possible that meets Davidson's standard, the phenomena are significant enough, and the interpretive language sufficiently clear, to warrant a competing framework" (115). Altieri follows Alvin Goldman and others in claiming that Davidson's theory fails to account for supererogatory features of actions. He uses Goldman's example of the debtor who repays a debt he owes to Smith. The debtor knows that Smith likes to collect two-dollar bills, and so he makes a point of paying him with a two-dollar bill. According to Goldman, the act of repaying the debt and the supererogatory gesture of paying with a two-dollar bill are acts with fundamentally different properties and, therefore, cannot be the same act. Altieri admits (*contra* Goldman) that it is not necessary for different descriptions of the same action to entail the same nonphysical property, but he claims that if it is the debtor's intention that his gesture be recognized by Smith, then "the act is not a physical event with a variety of possible descriptions. But the act here is what it is only under a description that recognizes the intention and clarifies the doing as a deliberate supererogatory gesture" (118). Altieri argues that, in contrast to Davidson's approach, a Wittgensteinian strategy would allow us to view such supererogatory reasons as constitutive features of events. Altieri makes a plausible case for his claim that a causal theory of action may induce a systematic insensitivity to certain features of action, features that are ordinarily described in "teleological" terminology, and my criticisms of Davidson tend to support this claim. I think, however, that Davidson's theory can accommodate the Goldman/Altieri counterexample. The supererogatory gesture does not have qualities that make it qualitatively different from other (re)descriptions of an objectlike event. As Lawrence Davis points out, there seem to be no arguments that demonstrate that one method of defining an event is, in itself, superior to others, since among the most influential action theories "whatever is said in terms of one theory can be restated in terms of any one of its rivals" (41).

McCormick is less interested in criticizing the theoretical framework of causal theories of action than he is in evaluating the descriptive models that have been developed by causal-action theorists. He focuses not on Davidson but on Myles Brand, whose *Intending and Acting* presents a psychological account of action based on causal-action theory. McCormick provides a detailed discussion of what he feels are the gaps in Brand's cognitive and motivational models of action, and he suggests some of the special difficulties that specifically literary accounts of action might present for Brand's theory. Brand eschews folk-psychological accounts of action, arguing that causal theories of action should provide an account of the cognitive and motivational "deep structure" of intention. Therefore, many of McCormick's criticisms of Brand do not apply to Davidson's much more informal scheme of causal explanation. One of McCormick's criticisms of Brand's argument, however, is particularly appropriate to Davidson's theory as well. McCormick notes the difficulty that Brand has in giving a suitably rigorous description of the relationship between the proximate and immediate mental events that cause an action, and I will argue below that Davidson's theory is plagued with a similar difficulty. McCormick also notes that certain literary descriptions of actions present special problems for a theory like Brand's. He observes, for example, that Thomas Becket's decision to wait at the altar in T. S. Eliot's *Murder in the Cathedral* is particularly difficult to describe in Brand's terminology, since that "decision" includes elements of both acting and nonacting. Such moments, surprisingly common in literature, present similar difficulties for Davidson's theory.

My criticisms of Davidson's action theory are generally congruent with the arguments of Altieri and McCormick, although my argumentative strategy of focusing on a single issue, pride, differs considerably from their strategies. Like both of these critics, I proceed by adducing examples of mental states and actions that I think present special difficulties for Davidson's theory. Yet, unlike them, I am concerned not so much with the theoretical rigor of Davidson's argument as with its usefulness in certain types of practical deliberation. This, however, is a matter of emphasis and does not reflect any conviction on my part that there is a necessary split between theory and practice.

I have chosen to discuss "Hume's Cognitive Theory of Pride" because it focuses on an issue of practical judgment, on the rationalization and justification of pride. Davidson argues that we can discuss and evaluate pride precisely because we assume it is caused by certain reasons; these reasons, he claims, take roughly the same syllogistic form as the primary reasons of his causal theory of action. The essay in question, then, provides a test case for assessing the adequacy of Davidson's theory to account for the explanations and judgments commonly found in everyday discourse. Such complex mental states as pride and shame are often the subjects of practical moral deliberation, and they are topics frequently addressed by literary critics. In the argument that follows, I will claim that Davidson's causal theory of pride is weakened by the fact that there are no adequate causal explanations for many common and presumably rational instances of complex mental states such as pride and shame. I also point out that many of the explanations and judgments that we commonly give and receive regarding these complex mental states do not include a causal explanation. That is, we are often satisfied with explanations that differ in kind from Davidson's.

In the final section of the present essay, I will use a discussion of two literary texts to illustrate some of the limitations of Davidson's causal theory of mental states. There I will also argue that some of the weaknesses in Davidson's causal account of mental states are also apparent in his causal theory of action, particularly as that theory is applied to literary accounts of action. Yet, I should point out that there is an important difference between Davidson's causal theory of pride and his more general causal theory of action. Unlike a *pro* attitude, the premises upon which a proud person's judgments depend are universalizable, according to Davidson. In this way, perhaps, a causal theory of pride is more rigorous and therefore more vulnerable than a causal explanation of action.

"Hume's Cognitive Theory of Pride" is Davidson's reconstruction of the theory of pride that Hume presents at the beginning of the second book of *A Treatise of Human Nature*. Both Davidson and Hume wish to assert that apparently subjective attitudes like pride can be explained in terms of a public discourse, and both claim that there is an essential contiguity between the act of self-evaluation and other, more public types of evaluative activities. This is important to Hume's liberal political agenda, since it means that self-love and public spirit can be shown to be contiguous rather than antithetical as they often are in the Christian view. Hume's argument provides the foundation for an associationist ethics like that of David Hartley or William Godwin in which social responsibility turns out to be merely an expanded form of self-interest. Davidson, however, is concerned with issues of intelligibility rather than with an affective theory of moral sympathy. As Davidson asserts in the conclusion to his essay, one of the primary lessons to be drawn from Hume's argument is that judgments are intelligible only to the extent that they embody complex logical and causal constraints. Identifying and acknowledging such constraints in the case of pride is thus a matter of both intelligibility and moral accountability. Meaning and morality, Davidson implies, are in this case inseparable.

Davidson describes his essay as a reconstruction of what Hume "*should* have meant" (*EAE* 277). He admits that there are many problems with Hume's argument but claims that Hume's cognitive theory can be separated from the flaws of Hume's atomistic psychology. In his description of pride, Hume freely conflates a sensationist model of causality, based upon the contiguity of pleasurable impressions, and a model of logical entailment whereby certain ideas necessarily lead to certain conclusions. Hume's argument is redeemed, according to Davidson, by eliminating any sensationist notions of pleasure as the cause of pride and by locating pride's cause exclusively in the domain of judgment. Hume is wrong, in Davidson's estimation, to suppose that pride always involves a "feeling or sensation," for although "frissons of pleasure" may accompany prideful thoughts, such sensations "are not necessary or typical" (278).

Davidson also dismisses Hume's attempt to provide an *a priori* specification of the kind of relationships that exist between a person and those praiseworthy qualities which might make that person proud. Hume claims that the qualities which cause a person to feel pride must be related to that person in at least one of a number of specific ways (ownership, kinship, bodily identity, etc.). Davidson, however, rejects this attempt to define pride in terms of a third-person observation. He claims that the relationship that produces pride is best suited to propositional s :ntences, and he formulates the relationship between the proud person and the quality that causes pride as a belief statement that could be attributed to the proud person: " 'I . . .' where the dots supply a predicate that may or may not contain a reference to some further object." As Davidson puts it, this builds the assumption of a relationship "into the central causal belief which is where it belongs" (279). This formulation makes it possible for Davidson to explicate the cognitive implications of what he considers to be one of Hume's most important insights: "in order to be proud that one has a property, the property itself must quite independently cause an impression that 'resembles and corresponds' to pride" (280). That is, the proud person must value the properties that cause pride—independently of the fact that she or he possesses them. It is the independent value of these qualities and not the proud person's possession of them that rationalizes or causes pride. Davidson summarizes:

I shall interpret Hume, then, as maintaining that, if someone is proud that he exemplifies a certain property, then he approves of, or thinks well of, others for exemplifying the same property. This approval is not to be distinguished from holding that anyone who has the property is to that extent praiseworthy, estimable, or virtuous. [281]

If the belief statement that causes pride is itself an application of certain universal norms, then the cognitive cause of pride can be formulated as a syllogism: all those who have property p are to that extent praiseworthy; I believe that I have property p; therefore, I am praiseworthy in that I have property p. Davidson is careful here to specify that judgment must be qualified to preclude unconditional conclusions. The phrase "to that extent" puts qualifications on the extent to which I am praiseworthy. To use Hume's example, if I believe that all those who own a beautiful house are praiseworthy and that I own such a house, then I am praiseworthy but only insofar as I own such a house.

This syllogism, Davidson argues, best represents the basic structure of the relationship Hume saw between pride and its causes, but Hume was prevented from formulating this relationship as clearly as he might have because he relied upon a faulty psychology and lacked a serious account of judgment. In reconstructing Hume's argument, Davidson incorporates what he sees as the infelicitous aspects of Hume's theory only insofar as they can be reconciled with the syllogistic model of propositional pride that he proposes. The syllogistic form of propositional pride is appealing because it renders pride intelligible in terms of arguments that can be formalized, questioned, and discussed. As Davidson puts it, "someone who is proud always has his reasons; the cause of his pride rationalizes it" (285). This means that while each person's assessment of her gifts is bound to differ, the relevant attitudes that inform the judgments of those gifts are universal. Davidson admits that although pride always has its reasons, this "does not show that such pride is always reasonable," since pride may be based upon mistaken assumptions about facts or values or it may be out of proportion to its grounds (286). Because of pride's propositional form, pride can be criticized, but "the criticism must concern the whole constellation of belief and attitude that is its direct source, since whatever forces for irrationality there are must operate to create the whole constellation" (287).

Davidson concludes the essay by reviewing some of the most common criticisms of Hume's causal theory of pride. Here he focuses primarily upon the types of criticism that might be directed either toward

Hume's argument or toward his own causal theory of action. The criticisms he reviews include the charge that Hume's description of the relationship between pride and the causes of pride is circular, and therefore inadequate as a definition of pride, as well as the charge that because the judgment which produces pride reflects a logical necessity, it cannot at the same time be a cause, since causes are contingent and not necessary. In defending Hume from the first charge, Davidson points out that because the premises of Hume's syllogistic account of pride are universal and imply a publicly shared and shareable set of values, those premises do more than repeat (in a circular fashion) the propositions found in specific acts of judgment. That is to say, I am not proud of having a beautiful house simply because I have a beautiful house; I am proud of having a beautiful house because I assume beautiful houses are universally valuable.

Davidson's response to the second charge is more elaborate. Here it is clear that Davidson is defending not only Hume's arguments about pride but also his own (more ambitious) assumption that we can understand how intelligibility is possible only by acknowledging that meaning is shaped by the constraints of both causality and logic (and by realizing that the two are not mutually exclusive). Whether or not Hume thought causality is contingent and therefore incompatible with logical necessity (Hume seems to present arguments on both sides of this question), Davidson is determined to dispute such an assumption; he argues that a phenomenon may be logically (and therefore necessarily) defined by a causal relationship. To defend this claim, he uses the example of a "snowblink," which is defined as sunlight that is reflected from snow onto clouds. Light reflected from snow onto clouds is both the cause of the snowblink and the necessary definition of that phenomenon. In a similar way, Davidson claims, the belief that one possesses praiseworthy attributes both defines and causes pride. The snowblink, he asserts, should prompt the question "How do you know that what we now see is snowblink" rather than "How do you know that the snowblink we now see is caused by the reflection of light from snow" (290). Similarly, pride should prompt the question "On what grounds do you believe that you possess this admirable attribute?" and not "How do you know that your belief that you possess this admirable attribute causes you to be proud?"

Opponents of this position complain that if causality were really a constituent feature of attitudes like pride, then first-person testimony would be open to challenge in a way that it is not. "I was proud of myself for keeping my mouth shut" would be open to empirical challenge in ways that it clearly is not. For Davidson, however, such statements are significant because we usually believe them and work to make them right. Although the causal relationship may be redescribed in physiological terms (and is therefore a contingent relationship), the real question is how a person gains authority when attributing propositional pride to himself. Such authority, Davidson claims, comes from the interpreter's assumption that interpretations are subject to complex restraints, restraints which are logical, causal, and both logical and causal. According to Davidson, the interpreter's assumption that such constraints exist bestows authority on the interpreted, and this assumption requires that causality and rationality be made to go hand in hand. Davidson summarizes this argument quite eloquently: "People are in general right about the mental causes of their emotions, intentions, and actions because as interpreters we interpret them so as to make them so. We must, if we are to interpret at all" (290).

In the following comments on "Hume's Cognitive Theory of Pride," I will be concerned primarily with evaluating Davidson's causal theory as an instrument for understanding a self-attitude like pride. As I stated at the outset of the present essay, my purpose will be to see whether a causal theory might replace or supplement the kinds of descriptions of human behavior that we find in the practical deliberations of less formal types of discourse. My remarks are not intended to engage Davidson's theory of meaning. Therefore, it is important to emphasize that Davidson may be correct in his conviction that logic and causality work hand in hand to produce meaning and, at the same time, wrong in his assertion that the types of attitude and behavior which we call pride are caused by the process of judgment he describes. That is, a description of pride may be rationally intelligible (and subject to constraints) without involving the kinds of judgment Davidson attributes to that mental state. I may, for instance, after a session with my psychiatrist or after reading a book by Norman Vincent Peale, decide that high self-esteem is necessary for mental health, and I may therefore attempt to develop a pride in my actions and attributes that is at least partially independent of objective criteria. Or, I may decide that pride is (contrary to what Davidson says) an instinctual disposition or inclination, that pride is best described in terms of sociobiology, and therefore needs no further justification in order to be intelligible. In either case, the intelligibility of pride does not depend upon my ability to rationalize an attitude according to Davidson's syllogism (although my second example may imply a departure from an intentional explanation of behavior). Descriptions of headaches, no less than descriptions of pride, are subject to complex restraints within Davidson's theory of meaning.

Apart from the broader issues raised by a theory of meaning, however, Davidson's reconstruction of Hume's argument raises a specific question about the intelligibility of certain types of practical judgment: Are acts of self-judgment intelligible only insofar as they may be said to include a syllogism based upon a universalizable premise? I will argue that while certain instances of self-judgment can be elucidated by Davidson's causal model, many cannot, and that in using Davidson's model to describe specific acts of self-judgment, we will often be led to overlook those features of the deliberative process which figure most prominently in our everyday accounts of our reasons for acting or assuming an attitude. Davidson's syllogistic model of self-judgment is inadequate for the following reasons: 1) the language that is needed to qualify the universal premise of the syllogism of self-judgment is likely to be vacuous, because it is often impossible to give an unambiguous and universally applicable account of what such qualification might mean; 2) the syllogistic model of judgment takes no account of the way in which our judgments are conditioned by our notions of character, including our notions of our own character; 3) the syllogistic model overlooks the role that narratives play in contextualizing and conditioning specific acts of judgment, and it also ignores the recursive features of judgment; 4) finally, Davidson's model provides an inadequate account of emotional affect (although other models of causal-action theory attempt to remedy this).[5]

According to Davidson's reconstruction of Hume, a cognitive theory of pride will allow us not only to provide rational accounts of the judgments that cause pride but also to see how such accounts imply important qualifications and, by recognizing these qualifications, to correct various forms of irrational pride. Yet, as I have just stated, it is often impossible to describe such qualifications in unambiguously universal terms, and because such qualifications cannot be formulated as universals, they cannot be built into the universal premise of the syllogism that rationalizes pride. According to Davidson, the qualifications of our judgments of pride or praiseworthiness take two forms. He stipulates that judgments of praiseworthiness must be qualified in terms of degree, noting that proud people may often be mistaken about the degree of their praiseworthiness and have a tendency to overrate their praiseworthy qualities; Davidson also claims that judgments of praiseworthiness must be limited to judgments of particular qualities. In other words, he cautions us not to assume that a person is generally praiseworthy just because that person has a specific praiseworthy quality. It is possible that the second qualification might be construed as a variation of the first— that is, that generalizing from the praiseworthiness of a specific attribute to the praiseworthiness of a person is merely a matter of mistaken judgment concerning degree. I think, however, that Davidson's insistence that we make a firm distinction between a person and her attributes raises thornier issues. Accordingly, I will deal with the second type of qualification when I discuss my second objection to the causal theory of pride: namely, my objection to the theory's insensitivity to the role that notions of personality play in conditioning our judgments.

Praiseworthiness is difficult to quantify because our judgments of self and others are usually extremely context-dependent and often employ a contrastive logic that resists translation into universal propositions. For this reason, it is not clear what kind of content can be given to the "to that extent" phrase which Davidson insists must be built into the universalized premise. Certainly it would be misleading to imply that praiseworthiness might be quantified in terms of an arithmetic specificity so that the ownership of a beautiful house might be assessed at, say, onetwentieth the amount of praiseworthiness granted an act of charity. Since Davidson insists that pride is primarily an act of judgment, not an emotion or a type of behavior, he must assume that the degree of praiseworthiness entailed by a specific attribute can be stated in propositional form. Yet, for many judgments of pride no such propositional form is available. I may decide that I have been too proud of my new monocle without being able to specify, in any propositional form, what the proper amount of pride might be. Furthermore, I might also be unable to specify in propositional form what my earlier, mistaken assumptions about monocles might have been. This problem is exacerbated by the fact that the overvaluation of a praiseworthy attribute is usually expressed not in a summary judgment but in a complex array of spoken and unspoken behaviors. My friends might point out that when I am wearing my monocle my speech patterns become affected and I tend to employ certain head-tossing gestures; they might further insist that such behavior is unjustified. Upon reflection, I might agree with them, but my agreement would in no way be dependent upon my ability to construct a universal proposition specifying the degree of praiseworthiness appropriate to monocles.

This difficulty with quantification points to a more general problem that appears when we try to imagine how the various limited grounds of specific judgments might be related to each other—how a person's ownership of a beautiful house might be related to her acts of charity, for instance. In practical judgments about ourselves and others, we tend to think holistically and to evaluate specific attributes of a person in terms of more general assumptions about her character. Thus, whatever universalizing premises we may be able to extract from practical judgments about others or ourselves will often include extensive qualifications based on judgments of character. For instance, a Davidsonian redaction of a judgment might produce such sentences as "Good manners are always appalling in men who are manipulative" or "Intelligence is a frightening quality in people who have no moral sense." It may be that, in some abstract way, the person who endorses the above premises may think that both intelligence and good manners are in themselves praiseworthy properties, or she may be indifferent to them. It seems to be begging the question, however, to analyze judgments about qualities in isolation from judgments about character.

The situation is further complicated by the fact that judgments about character as well as many other factors which might qualify and complicate a universal premise are accessible to us primarily in narrative form. When people are asked to explain a particular judgment, they characteristically produce not a universal premise but a loose, narrative account of the events that led to the judgment. In such a narrative, judgment will often be described as a recursive process. A decision will be made and then reaffirmed or modified on several different occasions over a period of time. Such a narrative may include clear, evaluative premises of universal scope, but often it will not. Sometimes such premises will help clarify the actions/judgments described in the narrative, but frequently the premises can do little more than repeat the narrative in question with all its gaps and uncertainties. Narratives are selective, limited by the interests as well as the knowledge of the narrator: they depend heavily upon a narrator's assumptions about character; they are usually organized retrospectively around already completed events; and they frequently suggest several different frameworks for evaluating/understanding an attitude or action without providing a clear synthesis of explanatory methods. The holistic quality of judgments about the praiseworthiness of character and the cumulative particularity that characterizes most narrative explanations do not rule out the possibility of giving a Davidsonian account of propositional attitude. But, they do call into question the actual value of such an account both as an explanation of what makes intelligible judgments intelligible and as an explanation of what procedures we should and do use to clarify ambiguous judgments.

Finally, Davidson's account of propositional pride gives us little help in understanding the complex emotional state usually associated with pride. It is not clear that assent to a syllogistic judgment is in itself sufficient to define pride. Those who are overwhelmed with a sense of unworthiness may, nonetheless, admit that they have praiseworthy qualities while insisting that those qualities give them no sense of self-worth. It seems counterintuitive to characterize such people as proud merely on the basis of their assent to a proposition.

Similar difficulties are apparent when we shift our attention from explanations of the way judgments cause pride to the actions that are caused by pride. Because pride is often stigmatized as an antisocial attitude, it is seldom mentioned in first-person accounts of specific actions. As the foregoing example of the monocle indicates, those who detect pride in the actions of others frequently describe pride as a supererogatory feature of those actions. Pride may not rationalize a particular speech act but may be evident in that speech act as it is revealed by tone and volume of voice, diction, gesture, and so on. Here, Davidson's formula would allow us to redescribe the act as both a conscious speech act, rationalized by a *pro* attitude and a belief, as well as an unintentional expression of a certain affect—say, the frisson of pride— but we would probably learn more from a phenomenologically based narrative.

Literary texts and the analyses of these texts tend to emphasize the features of practical judgment that, I have just argued, are most at odds with the spirit and sometimes the letter of Davidson's causal theory. Literary treatments of pride, for example, typically emphasize the way in which judgments by the proud individual are embedded in a narrative that, taken by itself, has a high degree of probability. Thus, in the moment of Aristotelian tragic recognition, the protagonist who has been duped by his own hubris is forced to revise an entire narrative framework of interpretation, and it would be difficult if not misleading to represent such tragic *anagnōrisis* as the revision of so many premises or pro attitudes. The example of tragedy also emphasizes the way in which literature typically requires its audience constantly to reconsider the relationship between free choice and contingency. This double awareness of agents as both determined and determining is difficult to capture in the language of primary reasons. In this section of my essay, I will use readings of two literary texts to illustrate some the limitations I have found in Davidson's causal theory. First I will show that Davidson's theory does not provide an adequate account of the humiliation of Gabriel Conroy in James Joyce's "The Dead" (humiliation, like pride, is a complex mental state based on self-evaluation). I will then show that similar difficulties are evident when Davidson's causal theory is used to describe the action in Joyce's "Eveline." Finally, I will consider some of the reasons why the types of actions that are often the subject of literary texts and the specifically literary features of literary representations might pose particular problems for a causal theory.

In *Pride, Shame, and Guilt,* Gabriele Taylor uses the conclusion of "The Dead" to criticize Davidson's theory of self-evaluation. Her reading illustrates the limitations of Davidson's model both as a tool for literary analysis and as an instrument of practical moral deliberation. The story's protagonist, Gabriel Conroy, and his wife, Gretta, attend a Christmas party given by Gabriel's aunts. Gabriel, his aunts' favorite nephew, helps them by making sure the party goes smoothly and delivers an oration at the party's conclusion. After the guests have left, Gabriel is suddenly smitten by his wife's beauty and loses himself in a series of romantic reminiscences about their shared past. When the couple arrives at their lodgings for the night, however, Gabriel notices that his wife is distracted, and he discovers that she is reminiscing about a boy, someone, she says, who once worked in the gasworks and who was once madly in love with her. Gabriel makes several ironic comments that are intended to convey his displeasure, but his wife is lost in memories and fails to notice. As a result, Joyce tells us, Gabriel feels

> humiliated by the failure of his irony and by the evocation of this figure from the dead, a boy in the gasworks. While he had been full of memories of their secret life together, full of tenderness and joy and desire, she had been comparing him in her mind with another. A shameful consciousness of his own person assailed him. He saw himself as a ludicrous figure. . . . [238]

Taylor claims, correctly I think, that it is impossible to construct the universal belief that will rationalize Gabriel's humiliation. According to Davidson's model, we should be able to construct Gabriel's universalizable assumption about what circumstances justify the feeling (or judgment, in Davidson's terms) of humiliation. This would allow us to understand why Gabriel believes his situation to be a particular instance of a set of universal conditions that everyone (universally) would find humiliating. Taylor constructs several hypothetical versions of the type of universal belief that would rationalize Gabriel's humiliation according to Davidson's model, and she finds them all to be deficient. Universalized generalizations about the most immediate causes of Gabriel's humiliation are likely to sound absurd. For instance, it would be silly to expect that Gabriel would agree to a generalization like "All those whose spouses fail to respond to their irony will feel humiliated." An entire range of reactions might be appropriate in such a situation, as Gabriel's earlier anger makes clear; and, as Taylor points out, we would think Gabriel insane if he assented to a universal premise like "All those whose spouses refuse to respond to irony about boys who work in the gasworks will feel humiliation," although the detail about Michael Furey's (Gretta's lover's) employment seems especially important in precipitating Gabriel's humiliation (*Pride* 9). Similar difficulties arise when we attempt to surmount these problems by building the appropriate qualifications into the universalizing premise. Say, for instance, we claim it is true of any husband that if he has been entertaining tender thoughts about his wife, he will be humiliated if he discovers she has been comparing him with someone else. As in the previous instance, many different responses to such a discovery can be imagined, and, as Taylor observes, Gabriel would likely admit that a more generous husband would and should respond differently in such a situation.

This last version of a universalizing premise contains a condensed narrative account of a fairly complex sequence of events, and subsequent attempts to provide an account of the universal grounds for Gabriel's humiliation are likely to involve the construction of a complex and highly personal narrative. If as Taylor suggests, for instance, we attempt to qualify the premise further by specifying that only husbands *like Gabriel* will always respond to a specific set of conditions by being humiliated, then we are moving away from a premise that explains self- . judgments by means of necessary reasons and toward an explanation that uses biographical data to explain why certain types of behavior are natural, though not inevitable, given a subject's past experiences. This is the direction in which most literary critics would be likely to travel when discussing Gabriel's moment of humiliation. Taylor summarizes her argument about Gabriel by asserting that "there would be no irrationality in Gabriel's refusal to commit himself to the truth of the relevant belief which is universal in form," and she observes that "maybe in such a tangled case the kind of intelligibility Davidson had in mind just cannot be had" (11). I would add that such tangled cases seem to be the rule rather than the exception, in literature if not in life.

Similar difficulties appear when we try to apply Davidson's causal-action theory to literary descriptions of actions. In its revised form, Davidson's action theory does not require that primary reasons take the form of universal statements; primary reasons need only present *pro* attitude judgments about the desirability of certain states of affairs. Such explanations are, of course, common enough in both literature and everyday discourse. Jack's boastful talk at the party is explained by the fact that he wanted to impress Sue and believed that by talking about his accomplishments he would do so. Typically, however, when actions are ambiguous enough to invite extensive interpretation, a causal theory of action proves to be of little help in integrating or synthesizing the various frameworks of explanation that are commonly invoked.

In Joyce's short story "Eveline," for example, the protagonist, Eveline, performs two actions which have been the subject of extensive critical discussion. In the first scene, Eveline sits by a window reminiscing about her childhood. She has decided to elope with a sailor named Frank. In her lap she has letters explaining her decision to her father and brother. As she reviews the reasons for her decision to elope, she is troubled by feelings of guilt and nostalgia. Her memories of the abusive behavior of her father in both the past and present are gradually displaced by memories of her father in his more pleasant moments. When she recalls that she promised her dying mother that she would keep the family together, she seems to be on the verge of changing her mind. At this point, however, she is overwhelmed by the vivid memory of her mother's misery and degradation; she flees in what Joyce describes as a state of terror: "Escape! She must escape! Frank would save her. He would give her life, perhaps love, too. But she wanted to live" (50). In the second and final scene of the story, Eveline is about to board a boat with Frank. In a state of distress and indecision, she prays "to God to direct her, to show her what [is] her duty" (51). As they approach the ship, she once again panics, overwhelmed with the feeling that "all the seas of the world [have] tumbled about her heart" and that Frank is "drawing her into them." Frank boards the ship ahead of her while she remains frozen, clutching the iron railing "passive, like a helpless animal" (51).

When we begin to construct primary reasons for Eveline's actions, we are confronted first with a general problem: primary reasons do not represent or summarize the introspective accounts of the decision-making process. Primary reasons may sometimes be inferred from such accounts, but they are seldom if ever directly stated. It is not clear, therefore, just what primary reasons will tell us about the drama of decision making that "Eveline" presents. More specifically, as I have already mentioned, primary reasons take no notice of the recursive nature of a decision-making process; they take no notice of the way in which certain primary reasons repeat and modify other primary reasons. In Eveline's case, this recursive aspect of decision making seems to be essential. Furthermore, Davidson's informal syllogisms provide little insight into the way that rational deliberation is conditioned by such factors as emotional compulsion and ideological systems of belief. Primary reasons give us no vocabulary for describing the relationship between Eveline's action and that state of nonaction which Joyce describes as paralysis.

Nonetheless, it is fairly easy to construct a plausible if necessarily vague primary reason for Eveline's flight: 1) she wishes to escape her present hardships and to find a better future; 2) she believes that eloping with Frank will allow her to escape her hardships and to find such a future; 3) this pair of *pro* attitude and belief rationalizes her action of leaving the house. Ambiguities, of course, remain: Does she really love Frank, or does she merely find him a convenient means of escape? Does she believe Frank is trustworthy, that he actually loves her, or is she trying to disguise her uncertainty about this? Constructing hypothetical primary reasons may help us describe what is ambiguous in Eveline's behavior, even if it does not dispel the ambiguities.

Yet, the critic's inquiry is likely to be focused upon a decision-making process as much as it is on the decision and act itself. We can discover quite a bit about this process without achieving certainty about Eveline's primary reasons. Furthermore, a summary of primary reasons alone is bound to distort the recursive nature of this process. Technically speaking, the mental event that affirms a primary reason must be temporally contiguous with the action it causes; this contiguity prevents the antecedental waywardness mentioned above. In Eveline's case, however, the decision to elope is, in fact, a sequence or series of decisions, and the action of leaving the house is best understood as both the affirmation and the modification of an earlier decision. We are led to believe that before the moment in which the story begins, Eveline has already decided to elope, and she has recorded her decision in letters to her father and brother. During the course of her deliberations, she affirms her decision several times, although at one point at least she seems poised to change her mind. In the instant before she leaves the house, Eveline repeats once more her reasons for leaving, but those reasons, familiar though they are, are no longer the same reasons that they were at the beginning of the story. They have been transformed by the panic Eveline experiences when she remembers her mother's madness and suffering. What once was a plan becomes an act of desperation. No longer is she weighing reasons as she was earlier in the story, as she presumably was when she wrote the two letters. Memory is Eveline's tool for deliberation, but it evokes emotions that are beyond her control, and Davidson's informal syllogism proves to be of little help in describing these dramatic changes in Eveline's thought.

Eveline's final paralysis is probably best described in Davidson's terms as an event, as pure panic that makes intentional action impossible. Yet, this scene's similarity to Eveline's flight from home is obvious, and her refusal to board the boat could also be rationalized. Her paralysis on the dock distills an entire spectrum of desires and anxieties: her worries about her father, her doubts about Frank, her desire to keep her promise to her mother, and finally her desire to do God's will. Any one or all of these reasons would be adequate to rationalize her "decision" to remain on the dock. Even her panic may be in some way intentional; like Eliot's Thomas Becket in McCormick's example, she may feel that she is acting out God's will by simply letting things happen. As was the case with the first scene, the story's conclusion invites us to weigh several frameworks of interpretation, to consider Eveline both as an agent and as a helpless animal. We may achieve a certain amount of clarity by using primary reasons to formalize some of these possible explanations for Eveline's behavior, but most of the critic's explanatory work is likely to be devoted to a synthesis of various partial explanations, a synthesis that is itself likely to take a narrative form. For this type of explanation, one that attempts to describe the relationship between doing and not doing, between reflective decision making and ideological thoughtlessness, between self-expression and self-surrender, a causal theory of action is likely to be of limited usefulness.

Up to this point, I have been discussing Joyce's fiction as if it contained transcripts of literal events. However, the conventions of literary representation and of literary criticism intensify some of the difficulties that, I have argued, are inevitable when one applies Davidson's causal-action theory to everyday explanations of human action. Literary representations of action are characteristically overdetermined; they manifest what Nelson Goodman has called symptoms of the aesthetic. These symptoms include such qualities as relative repleteness, multiple and complex reference, and exemplification.[6] According to Goodman, when a representation is replete, it obliges us to attend to an indefinitely large number of features or aspects. In literary fiction, for example, all aspects of a character's implied or specified past may contain information relevant to the explanation of an action; even the description of landscape and other seemingly unrelated details (as in instances of pathetic fallacy) can provide a reader with information necessary to understanding a character's action. Similarly, literary descriptions of actions are often produced by systems of multiple and complex reference. For instance, the actions of a character like Joyce's Bloom must be understood from mythical, literary, historical, and real/psychological points of view. Exemplification, the tendency of aesthetic works to pursue the representation of certain qualities (especially qualities pertaining to character and emotion) as an end in itself, is also apparent in literary representations of action. Some characters, usually minor ones, are presented as pure types, as the drunkard or the sentimental victim, for instance; their actions are to be explained primarily as the confirmation of a stereotyped pattern of human behavior.

None of these symptoms of the aesthetic is incompatible with the existence of primary reasons, but each symptom demands that the primary reasons we cite must be integrated within a larger, more complex, and open-ended sort of explanation. The repleteness of literary descriptions of action is naturally in tension with the rigorous economy of causal theories of action. Also, literary representations of action characteristically endow readers and characters alike with a heightened awareness of the way specific actions conform or do not conform to larger patterns of action: the way, for instance, that "Eveline" is an example of a fairy tale or popular romance gone wrong or the way we share Bloom's awareness that he is a stand-in for Jesus Christ in the Cyclops episode of *Ulysses.* Such supererogatory layers of explanation for action do not preclude the usefulness of causal explanations; but, as in the case of Eveline's ambiguous actions, a causal-action theory is unlikely to contribute much to the project of synthesis, in this case the synthesis of various systems of literary reference. Literary exemplification raises a similar issue for causal-action theory by rendering causal explanation unnecessary. The reader of Milton's "L'Allegro," for instance, would certainly be wasting time to construct primary reasons for the poet's celebration. More generally, as Charles Altieri has pointed out, causal-action theory seems to be insensitive to the performative or exemplificatory dimension of all actions, but especially the literary presentations of actions.

None of the characteristics that I have attributed either to practical deliberations about human action or, more specifically, to the literary presentation of such actions proves that a causal theory of action, Davidson's or any other, cannot contribute either to practical introspective accounts of human action or to literary analysis. Nor do my observations dispute Davidson's claim that the intelligibility of human action is made possible by the interpreter's willingness to assume that action is informed by complex logical and causal constraints. Rather, I think my discussion indicates that Davidson's action theory, in its present form, does not contribute much to the introspective folk-psychological language that is commonly used in practical as well as literary critical deliberations about the meaning of human action. Practical developments such as a more rigorous description of *pro* attitudes (particularly the conative features of *pro* attitudes) might change this. Literary critics are typically eclectic in the vocabularies they use to describe character and action, and I think that my argument supports an informed eclecticism. I suspect, however, that there will always be a tension between those descriptions of human action which attempt to capture the nuances of the decision-making process and those which attempt to specify in parsimonious terms the conditions that make such decisions meaningful.

NOTES

1. See "Problems in the Explanation of Action" (40ff.) for Davidson's description of the relationship between his formal account of action and the process of introspection.

2. For a helpful overview of recent theories of action, see Lawrence H. Davis's *Theory of Action*. The introductory sections of *Actions and Events* (LePore and McLaughlin, editors) provide helpful summaries of Davidson's work (as do many of the essays in that volume). I have also found the discussions of Davidson in Brand's *Intending and Acting* and Bishop's *Natural Agency* particularly illuminating.

3. See also "Moral Belief," in *Virtues and Vices and Other Essays in Moral Philosophy*, where Philippa Foot claims that notions of *pro* attitudes do not provide an adequate account of moral reasoning.

4. Davidson discusses such an account of desire in the third section of "The Structure and Content of Truth."

5. See Dan Bennett, "Hume's Pride," for criticism of "Hume's Cognitive Theory of Pride." Bennett argues that "it is my feeling of pleasure in and with myself which makes me pretty, and pleased with my house" (91).

6. Goodman discusses these and one other symptom of the aesthetic in the final section of *Languages of Art*.

WORKS CITED

Altieri, Charles. *Act and Quality: A Theory of Literary Meaning and Humanistic Understanding.* Amherst: U of Massachusetts P, 1981.

Bennett, Dan. "Hume's Pride." In Vermazen and Hintikka. 89–91.

Bishop, John. *Natural Agency: An Essay on the Causal Theory of Action.* Cambridge: Cambridge UP, 1989.

Brand, Myles. *Intending and Acting: Toward a Naturalized Action Theory.* Cambridge: MIT, 1984.

Davis, Lawrence H. *Theory of Action.* Englewood Cliffs: Prentice-Hall, 1979.

Foot, Philippa. *Virtues and Vices and Other Essays in Moral Philosophy.* Berkeley: U of California P, 1978.

Goodman, Nelson. *Languages of Art: An Approach to a Theory of Symbols.* Indianapolis: Hackett, 1976.

256   Allen Dunn

Hume, David. *A Treatise of Human Nature.* Ed. Ernest C. Mossner. London: Penguin, 1985.
Joyce, James. "The Dead." In *The Portable James Joyce.* New York: Viking, 1966. 190–242.
———. "Eveline." In *The Portable James Joyce.* New York: Viking, 1966. 46–51.
LePore, Ernest, and Brian P. McLaughlin. "Actions, Reasons, Causes, and Intentions." In *Actions and Events: Perspectives on the Philosophy of Donald Davidson.* Ed. LePore and McLaughlin. Oxford: Basil Blackwell, 1985. 3–13.
McCormick, Peter J. *Fictions, Philosophies, and the Problems of Poetics.* Ithaca: Cornell UP, 1988.
Sellars, Wilfrid. "Actions and Events." *Nous* 7 (1973): 179–202.
Taylor, Gabriele. *Pride, Shame, and Guilt: Emotions of Self-Assessment.* Oxford: Clarendon, 1985.
Vermazen, Bruce, and Merrill B. Hintikka, eds. *Essays on Davidson: Actions and Events.* Oxford: Clarendon, 1985.
Von Wright, Georg Henrik. *Explanation and Understanding.* Ithaca: Cornell UP, 1971.

Writing Action: Davidson, Rationality, and Literary Research

PAISLEY LIVINGSTON

Donald Davidson's work has many important implications for research in the literary disciplines, and in what follows I shall try to elucidate a few of them. I think it best to begin at a rather high level of generality, asking not how this or that Davidsonian notion or argument may be applied in the context of one of the particular ongoing debates in literary theory, but how different sorts of literary inquiry may be situated more generally in relation to some of Davidson's major philosophical themes. One fairly obvious approach to the topic would run as follows: Davidson has greatly clarified a number of issues surrounding the notions of meaning and interpretation, and his philosophy of language can, as a result, help us with some of the bedeviled questions of literary theory, beginning with the problem of the "validity" of interpretation, which concerns how critics can arrive at a (or perhaps even *the*) correct interpretation of a literary work. The intuition behind such an approach is straightforward enough: if David-son has a successful theory of interpretation, it ought to be applicable, *mutatis mutandis,* to the problem of literary interpretation. I think, however, that it is important to recognize some of the difficulties and limitations of this highly plausible way of adapting Davidson to literary theory. These limitations have to do, first of all, with aspects of the current situation in literary criticism, but they also involve ways in which Davidson's theory of interpretation is bound up with some of his

other philosophical views. I shall take up the latter point first, dealing
with it at some length before moving on in my second section to some
aspects of literary research.

My reservation about the most plausible and obvious manner of applying
Davidson's ideas to literary theory has to do with the place of the theory
of interpretation within his work. Davidson concludes "Belief and the
Basis of Meaning" by referring to "a holistic theory" that embraces every
interpretation and attribution of mental attitudes, or, in other words, the
whole of intentionalist psychology. In a highly significant phrase, he
writes that "indeterminacy is important only for calling attention to how
the interpretation of speech must go hand in hand with the interpretation of action generally, and so with the attribution of desires and beliefs"
(*ITI* 154). When we consider the massive importance that Willard Van
Orman Quine's reflections on indeterminacy have had for Davidson's
thinking (see, for example, "Meaning, Truth, and Evidence"), we realize
just how far-reaching the quoted phrase is; what follows will, in a sense,
amount to an effort to emphasize and follow up on this idea. I think it is
correct to say that this is anything but an isolated moment in Davidson's
work. Davidson explores the connection between decision theory and
semantics in "Belief and the Basis of Meaning," and his idea of a "unified
theory of meaning and action" is further developed in an article bearing
that title, large parts of which have been taken up more recently in the
John Dewey Lectures, published under the title "The Structure and Content of Truth." Here we read that "there is no chance of arriving at a deep
understanding of linguistic facts except as that understanding is accompanied by an interlocking account of the central cognitive and conative
attitudes" ("SCT" 315; "TUTMA" 2). Meaning, belief, and desire, Davidson claims, are the basic, irreducible trio of intentionalist psychology,
and he goes on to assert that no one of these three basic concepts can be
analyzed in terms of one or two of the others: "A basic account of any of
these concepts must start beyond or beneath them all, or at some point
equidistant from them all" ("SCT" 315; "TUTMA" 2). And what could
that point be? Davidson's idea is that it is a matter of fundamental norms
that govern the way in which these three interlocking notions are attributed in all processes of understanding. He rather modestly calls his own
descriptions of those norms "crude, vague, and incomplete" and makes a
basic suggestion about how his proposals might be fleshed out: "The way
to improve our understanding of such understanding is to improve our
grasp of the standards of rationality implicit in all interpretation of
thought and action" ("SCT" 325; "TUTMA" 12). In short, reflection on

implicit standards of rationality is basic to a Davidsonian perspective on meaning, understanding, and interpretation; his views on these latter notions are intimately linked to his theory of action explanations or "rationalizations," which are in turn grounded, along with the theory of interpretation, in assumptions about the nature and underpinnings of intentionalist psychology.

It would seem to follow from these points that an application of Davidson's theory of interpretation to literary criticism should begin by asking how standards of rationality could be fundamental to literary phenomena and their study. I shall be taking up precisely that question below, but first a clarification is in order. The very idea of bringing the notion of rationality into literary theory will be repugnant to many critics. Not only do many critics deem rationality to be a suspicious ideological notion in general, but they hold it to be especially inappropriate to literature and "textuality" (e.g., Adelman et al. 78). Now, this kind of romantic and postmodern attitude toward any and all concepts of rationality is an uninformed prejudice maintained in the absence of knowledge about the diverse conceptions of rationality that abound in the literature on the topic. (See, for example, the positions surveyed in my *Literature and Rationality.*) The prejudice in question here is especially inappropriate in relation to Davidson, whose views on rationality are joined by a keen interest in explaining the possibility of such serious forms of irrationality as *akrasia,* self-deception, mental partitioning, and nonrational forms of mental causation (see his "Incoherence and Irrationality," "Paradoxes of Irrationality," "Deception and Division," etc.). Thus, when Davidson suggests that norms of rationality play a fundamental role in any and every attribution of meaning and intention, he is not espousing any of the theses about rationality that literary theorists typically find so repugnant, such as the notion that all human activities are necessarily rational or the idea that rationality is the highest value in all things. Nothing that Davidson says about rationality implies that he believes the quality of literary works increases in direct proportion to their rationality, or that people should want to be the way Spock fancies himself in *Star Trek*—a creature of pure logic, unclouded by desire and emotion. Davidson begins "Incoherence and Irrationality" by noting that the term "irrational" is often used to stigmatize values and opinions that are simply different from our own, and he adds that such cases are not those with which he is concerned. Rationality is not just an ideological code word for expressing disagreement with someone else's attitudes; instead, Davidson is interested "in cases, if such there be, in which the judgment that the works or thoughts of an agent are irrational is not based, or at least not necessarily based, on disagreement over fact or norm—objective irrationality, one might be tempted to call it. This suggests that we should limit ourselves to cases in which an agent acts, thinks, or feels counter to his own conception of what is reasonable; cases where there is some sort of inner inconsistency or incoherence" ("II" 346).

The key to understanding this passage is a matter of grasping how Davidson can coherently claim that irrationality is plotted only in relation to norms that are the agent's own, while also contending that the identification of such a form of irrationality can be "objective," in the sense of not being merely the expression of a disagreement over norms or values. What reconciles these two claims is a deeper thesis: namely, the idea that there are certain standards of rationality that are held by all agents, so that violations of these standards are at once objective irrationalities *and* inner inconsistencies, relative both to the agent's own standards and to norms that are essential to agency as such. This thesis is presented rather directly by Davidson later in the same article: "all thinking creatures subscribe to *my* basic standards or norms of rationality. This sounds sweeping, even authoritarian, but it comes to no more than this, that it is a condition of having thoughts, judgments, and intentions that the basic standards of rationality have application" (351).

Davidson's claim, then, is that the language of agency and, along with it, the entire business of attributing meaningful mental attitudes to people and to their actions (of which utterances and writings are an important subset) can get started only if an interpreter or reader works with some basic standards concerning the "rationality" of the agent whose doings are under consideration. There can be no decision about whether to adopt these standards, because the very idea of a decision presupposes that the standards are already in place: "Agents can't *decide* whether or not to accept the fundamental attributes of rationality: if they are in a position to decide anything, they have those attributes" ("II" 352). That is why it is incoherent for postmodernists and neurophilosophers to try to persuade us to abandon the language of rational agency—the former because it is an illusory historical construct that obscures textual and discursive process, the latter because it is a "folk" theory that should be replaced by a scientific one. But suppose the language of rationality really were put out of play somehow—not as the result of a decision based on textual theory or progress in neuroscience, but as the result of some strange process (e.g., instead of making people shrink, the cosmic rays deprive them of the capacity to think about themselves and others as agents). We would then be deprived of all of the familiar kinds of coordination that we take for granted in everyday life, such as planning to run one's errands, deciding whether to finish reading an article in an anthology, making and keeping a rendezvous with a friend, and so on. Why? All of these familiar activities crucially involve ascriptions of mental attitudes to oneself and/or to others and, thereby, rely on the standards of rationality that make such ascriptions possible.

What, more precisely, are these standards? And how do we know that they are indeed a necessary condition of all intentionalist explanations and understandings? Here we need a brief evocation of Davidson's efforts to limn the norms of rationality that he considers to be basic to the entire framework of intersubjective understanding. I think it is fair to say that Davidson has attacked this problem from several different angles, just as he has made a proposal about a unifying theory, to which I shall return below. For example, his various analyses of interpretation and radical translation have led to descriptions of some of the principles that an interpreter must bring to bear on the material if he or she is to have a chance of successfully attributing anything like detailed, well-individuated propositional attitudes to another agent's linguistic behavior. The famous "principle of charity" belongs here, along with the analyses of "first person authority," truth, the relations between linguistic and speaker's meaning, and the debate over the role played by conventions in communication. Along with the aspects of rationality just evoked, we must include Davidson's references to "the basic principles of logic," to common sense ("PI" 302), and to certain inductive principles (e.g., Rudolf Carnap's principle of total evidence). Davidson has contended that one crucial aspect of rationality—and, hence, of the possibility of having and/or attributing well-individuated mental attitudes—is the capacity to formulate second-order beliefs, first and foremost of which is the concept of belief itself, for this is the notion that opens the door to the concept of objective truth and falsehood, and to the difference between states of affairs as fancied and as they really are (see especially "Rational Animals" for this argument).

In addition to making such claims about epistemic and semantic rationality, Davidson has outlined basic aspects of practical rationality, proposing descriptions of some of the causal and logical conditions on the reasonable production of action by such attitudes as belief and desire, which (when conjoined in the "right way") stand as the "primary reason" for an action. The "principle of continence" (the practical analogue of Carnap's principle of "total evidence") is another part of the standards of practical rationality: an agent deliberating over which course of action to choose may find that two mutually exclusive alternatives both find support; continence is a matter of acting on an evaluation based on all the considerations that the agent deems relevant to the choice in question. According to the principle of continence, the agent's intention to engage in the behavior is an "all-out" (unconditional) judgment in favor of this action, produced by the agent's desires and beliefs; to be rational, the intention must be consistent with the agent's "all-things-considered" (or "overall best") judgment of the action's value relative to the relevant attitudes (see "How Is Weakness of the Will Possible?" [in *EAE* 21–42]).

If we gather up these different elements, do they together constitute *the* basic standards of rationality to which Davidson frequently refers? In a context where he has just made a concise survey of some of these items, Davidson answers as follows:

> I have greatly oversimplified by making it seem that there is a definite, and short, list of "basic principles of rationality." There is no such list. The kinds and degrees of deviation from the norms of rationality that we can understand or explain are not settled in advance. We make sense of aberrations when they are seen against a background of rationality; but the background can be constituted in various ways to make various forms of battiness comprehensible. . . . [I]t does not make sense to ask, concerning a creature with propositional attitudes, whether that creature is *in general* rational, whether its attitudes and intentional actions are in accord with the basic standards of rationality. Rationality, in this primitive sense, is a condition of having thoughts at all. The question whether a creature "subscribes" to the principle of continence, or to the logic of the sentential calculus, or to the principle of total evidence for inductive reasoning, is not an empirical question. For it is only by interpreting a creature as largely in accord with these principles that we can intelligibly attribute propositional attitudes to it, or that we can raise the question whether it is in some respect irrational. ["II" 352]

I have reproduced this passage at length because I think it is indicative of a problem that Davidson's work usefully foregrounds but does not adequately resolve. The citation begins with the assertion that there is no definite and short list of the basic principles of rationality, which leaves open the question of whether there could be a definite but long list of such principles. Davidson seems to embrace the idea that there could not. In other words, if there is no list, that is not because we do not yet know enough about our practices of interpretation and understanding to be able to draft it, but because the principles are not themselves definite and unchanging, and hence could never be spelled out, even in a long list (or theory). But if we look more closely, this is not Davidson's claim—at least, it is not a claim he makes consistently. As the passage unfolds, the emphasis on a notion's being constituted in a variety of ways clearly pertains to irrationality, not to rationality. Davidson goes on referring to *the* norms of rationality, even as he suggests that different forms of irrationality may make sense in different ways against different backgrounds. And he does not hesitate to list three principles (of continence, logic, and induction) that definitely figure among the basic standards of rationality, for he asserts that it is "not an empirical question" whether human beings should be interpreted as being "largely in accord" with them (which implies that Davidson deems it empirically possible for someone to behave incontinently some, but not most, of the time).

To formulate the problem that surfaces here, we need to distinguish between two different sorts of claims and to take a close look at the relations between them. One claim is the thesis that standards of rationality are necessary (but not sufficient) to the enterprise of intersubjective understanding. Davidson offers a number of arguments along these lines, and I, for one, am quite sympathetic to them (not everyone agrees, however; see Levin). It is another thing to claim to have identified the objective (because universally subjective) standards of rationality; that is, all or some of the principles necessary to the framework and language of agency as such. It would seem that success in defending the first claim does not entail success in defending the latter, for one could be right about the necessity of norms of rationality in general, but in the dark (or seriously off the mark) about the precise nature of the universal and necessary norms of rationality. But is success with the first claim in no way dependent on success with the latter? Suppose we want to make arguments against the viability of a purely a-rational model of agency. Such arguments must hinge on some specific norms of rationality, for how can we go about testing the idea that norms of rationality are necessary to meaningful talk of belief and action unless we try to show that we cannot do without some particular principles or norms of rationality? Similarly, if we want to argue that a discourse of intentional agency is quite possible in the absence of standards of rationality, then we have to base our case on a reasonably precise description of at least some of those standards, showing how it is possible to engage in a systematic and meaningful ascription of individuated attitudes without in any way obeying or applying those standards. Thus, the general claim about the necessity of "some" standards of rationality may not entail the accuracy of any one list of those standards, but the cogency of our arguments in favor of that general claim does depend on a defense of some such list, because we cannot meaningfully argue over the necessity of some unspecified principles.

The upshot of all of this might seem to be that we should go back to Davidson's list and ask which, if any, of the principles of rationality mentioned indeed deserve to be granted the status of necessary and universal (but not sufficient) conditions of intentionalist psychology. And the question of *which* principles are *the* principles of rationality had better be cast as an empirical matter, even if we have good arguments for thinking that the issue of whether *some* such principles must be employed is already settled (e.g., arguments concerning the self-defeating nature of attempts to decide or to assert the contrary). We might begin, for example, by taking a closer look at the principle of continence as Davidson couches it, asking whether this formulation really deserves to be taken as a necessary condition on the rationality of an action. Along these lines, one might have serious reservations (see, for example, Bratman's contention, in "Practical Reasoning and Weakness of the Will," that the principle as stated is *ad hoc*). Or we might examine Davidson's particular claims about the logical and inferential standards that must be met by anything worthy of being thought to have a mind (and in such a context, one might take up the arguments presented by Cherniak, who proposes a significantly weaker formulation of the inferential capacities a rational agent must have).

But, at the same time, there is a way in which the approach I have just evoked misses the point of Davidson's remarks on rationality. Earlier I cited some phrases in which Davidson insists on the unity of the rationality principles. This emphasis suggests that, in his view, rationality is not reducible to a collection of disparate theses, to be picked over like tomatoes at the market. Decision theory and the theory of interpretation, Davidson contends, are the two main branches of a theory of rationality, and he is primarily interested in exploring their most fundamental relations. Along these lines, he has suggested that they are mutually dependent, neither standing as an independent basis for the other: "There is no way simply to add one to the other since in order to get started each requires an element drawn from the other. What is wanted is a unified theory that yields degree of belief, desirabilities on an interval scale, and an interpretation of speech, a theory that does not assume that either desires or beliefs have been individuated in advance, much less quantified" ("SCT" 322; "TUTMA" 8). What needs to be examined, then, is Davidson's proposal for a unified theory of meaning and action.

The proposal in question can be understood only once we have grasped some basic aspects of Davidson's perspective on decision theory. The kind of decision theory to which Davidson has himself contributed, along with Patrick Suppes and Stanley Siegel, pictures the decision maker as someone confronted by a choice between two or more "lotteries" or gambles. Davidson emphasizes the idea that the agent's choices, or revealed ordinal preferences, between different possible gambles are the product of two independent factors: 1) the agent's beliefs about the likelihood of different possible outcomes and 2) the agent's cardinal preferences in regard to those different outcomes. It may be useful in the present context to illustrate this idea by means of an example (with apologies to readers for whom these are elementary matters). Suppose I am traveling along a road that is new to me, guided only by someone's rather spotty description. I have reason to believe that there is an important first bifurcation in the road, and I have been told that one of the forks in the road will lead me to my goal for sure, albeit in a lengthy and more-or-less circuitous manner, depending on which of the different, reconnecting pathways I take after the first turn. The other main path, I am told, leads to a major shortcut, but it also leads in the wrong direction entirely if one makes the wrong turns after the first one. So when I reach the first fork, I have a decision to make. Option A is a path that will either (a) take me in the wrong direction entirely or (b) lead me very quickly to my destination; rightly or wrongly, I associate a particular probability with each of these two eventualities. Option B is the other fork in the road and will, I assume, lead either to (c) a very long, but sure, route to my goal or (d) a somewhat shorter, but equally sure, route. According to the theory, if I rationally prefer A over B, this choice is determined by my comparison of the products of the payoffs and odds that I associate with the two alternatives.

Three kinds of factors figure in a decision-theoretical analysis of my choice between the two forks in the road, and, given any two of them, we can arrive at the third. My beliefs (about the likelihood of different outcomes) and my cardinal preferences together yield my choice (ordinal preference) between the alternative courses of action deemed possible; from my beliefs and choices, my cardinal preferences can be inferred, and knowledge of my cardinal preferences and choices would allow someone to infer my beliefs about the probability of different outcomes. In practice, however, we have only the agent's revealed preferences to go on. The problem, then, according to Davidson, is that of knowing how information about two different categories of attitudes could be inferred from the agent's choices. That an agent freely chooses one of two alternatives does not allow us to infer that the choice directly reflects the agent's cardinal preferences, for these preferences could have been offset by a belief about the respective probabilities of the two outcomes. In relation to our example, the fact that I choose option A does not entail that I have a strong preference in favor of the shortcut; perhaps I only mildly preferred the shortcut, but happened to feel highly confident about my chances of finding it. On the other hand, I could have deemed my chances of getting lost very high, but nonetheless took the risky fork because I desperately wanted to reach my destination in a hurry, considering a late arrival just as bad as getting lost. It would seem, then, that even the most reliable knowledge of an agent's revealed preferences will not allow us to make any reasoned statements about the beliefs and cardinal preferences that shaped them, for so long as we know only the agent's choice, the other two factors remain indeterminate. We may know, or have good reason to assume, that the agent's ordinal preferences in regard to the example run $(b) > (d) > (c) > (a)$, but we are in no position to specify any precise cardinal weightings.

Davidson recommends Frank Ramsey's solution to this problem, which amounts to identifying the kind of situation where the agent's beliefs about probabilities can be isolated on the basis of revealed preference alone (see Ramsey and, for background, Sahlin). In other words, it is a matter of finding a case where one of the two unknown variables can be held steady, so that the value of the other variable can be known. Such a situation can be constructed as follows. We identify two outcomes, (a) and (b), between which the agent has an ordinal preference, say (a) > (b). We then specify an event, E, and two gambles: (1) if E occurs, then the outcome is (a), but if E does not occur, the outcome is (b); (2) if E occurs, the outcome is (b), but if not, the outcome is (a). If the agent is indifferent concerning the two gambles, we may then infer that the agent deems the events E and not-E to be equiprobable. Why? If the agent believed E to be more likely, then she would have preferred the first gamble; if the agent believed not-E more likely, she would have preferred the second. Once the subjective probability of event E has thereby been determined, it can be used as a basis for scaling cardinal preferences (given the assumption of a number of basic axioms) and can then be used to determine the subjective probability of other states of affairs.

What Davidson finds attractive in this analysis is that it "shows how it is possible to assign a content to two basic and interlocking propositional attitudes without assuming that either one is understood in advance" ("SCT" 317). Davidson suggests that Ramsey's approach can provide a basis for an analogous development in which the theories of interpretation and decision can be combined. Davidson has often insisted on the fact that the understanding of linguistic utterances and inscriptions requires two levels of interpretation, involving both the question of what the words mean and the question of what the speaker means in speaking them (what the speaker believes to be the case and is indeed asserting in the sentence). The revealed data are utterances, and the two categories of hidden, independent factors are 1) what the speaker believes and 2) what the speaker takes the utterance to mean. The problem, once again, is that of knowing how two different kinds of explanatory factors can be distinguished and extracted from the evidence, when only a third type of factor is "relatively directly observable," as Davidson puts it. He comments that "the problem is curiously like the problem of disentangling the roles of belief and preference in determining choices and preferences" ("SCT" 318–19).

The strategy Davidson recommends is that we should think of meanings and beliefs "as interrelated constructs of a single theory, just as we already view subjective values and probabilities as interrelated constructs of decision theory" (*ITI* 146). The theory of verbal interpretation and Bayesian theory are, Davidson comments, "made for each other" ("SCT" 322; cf. "TUTMA" 8). But one problem with decision theory is that it typically assumes that the problem of interpretation has already been solved: it is assumed that the meaning of the agents' preferences can be known by understanding their utterances, just as it is taken for granted that we know how they understand the gambles we propose to them. Thus, Davidson wants to develop a unified theory that does not simply give itself in advance the ability to ascribe well-individuated propositional content to agents' attitudes. The starting point of such a theory must be the definition of a simple attitude that can be recognized in an agent prior to the interpretive ascription of any other propositional attitudes. In a nutshell, Davidson's proposal is that this basic attitude must be the agent's preference for the truth of one uninterpreted sentence over another, conceived of as an extensional relation between the agent, two sentences, and a location. Davidson, then, accepts Richard Jeffrey's decision-theoretical axiomatics, but replaces propositions with uninterpreted sentences. Facts about preferences between uninterpreted sentences can be used to fix subjective probabilities and utilities as well as truth-functional connectives. A theory of interpretation, developed along Quinean lines, then explains the attribution of propositional content to sentences on the basis of the degree of belief in their truth (see "SCT" 315–28 for the outline of this project).

Davidson presents his unified theory of meaning, preference, and belief as a sketch of the ultimate theory of rationality. Yet aspects of this proposal, and of Davidson's own comments about its status, give us pause. My criticisms in what follows will focus on three interrelated topics: 1) Davidson's sense of the aims and status of the proposed theory; 2) the proposed theory's empirical adequacy; and 3) the relation of the proposed theory to some of Davidson's other important claims about action and rationality. These topics directly concern Davidson's defense of the two theses that were identified above: namely, his claim that norms of rationality are necessary to mental attributions and his claim that the norms he defends should be acknowledged as some (if not all) of those necessary norms.

To begin with the question of the status of the proposed theory, here are some of Davidson's most relevant comments (these remarks figure in the 1990 version, but not the 1980 version, of his proposal for a unified theory of meaning and action):

> The approach to the problems of meaning, belief, and desire which I have outlined is not, I am sure it is clear, meant to throw any direct light on how in real life we come to understand each other, nor on how we master our first concepts and our first language. I have been engaged in a conceptual exercise aimed at revealing the dependencies among our basic propositional attitudes at a level fundamental enough to avoid the assumption that we can come to grasp them—or intelligibly attribute them to others—one at a time. Performing the exercise has required showing how it is in principle possible to arrive at all of them at once. Showing this amounts to presenting an informal proof that we have endowed thought, desire, and speech with a structure that makes interpretation possible. Of course, we knew it was possible in advance. The philosophical question was, *what* makes it possible? ["SCT" 325]

One thing that strikes me as unclear here is the sense in which Davidson is using the notion of "making possible." One sense of the expression (though apparently is not what is meant here) is the sense in which we say that the electric current is one of the conditions that causally makes it possible for me to go on using my computer to write an essay. Evidently, the conceptual "exercise" was not meant to describe or defend any such thesis about what makes interpretation and understanding possible in real life. This would suggest that only conceptual or logical possibility is at stake here, so that what the exercise informally "proves" is that it is "in principle" possible (i.e., not incoherent) to sketch a theory in which the necessary conditions of rationality have a certain general configuration. This hardly seems a satisfactory result in light of the problem of stipulating which formulation of "the necessary rationality standards" can be used to demonstrate the actual, empirical necessity of some rationality standards as opposed to none at all. One cannot prove that all interpretation and all action explanation require some norms of rationality simply by drawing a sketch of *one* coherent theory of *some* rationality standards that *could,* in principle, be practicable; for the outstanding objection is that understanding can take place without anyone ascribing to, or in any way following, these particular standards, however unified and coherent they may be.

Many of Davidson's statements suggest that his ambition in talking of universal norms of rationality is that of articulating, by means of an explicit theoretical reconstruction, the actual unifying conditions of intentional attribution, conditions which effectively make possible intersubjective understanding—and this whether or not the agents themselves are aware of these standards or agree to them (for a statement of this sort of reconstructivist thesis, see Audi 117–18). Similarly, when Davidson-the-action-theorist speaks of explaining action in terms of belief and desire, his contention has always been that these attitudes together cause the action. Davidson's defense of the idea that reasons are causes is his most famous contribution to action theory, and it is hardly reassuring to see him abandon that thesis when he makes a proposal about a unifying theory of the norms of rationality. Yet, reconstructivist and causalist ambitions stand uneasily alongside the idea that the proposed framework is only a conceptual exercise, closer to "first philosophy" than to an empirical exploration of human linguistic and cognitive capacities and practices.

A trace of the same kind of ambivalence may be perceived in a footnote to the passage just cited: "Given the intricacy of any interpretable system of thought and language, I assume that there must be many alternative approaches to interpretation. I have outlined one; others may well be less artificial or closer to our intuitions concerning interpretive practice. But one should not take it for granted that the procedure I have sketched is totally remote from what is practicable" ("SCT" 325). I certainly agree that it should not be taken for granted that Davidson's proposal has nothing whatsoever to do with what could, in principle, be practiced, but nor should it be taken for granted that this theory actually describes a (or the) working procedure which effectively makes in-

tersubjective understanding possible and is hence necessary to a successful ascription of intentions and attitudes. By Davidson's own admission,
the light his proposal may shed on our everyday interpretive practices is
at best indirect. One wonders how Davidson's talk of "alternative approaches to interpretation" and "intuitions concerning interpretive practice" is compatible with his insistence on describing *the* standards of
rationality that are necessary to all understanding, even in cases where
the agents themselves must be interpreted as claiming to reject them.

These considerations become all the more important when we reflect
on a second topic, which concerns the empirical adequacy of the projected theory. The kind of decision theory that Davidson has adopted
depends on a number of major stipulations in order to define rational
choice as the maximization of a quantifiable, subjective expected utility.
For example, preferences must be definite (complete) and transitive;
there must be an invariance of preference between certainty and risk,
other things being equal, and so on. Davidson advocates the thesis that
decision theory specifies some of the standards of rationality, but the
empirical adequacy of the general sort of Bayesian subjective expected
utility (SEU) theory to which Davidson refers has been put in doubt by a
number of studies. (See Schoemaker and Slovic for fine surveys, as well
as the essays in Moser and in Gärdenfors and Sahlin; Davidson's failure to
refer to this work was already criticized in Suppes 192; more general
philosophical critiques of rational-choice theory are presented in Hollis
and in Slote.) Herbert A. Simon puts the main point as follows: "human
beings have neither the facts nor the consistent structure of values nor
the reasoning power at their disposal that would be required, even in
these relatively simple situations, to apply SEU principles" (17).

Often the axioms are violated by deep-seated intuitive preferences. An
historically important type of example, first proposed by Maurice Allais,
runs as follows. According to the theory, it is irrational to have both of
the following two preferences: (a) to choose getting ten million dollars
for sure over a gamble where one receives either twenty-five million,
five million, or nothing, with probabilities of .10, .89, and .01, respectively; *and* (b) to prefer the gamble of getting twenty-five million dollars, with a probability of .10, or nothing, with a probability of .90, over
the gamble of getting either five million dollars, with a .11 probability, or
nothing, with a .89 probability. In regard to the first preference, most
people agree that it would be best to avoid the small chance of missing
out on the opportunity of winning what will in any case be a very large
amount of money; at the same time, the second preference seems justified by the very large difference in payoffs, which offsets the small differ-

ence in probabilities. Yet the theory tells us that, taken together, these decisions are irrational (see Moser, Slovic 96–8; cf. Miller 332). Here we see that some judgments which may appear irrational in the light of Bayesian decision theory seem quite reasonable when understood in the agent's own terms. Davidson's claims are also challenged by a number of experiments in which subjects whose preferences did not correspond to some of the basic postulates of the theory (e.g., Savage's independence principle) were given a detailed argument explaining how their choices diverged from the standard; yet most of these subjects did not, when given the chance, change their preferences to bring them in line with the axioms of decision theory (Slovic and Tversky).

Davidson takes up this sort of objection in "Incoherence and Irrationality," where he entertains a number of ways of interpreting an interlocutor whose preferences in relation to three options violate the basic axiom of transitivity (if S prefers a to b and b to c, then S prefers a to c). Showing the agent that a "dutch book" can be made against intransitive preferences, which essentially amounts to proving that such preferences are self-defeating, does not suffice, and Davidson remarks that "plenty of questionable assumptions are needed for this argument" ("II" 351). And so, he continues: "I should never have tried to pin you down to an admission that you ought to subscribe to the principles of decision theory. For I think everyone does subscribe to those principles, whether he knows it or not" (351). But this seems high-handed. In cases where the agents refuse to accept the standards as their own, what warrants the confident assertion that the norms of rationality described by the theory really are those of the agents? The answer cannot be that some such norms are necessary to intentionalist psychology; for even if one grants that general point, one is not thereby required to assent to any particular formulation of the decision-theoretical axioms. The problem here is not simply that the agents themselves do not assent to the description of "their own" norms of rationality, but that even those researchers who agree there must be some such standards cannot agree among themselves as to what the standards really are. In such a situation, how can we be sure that it is right to call any particular standards the necessary and universal norms of rationality? Davidson has not given us a satisfactory answer to that question.

My third major criticism concerns the relation between this proposal and Davidson's own action-theoretical discussions of aspects of intersubjective understanding and rationality. Although it may be too strong to say that the former and the latter stand in direct contradiction, I think it can be shown that Davidson does not successfully make it clear how these two branches of his thought are to be unified. Most important, he does not establish that the framework adopted from Jeffrey is genuinely "necessary" to the kinds of action explanations he has elsewhere described. Davidson claims that his central goal in sketching the unified theory of meaning and action is to show that the attitudes are not grasped and attributed "one at a time," but in a unified and interlocking way. He is careful to point out that his idea is not that the theory shows how we can derive intentional states from nonintentional, directly observable data (e.g., uninterpreted behavior). The primary data are not directly observable in the complete absence of any theory of mind (or inferences about unobservable mental states). Instead, the "primary data" are only "relatively directly observable," taking the form of assent to sentences in a particular context, where the interpreter can observe the agent's linguistic behavior as well as the features of the environment to which the sentences may be related. So the data are already grasped under an intentional description that casts them as acts of preferring, assenting, and so on (e.g., it is assumed in Davidson's examples that the agent's ordinal preferences are "relatively directly observable" in behavior). What the theory purports to describe, then, is how we get from there to a finer individuation of attitudes and their propositional contents.

Thus, in light of Davidson's own qualifications, it seems fair to say that the problem of how mental attribution gets going is not solved by the unified theory. What is more, it is not clear that the details of Davidson's proposal have much to do with the kinds of semantic individuation that are most central to everyday practices of interpretation and action explanations. It seems instead that Davidson's proposal for a "unified theory" of rationality is a matter of a speculative decision-theoretical schema that is divorced from some of Davidson's own most important action-theoretical insights, which owe very little to the Bayesian axioms and to Ramsey's method of constructing cardinal preferences on the basis of ordinal ones. Davidson's elucidations of intersubjective understanding do not in fact rely on the apparatus whereby the relevant "pro attitudes" can be identified in terms of cardinal utilities. In fact, attempts to treat motivational attitudes like a "quantum of wantum" are notoriously unreliable (for an excellent argument along these lines, see Thalberg). Nor has it been shown that the probabilistic weighting of degrees of belief is a necessary condition of successful interpretive practice. One of Davidson's comments in another context reinforces my point, for he notes: "I do not mean that agents are rational or consistent in the idealized way that theories of decision demand, but that actual choices and decisions are governed by the sort of consideration that decision theories systematize" ("RE" 199). This seems a step in the right direction, provided we acknowledge that noting these differences between the "idealized way" and the "sort of consideration" will lead to rather different accounts of the necessary standards of rationality. What Davidson has yet to establish is that agents' practical reasoning is actually "governed" by the kind of schemata described in the unified theory.

According to the proposal for a unified theory, the norms of rationality constitute an unshakable and systematic theory that "in principle" unlocks the attitudes all at once. But that idea can be contrasted to another approach which Davidson himself has elsewhere followed. I have in mind passages where he speaks of interpretation as the strategic application of certain assumptions, from which we deviate only when the evidence against them piles up ("PI" 302). Following up on that suggestion, we may propose that rationality amounts not to a system of *a priori* principles, but to a bundle of privileged but fallible heuristics. These heuristics are privileged because they are indeed crucial to the business of interpreting each other's sayings and doings; yet they are also fallible, not simply because we are sometimes unable to discover the relevant attitudes, but also because intentionalist explanations, even when successful, cannot answer all our questions about human affairs. What, then, are these heuristics? Some highly plausible candidates for the role of necessary and universal rationality heuristics have already been described by Davidson. One very basic heuristic of practical rationality is the operating, or "default," assumption that we should try to understand and explain people's behavior in terms of their reasons—the beliefs, desires, and intentions that often guide their activity. This implies, in turn, that we work with the assumption that it is possible to discover meaningful, nonrandom connections between an agent's attitudes and behavior. A basic norm and pattern of practical reasoning runs as follows: if an agent's predominant preference is that a certain state of affairs obtain, and the agent believes that a certain action will bring this about, and if the agent is able and believes him- or herself able to perform that action, then the agent should form the intention to perform that action and should act on that intention. The related heuristic runs thusly: given an instance of behavior, try to interpret this behavior by inferring the wants (or predominant preference) and the beliefs that explain the agent's intentionally engaging in that behavior.

A general point to be noted here is that Davidson's insistence on explaining action in terms of two contrasting categories of attitudes— the motivational and the cognitive—correctly expresses, I think, an important aspect of the basic heuristic of practical rationality. Preferences as well as instrumental beliefs are required if we are to make sense of why someone intentionally does one thing as opposed to any other option deemed possible. Davidson's moderate variety of conativism is to be preferred to extreme cognitivist and conativist versions of action explanation—the one arguing that reference to belief and/or intention alone can suffice to rationalize action; the other contending that desire, in a narrow sense, is necessary to every adequate explanation of action (for background here, see Marks).

In regard to interpretation, Davidson usefully insists on the impossibility of successfully attributing fine-grained propositional contents in a vacuum: "it should not be thought that a theory of interpretation will stand alone, for as we noticed, there is no chance of telling when a sentence is held true without being able to attribute desires and being able to describe actions as having complex intentions" (*ITI* 162). The most basic point to be noted here is that meaningful utterances are events of a particular variety: namely, intentional actions. Thus: "Although we may sometimes say a group speaks with one voice, utterances are essentially personal; each utterance has its agent and its time" ("SCT" 309). Viewing utterances and inscriptions as actions means, first of all, that the interpretation of linguistic intentions and meanings requires reference to the speaking or writing agent's other attitudes, such as desires, beliefs, and present- and future-directed intentions. My way of understanding and extrapolating from this insight is to contend that the framework of action explanation, beginning with the basic heuristics just evoked, must be adopted in the interpretation of inscriptions and utterances, for only in that way can we successfully move from the multiple potentialities of unanchored linguistic meaning to actual communicative intent and purpose. Moreover, the application of rationality heuristics in trying to understand an utterance does not merely involve some assumptions about how one may go about linking this action to the agent's other attitudes and to what we may already think or know about them. We must also relate what the speaker utters to what we may observe or infer about the circumstances of the utterance, which "provide the most obvious evidence for the interpretation of these sentences and the predicates in them" ("SCT" 320). This point is reiterated in regard to the many indexical elements of speech (demonstratives, tense, shifters, etc.). The interpreter's assumptions about the rationality or coherence of the speaker's activities directly concern those episodes and situations in the world which we have reason to assume are salient to the speaker. In a key phrase, Davidson evokes the kind of basic situation within which the application of standards of rationality has some chance of success:

"The ultimate source of both objectivity and communication is the triangle that, by relating speaker, interpreter, and the world, determines the contents of thought and speech" ("SCT" 325).

To sum up, I have contended that we should not accept Davidson's thesis that the tenets and approach of SEU decision theory, as reworked in his proposal, are fundamental and "necessary" to all intentionalist psychology and thereby express (some or all of) the "universal norms of rationality." When we look more closely, Davidson seems somewhat ambivalent about the claims he wants to make for this proposal. Although he writes of schemata that are "practicable in principle," he does not consistently frame the proposal as a "transcendental argument" about the "a priori" foundations of intentionalist psychology (in the manner, say, of Apel). But, at the same time, he hesitates to stress the empirical claim that the schemata he has described are effectively at work in making all mental attribution possible—a hesitation which is more than understandable given Davidson's knowledge of the literature, for although that literature may not offer any definitive refutation of the descriptive adequacy of decision-theoretical axioms, it does shift the burden of proof onto the shoulders of those who want to insist that those axioms are the necessary scaffolding of all meaningful attributions of attitudes. Davidson cannot do without any empirical claims along these lines, for in their absence his proposal becomes totally divorced from his own previous attempts to defend a realist, causal theory of action. Yet, aspects of Davidson's action theory bear no relation to, and are ill-served by, the emphasis on the norms of SEU. Insofar as empirical claims about rationality are concerned, Davidson is on more solid ground with his action-theoretical clarifications of aspects of the language of intentionalist psychology. But even these descriptions of some basic rationality heuristics do not amount to an exhaustive description of necessary norms of rationality. Little has been said, for example, about the particular norms of epistemic rationality; nor has Davidson dealt with the crucial question concerning the relation between static and dynamic perspectives on rational choice (for background, see Bratman, McClennen).

I turn now to some implications for literary research. As I suggested earlier, there is a danger of wrongly assuming that it is obvious which critical problems and questions are the ones to which Davidson's results should be applied. Philosophers often think that literary criticism is a fairly unified field, a field made coherent, if not by some body of unanimously agreed-upon findings, then by an overarching unity of purpose.

Critics, it is assumed, embrace the common goal of describing and interpreting literary works of art. While this sort of interpretive activity, and
many standards and procedures that go along with it, is still pretty
common in the field, the fact is that literary scholars no longer agree that
the interpretive appreciation of literary art deserves to enjoy the priority
it once had. What has been put in question is not only the idea that the
art of literature should be at the center of critics' attention, but also the
idea that producing appreciations and interpretations is the critic's main
task. A wide variety of alternative goals and procedures has been proposed. To mention but one tendency, it has been suggested that instead
of doing detailed readings of literary works, critics should study the
larger discursive formations and social institutions within which literary
texts are historically inscribed (see Angenot for an elaborate version of
this approach). Other critics disagree, but even if they did not, the
decision to prefer historical and sociocultural topics over aesthetic ones
would not in itself entail any one specific method or avenue of inquiry.
In short, Richard Miller is right when he includes the literary disciplines
among the "self-questioning" fields.

In a context where there is fundamental disagreement over the basic
aims of literary research, a philosopher's work may have implications at
two different levels. First of all, there may be implications for the choice
between competing research programs: a philosophical doctrine could
lend support to, or put in question, different claims about the overarching goals, assumptions, and procedures of critical inquiry. Second, a
philosopher's ideas could have implications for how a particular research program may best be realized. When we turn to Davidson's views
and ask about their implications for critical theory, both levels should be
kept in mind. This means that applying Davidson's ideas about interpretation and radical translation to the literary debate over the "validity" of
interpretation would make sense only once we had made a number of
prior decisions about the kinds of interpretive questions critics should
try to answer; moreover, such an application could succeed only once
we had dealt with some significant differences between the role of interpretation in everyday communication and in a literary critical context,
for there is no reason to assume in advance that the *mutatis mutandis*
clause will in this case be easy to satisfy.

In what follows I shall focus primarily on the first level; that is, on the
general question of the choice between competing research paradigms.
On my reading, Davidson's philosophy of language points toward an
integrative, pragmatically situated approach to meaning, an approach in
which utterances are to be identified, understood, and explained as a

species of individual action. As far as Davidson is concerned, sentences (and, I presume, larger textual or semiotic units) are just abstract objects that have no truth-conditions unless "embodied in sounds and scribbles by speakers and scribblers" ("SCT" 309). If we speak of sentences as types of utterances and inscriptions, this is just shorthand for actual utterances and inscriptions of the same type; such shorthand makes it possible to describe what the truth-conditions of an utterance or inscription of that type would be if it were actually tokened. But the legitimacy of this sort of shorthand does not warrant the reification of textual entities, which are then granted a bewildering range of causal powers in the poststructuralist effort to short-circuit an ill-defined and poorly understood "category of the subject," itself accused of a remarkably implausible range of sociopolitical evils.

Thus, I take Davidson's assumptions to be strongly incompatible with the idea that the object domain called "literature" is populated by a collection of context-free items called "texts," "discourses," or "works." In other words, if Davidson is right, then conventionalist and pan-textualist perspectives on literary culture are mistaken. A Davidsonian emphasis on utterance as individual action would also militate against the various methodological holisms whereby discursive or textual macrosystems are made the object of literary historical inquiry. "Textuality" is not ontologically autonomous, nor can it be situated methodologically as an independent level of description or analysis. Instead of indulging in such underconstrained speculations about a pseudo-object called "textuality," literary researchers should focus on actual utterances, inscriptions, or acts of writing, which are basic to any real instances of literary meaning.

To repeat (with some minor substitutions) a phrase cited earlier, we may assert along with Davidson that every act of writing is an event of a special sort—an intentional action. Although we may sometimes say that a group, a genre, or an historical structure *writes,* when we speak more strictly we should say that *every writing has its agent and its time.* That is why I earlier insisted on the limitations of trying to adopt Davidson's theory of interpretation without also taking up his approach to action and rationality: Davidson's views imply that the interpretive process will be abstractive and underconstrained unless we are attuned to the pragmatic situations in which intersubjective understanding and practical rationality are made possible. The imaginary library, where all texts are dissolved within one vast intertext, and where meaning is a series of random firings among labyrinthine textual associations, is not a situation of this sort (for an early essay in which such themes are writ large, see Barthes).

These considerations help us to get clear about the kinds of items we should look for beneath the broad rubric of "literature." Davidson's views also establish some constraints that would have to be respected in any successful interpretation of these literary items. One major constraint is that any work or text must be indexed in relation to the agent whose intentional activities have brought it into being; and reference to features of that action (the agent's motivation, instrumental and background beliefs, beliefs about linguistic meaning, etc.), and to the world in which it took place, will be crucial to any reasoned interpretation of the literary item's meanings. Here is where we must insist on Davidson's basic claim that the ultimate source of communication is a triangle that, by relating speaker, interpreter, and the world, determines the contents of thought and writing. Of course, it remains true that our ability in actual cases to know the precise nature of this "ultimate source" is a matter of greater or lesser degrees of detail and precision. Yet even when the writer's specific identity and the precise time of the writing are unknown, there may still be enough evidence to formulate a detailed hypothesis about the desires, beliefs, and intentions that informed the writer's activity (a remarkable example is Lars Lönnroth's analysis of the pragmatics of the writing and reception of an anonymous thirteenth-century Icelandic saga; see my "Convention and Literary Explanations" for a discussion).

It should be clear that the constraint that I have just evoked must be observed if the literary work is viewed as part of a communicative process. It may be objected, however, that it is a mistake to view literary works as tokens in a communicative process instead of as autonomous aesthetic objects. At least one theorist has argued that reading a text as literature is precisely a matter of detaching it from the initial context of its writing and reception (see Ellis). One cogent response to that kind of objection would be to suggest that some degree of successful communication is a necessary condition to the identification and appreciation of any literary work of art (intelligent and carefully developed arguments along these lines have been presented recently by Currie and by Davies). The basic point is that the individuation of literary works cannot be based uniquely on semiotic or textual features: no function, not even a partial one, maps types of inscriptions (or texts) onto works of art; there are text-types that are not correlated with works at all, and, in some cases, a single text-type is correlated with more than one work. Nor is there a function from works to types of texts: some works are correlated with more than one type of inscription. What actually determines the practical identification of works are references to the agent or agents deemed responsible for the creation of the texts. For example, reference to the author's context, beliefs, and motivation can strongly influence decisions about the nature of a work's stylistic properties. Features that would be deemed archaic and imitative if the writing took place in one context are recognized as highly innovative and unconventional if we believe them to have been created in an earlier period. Decisions about genre also may depend on the reader's beliefs about the identity of the author and the nature of the author's other writings. Thus, some very basic aesthetic discriminations depend on beliefs about the "agent and time" of the inscription, a fact that puts in question the solidity of various prevalent romantic notions concerning the "autonomous," "organic," and "self-organizing" nature of literary works.

A second, and logically independent, response to the same objection would be to contend that in literary inquiry, concern with aesthetic goals or values is optional: not all avenues of genuine research in literary history are meant to contribute, or to be responsive to, aesthetic topics. It is a legitimate goal of literary research to ask what kinds of attitudes Edgar Allan Poe communicated to his magazine audiences with his mesmeric tales, and to answer such a question, it is not necessary for the literary historian to focus on what he or she takes the genuine aesthetic value of those writings to be. What is necessary is a realistic reconstruction of the writer's and readers' situations, attitudes, and strategic rationalities.

Another kind of potential objection to the interpretive constraint being proposed here is that there are legitimate and important avenues of literary research which are centered on neither aesthetic nor communicational topics. For example, a literary historian can study the ways in which Shakespeare's name and works have been appropriated in the building of a patriotic American ideology (for an excellent work on this topic, see Bristol). Some theorists might suppose that, in such an approach, Shakespeare's intentions and meanings are irrelevant, and thus the Davidsonian emphasis on the "agent and time" of writing would not be germane. Yet even a nonaesthetic, sociological approach to literary history cannot be based on a nonagential, a-rational approach to cultural phenomena. In the case of Michael Bristol's important study, the decision not to attempt a detailed reconstruction of Shakespeare's original authorial action is correctly accompanied by the decision to investigate the motives and reasoning of some of the influential figures who contributed to the building of the American institutions of "Shakespeare." Turning from the question of Shakespeare's authorial meanings to the unintended consequences and divergent appropriations of his complex literary artifacts does not remove the constraint of linking writings to their agents and times. If all such links were dissolved or ignored, we could no longer recognize the gulf that separates William Shakespeare, the hypothetical "ultimate source," from those whose practices have been aimed at establishing a monumental link back to that sacrosanct figure. More generally, we can hope to trace the boundary between a writer's intentional results and an artifact's various unintended consequences (including what the hermeneuticists call the "effective history" of a work) only by trying to make hypotheses about the rationales behind both the initial making of literary artifacts and their various uses and receptions.

My general thesis, then, is that agency and the rationality heuristics it entails are directly pertinent, and indeed necessary, to a range of significantly different literary research programs, ranging from literary aesthetics to sociopolitical analyses of the practices and institutions of literary history. It should be clear that my claim is *not* that turning to Davidson entails a return to one kind of author criticism and, with it, to the "intentional fallacy." On the contrary, a Davidsonian perspective on meaning and action serves to put in doubt the viability and coherence of certain poststructuralist tendencies in literary theory, while supporting a number of significantly different avenues of inquiry. In my view, Davidsonian constraints on interpretive practice are anything but a straitjacket; instead, it is a matter of identifying some heuristics that can help us try to answer a variety of questions, these interrogative activities being motivated by diverse goals and interests.

It must be acknowledged that to suggest, in a Davidsonian vein, that writing is action—intentional action—is to fly in the face of some of contemporary critical theory's most cherished dogmas. Many a contemporary theory tells us that the author is dead and that textuality and writing are the wolves in the manger of intentionality (for a recent evocation and critique of these themes, see Close). To many, Davidson's insistence on anchoring utterances and inscriptions to an agent and a time will sound like another instance of philosophical "logocentrism," with its emphasis on the "presence" of the speaking subject. Yet Davidson does not, in fact, return us to any discredited idea that a pristine, authorial intent must be viewed as the sole and ultimate source of legitimate meaning, an origin that stands prior to the complex process of writing. Here is a text by Davidson that can serve as a warning to anyone who might read him as the advocate of such naive doctrines: "Before one starts to write one thinks one knows what one is going to say. But in my case at least it is only as I write that I discover what I think, and this is almost never what I thought when I began" ("PR" 253). Our task in reading Davidson on interpretation is to understand how he can combine the latter observation with an insistence on the ways in which intentional attitudes can effectively inform the action of writing.

That Davidson's views warrant providing an "intentional action" description of instances of writing is made apparent by an example in which he does precisely that: "Let us consider a particular historical event, say David Hume's admitting in an appendix to his *Treatise* that he cannot see how to reconcile two of his theses" (*EAE* 254). Davidson goes on to say that making an admission has to be an intentional action and that, as such, it is explicable in terms of the agent's beliefs and desires; in this case, we ascribe to Hume both the belief that he cannot find a way to reconcile his two theses and the desire to reveal this fact. Not only do we attribute to Hume this desire and this belief on the basis of the textual evidence, but we make the additional explanatory inference that these attitudes were efficacious in generating the action(s) involved in the writing of the passage. This inference relies, in turn, on assumptions about the various complex dispositions and capacities that must be associated with the writer's knowledge of the language in which the passage is written. Unless we make such assumptions, we cannot grasp what the man meant when he scribbled certain words on the page.

But can the action of writing be explained and interpreted in terms of beliefs, desires, and dispositions alone? A negative response is suggested by Davidson's emphasis on the role of a range of concepts of intention. An early instance of his focus on intending happens to take the form of a reflection on the action of writing "action":

> For consider some simple action, like writing the word "action." Some temporal segments of this action are themselves actions: for example, first I write the letter "a." This I do with the intention of initiating an action that will not be complete until I have written the rest of the word. It is hard to see how the attitude towards the complete act which I have as I write the letter "a" differs from the pure intention I may have had a moment before. To be sure, my intention has now begun to be realized, but why should that necessarily change my attitude? It seems that in any intentional action that takes much time, or involves preparatory steps, something like pure intending must be present. [*EAE* 88]

To understand what Davidson is up to in this passage, we must recall that in his initial formulations of the basic schema of action explanations, the term "intention" was said to be purely "syncategorematic"; that is, not referring to any entity, state, disposition, or event (*EAE* 8). Beliefs and desires alone could cause intentional action without there being any intermediary states, such as acts of the will or the intention to perform the action. Yet Davidson altered this view as a result of various considerations, one of which was the existence of intentions in the absence of the intended actions: agents can fully intend to do something at some point in the future without necessarily realizing those intentions when the time comes. In writing these lines, I thought that I would get around to a more detailed discussion of the different notions of "intention" that have circulated in literary criticism, but I decided otherwise. This sort of "pure intending" is not only an isolated and idle possibility. The notion reflects back on the analysis of intentional action; for, as the example of writing "a" in "action" shows, there is an element of pure intending within an intentional act that unfolds in time and involves several discrete steps. Davidson entertains and rejects the possibility that intending can be reduced to belief (he critiques, in particular, the idea that agents must believe they can and/or will do something they intend to do), and he identifies it instead with an "all-out judgement that some action is more desirable than any available alternative" ("RE" 197). Intentional action is always accompanied by a judgment of this sort: namely, an evaluative attitude to the effect that the action is better than (or at least as good as) any alternative believed available. But this kind of evaluative judgment is distinguished by Davidson from another sort—the "all things considered" judgment which holds that an action or type of action is best given all of the relevant considerations known to the agent. The difference between these two types of judgment, which is central to Davidson's formulation of the principle of continence, is meant to explain how an action can be at once intentional and irrational: in the case of akratic action, the "all-out" or unconditional judgment that corresponds to the action is only a *prima facie* evaluation supported by some of the agent's attitudes and beliefs, and the agent's own all-things-considered judgment conflicts with the intention.

In Davidson's later accounts of action explanation, the notion of intention clearly plays an important role, and many more recent debates in the field have hinged on the several senses of the term (see especially Bratman, Mele, Wilson). An important aspect of a Davidsonian perspective on action is that intention, however central it may be to purposive action, is not a self-sufficient explanatory notion. Davidson emphasizes the idea that the intentions which lead to action are themselves produced by the agent's other attitudes—most essentially, the values the agent associates with various possible consequences of a contemplated course of action as well as the agent's beliefs about the likelihood of these possible outcomes. Thus, for Davidson, the meaning of an action and an adequate explanation of it cannot consist in an isolated, fully discrete mental state called "intention," for such attitudes are typically complex and are linked to a network of other attitudes and dispositions. Even if we single out the intention defining a discrete "basic" action, such as the act of pressing one's finger down on a particular key of the computer keyboard, the explanation of this action will inscribe that intention within the larger practical process within which it figures: the pressing down of the key is favored because the agent believes that it will suffice to generate the action of typing the letter "a," for example, which in turn is preferred because it is consistent with, and contributes to, the larger intention of typing a token of the word "action," which is in turn favored because the agent deems, at least provisionally, that the long phrase in question should at last be concluded—like this one— with the word "action." The chain of preferences and instrumental beliefs runs, then, both upstream and downstream of each basic act determined by an "I intend to perform the act x now." Such acts are woven together to form a complex texture of "in order to's" constitutive of ongoing practical reasoning and action: I perform this gesture *in order to* type this letter *in order to* type this word, my goal being to complete another sentence, so as to sketch in the missing element of this part of my argument, etc., which will, I hope, allow me to speak to some readers' potential queries and concerns. All of these intentions are themselves part of an ongoing, sustained effort to write an essay, an action that is motivated and guided by a number of interlocking yet separate goals and perspectives, one of which is to reach a better understanding of Davidson's complex and challenging writings by taking on the difficult task of trying to spell out a coherent response to some aspects of them.

To stress the importance of trying to analyze this kind of interlocking network of practical activity in intentionalist terms, then, is not to assume in advance that the analysis will succeed in reducing the complex to the simple; it is not a matter of presupposing that a single, pristine, global moment of conscious "intention" precedes and ultimately explains every writing. Before I began writing the present essay, the details of my argument were nowhere in sight, and, as the work unfolded, my initial project was altered in a number of significant ways, at least partly, I hope, as a result of reasonable reconsiderations of the wisdom of my initial, highly schematic plans (on the question of planning and the rationality of reconsideration, see Bratman, *Intention, Plans, and Practical Reason*). Nor do I dream for a moment that the only thoughts and responses my essay may give rise to will be those that I have intended, either explicitly or implicitly, in composing this piece, a fact which does not, however, imply that I am in no way responsible for, or aware of, any of its contents. You will, charitable readers, no doubt, interpret this essay in a number of strikingly different ways, but if you read *me* at all, you must at least begin by asking yourselves what my reasons in writing this could have been.

WORKS CITED

Adelman, Janet, Margaret J. Arnold, Linda Bamber et al. Letter. *PMLA* 104 (1989): 76–78.

Allais, Maurice. "Le Comportement de l'homme rationnel devant le risque. Critique des postulats et axiomes de l'école américaine." *Econometrica* 21 (1953): 503–46.

Angenot, Marc. *1889. Un état du discours social.* Montreal: Préambule, 1989.

Anscombe, G.E.M. *Intention.* Oxford: Basil Blackwell, 1958.

Apel, Karl-Otto. "Das Apriori der Kommunikationsgemeinschaft und die Grundlagen der Ethik: Zum Problem einer rationalen Begründung der Ethik im Zeitalter der Wissenschaft." In *Transformationen der Philosophie.* Frankfurt: Suhrkamp, 1973. II:358–435.

Audi, Robert. *Practical Reasoning.* London: Routledge, 1989.

Barthes, Roland. "De l'œuvre au texte." *La Revue d'Esthétique* 3 (1971): 225–32.

Bishop, John. *Natural Agency: An Essay on the Causal Theory of Action.* Cambridge: Cambridge UP, 1989.

Bratman, Michael. *Intention, Plans, and Practical Reason.* Cambridge: Harvard UP, 1987.

———. "Practical Reasoning and Weakness of the Will." *Nous* 13 (1979): 153–71.

Bristol, Michael. *Shakespeare's America, America's Shakespeare.* London: Routledge, 1989.

Cherniak, Christopher. *Minimal Rationality.* Cambridge: MIT, 1986.

Close, Anthony. "The Empirical Author: Salman Rushdie's *The Satanic Verses.*" *Philosophy and Literature* 14 (1990): 248–67.

Currie, Gregory. *The Nature of Fiction.* Cambridge: Cambridge UP, 1990.

———. *An Ontology of Art.* London: Macmillan, 1989.

Davidson, Donald, and Patrick Suppes. "A Finitistic Axiomatization of Subjective Probability and Utility." *Econometrica* 24 (1965): 264–75.

Davidson, Donald, Patrick Suppes, and Sidney Siegel. *Decision-Making: An Experimental Approach.* Stanford: Stanford UP, 1957.

Davies, David. "Works, Texts, and Contexts: Goodman on the Literary Artwork." *Canadian Journal of Philosophy* 21 (1991): 331–45.

Ellis, John. *The Theory of Literary Criticism.* Berkeley: U of California P, 1973.

Elster, Jon, ed. *The Multiple Self.* Cambridge: Cambridge UP, 1986.

Gärdenfors, Peter, and Nils-Eric Sahlin, eds. *Decision, Probability, and Utility: Selected Readings.* Cambridge: Cambridge UP, 1988.

Ginet, Carl. *On Action.* Cambridge: Cambridge UP, 1990.

Hollis, Martin. *The Cunning of Reason.* Cambridge: Cambridge UP, 1987.

Jeffrey, Richard C. *The Logic of Decision.* Chicago: U of Chicago P, 1983.

Levin, Janet. "Must Reasons Be Rational?" *Journal of Philosophy* 55 (1988): 199–217.

Livingston, Paisley. "Convention and Literary Explanations." In *Rules and Conventions: Literature, Philosophy, Social Theory.* Ed. Mette Hjort. Baltimore: Johns Hopkins UP, 1992. 67–94.

———. *Literary Knowledge: Humanistic Inquiry and the Philosophy of Science.* Ithaca: Cornell UP, 1988.

———. *Literature and Rationality: Ideas of Agency in Theory and Fiction.* Cambridge: Cambridge UP, 1991.

———. *Models of Desire: René Girard and the Psychology of Mimesis.* Baltimore: Johns Hopkins UP, 1992.

Lönnroth, Lars. *Njáls Saga: A Critical Introduction.* Berkeley: U of California P, 1976.

McClennen, Edward F. *Rationality and Dynamic Choice: Foundational Explorations.* Cambridge: Cambridge UP, 1990.

Marks, Joel, ed. *The Ways of Desire: New Essays in Philosophical Psychology on the Concept of Wanting.* Chicago: Precedent, 1986.

Mele, Alfred. *Irrationality: An Essay on Akrasia, Self-Deception, and Self-Control.* New York: Oxford UP, 1987.

———. *Springs of Action: Understanding Intentional Behavior.* New York: Oxford UP, 1992.

Miller, Richard W. *Fact and Method: Explanation, Confirmation, and Reality in the Natural and the Social Sciences.* Princeton: Princeton UP, 1987.

Moser, Paul K., ed. *Rationality in Action: Contemporary Approaches.* Cambridge: Cambridge UP, 1990.

Ramsey, Frank P. "Truth and Probability." In *The Foundations of Mathematics.* New York: Harcourt Brace, 1931. 156–98.

Sahlin, Nils-Eric. *The Philosophy of F. P. Ramsey.* Cambridge: Cambridge UP, 1990.

Savage, Leonard J. *The Foundations of Statistics.* New York: Wiley, 1954.

Schoemaker, Paul J. H. "The Expected Utility Model: Its Variants, Purposes, Evidence, and Limitations." *Journal of Economic Literature* 20 (1982): 529–63.

Simon, Herbert A. *Reason in Human Affairs.* Stanford: Stanford UP, 1983.

Slote, Michael. *Beyond Optimizing: A Study of Rational Choice.* Cambridge: Harvard UP, 1989.

Slovic, Paul. "Choice." In *Thinking.* Ed. Daniel N. Osherson and Edward E. Smith. Cambridge: MIT, 1990. 89–116.

Slovic, Paul, and Amos Tversky. "Who Accepts Savage's Axiom?" *Behavioral Science* 19 (1974): 368–73.

Suppes, Patrick. "Davidson's Views on Psychology as a Science." In *Essays on Davidson: Actions and Events.* Ed. Bruce Vermazen and Merrill B. Hintikka. Oxford: Clarendon, 1985. 183–94.

Thalberg, Irving. "Questions About Motivational Strength." In *Actions and Events: Perspectives on the Philosophy of Donald Davidson.* Ed. Ernest LePore and Brian McLaughlin. Oxford: Basil Blackwell, 1985. 88–103.

Wilson, George M. *The Intentionality of Human Action,* 2d ed. rev. Stanford: Stanford UP, 1989.

Davidson and the Politics of Relativism: A Response

MICHAEL FISCHER

When contemporary philosophers turn to literature, they often are responding to what they see as a crisis in their own discipline. Richard Rorty's use of George Orwell and Vladimir Nabokov in *Contingency, Irony, and Solidarity,* for example, is set up by what Rorty regards as the inability of philosophy to ground values in a common human nature. The default of philosophy brings about the need for novels, whose detailed descriptions of others become the glue keeping us together. Stanley Cavell's readings of Shakespeare, the English Romantics, Thoreau, and Emerson are similarly motivated by his dissatisfaction with philosophy's interpretation of skepticism. Finally, in *Love's Knowledge,* the failure of academic philosophy to address everyday ethical questions encourages Martha Nussbaum's attention to the novels of Henry James, which for her exemplify "the work of the moral imagination" (148).[1]

The essays collected in the present book take a different path, turning from literary criticism to philosophy, in particular the work of Donald Davidson. As commentaries on Davidson, the foregoing essays speak for themselves. But they also speak to a crisis in literary study that needs to be more fully described. I know why Rorty, Cavell, and Nussbaum need literature. I want to know more about why these writers think literary criticism needs Davidson.

My question is partly prompted by the fact that not everyone in literary study of course feels this need, much as not everyone in philosophy feels compelled to read Shakespeare and James. Nussbaum and Cavell account for this resistance to literature by citing many causes, among them what Nussbaum calls "the long-standing fascination of Western philosophy with the methods and the style of natural science" (19). The contributors to the present volume say very little about the neglect of Davidson. It is admittedly a difficult problem. Philosophical antipathy toward literature, for instance among some analytical philosophers, is undiscriminating; no writer or genre is spared. But literary critics have become more selective in their judgment of philosophers, favoring some (most notably Derrida, Heidegger, Austin, and Wittgenstein) while ignoring others.

Among these neglected philosophers I would put Davidson. For Michael Morton, explaining why Davidson is ignored by literary critics involves explaining why skepticism, or at least professing skepticism, is in vogue (see Morton essay, above). Somewhat impatiently, Morton asks *why*—why "so many have apparently found themselves irresistibly drawn to a position that a moment's reflection suffices to reveal as beset with a host of insuperable difficulties."[2] According to Morton, intellectual decadence has something to do with our skepticism, as does dissatisfaction with what Husserl called "the natural attitude." Both decadence and loss of confidence in "straightforward, unvarnished realism" enjoy in turn their "greatest currency in times of broad social and cultural decline," says Morton. Fighting for the "larger cause of basic good sense," Morton hopes that Davidson's work, like Kant's in his day, will at least help us show our literary colleagues "why they should stop talking a certain sort of nonsense."

Perhaps because I am not so pessimistic about the current age, I worry about seeing Davidson as a more sophisticated or analytical Allan Bloom. Picturing Davidson in this messianic way makes me want to join Mark Gaipa and Robert Scholes in pausing "before using his work as a blueprint for changes in literary study." In my opinion, the essays in the present volume describe a philosopher whose work more literary critics and theorists ought to use—not, however, as a blunt weapon against the skepticism, subjectivism, and relativism that presumably assault us. To borrow Gaipa and Scholes' opening analogy, before throwing these things out of our house, we need to understand what they are doing there. Or, adapting one of Davidson's key terms, we need a more charitable explanation of why literary theorists suspect rationality, objectivity, realism, and the other categories that Davidson rehabilitates. In his essay, Paisley Livingston notes: "this kind of romantic and postmodern attitude toward any and all concepts of rationality is an uninformed prejudice maintained in the absence of knowledge about the diverse conceptions of rationality that abound in the literature on the topic." I think it is much more than that.

For the sake of argument, I will assume that our skepticism entails 1) doubting that we can know other minds, 2) suspecting that there is no such thing as truth or fact, and 3) supposing that, in the absence of any objective evidence constraining us, we write the text we read. Although I am willing to call these ideas "skeptical," Samuel Wheeler's essay reminds me that our embracing them may not be the fault of deconstruction, as many opponents of critical relativism maintain. I am not sure who will be most disappointed by Wheeler's claim that Davidson and Derrida resemble one another: deconstructionists who want Derrida's work to be "startling" and "notorious" or Davidsonians who want to oppose his work to what they see as the irresponsibility of deconstruction. I still think that the differences between Derrida and Davidson matter more than the similarities, but I will not press the point here because in my view deconstruction (however defined) is not responsible for the skepticism that so many literary critics find attractive.

This skepticism results partly from the fact that, by and large, we still deal with literary texts, not with the oral communication that mainly concerns Davidson. As Thomas Kent notes in his essay, "Like his fellow analytic philosophers, Donald Davidson privileges spoken discourse over written discourse, and in his now-substantial array of essays concerning the philosophy of language, he has addressed directly neither the problematics of writing nor the character of literary hermeneutics." With this emphasis on speech in mind, Livingston rightly cautions us against mechanically applying Davidson's theory of interpretation to problems in literary criticism. (Coming from a different starting point— Davidson's theory of action—Allen Dunn reaches a comparable conclusion.) As Livingston concedes, critics have had good reasons for seeing literary texts as autonomous aesthetic objects rather than as "tokens in a communicative process," one of these reasons being that works of literature (as opposed to everyday speech acts) do seem to survive, maybe even thrive on, detachment from the initial context of their writing and reception. Once detached from the constraints of tone and voice, immediate context, and practical, often urgent intent—the constraints that Davidson's critical realism feeds on—literary texts seem more problematic, conflicted, indeterminate, and open-ended (to borrow some of the favorite words of current theorists). After disconnecting literature from intentional discourse, Livingston puts them together again and shows that Davidson's work (carefully applied) remains relevant to literary criticism after all, even to the nonaesthetic, sociohistorical approaches that seem most distant from Davidson's emphasis on intentionality and individual action. Nevertheless, Livington's circumspection, his sensitivity to the differences between literary interpretation and everyday communication, is well founded. For literary critics dealing with complex written texts, some degree of interpretive skepticism may come with the territory.

Steven Cole, in his contribution, touches on an even more important reason why a Davidsonian approach to interpretation may not come naturally to contemporary critics. Gayatri Spivak serves to illustrate what Cole calls "one of the oddities of recent literary theory" when she construes shared, common experience in largely negative and coercive— i.e., ideological—terms. Cole astutely shows how Spivak's analysis of the *"harm* of ideology" is at odds with her resignation to what I would call the omnipresence of ideology, which makes even the subject's (always illusory) sense of freedom and choice an effect of the ideology that Spivak wants to unsettle. As Cole puts it,

> it is hard to understand how ideology can be claimed to be a victimizer, since nothing in the account allows any description of what, exactly, might be harmed if ideology functions as that which is determinant of the very subject being harmed. The problem is that the description of ideology seems not to offer any explanation of what aspects of the subject might stand outside the determinations of ideology, and thus serve as a candidate for what ideology has itself victimized. If the subject is both the cause and the effect of ideology, and if such a relation to ideology is exhaustive of the subject itself, then there is literally nothing about the subject which ideology might victimize.

Instead of depriving us of our (again, illusory) sense of freedom, ideology nurtures it. We are not so much victimized by ideology as constituted by it, through and through. Compounding the problem, we lack public terms for articulating our grievances, public discourse being the product of the very ideology we would repudiate.

This is a crucial problem, and Cole deserves credit for posing it. But we need to look more closely at how this problem comes about before letting Davidson come to Spivak's rescue. Far from being an oddity, Spivak's predicament is an outgrowth of her concern with victims and victimization. Although rightly dissatisfied with Spivak's philosophical means, Cole fails to address her laudable political aim—to redress the victimization of women and others.

Given Spivak's early involvement with deconstruction, it is difficult to say which comes first, her politics or her epistemology. In other feminist critics, political objectives beget relativist-sounding philosophical positions, rather than the other way around. The experience of being excluded, silenced, shut out, and otherwise ignored motivates the demystification of the seemingly rational, objective norms keeping women and others out. Amy Ling, for instance, reports being told by her former chairman, "Give me one good reason why I should read your writers, other than guilt" (158). Perspectivism reinforces Ling's suspicion that her chairman's norms are culturally constructed; it encourages her to think that *he* cannot give her one good, ideology-free reason why she should read *his* books, other than her fear of his power over her. By "perspectivism" here I mean something roughly akin to what I earlier called "skepticism" and Morton calls "radical interpretationism," or the claim that putative facts, norms, and universals are made rather than discovered—made to legitimize the subordination of texts and people who deviate from the norm.[3]

Cole makes the good point that such perspectivism is a double-edged sword. By proclaiming the ideological basis of all normative claims, it undermines the victim's claims as well as the oppressor's, leading to the impasse, the quandary over victimization, that we saw in Spivak. But, again, I wish Cole would acknowledge Spivak's political motivations. Perhaps then he would not conclude by apparently scolding the "post-structuralist subject" for (stubbornly?) seeking "freedom in its denial of the intelligibility of any but its own determinations, and find[ing] finally only its own absolute." Admittedly, I may be reading into Cole's conclusion an unsympathetic tone that is not there. His unresponsiveness to Spivak's political aims, however, does create a vacuum that speculation like mine rushes to fill. In any case, substitute Amy Ling for the "post-structuralist subject" and we see someone longing for self-determination (hence, denying the determinations imposed on her) and understandably wishing to find an absolute that fits her experience instead repudiating it.

Cole unfavorably compares this poststructuralist subject to the "Davidsonian subject" who "is instead constituted by the limiting certainty of the truth of its own beliefs, and discovers the freedom of endless dispute." Compared to the poststructuralist, this subject seems confident, certain, and ready for disagreement. He finds endless dispute to be liberating rather than wearying or threatening. The comfortable social position of this subject is suggested by an earlier remark of Cole's:

> As Davidson puts it, before any disagreement is possible, the disputants must "interpret the words and beliefs of each other. In doing this each of necessity employs his own basis. For each, this supplies a ground of agreed-on standards, values and beliefs to which appeal can be made concerning their difference. Serious relativism provides no such common ground on which further intelligible discussion can be based."

Missing in this statement is any awareness that the two disputants might not be on equal footing—that one might be the male chair of an English department, the other an untenured, Asian-American woman. "Intelligible discussion" is already in progress here, not bullying or taunting. Perhaps the Davidsonian subject finds endless dispute invigorating because he usually wins—or has nothing to lose.

I am not defending what Davidson calls "serious relativism," only trying to understand its political appeal. It seems to redress the inequities that Davidson's statement overlooks. Whereas Davidson's disputants start out on equal terms, a more beleaguered subject might appreciate relativism for promising to even things up—for exposing the ideological basis of the established position and putting it on a par with the marginalized position it dominates.

I return to the opening conjunction of claims that Cole finds so odd. First, "the claim that the subject and its beliefs are themselves the effects of social causal mechanisms" is aimed at the privileged subject who evades the contingent social determination of his allegedly rational or universal views. Second, "the account of the subject as ultimately inscrutable" is an admittedly defensive, self-protective claim designed to ward off externally imposed definitions. Finally, "the insistence that the determining of the subject by social causal mechanisms should be unmasked by literary theory as a violation of the subject itself" gives literary theory an emancipatory purpose we should reinforce.

I agree with Cole that these claims get in each other's way. The assertion that "the subject and its beliefs are themselves the effects of social causal mechanisms," for example, undermines the rights of the victims as well as the privileges of the powerful, thus stalling the literary theorist's critique. Guided by Davidson, Cole has raised some excellent questions. For instance, how can we justify our claim to know that women really are more (or other) than objects of exchange—a claim essential to the political argument that women are victimized by such a description? But, having posed these problems, does Davidson help us resolve them? Having helped us see that relativism is logically incoherent, self-refuting, and impossible, does Davidson have a better alternative? By "better," I mean not just logically coherent, but politically effective, accountable to the democratic aspirations that literary critics such as Ling have thought relativism serves.

Cole's own answer to this kind of question would seem to be no: "As Davidson himself admits, there are no particular normative conclusions to be drawn from his account of the role which truth and rationality play in our knowledge." In a Kantian spirit, Davidson is not making judgments but is laying down their preconditions, not engaging in political critique but showing what it is that critique—more generally, communication—presupposes. Also comparing Davidson to Kant, Morton concedes in his essay that "as to the question of what the *substantive* implications of this development might be for the analysis and interpretation of texts, here, I think, it is still too early to speak with any confidence."

Gaipa, Scholes, and Reed Way Dasenbrock are less reticent, although they reach different conclusions about Davidson's work. Gaipa and Scholes picture Davidson taking a possibly alien word—"incommensurable" in Kuhn and Feyerabend, for example—and translating it into his own terminology "in order to get power over it, to make it more amenable to his own beliefs." Much as William Blake held that "pity would be no more / If we did not make somebody Poor," Gaipa and Scholes suggest that Davidson's vaunted principle of charity reflects an underlying imperialistic arrogance. We need be charitable only when we suspect others are wrong. Then, if we are Davidson, we generously assume that they are really one of us—that, for example, the term which they could be taking literally, they must be meaning metaphorically, "must" if we are still to regard them as rational, sane, or even human. I am of course adding to what Gaipa and Scholes say, but only in order to bring out the trenchant political critique of Davidson latent in their remarks. Although Davidson is "a somewhat reluctant or diffident absolutist," he is for Gaipa and Scholes an absolutist nonetheless, bent on seeing his own reflection everywhere and thus suppressing "historical change and differences in political or linguistic power."

Similarly, in his essay, Dasenbrock reads Stanley Fish as someone imprisoned in his own conceptual scheme and, consequently, never encountering or allowing for anything different. But for Dasenbrock, instead of reenacting Fish's narcissism, Davidson corrects it. According to this reading of Davidson, radical incommensurability puts other interpretive communities off-limits and, what comes to the same thing, encloses us within our own community. By denying the utter incommensurability of conceptual schemes, Davidson is trying to allow for difference, not eliminate it. Without mutual understanding, difference cannot emerge; we have no access to difference because we have no access to anything outside ourselves. In Davidson's terms, our "prior theory" about a text or culture remains our only one.

Dasenbrock's account raises as many questions as it tries to answer. In particular, why does difference come about? He notes: "It is not our different interpretive communities that keep us apart; it is simply our different interpretations." But this relocates the problem instead of solving it. Where do these different interpretations come from? Just as important, how should we respond to differnce? Dasenbrock's Davidson apparently does not have answers to these questions, but for him at least they *are* questions. Davidson's account, says Dasenbrock, makes possible a "productive encounter with difference," even if he does not define "productive" or, for that matter, "difference."

Although Dasenbrock reaches conclusions which are opposite to those of Gaipa and Scholes, all three seem to agree on what we literary critics need: namely, what Dasenbrock terms "a genuine hermeneutics of difference, particularly cultural difference, an interpretive method that can understand texts different from us and understand them to be different from us." This is a crucial concern for many contemporary literary critics, myself included. I have been suggesting that our desire to respect difference—not our decadence or uninformed prejudice—explains our uneasiness with absolutism as well as our attraction to what Ellen Messer-Davidow calls "perspectivism." Unlike "objectivity" and "uniformity," she says, perspectivism presumably

> requires us to include people with diverse perspectives, to learn a repertoire of cultural as well as technical perspectives, and to make knowledge collectively. Thus, perspectivity would restructure inquiry by institutionalizing a diversity grounded in cultural, personal, technical, and self-reflexive variables; by using viewpoints as a chief methodology; and by composing manifold knowledge. [89]

Not all of the contributors in the preceding pages think of Davidson as a resource in our effort to safeguard cultural difference and institutionalize diversity. Some—most notably Gaipa and Scholes—are apprehensive about Davidson. Others, taking their cue from Davidson's own

analytical approach to interpretive questions, offer rather more technical expositions of his thought. But all of them agree that Davidson, for
better or for worse, criticizes relativism. I think his critique *should*
matter to literary critics—not, however, because relativism is nonsense,
but because it shortchanges the political hopes that some critics have
invested in it. If Dasenbrock is right, Davidson may be just what we need:
someone who criticizes relativism while helping us carry out its democratic aims.

NOTES

1. To this list I would add Peter J. McCormick, who often finds in literature a richness and
particularity "from which philosophical reflection can only benefit" (156), and Richard Eldridge,
who argues that literary works respond to otherwise intractable philosophical problems.

2. Elsewhere Gorman also expresses his astonishment and disappointment that although
literary theory looks toward philosophy, it looks toward the wrong philosophy: "Indeed, the
main problem afflicting modern literary theory lies in the remarkable willingness of most
theorists to accept, with little examination, dicta of the philosophical authorities [Derrida, for
instance] who have impressed them for some reason, as opposed to thinking through such ideas
critically" (650). The phrase "for some reason" is noticeably vague here. I try to uncover some
of the political reasons for critics latching onto the poststructuralist ideas that Gorman finds
wrongheaded.

3. "Perspectivism" is Ellen Messer-Davidow's term for this claim. In the article to which Ling
is responding, Messer-Davidow argues that perspectivism should be the philosophical basis of
feminist criticism.

WORKS CITED

Eldridge, Richard. *On Moral Personhood.* Chicago: U of Chicago P, 1989.
Gorman, David. "From Small Beginnings: Literary Theorists Encounter Analytic Phi-
    losophy." *Poetics Today* 11, no. 3 (1990): 647–59.
Ling, Amy. "I'm Here: An Asian American Woman's Response." *New Literary History*
    19, no. 1 (1987): 151–60.
McCormick, Peter J. *Fictions, Philosophies, and the Problems of Poetics.* Ithaca:
    Cornell UP, 1988.
Messer-Davidow, Ellen. "The Philosophical Bases of Feminist Literary Criticisms."
    New Literary History 19, no. 1 (1987): 63–104.
Nussbaum, Martha. *Love's Knowledge.* Oxford: Oxford UP, 1990.
Rorty, Richard. *Contingency, Irony, and Solidarity.* Cambridge: Cambridge UP,
    1989.

Locating Literary Language

DONALD DAVIDSON

*L*iterature poses a problem for philosophy of language, for it directly challenges any theory of meaning that makes the assertorial or truth-seeking uses of language primary and pretends that other linguistic performances are in some sense "etiolated" or "parasitical."[1] The sources of trouble are to be sure far more ubiquitous than the reference to literature suggests: jokes, skits, polite nothings, ironies, all break the mold of sincere, literal, would-be truth-telling. But literature can serve as the focus of the problem if only by dint of its kinship with and employment of such verbal tricks and turns. Literature and these comrade conceits are a prime test of the adequacy of any view of the nature of language, and it is a test I have argued that many theories fail.[2]

Still, although the literary uses of language have long interested me, I have neglected to indicate, or even to think very hard about, how my account of the origins of intentionality and objectivity (which I see as emerging simultaneously and as mutually dependent) should be adapted to the case of literature. Indeed, it is clear to me now that any gesture in the direction of such adaptation will also reveal the need for a sharper focus on the role of intention in writing, and hence on the relation between writer and reader. I am grateful to the contributors to the present volume, and especially to its editor, for prodding me into considering these issues, even if all too briefly.

I will concentrate on two related problems: the role of reference in "storytelling" and the changes that occur when we replace the triangle of speaker-hearer-world with the triangle of writer-reader-tradition. Insofar as the geometry of the situation is concerned, I am a commentator on such triangles, as are the writers of the other essays in this book; and like them, I am also inescapably at an apex of various actual and imagined triangles of my own.

First, though, I should say a word about my general theory of action. One commentator labors to make the point that the theme of "Actions, Reasons and Causes" is of little value to the writer or critic of fiction. I certainly agree. If my analysis of the concept of action has any value at all for those who wish to look deep into the springs of action, it is to release them from the conceptual bind imposed on us, first by a series of nineteenth-century German philosophers, and then by Wittgenstein and his followers, who taught that the methods of the poet, the critic, and the social scientist not only are different from, but also opposed to, the methods of the sciences of (the rest of) nature. The latter, materialist, domain they saw as ruled by causality, laws, and the nomological-deductive method; the former, humanistic, domain ruled by insight, empathetic understanding, and teleological explanation. My contribution was to emphasize, somewhat as Spinoza had, that the two domains—of mind and body, intension and extension, law-governed events and thoughtful actions—were parts of radically distinct, but equally legitimate, ways of describing, understanding, and explaining phenomena, but that they nonetheless applied to a single ontology of events and objects. Causality, I argued, applied to both domains, but by distinguishing causal relations from the descriptions of events under which the events could be viewed as instantiating laws, I removed actions from the realm of deterministic nomological explanation. This view effectively reconciled, I thought, two apparently antagonistic intuitions. One intuition insists that the understanding of the thoughts and actions of people involves the imaginative adjustment of the interpreter's beliefs and values to the attitudes of the interpreted, a process that requires the accommodation of one normative system within another. The other intuition tells us that in the natural sciences such considerations are beside the point: physics strives to find categories from which norms, even causal concepts, are excluded, categories which lend themselves to incorporation in a system of laws with as few *ceteris paribus* clauses as possible.

It is a serious mistake, if I am right, to suppose that the relatively simple Aristotelian-Thomistic scheme I proposed for analyzing the concept of acting with a reason aims to assimilate this concept to the natural sciences simply because it invokes causality. This gets things backward: serious science strives to extrude the concept of causality in favor of strict laws. It is teleological explanation that cannot do without the concept of causality, and for that reason, among others, reason-explanations cannot hope to be reduced to, or incorporated in, the natural sciences.

It remains the case that my schematic account of the intention with which an action is performed is no positive help for someone who wants to construct an interesting psychology of action. The imagination might be caught, however, at the point where it becomes appropriate to identify, to give propositional content to, the various beliefs, desires, motives and attitudes that cause an intentional action, and by causing it, determine in turn its appropriate descriptions.

An ineluctable feature of teleological explanation is its normative character. This does not mean, as one of the contributors to the present volume thinks, that I confuse the purported norms of logic or of Bayesian decision theory with descriptive theories.[3] There is no definition of "perfect rationality," whatever we take that to be, according to which people satisfy the definition. My point has rather been that we can explain and understand irrationality only against a background of rationality, a background that each of us must, as an interpreter, supply for himself. There is no fixed list of standards, no eternal hierarchy of values, to which we all must subscribe, but some norms are so basic to intelligibility that we cannot avoid shaping thoughts to their patterns. Thus as W. V. Quine has pointed out, we can interpret some speaker's device as expressing conjunction only if the speaker generally treats that device in accord with the truth-table for conjunction; but then we have attributed a bit of logic to that person. The norms of decision making under uncertainty, of induction, and so on, are far more flexible, and we can understand deviations easily, including differences over what the norms are. But I would argue that we could not understand someone whom we were forced to treat as departing radically and predominantly from all such norms. This would not be an example of irrationality, or of an alien set of standards: it would be an absence of rationality, something that could not be reckoned as thought.

I now revert to the nature of interpretation. It is natural to state the central problem as that of determining the meaning of spoken or written words. This is not wrong, but it can be misleading. Words, Frege emphasized, have a meaning only in the context of a sentence. The basic reason for this is that the work of language, to give information, tell stories, ask questions, issue commands, and so on, is done by sentences; a word that is not being used to convey the content of a sentence cannot do any of these things. It is at the sentential level that language connects with the interests and intentions language serves, and this is also the level at which the evidence for interpretation emerges. But just as words have a meaning only in the context of a sentence, a sentence has a meaning only in a context of use, as part, in some sense, of a particular language. There would be no saying what language a sentence belonged to if there were not actual utterances cr writings, not, perhaps, of that very sentence, but of other sentences appropriately related to it. So in the end the sole source of linguistic meaning is the intentional production of tokens of sentences. If such acts did not have meanings, nothing would. There is no harm in assigning meanings to sentences, but this must always be a meaning derived from concrete occasions on which sentences are put to work.

The recognition that meaning of whatever sort rests ultimately on intention leads at once into the thickets of densely packed intentions through which philosophers (along with psychologists, historians, sociologists, literary critics and theorists) try to pick their way. For we can speak of "the" intention with which an act is performed only by narrowing attention to one among the tangle of intentions involved in any performance. Since most if not all the ambiguities of "meaning" spring from the varieties of intention, I begin by distinguishing some of those varieties.

There are, I think, three distinct sorts of intention which are present in all speech acts. First of all, there are ends or intentions which lie as it were beyond the production of words, ends that could at least in principle be achieved by nonlinguistic means. Thus one may speak with the intention of being elected mayor, of amusing a child, of warning a pilot of ice on the wings; one may write with the intention of making money, of proving one's cleverness, to celebrate the freedom of the will, or to neutralize a plaguing memory or emotion. Such ends do not involve language, in the sense that their description does not have to mention language. I call these intentions "ulterior." It is a striking fact (if I am right that it *is* a fact) that all genuine uses of language require an ulterior purpose. Using language is not a game: it is never an end in itself. Second, every linguistic utterance or inscription is produced with the intention that it should have a certain force: it is intended to be an assertion, or command, a joke or question, a pledge or insult. There can be borderline cases, but only when straddling a border is intended: so it is possible to intend an utterance of "Go to sleep" as somewhere between an order and the expression of a wish, or to intend the remark "See you in July" as part promise and part prediction. Third, it is a necessary mark of a linguistic action that the speaker or writer intends his words to be interpreted as having a certain meaning. These are the strictly semantic intentions.

Each of the foregoing categories may harbor more, in some cases many more, intentions but at least one intention of each sort is always present. A simple case: I shout "Thin ice" as you skate toward disaster. My ulterior motive is to warn you, the force of my utterance is assertory, and I intend you to take my words to mean that the ice toward which you are skating is thin. Even here, though, more intentions are present. I want to warn you, but I want to warn you in order to save you from a chilly plunge. I intend your grasp of the meaning and force of my utterance to be the means of your salvation. In this case, I have no reason to want you to be ignorant of any of my intentions, although it is not necessarily part of my intention that you should grasp all of my ulterior purposes. But here, as always, I use language with the intention that your grasp of my intended meaning and force should function to achieve my ulterior purpose. (This is the Gricean reflex.) A linguistic action is frustrated if its intended audience does not grasp the producer's intended semantic meaning and force. The speaker or writer may have good reasons, however, for wanting ulterior motives to remain undetected. Don Giovanni sings to Zerlina, "Là ci darem la mano." The semantic meaning of the utterance and its force (entreaty) seem clear enough, but of his ulterior aims Don Giovanni wants her to grasp only the most obvious, that she should give him her hand. Like a liar, he cannot afford to have his leading intention known.

It is perhaps obvious that ulterior purposes can be as complex as our thoughts about the relations between means and ends can make them. It is only a little less obvious that semantic intentions can be equally complicated. Thersites, looking at Ajax, says to Achilles: ". . . whomsoever you take him to be, he is Ajax" (Shakespeare, *Troilus and Cressida*, act II, scene 1). To point out only what is obvious: Thersites intends his words to be taken as literally meaning that whatever Achilles may think, the person in front of him is Ajax. Since Achilles of course knows this ("I know that, fool"), Thersites is not *asserting* that this is Ajax, but that Ajax is absurd beyond further description ("Ay, but that fool knows not himself"). The proposition Thersites asserts is not the proposition his words express. This is a mild case of what Grice calls "implicature"—something which the circumstances make clear the speaker intends to convey. The potential ambiguity which Thersites brings out in Achilles' reply (since the comma in "I know that, fool" cannot be spoken) is probably not intended by Achilles, but it does focus attention on the implicature in Thersites' first remark. The playwright wants us to catch what he may want us to think Achilles does not.

I have just spoken as if the distinction between the proposition expressed by a sentence and what is asserted by using that sentence were obvious. But sentences express something only as used on particular occasions, and what they express depends, among other things, on the intentions of the speaker or writer. How do the intentions of the author of a linguistic act allow us to distinguish between what her words convey and what she intends to convey by using them? Grice has given us some subtle and convincing principles for making this distinction in the case of certain sorts of implicature, but it is not clear that these principles are designed to handle the gamut of examples we find in literature; nor, surprisingly enough, are the principles based on the intentions of the speaker (see "The Causal Theory of Perception"). Fortunately, however, there is a simple principle which will serve our present purposes.

The intentions with which an action is done have an order: they constitute a chain built on the relation of means to end as seen by the agent. Thus someone moves his hand in order to move a pen across the paper in order to write his name in order to sign a check in order to pay a bill in order to . . . Or, someone moves her mouth and tongue in order to form the sounds "That is an emu" in order to speak words that will be interpreted by a hearer as true if and only if an emu is salient in order to inform the hearer that a salient object is an emu in order to instruct the hearer in how to identify an emu in order to . . . In this sequence, the first intention that has to do with what words mean, or are intended to mean, is the intention to speak words that will be assigned a certain meaning by an interpreter. I call this the *first meaning*. It corresponds roughly to what is sometimes called "literal meaning," but since this latter phrase has associations I do not want I have coined my own jargon.

The usefulness of the concept of first meaning emerges when we consider cases where what is stated or implied differs from what the words mean. "Sometime too hot the eye of heaven shines" means that the sun sometimes shines too brightly. But the first meaning of "the eye of heaven" purports to refer to the one and only eye of heaven. We can tell this because Shakespeare (we assume) intended to use words that would be recognized by a reader to refer to the one and only eye of heaven (if such a thing existed) in order to prompt the reader to understand that he meant the sun. We may wish to use the word "meaning" for both the first meaning and what the metaphor carries us to, but only the first meaning has a systematic place in the language of the author.[4]

First meaning is *first* in two related respects: it comes first in the order of the speaker's or the writer's semantic intentions, and it is the necessary basis for all further investigations into what words, as used on an occasion, mean. You do not begin to grasp what Shakespeare meant by "the eye of heaven" if you do not know the ordinary meaning of "eye"; and Shakespeare intended you to understand his metaphor by way of your understanding of the ordinary meanings of his words. The dependence of other meanings or implicatures on first meaning should not be taken to suggest that given the first meaning the rest follows. "He was burned up" has (let us say) an unambiguous first meaning, but what it implies depends on the context. When Herrick speaks of the liquefaction of Julia's clothes, how do we know the clothes did not fall into a vat of acid?

Similarly, first meaning and what it may in specific circumstances implicate are not enough to fix the force of an utterance or writing. Indeed, force and first meaning are entirely independent, a fact which literature makes particularly clear. H.L.A. Hart once suggested that in a sense the use of language in fiction is a "calculated abuse" (204). But what is being abused? We may say that the liar abuses language, but this does not mean it is the language which is badly used, but the victim. The victim of a successful lie understands the liar's words perfectly, both the first meaning and the force (assertion); what he gets wrong is an ulterior motive. Unless the liar may mean the same thing by his words as the honest man, it would be impossible to tell a lie, for to be understood would be to be unmasked.

Of course the fiction writer does not, in general at any rate, aim to deceive his readers. But neither does he pretend to use language: using language in play is not playing at using language. There are a few things I can pretend (e.g., that I can speak Tagalog) by pretending to use language; but I certainly cannot pretend, by only pretending to use language, that Oedipus killed Laius. But even this is a strained sense of pretense. The storyteller does not, like the liar, normally misrepresent his beliefs. He does not *assert* that Oedipus killed Laius. At most he pretends to assert it.

There are cases where we have trouble telling whether a work is fiction. On the page following the title page of the Modern Library edition of E. E. Cummings' *The Enormous Room* I read: "A note on the author of *The Enormous Room*. During the war Edward Estlin Cummings enlisted in the Norton-Harjes Ambulance Corps. With no charge against him, he was confined in a concentration camp in La Ferté Macé, France. It was there that he gathered material for his first and most successful book." In an introduction Cummings' father writes of the trouble he had in locating and finally freeing his son. The first sentence of the book reads, in part, "We had succeeded, my friend B. and I, in dispensing with almost three of our six months' engagement as *Conducteurs Volontaires*, ... had just finished the unlovely job of cleaning and greasing ... the own private flivver of ... a gentleman by the convenient name of Mr. A." How much here is true, or intended to be taken as true? Is the introduction really by Cummings' father, or is that part of the story? Surely no one was named "B." or "Mr. A." The simple point is that nothing that is said in the book can determine the force of these sentences. After all, the preface of *Moll Flanders* begins, "the world is so taken up of late with novels and romances, that it will be hard for a private history to be taken for genuine, where the names and other circumstances of the person are concealed." Should we say it is not really history if the names are altered? Of course not. But then we must apparently reject the popular view that proper names refer to a person only if their causal history ties them back to something like a christening.

Proper names are a problem whether we come at them from the point of view of sober fact-stating or of fiction. Seen from the former angle it seems natural to claim that if a name fails to refer it simply lacks a sense—a sentence that contains such a name fails to say anything, fails to express a proposition, while when studied in the footlights of fiction we feel compelled to assign as full a meaning to sentences with names of fictional characters as to any sentence. "Was Bloom married?" Yes, to Molly Bloom. "Was Bloom a real person?" No, of course not. Both answers cannot be true; but neither questions nor answers would make sense if nonreferring names had no meaning.

This is not the place to propose a detailed theory of the semantics of proper names. But I do want to insist on a principle to which any correct theory must conform: a meaning which can be grasped without knowledge of whether it was generated in the context of history or of fiction cannot depend on that context. Our response to a work may differ according to whether we think of it as fact or fiction, and it may differ according to whether we think of that work as intended to be fact or fiction (not quite the same question). This difference in response is appropriate, of course: if we are asking directions to the next town, or studying the sexual mores of the natives, we care whether our informant is spinning a tale or giving us the real dope. But our concern is pointless if we have not already understood the words. If we apply this simple thought to the case of proper names, I think we should reverse the usual strategy of making the "referring use" of names primary and the "nonreferring use" a play or pretend use. Using names in fiction is, as I said, a real use of language; so how names function in stories not only can, but must, be how they function elsewhere. (This is not to deny that we might never have come to understand the function of proper names had we not been exposed to cases in which names had a reference.)

I have been stressing the structured hierarchy of intentions with which sentences are spoken or written in part because it seems to me that many debates concerning the relevance of intention to the interpretation of literary texts overlook the differences among such intentions. It is time to turn to the larger picture in which those intentions play their parts.

We would not have a language, or the thoughts that depend on language (which comprise all beliefs, desires, hopes, expectations, intentions and other attitudes having propositional content), if there were not others who understood us and whom we understood; and such mutual understanding requires a world shared both causally and conceptually. I have argued for the primacy of this triangular relation at some length elsewhere,[5] and it is well explained by several of the contributors to the present book. Intersubjective interaction with the world is a necessary condition of our possession of the concepts of truth and objectivity; that is why I reject as unintelligible most forms of skepticism and of conceptual relativism. The triangle comes directly into play when two (or more) creatures react simultaneously to a common stimulus in the world and to each other's reactions. This is the causal nexus which must exist before there can be answers to the questions, What is the relevant stimulus of the response? and When are stimuli or responses similar? Much more is required for a complex of such relations to constitute the sort of communication we call language, but nothing less will do. The triangle models the primitive situation in which we take the first steps into language or begin decoding a totally alien language. It is easiest to think of its operation where there is a teacher (or informant) and a learner (or student), but it must apply also to the origins of language and to the most ordinary conversations.

The objectification of parts and aspects of the world which is made possible by intersubjective triangulation is appropriate to the origins of language and to what I have called "radical interpretation." But how does the primordial triangle bear on literature? On the one hand it is clear enough that the elements of the triangle remain: the writer, his audience, and a common background. But the distances between the elements have lengthened, the connections have become attenuated and obscure.

Almost at the start of language learning, modification of the primal triangle sets in. What begins with mutually observed reactions to mutually observed phenomena soon graduates to something more useful: the "speaker" observes the object or event (a snake approaches), and the "hearer," screened in one way or another from the snake, reacts to the speaker's reaction to the snake as he normally would to a snake. The communicative triangle triumphs over the loss of the direct causal relation between hearer and snake. Causal connections further attenuate: in the absence of the relevant objects, the hearer or learner masters words by connecting those words with words mastered more directly. Thus if you learn to apply "dog" and "picture of a dog" in the presence of the objects, you may understand "armadillo" by seeing a picture of an armadillo. More subtle but familiar devices allow us to give content to words and phrases that apply to objects and situations beyond the range of the senses, or remote in space and time. But without direct causal ties of language to the world at some points[6] no words would have a content—there would be no language.

In writing, the deictic and demonstrative machinery so readily available in speech cannot in the same way complete the triangle that relates writer, reader, and object or event or time. Ostension, which often serves to relate names and faces, or to help introduce a new color or sound or category, has no immediate analogue in writing. Writing has its ways, however, of establishing ties between writer's intentions, reader and the world. A personal letter can take advantage of a world of established mutual connections; a set of instructions can make demonstrative use of diagrams or of the apparatus to be assembled. Posted signs ("No Dumping," "Dangerous Curves," "Grasp the Handrail," "Trailhead") simply elide the obvious demonstrative reference to time, place or direction which is supplied by the location and orientation of the sign. Such props are not in general available to literature, but others are. Almost all connected writing that involves more than a few sentences depends on deictic references to its own text. The linear sequence of words and sentences often indicates the temporal order in which events are represented as occurring. A vast network of anaphoric references connects parts of a text to each other through the use of pronouns, demonstrative adjectives, tense and parataxis.[7]

Most of the words in a literary work have an ordinary extension in the world. Predicates, adjectives, verbs, common nouns and adverbs do not lose their normal ties to real objects and events when they are employed in fiction; they could suffer this loss only if their meanings changed, and if their meanings changed we would not understand them.[8] More puzzling, as I noted, is the use of proper names. Some proper names in fiction clearly fail to refer, and although this is a troubling semantic phenomenon, it is no more puzzling in fiction than in other contexts. What should we say, though, of names that have a reference when they appear in a newspaper if they are then employed in an historical novel, or of invented names in a *roman à clef?* In Trollope's *Phineas Phinn,* do "Daubeny" and "Gresham" refer to Disraeli and Gladstone? The *Daily Telegraph* chastised Trollope for putting real politicians in his novels and particularly criticized his "malignant" portrait of John Bright. Trollope claimed he had deliberately avoided any likeness to the real Bright, but another reviewer wrote that Trollope

> is cruelly careful that the veriest child shall not fail to recognize his pet aversion under the *alias* he has given him. With historical and needlessly elaborate minuteness [Trollope] describes his ro-bustness, age, hair, height, gait, complexion, eyes, nose, lips, coat, trousers, and waistcoat.... [T]he future historian may refer to [this novel] to discover what was the material of which Mr. Bright's waistcoats were made. [quoted in Hall 336]

Damon Runyon calls a newspaper writer "Waldo Winchester" (Walter Winchell), a restaurant "Mindy's" (Lindy's), and a street "Broadway" in a place he calls "Manhattan." But according to T. J. Binyon, "to imagine that Runyon's stories have anything to do with reality betrays a grotesque misunderstanding of the nature of art."

That depends on what you mean by having "anything to do with reality"; but the issue I raise is, it may seem, more parochial: namely, whether the names refer to real people and places. I raise the issue not in order to provide an answer, but to remark that the defense of whatever answer is offered must depend on two things: the intentions of the author and the relevance of those intentions to the correct interpretation of the text. The former concerns matters of fact, the latter matters of decision, aesthetic and otherwise. It is an empirical question, however difficult or easy it may be to decide, whether Trollope intended his readers to take his "Turnbull" to refer to Bright (in this case it does not seem hard to decide). But even this intention is not completely without its shadows. Which readers? Perhaps the "veriest child"—but surely only those reasonably in the know. Did Trollope have *me* in mind? If so, his intention failed until I recently learned more about the politics that interested Trollope. If Homer intended his audience to take "Troy" to refer to a real place, his intention misfired for many centuries until Heinrich Schliemann came along.

In any case, the intention by the originator that an utterance or writing be interpreted in a certain way is only a necessary condition for that being the correct interpretation; it is also necessary that the intention be reasonable. It would have been unreasonable of Trollope, if he gave it a moment's thought, to expect a reader unversed in the history of English politics and more than a hundred years later to have the key to his names. Joyce, annoyed that his readers did not spot the analogies between his and Homer's Ulysses, spilled the beans to Frank Budgen in a successful attempt to provide a hint his work had not. Here we come up hard against the questions of what intentions an author really has and what is "reasonable" for him to think his readers will make of his text. The questions are directly related, since one can intend only what one believes he has a chance of bringing off; and the issue ramifies in literature as the proposed or imagined audience fragments in time, place, background, education, politics and taste. At the same time, matters of fact about an author's intentions begin to depend in part on our judgment as to how reasonable those intentions were.

Joyce's desire to have his work read in the light of a tradition brings out a contrast between much literature and other uses of writing. The writers of proclamations, warnings, declarations of war, writs of habeas corpus, sales catalogues and political broadsides usually have a pretty good idea of the background knowledge and level of learning of their audiences; by comparison a novelist or poet can take relatively little detailed information about the everyday world for granted. But it is reasonable of the novelist or poet to assume that her reader has read other novels or poems in the same language, just as it is reasonable (usually) to assume that the reader has read the first half of a work of fiction before he reads the second half. Thus literature itself provides an important part of the background an author is apt to assume she shares with her audience. Other books help constitute the world which completes the triangle of author and reader, just as prior conversations provide much of what speaker and hearer depend on for good communication. A related idea is expressed as a constraint on interpretation by T. S. Eliot in "Tradition and the Individual Talent":

> No poet, no artist of any art, has his complete meaning alone. His significance, his appreciation is the appreciation of his relation to the dead poets and artists. You cannot value him alone; you must set him, for contrast and comparison, among the dead. [49]

I have been concentrating on first meaning and on the intentions which most directly affect it, but this should not obscure the fact that there are endless further intentions which an author is sure to have. I am not much interested in the question of which if any of these intentions are aesthetically relevant. I see little gain in legislation here, or in the kind of rhetoric that can "make" some critic's preferred standards "correct" by persuading others to go along. On the other hand, I see much advantage in admitting the potential contribution to the appreciation of an author's work of almost anything that can be learned about his or her life and interests. I take Freud to have been right in a sense he may not quite have intended when he wrote in *The Interpretation of Dreams* that

> all genuinely creative writings are the product of more than a single motive and more than a single impulse in the poet's mind, and are open to more than a single interpretation. [266]

Should we then agree with Hans-Georg Gadamer when he says that what the text means changes as the audience changes: "A text is understood only if it is understood in a different way every time"? (275). I think not. There can be multiple interpretations, as Freud suggests, because there is no reason to say one rules out others. Gadamer has in mind incompatible interpretations. It is true that every person, every age, every culture will make what it can of a text; and persons, periods and cultures differ. But how can a significant relativism follow from a truism? If you and I try to compare notes on our interpretation of a text we can do so only to the extent that we have or can establish a broad basis of agreement. If what we share provides a common standard of truth and objectivity, difference of opinion makes sense. But relativism about standards requires what there cannot be, a position beyond all standards.

NOTES

1. These words, and the idea behind them, are J. L. Austin's (see *How to Do Things with Words* 22).
2. See, for example, essays 8, 17 and 18 in *ITI*.
3. I have several times documented my own disillusion with the idea that such theories are experimentally testable (*EAE* 235ff.).
4. In my essay "What Metaphors Mean" (essay 17 in *ITI*) I was foolishly stubborn about the word "meaning" when all I cared about was the primacy of "first meaning."
5. See "MTE," "EpE" and "TVK."

6. No *particular* points are essential; different direct connections lead speakers by different routes into the same language.

7. In this paragraph I have tried to hold down overt reference in one sentence to an earlier sentence. But the "however" makes sense only in the light of what goes before, as does the "such props." There are many more subtle cross-references. If one spells out the reference, the text itself always plays a role: "such props" = "props such as those mentioned in the preceding sentence." Anyone who doubts the overwhelming frequency of such cross-textual demonstrative references should try writing a few paragraphs without them.

8. Of course a writer, like a speaker, may manage things so that in his work we interpret a familiar word in a novel way. But this cannot be the usual situation. We understand the word "cat," whether in fiction or in an advertisement for cat food, if we can tell a cat when we see one; the introduction of a fictional cat in a story does not change the list of objects to which the word applies any more than it changes the meaning of the word.

WORKS CITED

Austin, J. L. *How to Do Things with Words.* Cambridge: Harvard UP, 1962.

Binyon, T. J. Review of *Damon Runyon: A Life* by Jimmy Breslin. *Times Literary Supplement,* 20 March 1992: 6.

Cummings, E. E. *The Enormous Room.* New York: Modern Library, 1934.

Eliot, T. S. "Tradition and the Individual Talent." In *The Sacred Wood: Essays on Poetry and Criticism.* London: Methuen, 1960.

Freud, S. "The Interpretation of Dreams." *The Standard Edition,* vol. 4. London: The Hogarth Press, 1958.

Gadamer, Hans-Georg. *Truth and Method.* New York: Crossroad, 1975.

Hall, N. John. *Trollope: A Biography.* Oxford: Clarendon, 1991.

Hart, H.L.A. "A Logician's Fairy Tale." *Philosophical Review* 60 (1951): 198–212.

Grice, Paul. "The Causal Theory of Perception." In *Studies in the Way of Words.* Cambridge: Harvard UP, 1989. 224–47.

About the Contributors

STEVEN E. COLE earned his Ph.D. at the University of Washington and is Assistant Professor of English at Temple University; his essays on romanticism and critical theory have appeared in *Modern Philology*, *Studies in Romanticism*, and *Criticism.*

REED WAY DASENBROCK is Professor of English at New Mexico State University. He is the editor of *Redrawing the Lines: Analytic Philosophy, Deconstruction, and Literary Theory* (Minnesota, 1989), and his most recent books are *Imitating the Italians: Wyatt, Spenser, Synge, Pound, Joyce* (Johns Hopkins, 1991) and, with Feroza Jussawalla, *Interviews with Writers of the Post-Colonial World* (Mississippi, 1992). For the academic year 1992–93 he holds the Cardin Visiting Chair in Humanities at Loyola College in Maryland.

DONALD DAVIDSON teaches philosophy at the University of California–Berkeley and is one of the most eminent living philosophers. A selected list of his many publications is to be found in the Abbreviations at the front of this book.

ALLEN DUNN is Associate Professor of English at the University of Tennessee. He has published articles in *Boundary 2*, *Southern Humanities Review*, *Shakespeare Studies*, and the *Journal of Modern Literature.* He is currently at work on a book, *The Spectacle of Suffering,* which analyzes the dramatic representation of moral dilemmas in literature and philosophy.

MICHAEL FISCHER is Professor of English at the University of New Mexico and is the author of *Does Deconstruction Make Any Difference?*

(Indiana, 1984) and *Stanley Cavell and Literary Skepticism* (Chicago, 1989).

MARK GAIPA is a graduate student at Brown University.

DAVID GORMAN teaches in the English Department at Northern Illinois University. His writings on the history and theory of literary study have appeared in *Diacritics, Poetics Today, Critical Texts,* and elsewhere. He is at work on a study of literary history after historicism.

THOMAS KENT is Associate Professor of English at Iowa State University and is the author of *Interpretation and Genre: The Role of Generic Perception in the Study of Narrative Texts* (Bucknell, 1986).

PAISLEY LIVINGSTON is Professor of English at McGill University. He is the author of *Ingmar Bergman and the Rituals of Art* (Cornell, 1982), *Literary Knowledge: Humanistic Inquiry and the Philosophy of Science* (Cornell, 1988), *Literature and Rationality: Ideas of Agency in Theory and Fiction* (Cambridge, 1991), and *Models of Desire* (Johns Hopkins, 1992).

BILL MARTIN teaches in the Philosophy Department at DePaul University. He is the author of *Matrix and Line: Derrida and the Possibilities of Postmodern Social Theory* (SUNY, 1992). He is also the editor of *Deconstruction and Social Theory* (Humanities, 1992) and, with George Trey, of *Left Without Ground: Radical Possibilities of Postmodernity* (Maisonnueve, 1992).

MICHAEL MORTON is Associate Professor of German at Duke University and is the author of *Herder and the Poetics of Thought* (Penn State, 1989) and *The Critical Turn* (Wayne State, 1992).

SHEKHAR PRADHAN is Associate Professor of Philosophy in the Department of English and Philosophy at Central Missouri State University and is the author of the widely cited paper "Minimalist Semantics: Davidson and Derrida on Meaning, Use, and Convention," published in *Diacritics* 16 (1986).

ROBERT SCHOLES is the Andrew Mellon Professor of English at Brown University and is the author of *Textual Power* (Yale, 1985), *Protocols of Reading* (Yale, 1989), and many other books.

SAMUEL C. WHEELER III is Professor of Philosophy at the University of Connecticut. He does analytic philosophy of language and writes about ancient and contemporary metaphysics. His recent work combines deconstructive and analytic philosophical argument.

Index